Liners to the Sun

Other books by John Maxtone-Graham

The Only Way to Cross
Dark Brown Is the River
S/S Norway
Olympic/Titanic
Tribute to a Queen
From Song to Sovereign
Cunard: 150 Glorious Years
Monarch of the Seas
Majesty of the Seas
Safe Return Doubtful
Crossing & Cruising
Legend of the Seas
Under Crown and Anchor
Splendour of the Seas
Grandeur of the Seas
Titanic Survivor
Cruise Savvy

Liners to

the Sun

John Maxtone-Graham

S

SHERIDAN HOUSE

ACKNOWLEDGMENTS

CHAPTER 1: The second epigraph is a quotation by Clive James from *The 637 Best Things Anybody Ever Said*, by Robert Byrne, and is used by permission of Atheneum Publishers. Copyright (c) 1982 by Robert Byrne.

CHAPTER 4: The two-line excerpt from John Masefield's poem "Number '534'" is quoted with permission of The Society of Authors, literary representatives of the Estate of John Masefield.

CHAPTER 9: The excerpt from Kingsley Amis's article about cruising, in the London *Sunday Times Magazine* of July 26, 1981, is quoted by kind permission of the author.

This edition first published 2000 by
Sheridan House Inc.
145 Palisade Street
Dobbs Ferry, New York 10522

www.sheridanhouse.com

Copyright (c) 1985, 2000 by John Maxtone-Graham

First published 1985 by
Macmillan Publishing Company
New York, N.Y.

Library of Congress Cataloging-in-Publication Data

Maxtone-Graham, John.
    Liners to the sun / John Maxtone-Graham.
      p. cm.
    Originally published: New York : Macmillan, c1985.
    Includes bibliographical references (p.) and index.
    ISBN 1-57409-108-5 (hd. : alk. paper) — ISBN 1-57409-107-7 (pbk. : alk. paper)
    1. Ocean travel. 2. Cruise ships. 3. Ocean liners.

G550 .M22 2000
910.4'5—dc21

                             99-089712

Printed in the United States of America

ISBN 1-57409-108-5 (hardcover)
ISBN 1-57409-107-7 (paperback)

For Mary

Contents

Introduction

Regular transatlantic express service by sea came to an end in the early seventies. But fortuitously, at the same time, cruise ships began to abound in warmer waters, as though sea-loving man, deprived of transportation across the ocean, sought to perpetuate voyages elsewhere. Hence the current extraordinary cruise boom. For increasing millions of Americans especially, the one-week or two-week voyage has become a sometimes bi-annual rite, and to answer that demand, larger ships are sailing in increasing numbers

Readers in search of a comprehensive survey of those vessels and the companies that own them will find the ensuing pages disappointing. Guides of that kind are already in print, and others will doubtless appear. Together with an avalanche of travel magazines and Sunday supplements, they keep the cruising public informed about changing itineraries, ports, and prices.

My intent here is to document the shipboard that never really changes. Life on yesterday's ships, whether crossing or cruising, not only parallels what happens on today's, but still governs it as well. Years as a passenger have convinced me that what we enjoy about sailing, our parents, grandparents, and great grandparents enjoyed, too. They may have dressed differently, they may have thought differently, they certainly embarked from a social context ashore very different from our own, yet once afloat, a timeless bond of passengerhood, if you will, enveloped them. They conformed, as we do, to a universal shipboard behavior. Passengers are, after all, one of the three indispensable components of the liner triad—the other two are ship and crew. Together they shape every voyage; alone they cannot function. Visitors at a resort ashore never coalesce as do passengers at sea; ships devoid of clients have no raison d'être, and a crewless vessel is as inoperable as it is unthinkable.

My hope is that, having glimpsed cruising's antecedents, present-day passengers will find new insights into their life on board. As in all things, little of the contemporary springs full-blown from the present. Throngs celebrating a captain's gala are unaware that they are reliving, frivolously, the relief and gratitude of their humbler immigrant predecessors. Shorebound tender loads, hastening from cabin to cabana, have little conception of earlier excursionists who, in ship's boats towed to shore, blazed the trail. Few gathered nightly for cabaret realize how that packaged gaiety evolved from gentler, amateur theatricals in social halls and lounges of vessels long since vanished. Most passengers idling at the rail as their ship surmounts Panama's isthmus take their novel overland passage for granted, and whenever the on-deck heat oppresses, their retreat to air-conditioned equability conjures up no image of past agonies in stifling tropical saloons. My aim is to reveal cruising's historical underpinnings, to show that on board ship, as everywhere else, contemporary is no less than continuum.

This book was first published in 1985, amidst the earliest rumblings of our present-day cruise explosion, long before we had realized the extent of the colossal fallout to follow. Now, 15 years later, the shipping industry is experiencing the kind of newbuilding blitz that echoes the brave ocean liner scene of 1900. The following figures tell the tale: during the 1970s, 17 new cruise ships entered service. In the 1980s, that figure doubled. In the 1990s, 54 new cruise ships appeared over the horizon. And for the oughts—by which I suppose we must identify our new millennium's first decade—projected tonnage figures keep up the mind-boggling pace.

And it is not only the staggering numbers of ships, it is their staggering size as well. Giant predecessors from the North Atlantic have been easily surpassed and it is a rare Caribbean entry these days that accommodates less that 2000; a few can carry nearly twice as many. *Song of America*, Royal Caribbean's 1984 newbuilding documented within these pages, was recently sold off as too small. I saw her moored behind *Grand Princess* in Naples recently; she looked like a quaint toy. Similarly, *Royal Princess*, at 44,000 tons Princess Cruises' largest vessel in 1984, is now almost the company's smallest. *Tropicale*, Carnival's first purpose-built ship of 1981, is now dwarfed by a fleet of consorts displacing 100,000 tons. Small ships have proliferated as well: Seabourn, Renaissance and Silver Sea field flotillas of high-end, luxurious miniatures, for which *Sea Goddess I* of 1984 served as glittering prototype.

In contrast to this expansionist trend, cruising's corporate landscape has undergone drastic consolidation. Carnival has succeeded in corralling a formidable fleet that includes ships of Holland-America, Seabourn, Windstar, Cunard and Costa. Princess has absorbed Sitmar and Royal Caribbean now owns Celebrity's fleet. That Royal Caribbean Cruise Line recently changed its name to Royal Caribbean International betrays contemporary cruising's global ambition. Each summer, dozens of ships reposition eastbound from the Caribbean for Mediterranean or Baltic deployment; increasingly, Europeans are being bitten by the same cruising bug that infects Americans. Other vessels sailing westbound to Alaska are starting to incorporate round-trip jaunts to Hawaii en route.

I am convinced that what I set out to encompass nearly twenty years ago retains a timeless validity. Needless to say, all historical underpinnings remain firmly in place. Though hulls may be larger, décor more sophisticated and passenger loads more daunting, the essence of cruising's shipboard experience is as was. However few liners are left venturing to the sun, life aboard the towering white dream castles sailing in their wake remains surprisingly similar.

Indeed, the last survivor of those liners is enshrined on my cover. I must thank my son Ian, a talented writer and photographer alike, for allowing me use of his study of *Queen Elizabeth 2* moored alongside Bermuda's Royal Naval Dockyard. She is, as of this writing, the only liner left in service and, as a crossing/cruising hybrid, deserves pride of place on this volume's threshold. *QE2* has logged 30 years of service and her frequent Bermuda visits remind me that *Berengaria*, one of her proud Cunard forebears, undertook her first cruising venture to the same island during the depression of the 1930s.

A small caveat: I must apologize for some of the mechanical intricacies of the chapter entitled "Newbuilding." Nevertheless, in the same breath, I urge tentative readers to persevere. For us to ignore the gritty technicalities of ship design and construction is to sell these remarkable creations short.

Although writing remains an isolated profession, gathering source material involves vital collaboration. I am eternally grateful to countless passengers and crew, no less than historians and shipyard personnel, who told me their stories, answered my questions and, most important of all, shared memories with me that otherwise have been forgotten and lost.

I am indebted to Bård Kolltveit, director of Oslo's Norske Sjøfartsmuseum, a fellow ship historian, collaborator and cherished colleague. From Bremerhaven's Deutsches Schiffartsmuseum, the encyclopedically knowledgeable Arnold Kludas was a fount of wisdom and advice. In my own country, Norman Morse, who has at his fingertips details about nearly every North Atlantic deck plan, proved, as always, a formidable and ever-present ally. Fellow author William Miller also helped enormously.

Those who brought "Cruises Past" to life were invaluable and they are acknowledged chronologically. My gratitude extends to Mrs. Arthur Hays Sulzberger for her memories of the *Victoria Luise*'s cruise to Panama in 1913; to Carrie Wagner—"Miss Mini-Cunard"—for reliving her 1922 world cruise on board R.M.S. *Laconia*; to retired French Line stewards Raymond Guiheneuf and Pierre Troadec, who brought the *Normandie*'s fabled Rio cruise of 1938 into perfect focus; to Bill Archibald and Vaughan Rickard, whose recall of the *Caronia* of 1959 was flawless; and finally, to Jack Shaum, a fellow author who re-created his first cruise on board the *Queen Elizabeth*, to Nassau and back, in 1968. They all remembered so well and brought shipboard life of decades ago within entertaining reach.

For shedding light on the *Prinsendam* disaster, I am indebted to "B.K." Stephenson, Norman and Vivian Quillinan, Richard Ianni, Gene Reid, Beatrice Malon, Helena Grenot, Regina O'Malley, and Mary O'Hagan.

Innumerable ship's officers and staff offered the most useful input. From Holland America Line, Captains Cornelius van Herke, Conrad Menke, Cornelius Hoenderdos, Henk Westra, and Frederik van Driel as well as hotel managers Dirk Zeller, Fekko Ebbens, and Willem Dirksen were invaluable. Cunard masters who helped included Captains Eric Ashton-Irvine, Bob Arnott, Peter Jackson, Mortimer Hehir, and Doug Ridley, together with bridge officers John Hall, Ian Taylor, and Phil Rentell, and wireless officers Don Butterworth and Alan Holmes and Chief Engineer Willy Farmer. Royal Viking Captains Kjell Salbuvik and Haakon Gangdal lent their experienced hands, as did *Sea Goddess I*'s master, Captain Johan L'Orange, Chief Steward Ulf Guggenheimer, and the head of the company's hotel department, Arne Baekkelund. From Norwegian Caribbean Lines, Captains Torbjorn Hauge, Aage Hoddevik, Hartvig von Harling, and Ragnar Nilsen were extremely helpful, as was Chief Engineer Egil Fossen. On board Royal Caribbean Cruise Line's ships, Captain Eigil Eriksen and Chief Officer Kristian Skovborg-Hansen abetted my cause, as did, from company headquarters ashore, Robert Perez and Brenton Jenkins. On board Norwegian-American Cruises's *Sagafjord*, I am indebted to Captain Kai Julsen and, in the hotel department, Frank Simak and Flemming Wandahl.

At Wärtsilä shipyard in Helsinki, my task would have been impossible without the help of Tor Stolpe, Göran Damströmm, Kaj Liljestrand, and Mauri Francke. From Dubigeon-Normandie's yard at Nantes on the Loire, I am beholden to Engineer-in-Chief Roger Lefauconner and, at the Chantiers de L'Atlantique, the late General Manager Albert Laredo.

To the host of others who were kind enough to help, my undying thanks. What I trust is a complete alphabetical list follows: Heidi Albrecht, Susan Alpert, Edward Biedes, Arnold Brereton, Jane Dalton, Mrs. McClure Fahnestock, the late Herbert Frank, Ella May Fyfe, Basil Greenhill, John Hanbidge, Drs. Lyndon and Marjorie Hill, Chip Hoehler, Paul Hollister, John Kemble, Peter Kohler, Walter Lord, Georgiana Magolie, Alice Marshall, Eric Mason, Olivier Naffrechoux, Captain Carl Netherland-Brown, Bruce Nierenberg, Ken Norman, William and Pamela Nylen, Janet O'Rorke, Neil Osborne, Stanley Page, Bernard Pelletier, Jean-Claude Potier, Cecil Ridgely-Nevitt, Joseph Ryder, Victor Scrivens, Robert Smith, Russell Southern, Lynn Stafford, the late Jack Steitz, Helen I. Stoddard, Edward H. Turner, Petrus van den Bemt, Everett Viez, Lawrence Ward, Lex and Nora Ward, William Winberg, Barry Winiker, Sally Woodson, and Robert Zeschien.

My mother, born in the last year of the nineteenth century and now sadly deceased, proved invaluable at recalling countless imperishable snippets from her early steamship days. My dear friend and colleague Dolf Placzek has been extraordinarily kind in responding without complaint to so many demands on his valuable time, keeping the work on course and adding his urbane erudition when it was needed. Finally, warmest thanks to my wife, Mary, without whom I never sail, who contributed so much to this work, not only the index and endless proofing, but also continuous sagacity and support throughout.

With those indispensable formalities complete, we can now board and settle down for a long and, I trust, enlightening cruise. If passenger/readers enjoy it even a quarter as much as I have enjoyed mapping its itinerary, then we shall all have embarked on a bon voyage.

—John Maxtone-Graham

New York City, 1999

I soon found my fellow passengers and their behavior in the different places we visited a far more absorbing study than the places themselves.

—EVELYN WAUGH, WHEN
THE GOING WAS GOOD

A luxury liner is just a bad play surrounded by water.
—CLIVE JAMES

1.
Cruise Lines

Since the publication of *The Only Way to Cross* in 1972, I have lectured about life on the Atlantic liners all over the world. For audiences and lecturer alike, the tenor of these talks is one of nostalgic regret. Passengers embarked on long cruises are obvious devotees of the subject, and the same interest prevails ashore. The tales I share with older members of the audience always trigger wistful recall of forgotten journeys. It seems apparent to me that among the most pleasurably remembered episodes of lives crammed with riches are those involving ocean passage.

None are more articulate on this count than Atlantic regulars of the endangered species *Peregrinator transatlanticus inveteratus*—formerly indigenous to the northeastern United States, but more recently permanent

Sunbelt migrants roosting in tranquil, landlocked sanctuaries. The male of the species is most often found on the golf course save when it rains; then he rejoins the female at the bridge table. One of the rare delights of old age is reminiscing, and cocktail-fueled garrulity of *Peregrinator transatlanticus* often dwells, longingly, on sea voyages past.

After my talks, I have learned to anticipate familiar shipboard bromides. New York East Siders suggest that they never crossed to the West Side save when embarking for Europe. (Though I live on West 78th Street, that same joke was used by the member who introduced me at the Union Club.) Scores of ex-passengers have divulged the origin of POSH (Port Out, Starboard Home), mentioned in Chapter 7 of *The Only Way to Cross* as well as in Chapter 5 of this volume. Widows report roguishly that their husbands deliberately booked on French or Italian ships, where women and children might be presumed to have no priority in the event of disaster. Countless times, men repeat their boisterous remark to ships' captains following introduction of their officers: "Say, Captain, the thing I want to know is who's driving the ship?" Others, unhappy that conventional funnels and deckhouses have disappeared, complain that ships look different these days. Each storm at sea described to me is more parlous than any other, at least Force 10 on the Beaufort Scale and "the worst the captain had ever seen." I have heard about every celebrity with whom shoulders were rubbed in either Veranda Grill—where, my informants add, they ate every meal, not merely one for a treat. (I suspect that the number of passengers who "ate every meal" in both Veranda Grills comfortably exceeds the combined capacities of both restaurants for the entire life of the *Queen*s.) I have heard tell of splendid suites filled with flowers, of crossings sustained on jeroboams, of monumental shipboard binges and hangovers, and inevitably, tureens full of Beluga (see Chapter 3).

But once through this sargasso of platitudes, nothing is more fondly recalled than the delight of those crossings. In New York recently, a woman in her mid-sixties reminisced with me about transatlantic life. She was not a widow, merely parted momentarily from her banker husband, who was engrossed with cronies across the room. Charming and attractive, she wore a beautiful silk print dress and a grandmother's bracelet that chimed whenever she raised her glass. She had enjoyed my talk and it unleashed a torrent of memories about ocean travel: the ships had been comfortable, the stewards attentive, the captains entertaining, the service divine, the other passengers such lovely people. "It's a shame," she concluded, "that it's all over."

"What's over?" I inquired, though I knew what was coming.

"Sailing by ship, the life you talk about in your book."

"But it's not over at all," I countered.

"Oh, but it is," she insisted. "You can't cross anymore."

"But you can, if you care to, in the summer or on a positioning cruise—"

A light went out in her face. She grimaced with a miau combining resignation and regret. "But it's not the same, is it? Everything's changed nowadays."

My response, which fell on deaf ears, was that it was not the same; it was better.

I suppose her inference was—and it is *Peregrinator transatlanticus*'s recurring cry—that nice people stopped sailing at the same time as the nice ships. My firm recollection is that on every vessel, nice or not, crossing or cruising, a consistent proportion of the passenger load is unattractive. Parvenus, arrivistes, and assorted vulgarians have not arisen spontaneously with the cruise market; they have booked on steamships ever since the *Britannia* sailed out of Liverpool in 1840, in exactly the same proportion as is found on either shore.

What seemed to have concluded our dialogue so abruptly was the word *cruise*. For too many of these grounded birds of passage, "cruise," "cruiseship," and "cruise passenger" serve as benign pejoratives. And not only from *Peregrinator transatlanticus*. I am reminded of a man who books ships' entertainers; once, in an attempt to dissuade me from sailing on a certain vessel to Bermuda, he muttered disparagingly, "Nothing but Jersey roadhouse gang on that." Whence the sneer? Is it the polyester, the unpolished manner, or the baked Alaska? For my part, I find direct parallels with the snap-brim capped bore of the Atlantic smoking room and the same baked Alaska that Hamburg-Amerika always served its First Cabin passengers the night before docking in Hoboken. What surprises and saddens me is that passengers who so genuinely enjoyed life on board yesterday should recoil from sailings awaiting them year-round today. I spend about a quarter of my year at sea on cruise ships. As a dedicated passenger on anything that floats as well as a passenger liner historian, I find much to enjoy on board a wide variety of vessels. Some are better run than others; but what pleases me most is that more and more ships are sailing and more and more passengers are comfortably and pleasantly accommodated. For each of those holdouts who lament the vanished transatlantic days, millions more have found that life on board continues, no more changed, really, than life everywhere has changed. In sum, shipboard thrives.

How is cruising better than crossing? To begin with, in booking for pleasure rather than purpose, one stays on board longer. For my taste—and, I suspect, for many of my fellow passengers'—crossings were always too short, never more than a week on smaller vessels; on flagships, five days at the most. They were only part of the journey, preambles or finales bracketing longer sojourns abroad. Those delightful shipboard interludes, ordinary yet extraordinary every time, inevitably passed too swiftly.

Of course, that very haste gave crossings their special flavor. Unfortunately, when oil prices skyrocketed in the early seventies, adherence to ruthless transatlantic schedules made things prohibitively expensive. I am often asked why transatlantic ships disappeared. The answer is simple: crossing in five days required a service speed of 28½ knots; since fuel consumption escalates geometrically with increased speed, sustaining those knots consumed huge amounts of oil. The *France*, for instance, at 28½ knots, gulped a ton of oil for every mile of ocean traversed. Reducing speed would not have solved the problem. The first two *Queen*s sailed weekly, one in each direction; slowing down would have widened the discrepancy between their crossing time and the airborne alternative. Additionally, six- or seven-day crossings, though less expensive per se, would have curtailed the number of voyages and hence passenger bookings per annum. Regrettably, it is all as immutable as Cartesian logic. *Queen Elizabeth 2*, which steams far more efficiently than her two predecessors, still manages a couple of dozen crossings each year; but, increasingly, she is found, as are all her sisters on every ocean, steaming slowly and economically on cruises instead.

More than gilded passenger lists, I most miss a less tangible aspect of crossing—its sense of purpose. Beneath all the familiar excitement, every soul on board was preoccupied with what lay over the horizon. Eastbound crossings, despite their shorter days, were especially anticipatory. For American passengers, they heralded the start of the adventure; for crewmen, past their voyage's American apogee, each sea mile shortened the distance to families in their vessel's home port. An urgency permeated the crossing ship, embodied in the restless surge and plunge of her hull and the ceaseless, rattling chatter of her interior fittings. The view over the rail was consistent as well. My favorite was straight down to that turbulent spoil zone where shell plating met sea, where black Atlantic creamed white roiled impotently against steel as the ship and its shadow, in implacable tandem, hissed past. I always found that vision of demonstrable haste—seeming far faster than 28½ knots—all the more compelling since I realized it continued round the clock, long after passengers

4

Port of call: Holland America's *Nieuw Amsterdam* moored at Curaçao in the spring of 1948. Cruising's norm—steel and palms—was ever thus, rigid superstructure softened by a tropical foliage border. *(Everett E. Viez Collection)*

as besotted as I tired of watching it. Yet however exhilarating, its effect was to compact thousands of sea miles into inexorable five-day spans; long before we had drained the cup, our crossing was over, sea-motion quelled, creaking silenced, and Southampton or Cherbourg alongside.

At an average of 15 knots—crossing's compulsion halved—cruising's pace is languorous. The reduced number of propeller revolutions retards the tempo within as time, ship, and passengers are suspended in a watery limbo for a seductive week or more—an inviting prospect of days at sea alternating with days in port. We settle into cabins properly, every closet, cupboard, and drawer filled. There is no division of luggage as on a crossing—these suitcases for the ship (vestigial steamer trunks), those for London or Paris. The cruise's raison d'être is the sea voyage itself.

In enviable contrast to the Atlantic experience, no port save one signals voyage's end. Landfall can be enjoyed rather than endured. There cannot be any more pleasurable time-and-motion study than the ritual of port arrival, with decks and hull reassuring constants, harbor and weather intriguing variables. Incurable sidewalk superintendents all, we gather at the rail each time, enjoying an Olympian overview of the first emissary from shore, the pilot. He makes his purposeful approach alongside, then a laddered clamber inboard. Revolutions increase again. Shepherded by evermore cautious tugs, we forsake sea for shelter. Near land, messenger lines arc gracefully ashore; hawsers follow, splashing down and, uncannily serpentine, nosing landward where they are hauled up and bollard-snugged. Winches on board raise the sinuous lengths from the water until, drawn bar-taut and dripping, they bridge and shrink the final ribbon of fetid harbor to nothing. Hull nudges pier with a groan of resignation. If it is a maiden arrival, a welcoming band struts dockside, snaredrums echoing in contrapuntal ricochet between hull and shed. At routine ports of call, the cries of laconic dockers and the clatter of gangplank on pier indicate a tenuous linkage with land. The cruise's sea circuit is momentarily shorted by overland digression.

With only daylight at their disposal, passengers disembark from the cleared ship in haste, dressed for comfort rather than boat train or city, unencumbered save by camera or bathing suit. But whatever ruin, shops, beach, or luncheon await, most endearing for me is guaranteed reembarkation by dusk. (I still remember only too vividly my first Caribbean arrival on board the *France* in the sixties. A cruise novice, I fought my way ashore on Martinique with four children, endured a humid jitney trek, and, at noon, found myself queued up for an appalling barbecue. Over my shoulder, I saw a Tantalus vision of the *France* at anchor, where a superb

6

A "Tantalus vision": *France* on the horizon off St. Thomas at the end of a day ashore. *Below,* mooring at Kusadasi. *Danae, Stella Solaris,* and—stern-to in the distance—*Atlas* discharge passengers for a day's visit to nearby Ephesus. *(Author's collection)*

luncheon—for which I had already paid—would be consumed without us. From that moment on, I realized that the best islands in the Caribbean have propellers.)

Indeed, one's tethered vessel remains a potent lodestone throughout the day, a citadel looming over a medieval town. Upperworks glistening like polished ivory, funnel capped by a shimmering heat haze, she stands aloof from the turmoil and decay below. Her halo of rainbowed signal flags, flown each port day, hangs torpid now. Even motionless, hawsered down like a captive Gulliver, a ship's inherent design strains forward, suppressed tension in the stance of her bows and throughout her coiled haunches astern.

Among the advantages of staying on board is the opportunity—never granted on crossings—of observing a vessel deserted by most of her impulsive human cargo. The day's only disruption is crew boat-drill; serious stuff, this, lifeboats lowered to the harbor and fire and watertight doors closed as goggled damage-control parties carrying respirators and fire axes respond to contrived emergencies in public rooms and lobbies. But later, a surreal, preprandial torpor descends, the peace disrupted only by the distant whine of vacuums along cabin passageways or, on deck, the chatter of idled stewards and perhaps the disparate *chinngg-chinngg* of unseen but ubiquitous paint scalers. Off-duty officers surround the pool. The weather deck chiaroscuro is completed by a shadebound passenger residue prostrate in deck chairs, save an inquisitive few who, unsated by the morning's docking, cluster at the forward railing to oversee the loading of stores.

Below the battlements, where passenger meets native on the disputed castellany of the pier, loafers, taximen, and souvenir-sellers lay patient siege, withdrawn watchfully into the sparse midday shade. Our only postern is the single gangplank, drawbridge access to the towering steel ramparts it breeches. Scrutinizing those venturing along its length is the duty quartermaster, a solitary picket whose bronzed squint is the legacy of a hundred pierside vigils. Forward, paint crews on a listing, spattered coracle maneuver through the water segment under our bows; one of their number, suspended in a bosun's chair above a half-lowered anchor, daubs at rust in way of the hawse plating.

Near dusk there is a final pierside skirmish as buses and taxis disgorge weary, spoils-laden foot soldiers for what Kingsley Amis once called "the plunge back into the grateful bosom of the ship." Practiced now, they parry the last thrusts of peddlers sprung from ambush and crowd the gangplank, jostling passengers and crew alike as they regain their common abode. Reentry within that domain is exquisite: the campaigners' trium-

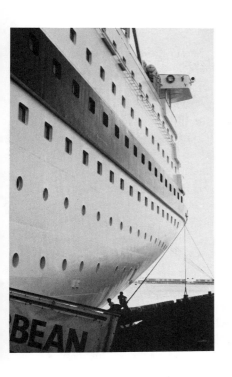

Midday in port. The cruise ship as castle. During her maiden voyage in December 1982, the *Song of America* provides a shady respite for two young Bahamians. The steel ramparts loom overhead, remote, unassailable, and serene. *Below, Fairsea* crewmen touch up their vessel's shell plating at Aruba. *(Author's collection)*

phal return from the dust, heat, and clamor to the cool, ordered familiarity of their ship; intruders ashore, on board they belong. There is, already, an observant and sometimes vociferous gallery along the upper railings to which last-minute excursionists will repair after strewing parceled loot over cabin berths. Passengers about to sail are victims of the same fever infecting crowds in football stadia: there is a compulsion to be up for the kickoff.

Except for the first, sailings are especially evocative. A cruise ship's departure from its home port is an orchestrated carnival of forced gaiety, streamers, confetti, and "Auld Lang Syne." Passengers at the rail commune not so much with their fellows beside them as with well-wishers screaming from atop the neighboring pier. Only sea air will erode that bittersweet, shoreside pull, displacing it with a shipboard symbiosis that prevails regardless of digressions ashore. The cruise forges a unique maritime community, embracing every soul on board. Now, having foraged in the hinterlands, the occupants withdraw into their castle's keep, throng the battlements, and await the raising of the drawbridge that will reestablish the sea moat sustaining their languid, enchanted quest.

From ashore, routine port departure is as prosaic as the word sailors use to describe it: undocking. Indifferent longshoremen slip our cables and turn away as, tug-assisted, we float clear. I never sail in the evening without being reminded of Mazatlán, a port on Mexico's Pacific coast due east of the tip of the Baja Peninsula. I must have called there a dozen times. Though there are splendid beaches somewhere, the dock area is, save for Cartagena's blighted pierscape, the most insalubrious I know. Mazatlán's most notorious nineteenth-century exports were shiploads of prostitutes bound north for San Francisco's gold-rush brothels; a legacy of that corrupt odium seems extant today over the arid, flyspecked town.

But, with the onset of what the French call *l'heure bleue*, there is a crepuscular reprieve. The withering day relents as a fairy-tale twinkle of lights laces the indigo dusk. Towering cumulus to the south catches the dying sun as do mellowed ocher promontories guarding the port. In captivated silence, we slip past that twilit panorama. Beyond the winking breakwater light we slow, breasting gentle Pacific swells as the pilot quits our side, his craft scarring the oiled surface with a crescent of foam in its retreat to shore. An accompanying tug turns back more sedately, bleating in salute, awakening above our heads a measured, sonorous triple blast. The traditional exchange of farewell, its conclusion is a single, abbreviated toot—a farewell peck—that echoes off headlands receding astern. Then we are alone, postern sealed once more, girdled in monocoqued perfection, standing off into the balmy, tropical night.

We leave the rail reluctantly, hoping to retain the spell intact. There is not—nor ever was—anything comparable on the North Atlantic.

Welcome aboard. This is not only a volume for cruise passengers; though experienced travelers will find familiar pleasure herein, I hope that others, neophytes as well as disenchanted Atlantic hands, may become intrigued enough to book passage. I can guarantee them one imperishable memento, hinted at by a symbolic and appropriate coincidence: in radio traffic between home office and ship, the cable-ese abbreviation for "passenger" is "pax," also the Latin word for peace. More than any other shipboard dividend, more than tans, ports, adventures, souvenirs, friends, or gluttony, I think they will discover a soothing, shipboard peace, an unlimited duty-free passenger allowance that can be brought ashore at cruise's end regardless of the Customs inspectors' vigilance.

(Curiously enough, there are several companies that are doing their best to suppress the term "passenger" in favor of the hotelspeak "guest." It is a distressing move; a guest is an invited client whereas the passenger has paid for passage. Moreover, it is an ancient and authentic name that demands preservation.)

Thus briefed, let us begin at the shipyard and the hull on the ways, that germinal disc of the cruise industry. For it is there, in those distant, waterside workshops, that the magic begins.

*Welding [is] the only satisfactory
means of joining many metal parts.*

—EARL R. PARKER

2.
Newbuilding

"Newbuilding" is an English generic with universal meaning for ship-builders of every nationality; in yards all over the world, whether Korean, Finnish, German, or French, "newbuilding" describes any and all created tonnage, vessels being started from scratch rather than converted. The amount of newbuilding is a register of shipyard vitality, and it can embrace many kinds of ships—tankers, container vessels, icebreakers, bulk carriers, warships, or car ferries.

Recently, a significant percentage of newbuilding has included a latter-day generation of passenger vessels, produced in record numbers for the cruise trade. During the summer of 1981, I toured half a dozen ship-yards, from the Baltic to the Mediterranean, where nine new cruise ships were either projected, on the ways, or fitting out. All displaced at least 30,000 tons or more. They were not giants from the glory days but, rather, new contemporary medians, about 700 feet long with shallow draught, dense capacity, ingenious propellers, and double rudders to assure tug-free access to island ports. I was anxious to see firsthand the changes in methods of construction from the days of the Atlantic Ferry; not only were the silhouettes of this newbuilding different, their assembly was different as well.

First, I stopped in Scotland for a nostalgic visit to John Brown's yard on the Clyde. The legendary works no longer builds ships at all—a French consortium has leased a portion of the yard to construct offshore drilling platforms. Clydebank is an industrial ghost town. The ways that launched the *Lusitania*, the *Aquitania*, and all three *Queens* are no more. I stood in front of the familiar brick façade of the works, at the top of what had been building berth number 4. That precise cement slope down to the water is now a wasteland of coarse black sand. On the far shore, where the little river Cart winds through the Inchemann fields to join the Clyde, dairy cows graze, just as their forebears had chewed contentedly decades earlier, raising incurious bovine eyes to see "a rampart of a ship"—as Masefield dubbed the *Queen Mary*—thunder into the peaceful waters. Only two vertical derricks remained of the dozens that had once flanked the ways; apart from the cattle, all that moved within that skeletal proscenium were passenger jets lofting up regularly from Glasgow Airport, each defiant takeoff roar rebuking the vanished champions they had supplanted.

Half-buried at my feet lay a symbolic fragment, a rusty, twisted steel plate studded with rivet-heads, a memorial to those staunch hulls that had been wrought here. It was also a curiosity, a relic from a vanished industrial era. In no yard I would visit that summer would the sustained *rat-tat-tat* of the pneumatic riveting gun prevail; that familiar staccato, which had echoed throughout shipyard scaffolding since iron ships were first conceived, has been replaced by the persistent crackle of the electric arc weld.

For almost exactly a century—from mid-nineteenth to mid-twentieth —rivets dominated ship construction. Indeed, the humble iron rivet was the linchpin of the Victorians' machine age, studding ships, buildings, railways, bridges, and machinery—every grandiose marvel of its time. Rivets were the inevitable connectors, the preferred—the only—means of attaching girder to girder and girder to plate. In shipyards, steel plates all along the hull had edges lined with serried holes punched out dozens at a time by stamping machines in the plate shop. Then the plates would

Mute relic from shipbuilding's recent past. A riveted plate lies discarded at John Brown's Clydeside yard. *(Author's collection)*

be bolted temporarily in place at the corners, their perforated edges neatly overlapped. Red-hot rivets were thrust through each aligned hole, their protruding shanks battered into a crude facsimile of the button head at the opposite end. Brutal and noisy, it was a technique that nonetheless required dexterous craftsmen. The skill of the riveter lay in his ability to flatten the rivet point speedily, before it cooled, without bending the shank in the process. An accomplished worker could drive home two hundred rivets during an eight-hour shift.

Where there was room for them to intrude between frames, pneumatic riveting machines—huge, cast-iron lobster claws tall as a man— would flatten rivet points with one convulsive, shuddering hiss of compressed air. As the rivet cooled, it would contract, drawing adjacent plates together (appropriate use for the homonym verb "to rivet: to engross or hold the attention"). To make an even tighter fit, adjoining plates were caulked, not with the oakum that had been hammered between wooden planking, but in a different fashion. Steel plates are caulked by battering the overlapping plate with a pneumatic caulking tool. Using the chisel blade, workers split the edge, forcing a portion of sprung steel against its overlapped neighbor.

Overall, that riveted plating was immensely reliable. It was easy to inspect, and a clenched or crooked rivet could be punched out and replaced with ease. For shipbuilders and sailors alike, there was something reassuring about the strength implicit in a rivet-studded hull, its flanks seamed with quadruple rows of button heads. And if riveted joints sometimes leaked, seeping seawater was the ultimate caulker, rusting offending rivet holes into impermeability.

Airplanes, the most advanced and fastest means of transportation, are still flush riveted because scrupulously fashioned aerodynamic surfaces demand it; even the most discreet welding bead cannot be tolerated. Bridges and buildings are also riveted. But in shipyards, rivet buttons have been replaced with welded zippers. The riveting gun has vanished, gone the way of the stoker's shovel and the sailmaker's palm. During my summer's shipyard tour, every bracket, stringer, stanchion, and plate I saw was welded within the structure. It is a method with all the advantages: it is faster, cheaper, stronger, and lighter. It has even been estimated that, since the steel plates did not have to overlap, Cunard saved 2,000 tons deadweight by having their third Queen, the Queen Elizabeth 2, welded rather than riveted.

After Scotland, I flew to Finland to visit the Helsinki yard of the Wärtsilä Company. Six percent of Finland's population speak Swedish,

Wärtsilä's Helsinki yard in two seasons two years apart. *Above*, 1982: New-building 431, Royal Caribbean Cruise Line's *Song of America*, moored at fitting-out berth number 3. The square box of the Building Hall has its water-borne exit door closed; an opening at the extreme left admits hull sections for assembly. *Below*, 1984: Newbuilding 464, P&O's *Royal Princess*, berthed alongside a new fitting-out complex, built since 1982 and visible over the vessel's uppermost deck. Down left lies *Sea Goddess I*, Newbuilding 466 (Wärtsilä's *Helsinki Shipyard*)

and this lingual duality is reflected in the company's formal letterhead, Oy Wärtsilä Ab: the company name is bracketed, respectively, with the Finnish incorporation abbreviation (Osakeyhtio) and the same in Swedish (Aktiebolag). Wärtsilä itself was a port to the east, in Carelia, where, in 1834, a sawmill was established with the later addition of a blast furnace that processed local iron ore. But Wärtsilä remains only a company name now, with shipbuilding production centered in three different locations, the Helsinki yard and two others farther along the coast at the port of Turku on Finland's southwest corner at the entrance to the Gulf of Bothnia. The Turku and Perno yards are much newer than their Helsinki predecessor; Perno has been built on a broad expanse of virgin shore where there is room to launch 100,000-ton tankers. The Turku yard produces specialized vessels, from cement carriers to cable-laying ships. But the oldest and original Wärtsilä yard is in the midst of Finland's capital, nestled within Helsinki's boundaries since its founding in 1865.

Wärtsilä owes its present-day success to an aggressive and technologically sound building program. The Russians buy all their icebreakers from the Finnish company, and at the opposite end of the thermal spectrum, the Wärtsilä yard in Helsinki has produced more new cruise ships than any single yard. During the cruise explosion in the early seventies, 30 percent of the world's passenger newbuilding was launched at Wärtsilä. Those six new hulls launched, in turn, two phenomenally successful cruise lines: Royal Viking Line, headquartered in San Francisco, whose trio of Wärtsilä ships roams the oceans of the world, and Royal Caribbean Cruise Line (RCCL), a Miami company whose trio established a successful Caribbean operation at the same time. All six of those Wärtsilä profiles, with their graceful clipper bows, are visually interchangeable from a distance. Two of the Royal Caribbean ships—*Nordic Prince* and *Song of Norway*—were later lengthened at Wärtsilä's Helsinki yard, a successful technique for enlarging passenger vessels that was pioneered at the yard. Royal Viking Line has stretched their trio of Wärtsilä hulls at German yards in Bremerhaven.

In June 1981, during the week I was to spend at Wärtsilä, New-building 431 was under construction. She was the Royal Caribbean Cruise Line's fourth vessel, to be officially christened *Song of America* by Beverly Sills in Miami in 1982 just prior to her maiden voyage. (Musical themes haunt Royal Caribbean: *Song of Norway* boasts a "My Fair Lady Lounge," and on the *Sun Viking*, one dines in the "H.M.S. Pinafore Dining Room.") She would be larger than her six predecessors, with a beam of 93 feet, as opposed to the *Song of Norway*'s 80 feet. She would

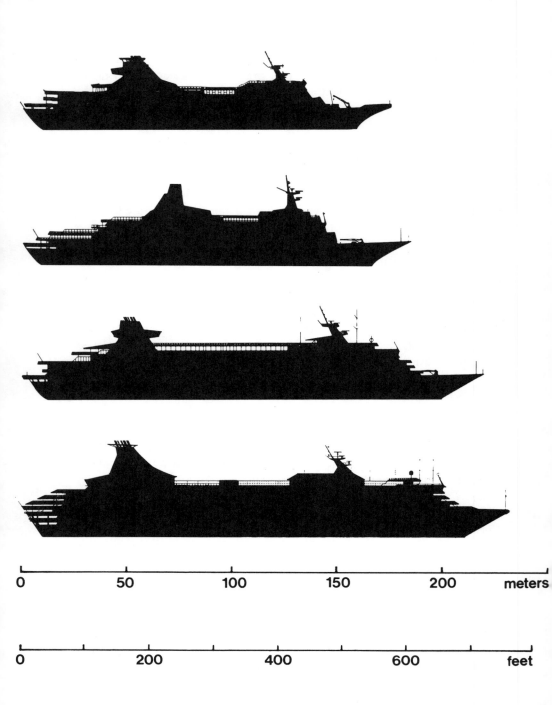

Genesis of the Wärtsilä cruise ship silhouette, reflecting the hulls' relentless growth. *From top to bottom, with dates of construction: Song of Norway* (1970); *Royal Viking Star* (1972) as originally built before she was stretched; *Song of America* (1981); *Royal Princess* (1983). (*Wärtsilä's Helsinki Shipyard*)

be 700 feet long, built from scratch to the dimension two of her sisters have achieved by being lengthened. Like most of their rivals, Royal Caribbean has planned for an abundant passenger capacity for the eighties and nineties, "stretching" already incorporated into the hull.

I arrived in Helsinki on a Sunday morning and, while awaiting the opening of the yard the following day, took a blustery harbor tour in hopes of at least seeing the *Song of America*'s hull, half-completed against the sky. I saw not a sign of it, though my excursion vessel passed the Wärtsilä yard twice. I found out why the following morning. After I had qualified for admission to the yard—security is very tight—I was ushered within an enormous gray steel shed. Inside, the *Song of America* lay at my feet, her upper decks almost even with ground level. She was being built in a dry dock, concealed beneath the 700-foot steel shed that Wärtsilä officials call the Building Hall. It is the world's largest covered dry dock and owes its existence to the extremes of local weather. The Gulf Stream does not penetrate into the Gulf of Finland, and Helsinki shipyard workers, at sixty degrees north latitude, need protection from the cold much of the year. Wärtsilä's is a Building Hall for all seasons. During the summer, bottom panels along three walls can be raised to admit fresh air and sunlight, but in winter, they are lowered, buttoning up the entire structure.

Building ships in dry dock has not completely supplanted the traditional sloping launchways, although it is increasingly popular. One of the first liner hulls constructed thus was the *United States*, built at Virginia's Newport News in 1950. Of the hulls I was investigating that summer of 1981, launch methods were divided: *Song of America, Nieuw Amsterdam,* and *Noordam* took shape in dry docks while *Atlantic, Fairsky, Europa, Tropicale,* and *Scandinavia* slid into the water in traditional fashion. Dry-dock construction ties up a dry dock for months, and so large yards with more than one dry dock can afford the convenience. And it is a convenience—large sections of ship are easier to assemble on a flat rather than an inclined surface, and more weight can be added to a land-bound hull that will not have to face the stress of a sloping launch. Dry-dock construction began during World War II, when shipbuilders at Newport News realized that hoisting armor plate up to an aircraft carrier's flight deck high above a conventional launchway necessitated enormously tall—and expensive—cranes; built in a hole in the ground, so to speak, the upper decks were conveniently within reach of much shorter cranes. Certainly, a dry-dock launch is less than spectacular. Sluice gates are opened, water seeps in, and hours later, nearly imperceptibly, the completed hull floats silently off its blocks. There is no stupendous splash into the water. "*La*

Contrasting building techniques. *Top,* in 1913, the *Imperator*'s steel components were assembled piece by piece on the ways. *Bottom,* the first of several keel sections put in place on building berth number 4 at John Brown's yard. From it grew the *Queen Elizabeth 2. (Hapag-Lloyd and Cunard)*

magie s'évanouie," remarked Albert Laredo, manager of Saint-Nazaire's shipyard as he showed me the kilometer-long dry dock where *Nieuw Amsterdam* would be assembled. Nearby, the legendary ways that had launched *Normandie* and *France* were cemented over and lost.

"Assembled" is the operative word for contemporary newbuilding. In the past, shipbuilders adhered to a constructional unity, derived from a mammalian vertebrate original. Ribs radiated from a spinelike keel and were covered with a skin of wood, iron, or steel. From the earliest coracles and canoes, to Viking long ships, to galleons, frigates, and clippers, to battleships and ocean liners, this was the invariable naval architectural principle: a clad framework. The vessel grew on a centrally located building berth. Components came from every corner of the surrounding yard, frames from the frame-bender, plates from the plate shop, and machinery from the engine works. The focus of delivery and construction was the launchway. Only the growing hull bore any resemblance to the finished ship; all else was raw material.

Though the spine/keel still exists, it is not necessarily the first element of the ship laid down ceremonially. Nowadays, hulls are made up from sections, recognizable chunks of ship put together at widely scattered yard locations. Guests at a keel-laying ceremony today will see a keel *section* lowered into place on the blocks—perhaps the port side of the midships double bottom—scrupulously positioned fore and aft by lasers. Midship sections are always put down first; as the widest, solidest part of the ship, they serve as the base for the engines, a central starting point to which additional sections will be attached in either direction as construction progresses. Every ensuing section will have been prefabricated elsewhere in the yard—huge building blocks weighing several hundred tons, often made heavier by the inclusion of tanks, piping, and auxiliary machinery. By installing these elements before the sections are assembled and still have open ends, subsequent time and labor can be saved. Sections move either suspended from cranes, indoors or out, or carried on flatbeds from their point of origin, first to the paint shop and then to the berth.

So at Wärtsilä, sections of the *Song of America* lay everywhere, huge, reddish "Lego" blocks ranged along the inboard wall of the Building Hall. Bow and stern sections were inverted, not only because it was easier to build them upside down, but, additionally, because they would not balance on their rounded bottoms until temporary legs had been attached. So they lay face down with lifting lugs—pierced, steel rabbit ears—spot-welded onto their convex slopes. The *Song of America*'s twin rudder posts stood upright atop the inverted stern, resembling lookout periscopes crown-

Song of America sections in waiting. *Above,* lined up alongside the Building Hall. Over the ladder at left, a "rabbit ear" lifting lug has been temporarily welded to the steel. *Left,* the bulbous bow stands on end; together with the prow, it will be the last forward section to be attached. *(Author's collection)*

Above, the inverted stern section awaiting transportation. Once attached to the hull, the welded legs will be removed, leaving rudder posts only projecting below. A transporter waits at left. *(Author's collection)*

ing a concrete bunker. Upper-deck sections stood right way up, balanced on splayed lower walls that would ultimately be attached to a lower deck. In consequence they looked fragile, like rusted card houses, the open ends of each level framed with temporary white handrails. Once these loose ends are tied into the hull's structural whole, a honeycomb strength would obtain; separated, awaiting that day of assembly, the sections were as graceless as jerry-built houseboats sitting out the winter onshore. Structurally completed sections, on the other hand, had massive, inherent strength: the *Song of America*'s underwater bulbous bow was parked upended outside the paint shop, its steel tip pointing heavenward like an eleventh-century Norman helmet, or perhaps a towering sentry box with a jagged triangular opening marking its point of attachment at the base of the stem.

My Wärtsilä timing was admirable in that I saw a completed bow section—not the prow but the one directly behind it—moved from the paint shop to the Building Hall. (Amidships, where the hull is broadest, sections are two abreast and several decks high; at bow and stern, the hull narrows so that a single section suffices. These single slices of ship, so to speak, are the most readily identifiable.) The section in question had just been sandblasted, primed, and painted. The carborundum grit used to scale off rust before painting had been scattered by the wind, coming to rest everywhere, crunching noisily underfoot.

The sliding doors of the paint shed drew back to admit the motorized flatbed that would carry the bow section to the Building Hall. These flatbeds are 50 feet square, but only 6 feet high. They roll on dozens of tires the size of rear tractor wheels, wheels that are mounted on pairs to either side of steering posts, like aircraft landing carriages; all the flatbed's dozens of wheels can be turned at once for maximum, exquisite maneuverability. The driver rides below the flush deck of his vehicle, confined within a low-slung claustrophobic pod about the size of a ball turret from a World War II Flying Fortress. Suspended within his underbelly perch, he backs the flatbed beneath the freshly painted bow section standing keel down, its sloping sides buttressed with I-beam legs to keep it on point.

Once lowered by jacks onto the flatbed, the 60-foot-high load was inched out into the daylight and began its cautious journey down an *allée* of sheds toward the Building Hall, where a vast door had been slid aside to admit it. The flatbed was driven inside and positioned beneath a pair of cranes that track the length of the Hall's ceiling. They hoisted the gray, V-shaped section from the flatbed, moved it in tandem over the smoky depths of the dry dock, and lowered it onto the muddy, puddled cement

Top, balanced atop a transporter, the penultimate bow section, its machinery already in place, leaves the paint shop for the Building Hall. *Bottom,* the same bow section in place, ready to be attached to the lengthening *Song of America* inside the Building Hall. *(Author's collection)*

floor. This was rough positioning only: within a few days, the *Song of America*'s number 2 bow section would be mated precisely to the number 3 section already in place, and shipfitters—so called because they literally fit sections of ship together—would attach shell plating and framing, transforming the new section into an intrinsic extension of the hull. Although I was not present for that process, I did spend an afternoon down in the dry dock. I clambered down a long, grated steel staircase fast by the gouged rock walls of the dock and, stooping low to avoid the bottom plating only 4 feet above the dock floor, walked underneath the length of the *Song of America*'s clangorous hull, skirting cast-iron keel blocks and stumbling over a tangle of pipes, cables, and hoses.

The cranes that had lowered the bow section that morning were confined to the Building Hall's interior. Crane operators rode in glass-enclosed cabs high above the floor; the carrying beam, from which they and their loads were suspended, enabled them to move the length and/or width of the Hall's roof on fixed tracks, thus positioning the load anywhere over the dry dock. Outdoor shipyard cranes are different; unable to follow ceiling tracks, they must stand alone. There are two types. The first is called a T-crane, quite simply because it looks like an enormous capital *T*. It is supported on a central, vertical member that carries an unbalanced crossbar at its top. The short end is cantilevered, allowing the longer end to swing in a wide arc with its load riding anywhere along the crossbar's underside. These are familiar fixtures on building sites all over the world, either resting on the ground for low buildings or erected high up in a taller building's girders so as to retain their height advantage. The other shipyard crane is called, in the United States, a whirly crane, quite simply because it can whirl a sloping, lifting arm in a circle. The whirly crane has the added advantage of mobility. Four stout legs are mounted on wheeled bogie trucks that ride the length of a pier or slipway along parallel railway tracks. The moving crane can straddle objects stored carefully between rails. As it moves, an electric traveling bell rings, and from a huge spool attached to a lower leg, yards of a thick black umbilical cable either wind up or pay out, depending on the direction of movement.

Shipyard cranes must be able to span both sides of a launch berth and, sometimes, must work in ganged pairs for especially complex tasks. Later that summer, in Nantes, at the Dubigeon-Normandie yard, I watched the stern section of the *Scandinavia* being inverted in midair. It had arrived upside down from the paint shed, propeller brackets uppermost; now, thanks to some ponderous, midair juggling by a pair of cranes, it was to be turned right side up for the first time. It was delivered by flatbed to a

Midair juggling. One of the *Scandinavia*'s stern sections, incorporating a shaft bracket, being flipped over at Nantes. *Below,* a colony of whirly cranes hovers solicitously over the *Nordic Prince* at Wärtsilä in 1970. *(Author's collection and Wärtsilä's Helsinki Shipyard)*

cleared space beyond the landbound *Scandinavia*'s bow at the top of the berth. Two identical whirly cranes put their heads together over the newly arrived section. (Whether in shipyard or pier, whirly cranes drawn together on the same track huddle in a lifelike fashion, their swan neck jibs leaning inward like the beaks of solicitous parent birds conferring over the nest.) The stern section was lifted high in the air by both cranes. Then one slacked off so that the other carried the entire load on edge. The partner crane's hooks were detached, then reattached to a different set of lifting lugs on the section's upper side; deftly, the massive piece was rotated elegantly in midair until it hung keel-side down. Then, in concert, both cranes hoisted it even higher and carried it triumphantly over the length of the *Scandinavia*, traveling bells chattering shrilly at each other, and deposited their load where it belonged, at the hull's after end down by the Loire.

During the week following the one I spent at Wärtsilä, I visited the yard of the Aalborg Werft, located in the town of the same name that produces most of the world's aquavit. Carnival Cruise Lines's *Tropicale* was fitting out there, and for the morning of my last day in Denmark, I left a 2:00 A.M. wake-up call so that I could see the *Tropicale*'s single, branching *France*-like funnel hoisted from pier to upper deck. Works engineers had predicted—correctly—that minimal wind conditions would be encountered just before dawn. They were right, although a fine penetrating drizzle was falling. But even with the assistance of a huge floating crane moored alongside the *Tropicale*'s outboard flank, the rigging for its combined lift with the land-based whirly cranes was inadequate to raise safely the red, white, and blue fixture from the pier to its floating base 80 feet in the air. Yet even though that early-morning lift was temporarily abandoned, it was exhilarating to have seen it initiated.

That kind of spectacular move is the exception. Normally, there is frustratingly little movement in a shipyard. Ship sections seem permanent structures rusting dolefully in place, awaiting their summons to the berth. New Yorkers are familiar with the phenomenon: skeletal framings for office or apartment towers proceed in fits and starts, with enormous growth one week and none for several to follow. It is the same in every shipyard from Wärtsilä to Saint-Nazaire. The minutiae of construction are best observed away from the berth, out in the complex of sheds where individual welders are prefabricating the sections. But even there, at the start of the construction chain, apparent immobility suffuses the work as well. Motionless welders are everywhere, draped prone atop a curved section

28   LINERS TO THE SUN

Two views of the *Tropicale*'s funnel. *Above,* surrounded by scaffolding, the branching stack nears completion. *Left,* the funnel base was ready above, the funnel itself ready below, but the cranes were not ready to make the final lift. *(Author's collection)*

of hull or crouching out of sight within a giant grid of floor plates, their presence betrayed only by the flare of their arcs.

Close up, the welder seems a graven image, genuflecting in devotion over an eternal flame. He is swathed in protective clothing, as anonymous as a space suit: a leather apron, stout canvas coveralls, asbestos spats, huge gauntlets, and even trouser clips keep red-hot steel fragments away from his skin. A curved shield conceals his face; the thick, glass viewing port must be replaced frequently because it pits and discolors so. Although intermittent welding chores require goggles only, the shipyard welder, remaining within inches of his searing work for hours at a time, needs substantial protection from continual infrared and ultraviolet radiation. It is stifling work. Outdoors in cold weather, the welder's garb is an asset, but it is appalling overdressing for summer, when welders doff their hoods to reveal flushed, dripping faces. During the warm months at Toulon's Seyne-sur-Mer yard, the day shift fitting out the *Atlantic* started at 6:00 A.M. in order to finish their working day before the worst of the afternoon's heat.

How does a welder join two flat plates together? At Wärtsilä, I was allowed to try welding some scrap. My only tool was primitive, a stout spring clip with an insulated handle. Held in its jaws was a 14-inch steel rod, called an electrode, coated with a sleeve of rutile, or titanium oxide. Only the half inch grasped within the spring clip was bare to ensure sound electrical contact; the reason for the coating covering the rest of the electrode will emerge shortly. One wire from a high-voltage source—direct current—led through the handle of my clip to the electrode; the other was clamped onto the steel I would weld. I was to weld two steel plates together; each of the two had its facing edge sloped so that, placed close together but not touching, their joint bevels, or scarfs, produced a V-shaped valley between them. I was to fill that valley with several layers, or beads, of molten steel.

Wearing gloves, apron, and mask, I touched the electrode to the plate. With an audible snap, a glaring spark leaped between them. That first encounter is known as striking the arc, and I had been warned to withdraw at once after that initial jab, to avoid gluing electrode to plate. It is the novice welder's inevitable error, and true to form, my electrode remained adhered to the steel plate, as though embedded like a dart. After four false starts, I finally managed to strike and maintain the arc correctly. It fizzed and sparked away, developing the necessary high temperature: 3,500 degrees centigrade. Within seconds, through the glass of my mask, the electrode tip and both valley slopes boiled into a molten pool. By drawing the electrode steadily toward me, I was to form a smooth, con-

Welding at Wärtsilä. *Above,* lost in a steel thicket, welders assemble *Song of America* deck beams. Although large steel sheets can be seam-welded by machine, awkward or inaccessible welds like these must be achieved by hand. *Below,* an inverted hull section under construction. The rat holes—individual bites along the floorplates' edges—are there to avoid contact with longitudinal welds along the shell plating. The sections here became part of *Royal Princess.* *(Author's collection and Wärtsilä's Helsinki Shipyard)*

tinuous bead along the deepest part of the valley. After a few ineffectual tries, I called it quits, doffed the already stifling mask, and passed the electrode to more experienced hands. Only then did I comprehend the welder's intense concentration. The electrode must be held just so, sixty degrees to the horizontal, as well as at exactly the right distance from the plate. The speed of movement is also crucial: too quick and a skimpy bead is formed, too slow and a lumpish accumulation builds up in its wake.

Whereas rivet-joined plates represent a simple, physical union, welding is a complex bonding process. The enormous heat of the arc sucks oxygen and nitrogen from the surrounding atmosphere. Yet air must be excluded, for when absorbed into the molten pool, it creates bubbles that make the finished weld crumbly with porosity. The oxide coating I mentioned earlier is designed to foil this atmospheric contamination. In addition to being nonconductive and noncombustible, the oxide has a slightly higher melting point than the steel it surrounds. The melting sequence works as follows: The moment the arc is struck, the electrode's steel core is liquefied. Milliseconds later, the oxide coating melts. It vaporizes at once and forms a gaseous shield around the weld, excluding oxygen and nitrogen until the molten steel has cooled and hardened, impervious to atmospheric interference. Remnants of oxide coating either form slag atop the cooled weld or shower down around the welder's feet—hence his protective spats and apron—to cool on the floor. They crunch underfoot, the detritus of welding, like sand on the porch of a beach-front house.

A deep V-shaped valley requires several layers, or passes, of weld material to fill it. After each pass, surface impurities must be wire-brushed off. A good finished weld has the look of a slightly wrinkled silver worm that just overfills the V-shaped valley, rather the way water bulges at the top of a full glass. This domed top is called the reinforcement of the weld, and to either side, it must join the top of each valley slope—the "toe" of the weld—precisely. Overflowing the valley is as bad as not filling it completely; it must be filled exactly to the brim and no further, save for its gentle meniscus. On the underside of the joined plates, beneath the valley, a small bead should have been extruded—this is called "good penetration" —so that a smaller, glistening worm also bridges the bottom of the joint.

While a good weld may seem apparent from its outward appearance, the unseen subsurface requires sophisticated checking. Any number of failures can contribute to a flawed weld: air bubbles, porosity, interior slag not brushed from an early pass, or, worse, malicious neglect. A welded barge built in New York during World War II had a steel rubrail around

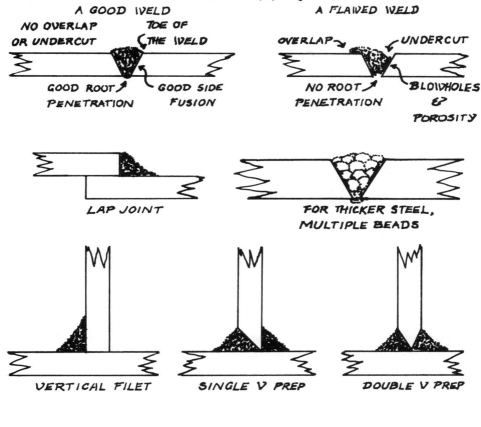

"FILLING THE VALLEY"

A GOOD WELD

NO OVERLAP OR UNDERCUT
TOE OF THE WELD
GOOD ROOT PENETRATION
GOOD SIDE FUSION

A FLAWED WELD

OVERLAP
UNDERCUT
NO ROOT PENETRATION
BLOWHOLES & POROSITY

LAP JOINT

FOR THICKER STEEL, MULTIPLE BEADS

VERTICAL FILET

SINGLE V PREP

DOUBLE V PREP

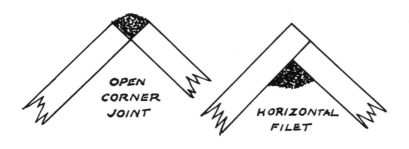

OPEN CORNER JOINT

HORIZONTAL FILET

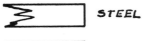

STEEL

WELD

SHIPBUILDING'S WELDING TECHNIQUES

JMG

its hull crack, inexplicably, after only a week's service. Close inspection revealed that a welder had merely stuffed most of the weld valley with unused electrodes and finished over the top into a facsimile of completion. Simple fluid penetrants can be used to check a spurious weld, but these will only detect surface cracks. Complex machinery—portable X-ray equipment or ultrasonic scanners—is required to see deeper. (The welding inspector at a power plant constructed in France was a stunning Danish blonde. Although she had the highest technical qualifications for the post, it was her extraordinary beauty that served the project best: all the welders on the site outdid themselves in their attempts to make the best possible welds, to please their enchanting forewoman.)

Although welded ships are commonplace today, their birth followed an extended and troublesome period of gestation. Washington ordered its first experimental welded cargo ship during World War I, but the contract was canceled after the armistice. So production of the world's first all-welded vessel was left to the British. The little coastal steamer *Fullagar*, launched into the River Mersey in 1919, was 150 feet long. She sailed for twenty years in English and Canadian waters and might have sailed longer had she not sunk after colliding with another vessel off British Columbia in 1937. She was an experimental rarity; in postwar American and European shipyards, welding was used only for repairs. In the 1930s, small, welded tanker barges appeared, followed by self-propelled tankers for inland waters. Within ten years, all American vessels under 300 feet were welded, and the *J. W. Van Dyke*, launched in 1937, was the prototype of the first welded, seagoing tanker. (Even so, the *J. W. Van Dyke*'s bow and stern sections were riveted as a strength precaution.) By the time World War II broke out, nearly all deep-water tonnage was still being riveted.

The wartime maritime emergency hastened sweeping changes. Fleets of new, cheap cargo ships had to be built quickly, identical hulls had to be turned out in the hundreds. By war's end, 2,500 Liberty ships, 500 T-2 tankers, and 400 Victory ships would be launched. It was a huge undertaking, initiated in new yards where new workers would have to be trained. Since it was easier to train welders than riveters, all-welded oceangoing cargo vessels were prescribed. The new yards were laid out to accommodate prefabrication, and identical subassemblies were built that allowed new welders to perfect their skills by repetition. The construction of ships by section was begun, and the innovation of working on those sections upside down became commonplace. With every prospect of success, America's new wartime shipyards geared up for full production, and the first all-welded, mass-produced merchant ships soon joined the war effort.

But within a year, over the winter of 1942–43, disquieting reports came back to the yards. Something was disastrously wrong with the new hulls. In Oregon, the *Schenectady*, a brand-new T-2 tanker tied up at a Portland dock, suddenly broke in half before dawn with a report heard a mile away. Bow and stern sagged to the bottom, and the vessel lay pierside like a broken match. Alarmingly, it was not an isolated incident. Another T-2 broke up spontaneously at the entrance to New York harbor. A Liberty ship unloading at an East Coast terminal cracked wide open, and a freighter hull under construction on the Great Lakes separated into two halves. Altogether, there were nine welded ship failures that winter; another was unauthenticated but presumed because ship and crew vanished in mid-Atlantic, far from enemy submarines. The culprit, unmasked by the American Bureau of Shipping, was brittle fracture.

Brittle fracture is a phenomenon as old as modern steel. The first recorded instance occurred in 1879, shortly after the Bessemer process had been perfected. Brittle fracture is an apparently spontaneous rupture of a steel member, resulting from residual stresses within the steel itself, stresses amplified by the severe expansion and contraction cycle of the welding process. In fact, no piece of steel is immune from brittle fracture; there is in the records of one steel mill a bizarre instance of a stout I-beam, lying on the floor unattached to anything, suddenly and devastatingly splitting down the middle like a pine log.

Brittle fracture has destroyed a wide variety of structures. One of the most spectacular and tragic occurred in Boston on a cold January day in 1919. At noon, a large molasses storage tank, 50 feet high and 90 feet in diameter, suddenly collapsed, engulfing adjacent streets in a lethal brown tidal wave. Vehicles and their drivers were swept along by the sticky flood. Twelve people died, many more were injured, and dozens of horses had to be destroyed. Supports for the Boston Elevated Railway were knocked down, putting the branch line out of service for a month. (They say along Boston's piers that on a hot summer's day after a rainstorm, there is still a faint reek of molasses.)

At a subsequent trial, the tank's owners insisted at first that a bomb had caused the damage; anarchists were popular postwar scapegoats. Then they claimed that a streetcar had rammed the tank's base. But city engineers proved that the overloaded tank had self-destructed spontaneously from brittle fracture. They submitted photographs in evidence, showing the edges of the torn plates: telltale herringbone patterns in the steel gave clear indication of brittle fracture, a characteristic that had first been identified by the French engineer Charles de Fréminville five years earlier in his *Recherche sur la Fragilité*.

But on riveted hulls, such total structural collapse was rare. Rivets offer the advantage of giving a little; when brittle fracture reaches the edge of a riveted plate, the rivets bend slightly, the stress is thus relieved, and the rupture is contained within the original, offending plate. At least four Atlantic superliners suffered from brittle fracture. Between the wars, portions of the shell plating on the German-built *Leviathan* and *Majestic* cracked. The cracks were plated over on the exterior and painted over within the affected cabins. The *Europa*'s foredeck cracked around a cargo hatch, as did the *Queen Mary*'s. But, consistently, all four fractures were contained *because riveted joints gave*. Welded hulls, on the other hand, are notoriously rigid; when brittle fracture reaches a seam as strong as— if not stronger than—the plates it joins, it continues across plate after plate, creating a catastrophically long rupture.

This is what was destroying those first wartime welded hulls. Shipbuilders were unaware of the residual stresses that the welding process had unleashed in their hulls. Strictly speaking, cooling rather than heating sets the stage. As welded seams cool, the adjacent steel contracts, creating a network of hidden stresses throughout the hull, a time bomb waiting to go off. Small differences in temperature proved critical. One ship, on leaving the relative warmth of harbor water at fifty degrees for the waters of an incoming river at forty degrees, suffered explosive brittle fracture right across the bottom plating. In Boston Harbor, in 1947, the T-2 tanker *Ponagansett* was having a 2-inch clip welded onto her strength deck. The heat from this trivial repair triggered a massive release of stresses within the ship's plating, and she burst apart on the instant, bow and stern sections coming to rest on the bottom, grotesquely misaligned.

Wartime failures created distrust among America's allies, in particular the traditionalists of Britain's Royal Navy. In the summer of 1944, I crossed the Atlantic eastbound on board H.M.S. *Patroller*, a welded escort carrier built in the United States for the Royal Navy. The crew assured me that their "Woolworth carrier"—their own pejorative—would go to the bottom in ten seconds if struck by a torpedo. They had concluded, incorrectly, that any welded seam was suspect, that the process was merely a wartime expedient for more reliable riveting. But they were wrong; although fatal Liberty ship cracks might originate in a faulty weld, the line of fracture did not follow the seam but marched across the plates. The

36

hulls themselves were tearing apart because no one understood the stresses imparted by improper welding techniques.

Dozens of damaged plates were removed from the ships and examined by the National Bureau of Standards. Laid out in a warehouse, they were separated into three categories: Source, Thru, and End, according to whether brittle fracture had begun, continued, or terminated in them. After exhaustive tests, the pattern of destruction emerged, and new welding directories were rushed to the shipyards. Steel crack-arrester straps were to be riveted across eight potential stress points, some on deck, others below water. The system of plating was rearranged: larger plates meant fewer welds, and close parallel welds were prohibited. Welds were never to cross one another; where a stringer crossed a plate seam, its edge was to be scooped out—leaving an indentation called a rat's hole—vaulting over the transverse weld before reestablishing contact on the far side. Rounded rather than square corners were ordained for cargo hatches (shades of the *Europa*'s and *Queen Mary*'s troubles). Materials to be welded were to be preheated or annealed after welding. Bulkheads above the strength deck were to be kept low, and openings with right angles were forbidden. As these reforms were adopted, the wartime hulls assumed the reliability that had originally eluded them.

Just after the war, the S.S. *United States*, assembled in a dry dock at Virginia's Newport News, swept the seas as the world's fastest passenger liner. She embodied several firsts, among them her smooth, almost rivet-free hull, which inaugurated the age of the all-welded passenger liner, prototype for all newbuilding today. Yet some of her other revolutionary specifications did not catch on. William Francis Gibbs, her naval architect, pioneered extensive use of aluminum in her superstructure. An entirely new welding technique had to be developed and workers trained to implement it. Ultimately, 2,000 tons of aluminum were used, although the *United States*'s superstructure was not all aluminum by any means. The fore-and-aft framing and some of the plating were aluminum but the transverse members were steel. Structural aluminum bends, so no expansion joints were needed on the ship's upper decks. (The next most heavily aluminized ship was the *France* of 1962, containing 1,600 tons. The *QE2* used 1,100 tons initially, though additional aluminum cabin units have since been added.)

But the great difficulty of the new material was not welding the aluminum to itself, but to the steel of the hull. Where the two metals touched, spontaneous electrolysis occurred, and strips of rubber-coated fiberglass had to be inserted painstakingly between every ferro-aluminous

Cunard's first aluminum deckhouse. On an early spring
morning in 1967, this was how the strength deck of the
Queen Elizabeth 2—or, as she was known then, the
Q4—appeared, high above John Brown's yard beneath
a trio of motionless T-cranes. The large public room
nearest the camera is the Queen's Room, the First Class
lounge. *(Cunard)*

joint. Consistently, today's shipbuilders avoid aluminum altogether. Although light and corrosion-resistant, it is expensive, requires specialized handling, and is awkward to link to steel. Also, as demonstrated when an Argentine missile struck the H.M.S. *Sheffield* off the Falklands, aluminum is unpleasantly susceptible to fire. In fact, crewmen serving on board the *Queen Elizabeth 2* in the South Atlantic that spring favored nonaluminum sections of the vessel until they were out of the war zone.

Steel, then, remains the basic component. It arrives from the mill in a variety of shapes and thicknesses, most of it plates over 200 feet square. Stacked alongside are lengths of structural steel—channel (U-shaped) or bulb angle or bulb plate. (The bulb in each case refers to lengths with one running edge swollen to a bulge for strength.) Elsewhere are what look like bundles of rusted pipe—rolled hollow columns that, cut to 'tween-deck height, will support interior deck loads as stanchions. On demand, loads of steel are delivered into the adjacent plating shop. The largest pieces travel via roof crane, with bell-shaped electromagnetic cones sustaining several tons of flat plate through the air. Ensconced, God-like, in his enclosed cab high above the floor, the operator pilots that quiet flight through the dust-moted sun of the shed's interior; above the appropriate cutting table, he lowers the load, cuts the current to his magnets, and delivers the steel with a thunderous crash.

Cutting it to shape is the next step. Where possible on his plans, a naval architect will specify identical brackets, in the hundreds, throughout the hull. These steel multiples are turned out with ganged oxyacetylene cutters, slicing through half-inch steel as though it were butter. The machines operate by computer: a punched paper tape spools past a control head, governing the movement of a trio of cutting flames. Once the three torches have been ignited, they move in eerie, purposeful precision across the surface of the steel plate. A triple shower of brilliant tracers spatters the floor. In half a minute, the cutting heads have returned to their starting point and three identical pieces, edges blackened and slightly scalloped by heat, fall with a clatter. The cutting heads continue relentlessly, tackling a second triptych, pouring a torrent of sparks onto the cooling prototypes as it produces yet another three. Left on the cutting surface at the end of the run is a lacy framework of waste, fragments of which will be gathered up and returned to the steel mill as scrap.

Thicker steel is cut to shape by a plasma arc, an American invention that has become part of most European shipyards' increasingly expensive arsenal of sophisticated, computer-controlled equipment. A plasma arc is several times hotter than an electric arc, firing at temperatures in excess

Light and heavy automated steel cutting. *Above,* brackets three at a time are cut by the dozens for the *Scandinavia* at Nantes. *Below,* the plasma arc-cutting head, submerged below water, slices effortlessly through two-inch steel plate. *(Author's collection)*

of fifty thousand degrees Fahrenheit. It produces a projectile flame so powerful that it burns through 6-inch steel with ease, literally blowing away all accumulating dross to leave a clean, usable edge. The cutting head rides suspended from a motorized gantry trailing festoons of cable and hose, including a pleated accordion-pipe to vent off gases. The cutting must be done underwater; this submerging of the process helps to contain the noise, radiation, and fumes emitted. Ignited, the plasma arc fires, producing a flowerlike, pink eruption that bubbles around the nozzle. Operated by programmed instructions, the torch rides on its ordained path, slicing along an inch a second. After completing its route, the arc is extinguished and the pink froth subsides; when the water has been drained off, a pristine steel contour is revealed, its cut margin unruffled and scarcely scorched.

The minute each plate is cut, it must be tagged for identification. Daubed in yellow paint across one random steel plate at Wärtsilä, I saw the following numbers:

$$431 \quad 2214 \quad 41.26$$
$$8062 \quad (11) \quad BB$$

The *Song of America*'s hull number was 431. The next group of numbers —2214—indicates the number of the drawing that contained the original design of the piece in question. It was destined for inclusion in the section numbered 8062 and the number 11 indicates the location of that particular detail within the section. The piece weighs 41.26 kg and the notation BB is the abbreviation for the Swedish word *babord*, meaning the port, or left, side of the ship. (Curiously, the Finns have no words for the traditional maritime terms "port" or "starboard.") When a BB or SB appears on a piece of steel, it means that somewhere else in the yard, among thousands of steel plates, is its reflected twin, a mirror image destined for installation on the opposite side of the vessel. The shipyard's master computer keeps track of all the individual steel components from the moment they are designed, through their cutting out and assembly within the appropriate section.

Some plates must be bent before they are incorporated into the hull. Putting precisely the right curve into flat steel cannot be trusted to a computer; plates are rolled today, I was somehow pleased to find, exactly as they were a century ago, the final arbiter being the critical eye of the craftsman. They are rolled cold, fed between the rollers of a machine much like an old-fashioned clothes wringer. It has three immensely strong steel rollers, one up and two down. The single upper roller can be raised

The *Normandie*'s port side at New York
in the late thirties. The promenade deck's
overhang betrays a slope-sided hull below
with tumble home incorporated into its
plating. *(Photograph by Paul Hollister)*

or lowered hydraulically to produce varying degrees of bend in the plate. The process is cumulative, each pass back and forth producing additional curl. Carried to the ultimate, a flat plate can be transformed into a cylinder. The *Queen Mary*'s mast, for instance, was made from sections of plate rolled into a complete circle.

Increasingly, modern hulls contain fewer and fewer curves. "Tumble home," for example, that picturesque legacy from wooden ships, is no more. The tumble home was that graceful, inward slope of a ship's side from waterline to strength deck that originated on wooden warships as a means of increasing stability above the waterline. The higher the decks, the lighter the ordnance carried there: if guns and their carriages were smaller, they not only were lighter in weight, they needed less room for recoil. Therefore, naval architects narrowed upper decks, continuing the practice in the evolution to large passenger vessels. The superstructure on many twentieth-century liners with tumble home would perch atop a narrowing hull. Although a liner's tumble home might be almost indistinguishable, only a matter of a foot or so, the device saved considerable upper deck weight. Both original *Queen*s and the *France* had tumble home, as do Cunard's *Countess* and *Princess* today; but the *Queen Elizabeth 2* is, as are all contemporary newbuildings, slab-sided. Square flanks are faster and cheaper to build; the only hull curves remaining are those at either end.

The old overhanging counter, like those on the *Olympic*-class vessels of 1911, rich with compound curves, has become prohibitively expensive. The last two passenger vessels incorporating this graceful feature were the American Export Line's *Constitution* and *Independence* from the fifties, now restored to cruising among the Hawaiian Islands. By the thirties, there was a vogue for cruiser sterns, with after ends like rounded knobs with an above-water slope paralleling the fall of the bow. Both of the earlier *Queen*s boasted cruiser sterns. During the last decade, the simple rounded counter emerged as a favorite; it can be found on all seven new Wärtsilä hulls and for the Peninsular and Orient's *Royal Princess*.

But the stern of the future is already with us. An abrupt, chopped-off transom is found on six contemporary hulls—*Royal Princess, Tropicale, Europa, Nieuw Amsterdam, Noordam*, and *Scandinavia*. The stern of the *Scandinavia* is the most radical, for it is a car ferry as well as a passenger liner, and the bottom half of her stern houses twin loading ramps for cars. This completely square after-plating provides interior designers with maximum cubic enclosure from the waterline up, the same logistical dividend that modern freight carriers enjoy as well.

A *Scandinavia* portfolio. The *Scandinavia* on trials in October 1982. The window row across the counter stern is unique. *Below,* the view from inside as the vessel returns to New York on her maiden voyage. *Opposite top,* the inadequate bow before it was distorted by heavy seas off Cape Hatteras. *Opposite bottom,* Kamewa skewback propellers. Once mounted on their central boss, the blades' pitch can be changed from the bridge. Thus, the vessel can maneuver forward or in reverse without ever changing the shafts' direction of rotation. (*Author's collection*)

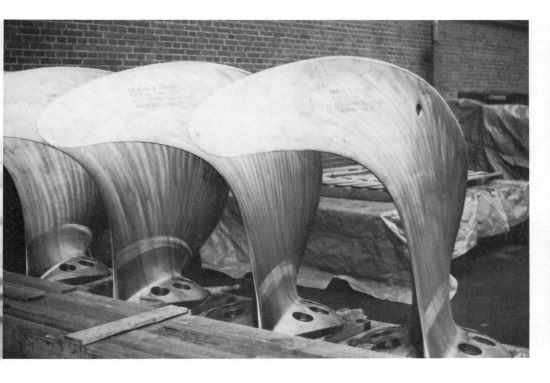

For passengers on board the *Scandinavia*, there is an aesthetic dividend, too. Her public rooms are grouped on three consecutive decks aft. The handsomest, the Blue Riband Lounge, has floor-length windows cut through the stern plating so passengers seated at the aftermost tables can enjoy a unique indoor vista over the wake. There is nothing like it anywhere afloat, and it recalls the elegant stern castles of seventeenth-century Spanish galleons. In those days, before engines existed, a vessel's quietest quarters lay aft. They remained so through the brief paddle-wheel era until they were displaced amidships by propeller vibration. But by some engineering miracle—most importantly, their brace of Kamewa skewback propellers—the *Scandinavia*'s builders have reduced stern vibration to an almost imperceptible minimum. During the vessel's maiden voyage in October 1982, those stern windows of the Blue Riband Lounge were incomparable vantage points, not only at sea but during entry into port, New York as well as Freeport, when chilly and humid weather respectively discouraged a vigil at the rail.

But if sterns have been simplified, bows grow paradoxically more complex. Contrast, if you will, the four-square vertical cutwater of a Harland & Wolff hull of 1900 with the soaring curve of a Wärtsilä stem of the seventies. It has nothing to do with advanced technology or the change from riveting to welding—turn-of-the-century shipbuilders could have achieved the same effect had it been desired. Indeed, the clipper bow of today is used for two reasons only, one practical, the other aesthetic. First, the overhanging prow provides those navigating with a protective override in advance of the underwater bulbous bow; second, the prow soars forward because, quite simply, it is the fashion.

That pointed beak has expensive ramifications, among them the need for a great deal of flared bow plating. It is a question of shaping: on that traditional Harland & Wolff hull, the forward bulwark—the solid railing enclosing the fo'c's'le deck—was a vertical continuation of the stem and sides. However, when the stem arches forward, to complement the line, the surrounding bulwark must arch with it, creating a flare of sloping plating almost as far aft as the bridge. It is not only expensive, it can be awkward as well. On a 1982 cruise, the *Royal Viking Star* raised a fouled anchor three times, once each off Lerwick, St. Pierre, and Bar Harbor. In each case, the anchor flukes had tangled with discarded steel cable on the bottom. Crewmen on the fo'c's'le trying to clear it could not even see it; the flaring overhang of the bow denied them sight of, let alone access to, the problem. A seaman suspended over the rail in a bosun's chair was still yards away from the offending tangle he had been lowered to cut free. The job was finally done by solicitous pilot-boat crews.

Then, too, that Wärtsilä bow is not prudent for the most punishing seas—though it is adequate for RCCL ships confined to the largely placid Caribbean. But Royal Viking vessels, roaming on world-wide itineraries, often encounter dirty weather, and when they do, they must ride it out. One passenger on board the *Royal Viking Sky* during a heavy blow off Canada's maritime provinces in 1981 took note of a lighthouse's gleam through her porthole; its bearing never changed throughout the storm even though the vessel was ostensibly under way. The *Sky*'s master was merely keeping his vessel's head into the storm, not risking his handsome bow by pressing into it at cruising speed.

On their two newest ships—*Nieuw Amsterdam* and *Noordam*—Holland America Line has opted for a traditional if less graceful choice. Both vessels are identical from the exterior and are designed for round-the-world service. Aft and amidships, they are relentlessly modern with a contemporary transom stern, a single stack aft, and a kind of Bauhaus superstructure reminiscent of the *Prinsendam*. But forward, the Penhoët builders have hedged their bets. From either side, the bows appear to swoop to a graceful point in Wärtsilä fashion; from ahead, the bow plating is flared modishly—more bowl than beak—with reserves of strength that recall the lines of their two predecessors, the 1938 *Nieuw Amsterdam* and the 1959 *Rotterdam*. Whenever those successive flagships were in adjoining dry docks in Rotterdam, it was interesting to see that, despite their contrasting superstructures, separated by two decades of maritime fashion, their hull configuration at the bow was almost identical. The same genes are apparent in the latest *Nieuw Amsterdam*'s bow with a new wrinkle added: from the shear strake down through two lower strakes, the plating to either side falls almost vertically before a pronounced horizontal corner heralds an inward slope of steel down to the waterline. It not only increases the interior cubic capacity, it adds immeasurably to the vessel's high-tech look—a look, curiously, of which the company seems somehow ashamed. In the eighties, Holland America patented the words *Ocean Liner* (a lexicological presumption of the highest order!). But the new high-tech bow did not sit well with the company's marketing arm, did not embody what they perceived as the correct "ocean liner" profile. So, for the brochures, artists air-brushed out that intriguing plating wrinkle, leaving intact a conventional swooping bow with far less character than the rest of the ship.

What's in a bow? Two contrasting views of Holland America's latest *Nieuw Amsterdam*. *Top,* in profile during trials off Saint-Nazaire, the soaring prow belies its bulk. *Bottom,* from ahead, as she approaches New York on her maiden voyage, the impressive brute strength of her forward hull configuration, a perspective the company eschews. *(Holland America Line)*

Recapturing a former look can be elusive. A case in point is the Home Lines's *Atlantic*, designed as a visual companion to their earlier *Oceanic*. Yet the subsequent ship, which entered service in 1982, falls aesthetically short of the prototype. Both have midship pools covered by Magrodomes and a substantial and handsome single funnel aft. But the *Atlantic*'s designers fell prey to a shortcoming common to many new vessels: the foreshortened bow. Owners tend to pack as much superstructure, which earns income, forward, at the expense of a projecting fo'c's'le, which earns nothing. As a result, the *Atlantic* has little of her older sister's long, lean grace, and company brochures for the second vessel favor overhead shots taken from astern, avoiding her abbreviated and hence disappointing bow.

The same problem haunted the *Scandinavia*, built upriver from Saint-Nazaire at Nantes. She had a radically new silhouette, commonplace in the Baltic, where car ferries reign supreme, but novel in the Western Hemisphere. In simplest terms, she was built like a shoebox with a bow, a minuscule token bow so ruthlessly foreshortened as to be aesthetically as well as functionally imprudent. She was destined not for the Baltic but as a year-round liner between New York and Freeport; her course cut across one of the most notorious winter storm regions in the world. "Cape Hatteras" were the two words haunting all on board the maiden voyage in October 1982. A few voyages later, they made their persuasive mark on the ship: 14-foot seas off the Carolinas in November of the same year wreaked havoc with the forward bulkhead stiffeners supporting that inadequate bow. Fortunately for Scandinavian World Cruises, their flagship was the only ship that backed into her New York slip in order to load cars through the stern; hence, her damaged bow was spared scrutiny from observers ashore.

But more often, the look of a bow is related less to cost or expediency than the demands of the shipyard's clients. Invariably, owners strive for a modish, contemporary look to their ships, and during the early design phase, when anyone can sketch something on the back of an envelope, company executives will agonize over the proposed look. Like their opposite numbers in Detroit, ship owners are front-end fetishists; consistently, automotive newbuilding's annual changes occur within the design complex of grille, hood, and windshield. (It is, incidentally, a curious obsession for carmakers, since the majority of today's drivers—confined to one-way, multilaned thruways—stare for most of their driving time at trunks rather than hoods.) To carry the automotive parallel one step further, both cars and ships have been similarly foreshortened. A Packard of the twenties, with its vertical grille, long horizontal hood, and vertical windshield, had

Oceanic and *Atlantic*. The older ship *(above)* has a splendid grace, while her newer consort falls somehow short. *(Home Lines)*

as its oceangoing counterpart the straight stem, extended fo'c's'le, and vertical bridge-front of the contemporary *Laconia*, for instance. Forty years later, those right-angled elements were softened and compressed; a rounded grille vanished into a hood that flowed sinuously into a windshield. Afloat, the fo'c's'le head has been withdrawn into an angled screen bulkhead with a slipstream configuration. The only reverse slope in a ship's forward end is the swoop of the bow and it, in conjunction with the ski-slope of the bridgescreen, makes for that pervasive newbuilding profile, the wedge. That seems to be the look that sells.

Ship styling is increasingly important. The cruise business prospered in the seventies because it offered new mass market clients a gleaming, styled product akin to the latest refrigerator or dishwasher. And, as with any new product line, there have been problems. Though the exterior look of the wedge ships is sleek and carefree, their internal systems are frighteningly complex, complete with sophisticated electronic components sometimes beyond the capabilities of the engineers on board. The repeated delays of the *Nieuw Amsterdam*'s entry into service during the spring of 1983 serve as a case in point: had Holland America been unable to pirate the necessary spare part from the yard-bound *Noordam*, it would have taken five months to manufacture a replacement for the defective electrical relays that stalled the originally scheduled maiden voyage from Le Havre.

This was the newbuilding I saw over the summer of 1981. All of those ships are now in service, though the *Scandinavia* was transferred back to the Baltic after a flawed start between New York and Freeport and, more recently, has been sold to Seattle's Sundance Cruises and been rechristened *Stardancer*. As cruising's impetus continues, even larger hulls are in train. In addition to P&O's *Royal Princess*, built in Wärtsilä's Building Hall—so long that her bow was added after she was afloat and launched—Carnival Cruise Lines has three more ships under construction, all in excess of 45,000 tons. The *Holiday* was completed at Aalborg, *Jubilee* and *Celebration* at Kockum's yard in Malmö, Sweden. In 1984, Klosters Rederi A/S, parent company of Norwegian Caribbean Lines, announced plans for the *Phoenix* project, an ambitious and extraordinary scheme to launch the largest passenger vessel ever built, a kind of late-twentieth-century *Great Eastern*.

But these new hulls are only the frame of the cruise picture. New passengers are booking, and it is important to understand how they relate to their predecessors, how they are accommodated on board, and how they find amusement and contentment at sea.

In travel, separate class accommodation
as a reflection of a hierarchical social structure
is clearly out of date. . . . All passengers can walk
from end to end without let or hindrance.

—SIR BASIL SMALLPEICE, DESCRIBING
Queen Elizabeth 2 BEFORE LAUNCH

There was another ship in port along with our
own and the quaint streets of Willemstadt were
sprinkled with tourists. It was amusing to watch
the different batches of tourists pass each other.
They would pause slightly, recognize each other as
tourists, but would not speak or give any signal
and after a moment would pass on like ants from
different nests sniffing at each other for the scent
of their own formicary.

—T. S. STRIBLING, "NINETEEN
BOILED SHIRTFRONTS"

3.
Class Distinctions

A casualty on board nearly all of today's ships is multiple-class accommodations: that historic double, triple, or even quadruple standard—a perennial Atlantic fixture—is no more. Contemporary cruise ships are single class because cruising, from its inception, has traditionally been single class. All passengers vacationing at sea were conceived by shipowners and operators to be compatible, capable of sharing an entire vessel without friction or embarrassment. Just as numbers of Atlantic vessels in the past were designed exclusively for immigrants or Cabin Class, so shipboard today is restricted to one amorphous cruising class.

Today's shipowners pack their hulls democratically. But, despite that egalitarian intent, a class system of a different sort has emerged to replace the discarded one. Moreover, the barriers between these new classes are harder to circumvent than of old when no Tourist passenger worth his or her salt did not occasionally masquerade—if only for an evening—as a member of First. To change classes today, as we shall see, one must change hulls as well, depending on one's taste for ritz or glitz.

We shall better understand these contemporary class distinctions by reexamining the originals, outlining the ways in which the earliest Atlantic passengers were segregated. It was a system resting less on snobbism than on sound business practice, and it arose out of an appreciation by ship-owners that they should provide berths for every purse. Indeed, the great cabin synonym is "accommodation," utterly appropriate shipboard usage; company owners were predisposed to accommodate passengers of every background. If they did not, they could not possibly compete.

On the earliest Atlantic steamers, passengers were separated and identified by the type of accommodation they sought. Those who could, booked individual cabins and were described, perforce, as Cabin passengers. Humbler travelers, usually immigrants, were crowded into compartments, plebeian dormitories aft, often near the steering mechanism—hence, in the steerage. As the years passed, Steerage encompassed mass berthing any-where in the hull, fore or aft, while the stabler and quieter midships section was reserved by naval architects and company planners as the domain of Cabin passengers.

Among the perks enjoyed by this superior class were abundant light and fresh air, denied their Steerage shipmates below. Cabin Class state-rooms and public rooms—all save the dining saloon—were invariably situated on upper decks, high in the vessel. Ironically, occupants of those lofty quarters suffered badly in rough weather, located as they were at the extreme end of an inverted pendulum whenever their ship pitched (its bow rising and falling), rolled from side to side, or, worst of all, scended, a ghastly combination of the two motions produced by a following sea. Yet to this day, cabin locations high in a vessel remain the most enviable and expensive. On board *Queen Elizabeth 2*, for instance, the Queen Mary and Queen Elizabeth Suites, perched aft of the bridge, offer incomparable views ahead and to either flank but turn into heaving, creaking torture chambers in a gale. At such times, occupants of downscale accommodations below relish their advantageous placement nearer the ship's pivot point.

In the last decade of the nineteenth century, larger liners offered larger numbers of passengers a larger choice of accommodations. A new intermediate class bridged the gulf between steerage and stateroom. Hence-forth, Cabin passengers were economically subdivided. First Cabin, or

First Class, encompassed the most lavish and expensive staterooms on board. The new class, Second Cabin—hence Second Class—occupied small quarters at the after end of the main deckhouse and below. Their cabins were furnished modestly, they slept in bunks rather than brass beds, and made do with communal bathrooms and lavatories down the passageway. But passengers who booked in the Second Cabin were eminently respectable, bourgeois voyagers who shared a genteel seagoing kinship with their richer shipmates forward, and kept aloof from the "huddled masses" they observed below the railing of their after promenade.

At that moment in transatlantic history, First, Second, and Steerage afloat reflected precisely the prevailing upper-, middle-, and working-class structure ashore. Each class kept to itself, an autonomous neighborhood within the urban microcosm of the ship. Steerage passengers got short shrift, with no public rooms or even formal deck space of their own. When they took the air, they sat on winches or hatchcovers in either well deck. But First and Second Cabin passengers had not only their own contiguous blocks of cabins, but their own decks, sheltered and open; their own dining saloons and smoking rooms; and their own libraries, writing rooms, gymnasia, and purser's office. There was no crossover point and no official intermingling of classes save on one occasion: every Sunday morning, Second Cabin worshippers would flock into the otherwise forbidden First Cabin lounge or dining saloon for divine services conducted by the master of the vessel. (It is a revealing socioarchitectural fact of interior steamship design that First Class, the least populous class on board, nevertheless boasted the most capacious public rooms.) This divine dispensation did not extend to Steerage; their orisons were either voiced informally or were led by a traveling cleric who might volunteer to officiate at a Steerage-compartment service. At all other times, separation of the classes was rigidly maintained by company and client alike, save for those boorish few from the First Class who ventured on slumming expeditions down in Steerage. First Class never slummed in Second—that had no vicarious spice at all; only a descent into the lowest depths intrigued.

Quite naturally, the next overdue refinement in transatlantic class structure involved Steerage. By 1910, the moment was ripe. Competition among steamship companies for a larger share of the emigrant traffic triggered far-reaching improvements in their humblest passengers' lot. This was less a question of Fabian altruism than shrewd business; the immigrant was, consistently, the most profitable passenger on board. Albert Ballin, astute head of the Hamburg-Amerika Linie, was the first to capitalize on this economic fact of life by upgrading his lowest passenger accommodation on board the new *Imperator*-class monsters of 50,000 tons in 1912. Steerage was transformed into Third Class; the old dormitories were gone and in their place were blocks of spartan but private rooms. Astonishingly, immigrants on board Hamburg-Amerika's newest tonnage had proper berths in cabins. They also had interior public spaces—smoking rooms, lounges, and dining saloons. None were lavish; dining tables were covered with oilcloth rather than linen and there was no attempt at a menu. But it was a vast improvement over supping indifferently in the Steerage compartment of old, and it served notice that, within the obvious limitations of the cheapest fare, a discernible if remote facsimile of life in First and Second had been established.

It was a class improvement interrupted by World War I. Postwar political developments mandated further class ructions. In 1920, when Congress cut off the unrestricted flow of immigrants, shipping companies upgraded the recently inaugurated Third Class even further. Redundant immigrant quarters were spruced up—if only just—and emerged in company brochures with a new accommodation label: Tourist Third Cabin. It was a stroke of genius. The two peripheral embellishments—a "Tourist" prefix and an obligatory snob suffix, "Cabin"—diluted the undeniably proletarian stigma of "Third." As a piece of sales strategy, it had been designed to reach and attract eastbound summer traffic.

And beyond anybody's wildest expectation, it did. Atlantic schedules became seasonal for the first time as tourists of all kinds—undergraduates, academics, farmers, clerks, even nouveau riche, second-generation immigrants sailing home for a visit—embarked for Europe. Tourist Third Cabin was a class for all classes, as cheap as it was romantic. The vast majority of its summer occupants referred to it as the "white-collar Steerage," a cognomen indicative of the mixed class origins of the passenger booking Tourist Third Cabin. It catered to a wide social spectrum, including children of families who, traveling alone as adults, might have booked with their parents in a First Class suite on the same ship before the war. Tourist Third Cabin was a heady, bohemian adventure. More than any other single marketing device, it established Americans of all classes as the predominant ocean travelers, a position they still occupy to this day.

Those three basic classes—First, Second, and Tourist Third Cabin—remained the rule throughout the twenties, or at least on the flagships sailing between New York and European ports. There were occasional deviations. On the *Aquitania* in 1927, for instance, those in First Class were referred to in the passenger list as Saloon Passengers. To the north, smaller Atlantic vessels sometimes carried only one or two classes. On what the

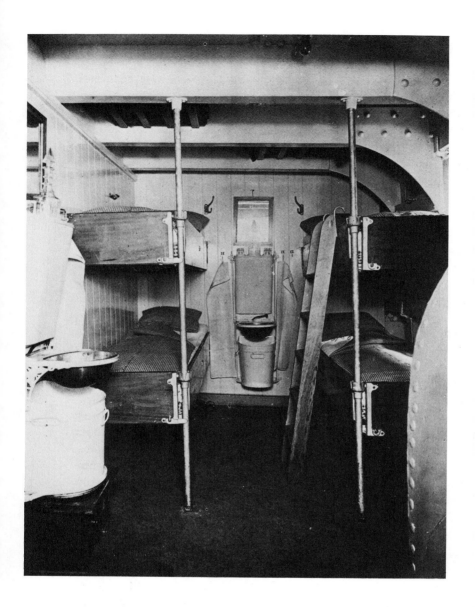

A four-berth Third Class cabin on board the *Imperator*.
Although spartan to contemporary eyes, for immigrants
boarding in 1913 it was an astounding advance into
oceangoing respectability. They were quite content with
the narrow berths, primitive washstands, and naked
steel deckhead; one only marvels at the elegance of the
water carafes. *(Hapag-Lloyd)*

Canadian Pacific referred to as "the mighty water boulevard to Canada," the little *Minnedosa* carried a single intermediate class from Liverpool to Quebec in 1930. Moreover, that single class could not be called First Class —a natural temptation for unscrupulous operators—for, according to the regulations of the self-governing Atlantic Conference, an accommodation so labeled had to *be* First Class; specified perks had to be provided at specified rates. So smaller ships called their best quarters Cabin Class, re-suscitating the old nineteenth-century term. On board Cunard's *Samaria*, sailing from Liverpool to New York in 1931, only two grades of accom-modation were extant: Cabin and Tourist Third Cabin; Second Class did not exist at all. On the one hand, this two-class mode was a foretaste of the postwar forties. But on the other, that specific use of Cabin Class pro-vided more than a nineteenth-century term of convenience; smaller and slower ships offered this less-than-First-Class as their top category.

Cabin Class would precipitate a divisive North Atlantic class struggle that made for a fine confusion during the thirties. The Sturm und Drang began with Norddeutscher Lloyd's *Bremen* and *Europa* of 1929 and 1930 respectively. With the Blue Riband to their credit, both were enormously popular, intensifying the already fierce competition among rival lines. In the Depression years, fewer passengers were sailing; quite naturally, the latest and fastest liners attracted the cream of the traffic. The Germans in-creased their appeal by widening their accommodation spread; each ship offered four classes instead of three—First, Second, Tourist, and Third. The Italians followed suit. Hot on the heels of the German record-breakers came another pair from the Mediterranean, the *Rex* and *Conte di Savoia*. They also boasted four classes, but with an upscale emphasis: two First Classes—First and Special—were listed in addition to Tourist and Third. When the French liner *Normandie* entered service in May 1935, she re-mained a three-class ship—First, Tourist, and Third.

But it was the advent of the *Queen Mary* the following summer of 1936 that upset the apple cart. In an effort to undercut what was considered the overpriced *Normandie*, Cunard White Star ignored the Conference listings and christened their top class Cabin Class, an amalgam of First and Second; below were Tourist and Third. In retrospect, the names seemed so similar to the *Normandie*'s class definitions—also without an intermediate between First and Tourist—that one wonders at the ensuing uproar. But uproar there was, and it seems to have been the abuse of the name Cabin Class that rankled. As a result, all of Cunard White Star's competitors fol-lowed suit. At the Paris meeting of 1936, the members of the North Atlantic Conference abolished the term "First Class" altogether with the result that,

The last of the three-class giants: *Normandie (top)* and *Queen Mary (bottom)*. The French vessel is seen as she was in her earliest after-deck configuration, the Grill Room esplanade intact. (*French Line and Cunard*)

until the war, the most splendid staterooms and suites were described as Cabin Class.

Historically, the name was inappropriate and inaccurate: by the mid-thirties, *all* passengers were berthed in cabins, so the term "Cabin Class" lacked any etymological validity. Another and even more significant change of the thirties was the emergence of Tourist as a generic without the supplemental "Third Cabin." Second Class vanished during the decade, never to reappear on the North Atlantic. It has remained, curiously, a historical unknown, the class of neglected remembrance adrift in a limbo between the gilt of First and the grime of Third. Significantly, Second Class carriages on most British railway trains were withdrawn soon after World War I.

Reversing that maritime class reduction, today's airlines seem bent on an opposing course. Throughout the long war of attrition between liner and jet, First Class and Tourist Class obtained aloft as well as afloat. But once the aircraft had achieved mastery of the Atlantic, they began skirmishing with one another. Laker's bargain fares set off an international wrangle that has seen airborne classes proliferate. Business Class—a kind of wide-body Second Cabin—has bridged the gulf between First and Tourist or, as it is sometimes called, Economy. Designed to separate cut-rate goats from full-fare sheep, it has also created the same divisive imbroglio that plagued the Atlantic Conference half a century ago.

Regardless of how the classes were contorted, the barriers separating them remained consistent. In cutaways of any multiclass vessel, space was invariably assigned as follows: premier reigned high amidships, intermediate nestled just aft, and the groundlings filled all spatial leftovers. Hulls were segmented according to this time-honored formula, separated by vertical class delineations.

But when passenger numbers dwindled alarmingly during the Depression, the companies sent some of their most elegant tonnage south. And when those ships cruised rather than crossed, the immutable barriers disappeared. Cruise passengers booked in one huge class. The only distinction between them was discreet, as higher fares commanded the larger staterooms. But in public rooms, on deck, or in launches headed for shore, instant sun-drenched democracy prevailed. It was as abrupt as a Central American coup d'état. When the *Mauretania* steamed up the Narrows from Southampton, her passenger load was traditionally segregated. But when she sailed for the Caribbean, banker and busboy commingled at the rail, in the dining saloon, or in a makeshift canvas pool, glacial class strata melting in the sun.

Class comparatives on board *Imperator*. *Top,* Third Class general room; *bottom,* First Class music room. In each room, swivel chairs are bolted to the deck and both are illuminated by skylights. But there the similarities end: every decorative element, from carpet to painted ceiling, is superior in the lower photograph. *(Hapag-Lloyd)*

Two views of the cruising *Mauretania*. *Top,* at anchor off Nassau's Hog Island Light, the Cunarder awaits shore tenders. *Bottom,* making heavy smoke from all four stacks, the newly white-painted *Mauretania* sails from Pier 54 in the winter of 1934. Several crew cabins forward are equipped with wind scoops. (*Everett E. Viez Collection, Everett E. Viez*)

The reason for this social volte-face arose from the contrast between the two kinds of passage: crossing was business, cruising was pleasure. Liners shuttling between continents on the North Atlantic sailed on voyages of intent. With no other means of crossing at their disposal, passengers were of every socioeconomic level. Companies had to provide appropriate and affordable accommodations for clients of every rank—a class for every passenger and a passenger for every class. Haut monde may have been insulated from hoi polloi, but all crossed at the same speed for different fares. It was this diversity of accommodation *within the same hull* that distinguished liner from land-based hostlery. In port, before they sailed, prospective passengers booked for the same crossing would gravitate to predictable overnight accommodations—the rich to *grande luxe* hotels, the bourgeois to less splendid family establishments, the poor to rooming or doss houses. The following morning at the pier, all would be welcomed aboard the same vessel. Therein lay the liner's unique adaptability. People who refer to transatlantic ships as "floating hotels" miss a crucial point: whereas the *Berengaria* embarked a broad social spectrum, the concept that the Ritz might offer Second or Third Class quarters was inconceivable. (Yet another pivotal difference between hotel and ship was that, if unsatisfied, patrons could not check out in midocean!)

At the same time, symptomatic of those hulls was that a week's enforced stay on board could be, for many, as unpleasant as it was unavoidable. The North Atlantic is cold, rough, or foggy for much of the year, and save for the incurably peripatetic or hardiest sailor, a crossing can combine ennui, illness, or terror in equal doses. Crossings were scarcely pleasant excursions. In the 1950s, Cunard tried popularizing them with a slogan that remained so firmly imprinted on the public conscience that it has recently been redeployed: "Getting there," prospective clients were advised, "is half the fun." It had been a weapon in the "air war" as the company wooed passengers debating between ship or plane: ocean passage was marketed as a resort vacation, compensation for the airlines' undeniable advantage of speed. It was, moreover, the first—and an unlikely—suggestion, for company and customer alike, that North Atlantic shipboard might be more than a bumpy ferry service.

Yet even those "getting-there-is-half-the-fun" travelers shared one common preoccupation: a destination. Cruise passengers have none; traditionally, they embark and disembark at the same port, having accomplished nothing more pressing than an idle round-trip. Spared that obligatory rough week at sea, cruise passengers serve seagoing time in a minimum-care facility on which dispatch has dissipated into drift. And from the very beginning, the poor and working class were not among them. They had neither the income nor the inclination to sail to Nassau or Havana. Later on, as the market broadened, as everyone traveled, as jet air buses were linked with ship buses, they would. But cruising began as a floating holiday for the middle class, a kind of resurgent Second Cabin outing. There was no reason to expect or accommodate denizens of the old Third Class, who, in former years, had more than half-filled the same ships on crossings. In sum, steamship company booking agents decided that, since only First or Second Class types would board, they could be carried indiscriminately together.

Of course, there were complications. Even though the entire ship's interior was available to this one congenial class, nagging architectural inequities contravened. Each established class area had its own design gradations, as scrupulously observed as office perks for civil servants. Whatever the itinerary, these aspects of the vessel's decorative infrastructure could not be changed. So, it was all very well for thrifty passengers in 1935 to have booked a modest Second Cabin on the *Aquitania* for a cruise to Nassau. Having boarded, they quite naturally expected, as members of one universal class, to live and dine as well as their shipmates who had paid for First Cabin. In effect, they did. Yet though they ordered from identical menus, they ate in Second Cabin surroundings, lacking the decorative finesse obtaining in First. Moreover, the most desirable public rooms were seriously overcrowded: throngs of egalitarian dancers would pack the Palladian Lounge each night at sea, overflowing space designed to accommodate less than half the cruising passenger load. This same problem— one-class passengers swamping First Class space—was a perennial headache on Atlantic vessels cruising the Caribbean, most especially, as we shall see, on board the *France*.

As a result, on postwar liners built for the Atlantic trade, contrasts between the class interiors were gradually but purposely blurred. Shipping companies were facing reality; their two-class ships might operate half the year in a single-class mode. So throughout the fifties and sixties, Tourist Class was continually improved. More of their cabins had bathrooms attached, they grew comparable in size to their First Class counterparts, and Tourist Class public rooms were dressed up to be more than genteel hotel lobbies. A unified decorative parity was the objective, as effortless a conversion from crossing to cruising as could be executed. The most significant crossing advantage—a higher servant ratio—could be amended without a trace.

The most efficient changeover formula involved reshaping traditional

Shuffleboard in bathing suits as R.M.S. *Berengaria*
sails home from Bermuda in the summer of 1936.
Cruises on this Atlantic stalwart during the Depression
were so cheap that, as William Miller tells us, she was
referred to as "the bargain area." *Opposite top*, the
Aquitania steams toward Nassau in the mid-thirties. It
is still too cool for horse racing outdoors, to judge by
canvas windscreen along the boat deck and the sweaters
and overcoats in evidence. *Bottom*, a well-attended
children's party in the Second Cabin dining room
indicates either a Christmas or Easter cruise. *(Everett
E. Viez and Joseph Rider)*

class areas. It was on board Holland America Line's new flagship, the *Rotterdam* of 1959, that a most successful innovation in this respect was introduced. Instead of occupying vertical hull segments, First and Tourist Class each inhabited their own deck of public rooms and promenades, one above the other: a class sandwich ran the entire length of the hull. First Class passengers occupied all of Upper Promenade Deck, surrounded by their own wraparound promenade. Aft, they drank and danced in the double-decked splendor of the Ritz Carlton—the last room of that name afloat—and, passing forward, had at their disposal a smoking room, card room, library, shopping area, and the Ambassador Lounge. Farthest forward was the balcony of the cinema, where they enjoyed movies within hailing distance of but apart from their Tourist Class shipmates occupying the orchestra floor below.

That lower theater level was, in turn, the forward interior extremity of Promenade Deck, devoted exclusively to Tourist Class. Moving aft, they had available a large, low-ceilinged lounge, a library, their own shops, the Club Room (it was not called the card room in those days), the Café de la Paix (now the Lido), and finally, a veranda aft that gave onto an open-air swimming pool. (On the Tourist Class's deck, that pool was a useless fixture on the cold North Atlantic, where no one in their right mind swam outdoors. On crossings, all passengers shared an indoor pool down on D-deck.)

With two classes of passengers grouped on two consecutive levels high in the ship, Holland America faced the problem of connecting them with their respective cabins and dining rooms below. On segmented class ships, vertical access had always been simple: each class had its own staircase. On board the *Rotterdam*, the problem was solved uniquely with an ingenious Main Staircase that could carry two segregated classes simultaneously. It had as its inspiration a novel architectural feature first seen in François I's palace at Chambord: a double cylindrical staircase. In the form of two interlocking but untouching corkscrews, it had been conceived to ensure that the royals and their intimates could roam the palace unobserved by the court. The seagoing Dutch version of the French original called the "secret staircase" was the inspiration of Willem de Monchy, Holland America's president. Though in scissors rather than circular shape, it achieved the same effect. In open form, it merely connected each deck with two alternate flights; but when sliding doors on the appropriate landings were closed, the two classes were completely and mystifyingly separated. In that crossing mode, First Class passengers descended past one closed-off landing—the Tourist Class main square—down to their cabin deck, then down past two additional closed-off landings to their Odyssey Dining Room. Tourist Class passengers, in turn, had no reason to ascend above their public rooms on Promenade Deck but could descend past a single closed-off landing to their cabins or, farther still, down to their La Fontaine Dining Room. Elevators bracketing the Main Staircase were segregated as well: numbers 1, 2, and 3 were reserved for First Class passengers and destinations only, while Tourist Class were transported exclusively on numbers 4, 5, and 6.

Regrettably, the *Rotterdam* no longer crosses the Atlantic. She is restricted to one-class cruising these days, so the staircase baffles remain withdrawn into the walls lining the banisters. Nevertheless, that Chambord effect often mystifies newcomers. The foyers on both Lower Promenade and A-decks look identical forward and aft, as well as port and starboard; descending one of the scissors staircases is momentarily disorienting. But experienced passengers know the trick, which is to memorize the appropriate bronzes adorning each landing corner. All are different, delightful miniatures from *The Tempest*. Ariel guarded the entrance to my particular cabin passage when I was first on board some years ago, and using him as a talisman, I found my way home no matter into which corner of the landing I had emerged from the stairs.

The endearing thing about the *Rotterdam* today is that the company has preserved her so well, sustaining those interiors almost exactly as they appeared at the time of her maiden voyage. There are some necessary one-class changes—the Café de la Paix has been transformed into a Lido Restaurant serving the entire passenger load. Another change, on the forward end of Promenade Deck, is puzzling: the wraparound interior space on the old Tourist Class deck, forward of the theater's orchestra floor, is a kind of ghost town. Originally, the port side had been devoted to high school–age children, the starboard for younger passengers. Nowadays, the port side remains an underutilized teen hangout while the portion to starboard has been appropriated as a dressing room for large casts performing in the theater as well as a workshop for the Indonesian upholsterers and tailors who are carried on board. (Every uniform worn on board *Rotterdam* is made on the ship.) There is talk of converting the starboard space to cabins but the expense for such work on a twenty-five-year-old vessel makes it an unlikely prospect. Overall, it is a terrible waste of prime space, with its splendid view over the bows, for there is no room, anywhere on board, that faces forward. Moreover, there is a curious open deck omission: the forward curve of the Sun Deck, which could easily be railed to accommodate a forward-facing passenger gallery, is inexplicably blocked

FROM CROSSING....

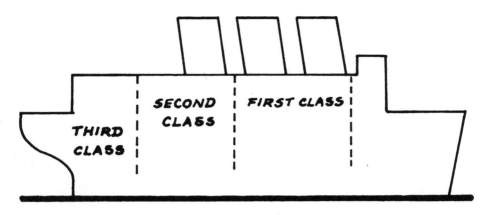

TRANSATLANTIC CLASS BARRIERS : VERTICAL

...TO CRUISING

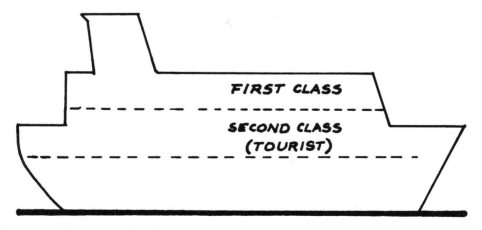

EASIER CONVERSION TO ONE CLASS CRUISING:
THE HORIZONTAL CLASS SANDWICH

JMG

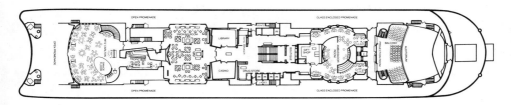

Rotterdam
UPPER PROMENADE DECK

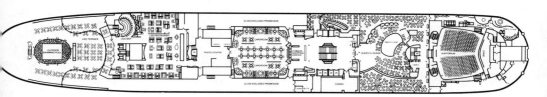

otterdam
ROMENADE DECK

The *Rotterdam*'s class sandwich. Plans of the two
adjacent decks that were the domain of First and
Tourist Class on board the ship originally. It is interesting
to see how much more promenading space First had
than their more numerous shipmates one deck below.
But Tourist Class did have the after-pool surround
for their use on the North Atlantic. *(Holland America
Line)*

Rotterdam interiors. The famous double
staircase with its baffles withdrawn into
the walls. *Right,* Ariel in bronze, one of
the decorative features that guide
confused passengers back to their proper
cabin corridor. *(Author's collection)*

off, serving only as roof rather than deck. Although the *Rotterdam* cruises year-round, the Ambassador Lounge, on Upper Promenade Deck, remains a relentlessly interior North Atlantic room; its large bow windows facing out onto the upper Promenade Deck are shrouded permanently in Austrian shades and bull's-eye glazing.

That curious neglect notwithstanding, the *Rotterdam* today survives as a memorable design exercise, the ideal, effortless crossing-to-cruising conversion. Half a dozen sliding doors on the staircase as well as another two that open up baffles on the stairs connecting the theater's balcony and orchestra do the trick. A tour today of the ship's public rooms gives some indication, too, of the comparative decorative perquisites of each class. Both card rooms, for instance, are exactly as they were when the *Rotterdam* crossed the Atlantic. In fact, Tourist Class is the more practical of the two; Tourist Class passengers played bridge on baize-covered tables in sensible armchairs, while First Class were given hopeless marble-topped card tables and overstuffed, awkward club chairs. There are, however, delights in First Class—a paneled ceiling that remains one of the prettiest on board any ship, and a row of ingenious reversing loveseats that line the tall windows to either side.

But the difference between the rooms is marginal. Both were designed with equal restraint and ambition, with contrasting style rather than pretension. The two adjoining decks, impeccably preserved, exist as an invaluable and remarkable working museum that demonstrates, far more cogently than reams of commentary, how cleverly the Holland America Line's class differential was minimized for sailing into the sixties.

The *Rotterdam*'s design breakthrough would be duplicated three years later on the *France*, the last great Compagnie Générale Transatlantique flagship, which appeared in New York harbor for the first time in the winter of 1962. Once again, the company had cruise conversion in mind: *France*'s public rooms were spread along a similar class sandwich on two adjacent decks the length of the hull. First Class occupied the uppermost; from the Smoking Room aft to the theater balcony forward, Veranda Deck was the domain of five hundred First Class passengers. Fifteen hundred Tourist Class passengers were confined one deck below on Promenade Deck. (A misleading name, this, for each of the public room decks had its own wraparound promenade.) There was no Chambord staircase trickery on the *France*. Tourist Class passengers were restricted to their own stairwells forward and aft, smaller and less lavish than *la grande déscente* amidships trod exclusively by First Class. But the conversion modus was the same;

Inboard/outboard. A row of reversible
sofas affords passengers in the
Rotterdam's Smoking Room the option
of a view out to sea or into the center of
the room. *(Ian Maxtone-Graham)*

for cruises, all baffle doors segregating staircases from taboo decks were opened to permit free circulation throughout the vessel.

In her two-class Atlantic configuration, the *France*'s Tourist and First Class passengers were, for the most part, kept geographically isolated. There were, however, three crossover points—two by day and one by night —Check-point Charlies between facilities designed to serve both classes. There was a discreet staircase between the Galéries Lafayette and Veranda Deck. Then again, forward on the First Class promenade, the chapel, hairdressers, and children's playrooms were clustered about a violable frontier barrier. (It was a barrier in another sense, for the playroom stewardesses used to keep their glass doors locked, thwarting First Class passenger/ walkers anxious to complete a circuit of their promenade.) Although the playroom complex served the children of both classes, it had not initially been planned that way. Just aft of the Salle de Jeux on the starboard side, firmly within First Class territory, was a small, exquisitely decorated but otherwise barren chamber, identified on early deck plans as the First Class Children's Playroom. Not once did I ever see it in use. It was so preciously sterile that all First Class children took one horrified look and abandoned it immediately in favor of Tourist Class's Tivoli-like spread just forward or, better still, the adolescent heaven—all pinball and soda fountain—to port in the Club des Jeunes.

But though the *France*'s planners had intended to keep First and Tourist Class toddlers apart, they instigated an unusual scheme to bring at least some of their parents together. The innovation—revolutionary for the French Line—was to have taken place only after midnight, a reverse of the Cinderella story allowing prince and commoner to continue mingling. They were to do so in the heart of First Class country, within a late-night boîte along Veranda Deck's starboard side known as the Cabaret de l'Atlantique. (Another naming anomaly—there was never any cabaret in the place at all, just dancing.)

The Cabaret de l'Atlantique satisfied every requirement of a successful nightclub: elegant, claustrophobic, dim, and deafening. At the forward end of the narrow room was a murky bar that stayed open twenty hours out of every twenty-four. (All ships, crossing or cruising alike, have one hidden bar with long hours, a haven for chronic drinkers. Many book passage specifically because they can drink day and night, arousing neither comment from their shipmates nor reproof from their exhausted families at home.) Aft of the bar were some crowded tables and banquettes surrounding a postage-stamp-size dance floor, music for which was supplied by an inexhaustible rhythm section sprung from their recent gig in the adjoining

The tiny original First Class Children's
Playroom on board *France* with much of
its splendid trompe l'oeil decor crowded
out by video games for young *Norway*
passengers. *(Author's collection)*

lounge. At the after end was a horseshoe-shaped Snack Bar, the domain of a genial sous-chef from midnight on who, resplendent in starched toque and fichu, stood ready to dispense a steaming gratiné or croque-monsieur or, within reason, whatever delicacy he could cajole from his colleagues toiling below in the main galley.

But never caviar. Through rose-colored spectacles focused longingly on that vanished era, Proustian passengers inevitably recall unlimited caviar, a *mémoire volontaire* grown now into hoary Atlantic cliché. To be accurate, caviar has always been expensive and, in consequence, was never dispensed with a trowel. It could be found on canapés in the bars or ordered at dinner, but never in those Brobdingnagian portions conjured up in wistful retrospect.

Whatever First Class passengers enjoyed in the Cabaret de l'Atlantique was shared, mirabile dictu, with Tourist Class. Tucked away in an after corner was a staircase up from Promenade Deck that, after midnight, admitted night-bloomers from below. But that nocturnal dispensation lasted for only a few crossings. I asked Jean-Claude Potier, the French Line's North American president, why and he replied, deadpan, that the company felt that Tourist Class livers should be spared from too much pâté de foie gras. In truth, so many upwardly mobile from Promenade Deck were attracted that the anticipated trickle turned into a torrent and legitimate patrons from First Class were crowded out of their own room. The staircase was closed, the experiment concluded; Tourist Class insomniacs were restricted to their own Smoking Room. Very shortly thereafter, the late-night flow was reversed: the early sixties marked the debut of the discotheque and the more agile amongst the First Class forsook dancing cheek-to-cheek in the Cabaret de l'Atlantique for the amplified racket one deck down. The Cabaret de l'Atlantique continued as a strictly First Class public room save for cruises, when it welcomed all comers.

In fact, when the ship made its first cruise, two glaring miscalculations emerged—one easily correctable, the other not. Both gave indication that the company, wedded to a crossing philosophy of old, had neglected its warm-weather homework. For a start, adhering to traditional French Line policy, public room names throughout the ship had been identified generically. The only exception were two music rooms bracketing the main staircase on Veranda Deck—the salons Débussy and Ravel—and the aforementioned Cabaret de l'Atlantique. For the rest, prominent class indicators were used: the two dining rooms, for instance, were called First and Tourist Class Dining Rooms, a self-defeating embarrassment for cruises. Helpful stewards would direct lost one-class passengers toward two-class public rooms.

At company headquarters, a list of new names was decreed, and within hours of the ship's return to New York, a crop of euphemisms had blossomed the length of Veranda and Promenade decks. First Class passengers were now assigned to tables in the Restaurant Chambord rather than the First Class Dining Room; they repaired to the Salon Fontainebleau instead of the First Class Lounge and played bridge or took their cocktails in the Salon Riviera, né First Class Smoking Room. One deck down, Tourist Class took their meals in the Restaurant Versailles, danced in the Salon St.-Tropez, and stayed up late in the Café Rive Gauche. For cruises, at least, the *France* had been rendered déclassé; those names remained in effect for the rest of the vessel's French life and stewards were instructed to use them exclusively.

Unfortunately, what began in that instance as a specific marketing palliative has spread throughout the world's cruising fleets like a plague. On contemporary one-class vessels, where no need to camouflage dual-class origins exists, fantasy names for public rooms are the rule. On board *Norway*-ex-*France*, there is still only one theater, the former Salle de Spectacle; but instead of being called simply "the Theater," it has been dubbed the Saga Theatre, in line with Norwegian Caribbean Lines's relentlessly Nordic concept. ("Concept" is so chillingly inevitable: it springs from corporate cruisespeak's overworked lexicon in the tradition of "duty-free," "hand-carved," and "gourmet dining.") Similarly, the *Royal Viking Star* has only one theater; located in the bowels of the ship, it is known on board as the Starlight Theatre, although it is as far from starlight as it is possible to be. Carnival Cruise Lines offers the most extraordinary public room misnomers: their *Carnivale*'s discotheque is captioned on deckplans as the Fly-Aweigh Disco, an appellation that is, on any level, redundant, overcute, and obfuscating. What "Fly-Aweigh" means is not clear; a giddy concept has gone overboard. Surely, no passenger bound for dancing on the *Carnivale* has ever actually articulated, "Let's go to the Fly-Aweigh Disco!" Far more sensible, they doubtless rely on the simple generic word *disco*, just as New Yorkers have rejected "Avenue of the Americas" in favor of "Sixth Avenue." On board Royal Caribbean Cruise Line's *Song of America*, the only dining room is called the Madame Butterfly Dining Room; compounding the confusion, after extensions within the same space are identified as the Ambassador Room and Oriental Terrace. On the same ship, there is only one main lounge: in line with RCCL's musical theme concept it bears the unfortunate name of the Can-Can Lounge, a choice

Luxury cruising. The S.S. *France* at
anchor off Nassau's Hog Island Light.
Dernier cri on the North Atlantic, she
had shortcomings in the Caribbean.
(Everett E. Viez Collection)

Neither indoors nor out: the *France*'s Tourist Class pool. It was very crowded in warm weather and somehow disappointing in cold. *(French Line)*

with vaguely lavatorial overtones. Curiously, cheek-by-jowl with these fanciful concoctions, traditional Card Room and Cinema coexist. There is no reason to trivialize a ship's public rooms by any but the clearest expedient—to whit, after their use. A lounge should be a lounge, not an experience.

But, back to the *France*'s other shortcoming as a cruise ship. More serious than the problem of public-room names was the lack of an open-air swimming pool. The naval architect's flawed solution was the creation of what was hoped would be a dual-purpose pool for Tourist Class. Located aft on Promenade Deck, it was half-indoors and half-outdoors, an on-deck pool situated beneath an immovable, skylit shell with glass doors at its after end. In practice, it proved a disappointment on both counts. On the North Atlantic, that glass roof was both an oppressive, inadequate psychological protection against rain and a stuffy frustration when the sun shone. In the Caribbean, though the doors were flung open, the pool afforded little pleasure to bathers lounging around its muggy, shaded margins or crowded onto the sunny fantail immediately behind it. It seems strange that the French did not equip that pool with a Magrodome, one of those genuinely convertible glass roofs that HAPAG-Lloyd, Home Lines, Scandinavian World Cruises, and Cunard have incorporated so successfully over their upper-deck pools. At the touch of a button on the bridge, motorized cables withdraw a sectional glass roof, opening a covered pool to the skies. There seems no valid reason not to have done so on the *France*; the technology was there because the *Oceanic* sailed only three years later. Perhaps the French were reluctant to install a Magrodome because, in its open position with overlapping sections nested forward, the ship's profile might have been disrupted. In addition, the view over the stern from the veranda, where First Class passengers sat outside the Salon Riviera, would have been obstructed. Yet it does seem strange that the company should have denied itself the advantage of a successful, one-class facility appropriate for the Caribbean. Small wonder that, when the *France* was transformed into the *Norway* at Bremerhaven in the winter of 1980, one of the first orders of business was the installation of two open-air pools.

In 1969, seven years after the *France*'s maiden voyage, Cunard's *Queen Elizabeth 2* entered into service. Symbolically, she often made a crossing as well as a cruise, a passage for every season, originating in Southampton and terminating in New York, but touching at Las Palmas, Barbados, and Kingston en route. From bleak midwinter North Atlantic to the Caribbean's turquoise indolence, there seemed no better way for Cunard to demonstrate the splendid duality they had embodied within their latest

Opposite, the last *Queen*: Cunard's flagship at her New York pier. *Above left, Queen Elizabeth 2* in post-Falklands gray, showing her spread of terraces down from First Class atop to crew space on the fantail. *Right,* following a Bremer-haven refit in December 1983, the First Class pool on Quarter Deck has been equipped with a retractable Magrodome, creating an indoor/outdoor option at the touch of a button. *(William Nylen and Cunard)*

flagship. She was far better equipped for the tropics than her French predecessor, easily and expeditiously convertible from crossing to cruising. She boasted four swimming pools—two on deck, two below—a warm- or cold-weather option for each of her two classes. Those options were expanded in the early eighties when Bremerhaven shipyard workers installed a Magrodome over the First Class pool. It differs from the Home Lines's prototype in that it divides in the center, along the keel line, and opens to either side, the roof sections nesting and disappearing within a new thickness built into Upper Deck. When the Magrodome is in open position, the two on-deck pools are incorporated into a stepped terrace complex that starts amidships aft of the funnel and continues down to the fantail.

As the last multiclass liner in service, *QE2* merits special attention, all the more since she was conceived originally as a three-class ship. Sadly, she is the last vessel (save for the little *Stefan Batory*, running between Montreal and London) making scheduled transatlantic crossings, but she has been designed equally well for the cruises that comprise most of her annual service. She is, in fact, Cunard's fourth *Queen*-class vessel; the third was never built. Designated *Q-3* to distinguish her from her two forebears—*Q-1 Queen Mary*, *Q-2 Queen Elizabeth*—that abandoned concept was to have been an impractical 75,000 tonner, a star turn to maintain Cunard's "big ship" prestige on the North Atlantic, hopelessly miscast for modern cruising. In the early planning stages of that single successor to the two legendary *Queen*s, Cunard had been slow to realize the crippling inroads that airlines would make on the transatlantic passenger market. Wisely, Cunard aborted *Q-3*, turning instead to *Q-4*, the working designation that would sail as *Queen Elizabeth 2*. (Never, incidentally, should the vessel's name incorporate a roman *II*; that identifies the sovereign who christened her. The ship's numerical suffix is correctly written with the arabic 2.)

One vestigial specification retained from *Q-3* and incorporated into the early planning for *Q-4* was a provision that the vessel offer three grades of accommodation—First, Cabin, and Tourist. Just as Cunard White Star had precipitated an Atlantic Conference brouhaha with new class names for the *Queen Mary*'s debut in 1936, so Cunard seemed bent on instigating a duplicate flap with *Queen Elizabeth 2*. But this time, there were few multiple-class competitors left to care, and the idea was abandoned in favor of the conventional two classes. But the reduction from three to two was mandated *after* the structural designs for public rooms in triplicate were complete. All three lounges had been located one above the other amidships, Cabin Class over Tourist Class, which was, in turn, atop First Class. With an inspired stroke of his pencil—or, rather, eraser—Dan Wallace,

Cunard's naval architect, opened a well through the redundant top lounge's dance floor, uniting it with and enlarging the Tourist Class lounge below. A handsome sweep of coiled staircase connected the two levels and, phoenix-like, the famous Double Room emerged from the ashes of Cunard's projected three classes.

The Double Room remains not only the largest public room ever seen on a liner, but one of the most successful as well, as practical as it is huge. Its double height is impressive, yet the scale is manageable. Passengers remain in touch with the ocean to either side and have at their disposal a large central dance floor and a cabaret stage with excellent sightlines. There is comfortable seating for morning bouillon or afternoon tea as well as an upper gallery ideal for casual participation in the spectacle below. That upper level was enriched when, in 1971, two years after the ship's maiden voyage, all but one of the shops on board were installed along its outboard flanks. It was a sensible accommodation; the upper level's outer reaches were so remote from the central well that they had remained underutilized. Turning them into a shopping arcade has given the Double Room's upper level a life of its own, complementing the activity below. The entire Double Room—Double Up and Double Down—has evolved into a busy, cheerful thoroughfare, in continuous use throughout every shipboard day.

Relocating the shops from their original midships position was serendipitous; however, it was a move made not to improve the Double Up, but because the shops were being replaced by new cabins. Before we explore the background of those upheavals, it is worth a moment's pause to see how each of the *Queen Elizabeth 2*'s classes fares in the matter of main lounges. Contrary to ancient convention, Tourist's is superior. Although the Queen's Room, which was built for the use of First Class passengers, may be lighter and quieter, it is less successful as a working space than the Double Room one deck higher. Both lounges, incidentally, expand to the full width of the vessel, incorporating within them space that, normally, would have become flanking promenade decks. The omission of those traditional Atlantic fixtures remains a controversial feature of Cunard's and Wallace's design. The intention was clear: creation of a useful cruise conversion factor. Promenade decks—interiors in prime sections of the ship that are deserted after dark—have always been lavish space wasters. By adding that space to the respective lounges, Wallace increased each room's capacity: many more passengers can be accommodated, however remotely, along their outer margins, making a single evening's performance available to, if not quite all, at least a larger percentage of the passenger load. For Atlantic crossings, when the Queen's Room reverts to a First Class domain,

Although here flattened by a fish-eye
lens, the Double Room on board *QE2*
is a commodious and successful
shipboard space. The deep reaches to
either side of the upper level are lined
with shops. *(Cunard)*

curtained partitions can be closed, cutting off the additional width of "promenade deck" and reducing the room's dimensions, and at the same time, insulating passengers from the gray Atlantic. (In practice, these partitions are seldom closed.) Since the Double Room must accommodate a larger crowd whether crossing or cruising, it need not be narrowed for the Atlantic.

The primary function of both rooms is presentation of cabaret. In this respect, the Queen's Room falls woefully short. Its designer, Michael Inchbald, was originally unhappy with the room's dimensions, convinced that the allotted space was not only too low but too wide as well. All he could do about the height was to attempt to raise the roof visually by cloaking the obligatory row of stanchions midway between keel-line and shell plating with upward-flaring trumpet shapes. He tried correcting what he felt to be the room's troubling second dimension—its width—by tampering with its length, making it seem narrower, in effect, by making it seem longer. Mirrors were sited athwart room dividers to each side, and at the room's fore and aft ends, Inchbald specified what he described as "sculptured woodblocks," handsome mahogany boxes apparently stacked as a pierced lazaret, their interstices mirrored to extend the lounge's long axis.

Though Inchbald's end-wall effect is pleasing, his stress on the length makes the Queen's Room difficult for performers. Cabaret works best when played in close proximity, allowing interaction between artist and audience. Up above, in the Double Room, passenger/spectators flank the dance floor/playing arena; there is only a narrow stretch of floor between the edge of the bandstand and the staircase railing, the effective back wall. In the Queen's Room, that distance is twice as long; the bulk of the First Class audience sits on the far side of the dance floor, a parquet no-man's-land several critical yards wide, separating entertainer from objective. And whereas the Double Room vaults into a hall, the Queen's Room oozes into unfathomable reaches. Farthest from the stage, the forward pierced lazaret wall houses Oscar Nemon's excellent bust of the monarch who christened the vessel; Her Majesty's head is turned characteristically to one side, recoiling in sympathy, I always feel, for the valiant artistes who, each evening, strut and shout to so little avail at the far end.

Worse, those remote spectators are cradled soporifically within Inchbald's Queen's Room chairs. They are undoubtedly smart; the swivel bases are inverted echoes of the neighboring column shapes. But they are too comfortable by far—splendid for a nap after tea but forcing what should be an attentive audience into postures of somnolent repose. Thus inad-

The *Queen Elizabeth 2*'s First Cla
lounge, the Queen's Room. Although th
illuminated coffered ceiling helps, th
room's troublesome dimension f
performers is its length. *(Cunar*

vertently reclining, Queen's Room audiences remain aloof rather than alert, uninvolved with what is happening far beyond their extended feet.

No discourse about the *QE2*'s lounges would be complete without reference to a bizarre interaction between the two. I sat one night at the edge of the Queen's Room dance floor while, overhead, Double Room occupants, dragooned into some "Knees Up, Mother Brown" high jinks, had swarmed onto the dance floor and were jumping in unison. Soldiers crossing bridges are ordered to break step to discourage sympathetic vibrations; no such admonition had been given to Tourists crossing to England. The Queen's Room ceiling was swelling and contracting like an enormous pulse in time to the thump of their band. Those seated beneath it pulled hastily back beneath Inchbald's trumpet columns. The chief engineer later observed that, though distressing to watch, the pliant ceiling would never collapse. He has been proved right—it has survived the booted feet of thousands of soldiers bound for the Falklands. But learning to live with flexing aluminum on board the *Queen Elizabeth 2* takes time. The outdoor staircases connecting the after sun decks are modernistic in form, each riser welded at its center to a sloping pipe. If graceful to look at, they are alarming to climb, with as much bounce as the Queen's Room ceiling. But they are reliable, as sturdy as the traditional mahogany flights connecting the promenade and boat decks of the earlier *Queen*s.

That Tourist Class's Double Room is situated *above* First Class's Queen's Room indicates that on board Cunard's flagship, the class sandwich was reversed from the Dutch and French prototype. Tourist Class roam the Upper Deck, one flight above their First Class shipmates, whose public rooms are spread along the Quarter Deck. (A curious name, borrowed from the Royal Navy; better that, however, than Biscayne or Emerald!) This inversion was dictated by the choice of location of what was, originally, the ship's only galley, a large facility on the forward end of Quarter Deck, designed to provide food for all dining rooms on board. The *QE2*'s original restaurants have the same approximate area, the First Class Columbia accommodating five hundred while the Britannia packs in eight hundred Tourist diners at a time, a process repeated at a second sitting when capacity warrants it. At one time, confusion reigned because the *Britannia* Cup, a large silver trophy presented to Cunard's first ship by Boston's city fathers in 1840, was prominently displayed on the front buffet of the Columbia Restaurant. But that confusion is academic now; the Britannia Restaurant has become Tables of the World, just as Tourist Class is now referred to as Transatlantic Class.

Just forward on the port side, beyond the Columbia Restaurant, is the Princess Grill, reached by its own discreet maroon leather staircase from One Deck. This is the *QE2*'s version of the legendary Veranda Grills that were such popular fixtures on both *Queen*s. The difference between the Princess and its predecessors is that it is simply a restaurant and need not be transformed into a nightclub after the evening's last diners have been accommodated. Neither *Queen Mary* nor *Queen Elizabeth* had a nightclub per se on board, and so utilizing the extra-tariff restaurant for late-night use made sense. The Princess was, originally, for occasional, special use only, the last extra-tariff restaurant afloat, where First Class passengers who wished to do so could book a table with companions and, at an hour of their own choosing, have lunch or dinner away from assigned seats in the Columbia. It is a small room that seats only a hundred diners with the same elegance that I remember from the Veranda Grills. There is no sculpted steel or chrome but a mellow atmosphere of warm plum velvet and leather contrasted with pink tablecloths. Janine Jane's quartet of life-size nudes— the Four Elements, she called them—have fortunately been removed else- where, two to the Columbia. Although striking, they were hopelessly over- scale for the little Princess.

Genuinely missed is a tiny, anticipatory bar located at the foot of the spiral staircase entrance. It could accommodate no more than ten people, including the barman, and its very diminutiveness gave it a chic exclusivity. Now, sadly, it is locked, no longer even indicated on deckplans. Apart from use as a storage room, I have seen it occupied only once: during a North Cape cruise it was used as a meeting place for Cunard and union officials hammering out a new contract. After menacing each other all day in a fug of cigarette smoke, they would ascend wreathed in smiles to dine in genial splendor at a window table in the Princess Grill.

Rather than looking over the stern as did the Veranda Grills on both earlier *Queen*s, Princess Grill windows are confined to the vessel's port side; those seated inboard have been compensated with a raised platform along the wall. In fact, as regards interior views looking ahead or astern, First Class passengers on board *Queen Elizabeth 2* have always been thwarted. Whatever the implied elegance of Quarter Deck, it terminates at either end in blind anonymity: forward the kitchen, aft the nightclub. Once again, as with their superior Double Room, Tourist Class came up trumps. Over- looking the bow forward on Upper Deck they had a Lookout Bar, and aft, behind the Double Room's staircase, the Double Down Bar commands a view over the stern. The Double Down Bar remains to this day, but the Lookout Bar, the *QE2*'s sole forward-facing interior, has been turned into a Tourist Class galley, its crescent of plate-glass windows covered with steel blanks, its handsome cubist furniture diverted to the petty officers' mess. That regrettable curtailment of prime passenger space occurred after Cunard, the company that had conceived, designed, and built the ship, had been absorbed within a holding company called Trafalgar.

The transfer was made within two years of the *QE2*'s maiden voyage, initiating some drastic changes on the relatively new ship. The new owners decided that it was essential to increase passenger capacity. Hence the transfer of the shops from amidships to the Double Up. Two rows of supplementary cabins were installed in their place. (Those on the starboard side are noisy; I occupied one once and marveled at the rich depth of carpeting into which one sank almost up to the ankles. Only when my head hit the pillow that first night at sea did I realize that the layers underfoot had been added—ineffectually, I found—as insulation against the throb from the Theatre Bar's amplifiers one deck down. The reverberations continued until dawn.)

In addition to those new Boat Deck cabins, a prefabricated aluminum complex of suites—crewmen called it "the motel"—was attached atop the Sports Deck. Subsequently, two additional supersuites, the Queen Mary and Queen Elizabeth, would be installed just forward. To feed the occupants of these splendid penthouses, as well as those traveling in the largest cabins amidships, Trafalgar created a new dining room directly below "the motel," connected to it by a special staircase and elevator. This was done at the expense of several original First Class features on Boat Deck, among them a circular open area, similar in nature, if not intent, to the Patio Provençale situated amidships on the *France*'s Sun Deck. Whereas the French well was merely a means of converting inside into outside cabins, the *QE2*'s well was a place for First Class passengers to enjoy a sun-filled exterior sheltered from Atlantic winds. But it, together with a soda fountain, gallery, and discotheque, was obliterated. The space was refashioned into a new cocktail lounge and grill, complete with its own galley. Over a hundred welders and fitters from Vosper-Thorneycroft, the Southampton yard, spent the summer of 1972 shuttling back and forth across the Atlantic, completing the new installation; it was an unsettling business, most especially welding at sea with passengers aboard. But once the work had been completed, a second grill emerged, elevated geographically and royally above the existing Princess, to be known as the Queen's Grill.

Of the two *QE2* grill rooms, the Princess is decoratively superior. Save for the unlamented departure of the nude quartet, its decor remains unchanged since 1969, part of a handsome original. As originally conceived and executed, the *Queen Elizabeth 2* was a superb, total design achievement: no other vessel has ever matched the success of her design teams. The color choices of the exterior hull no less than the look inside were memorable and sounded a new and refreshing note everywhere. The *QE2*'s interiors overshadowed in every respect those on board the *France*, her nearest chronological rival. Dennis Lennon's First Class Midships Bar, for instance, with its bottle green and brass, is extremely successful, rich, restrained, discreet, and cozy. (The barmen tried making it even cozier by encouraging passengers to donate awful tavern memorabilia—postcards, short-snorters, and muppets—with which the bar's reredos, so to speak, was festooned for years. These have been removed on orders from ashore and the room has resumed its former dignity.)

But the hastily conceived Queen's Grill is betrayed as a decorative orphan. It has undergone three renovations, none necessarily improving on its predecessor. Done originally in early Statler, it then suffered royal overkill: carved mahogany arms, complete with lion, unicorn, and DIEU ET MON DROIT, dominated the after wall. That was replaced, post-Falklands, with Erté prints. Part of that same refit saw redecoration of the outer bar; it was crammed with overstuffed chairs and sofas. The change not only reduced the space's capacity—seats are at a premium before lunch or dinner —but makes it look for much of the time like an unmade bed since the stewards never reinvigorate the pillows between meals. Throughout, neither grandeur nor elegance has quite been achieved.

When Trafalgar increased the ship's capacity, the Princess no longer remained an extra-tariff restaurant, accessible to First Class passengers anxious to sample grill service. Now, tables in the Princess, as in the Queen's Grill, are permanently assigned to occupants of the vessel's most expensive cabins, and Columbia Restaurant clients can no longer enjoy an evening out, save in the rarest instances. It is interesting to compare the food and service provided in the grills with those in the Columbia. Ostensibly, all three rooms offer First Class fare and, to a large extent, they do: an identical menu is used throughout, and given adequate notice, one can order almost anything in advance in any of them. But there are special perquisites in the grills: more room, more caviar, and—extremely important—more stewards with more experience. (I was rather taken aback one summer when the *commis* waiter at my table in the Columbia Restaurant confided that he was not really a steward, only an accountant earning some extra pocket money! That stewarding was *not* his calling he made abundantly clear; he never once pulled out my wife's chair nor brushed crumbs from it either throughout the voyage.) Moreover, though not as well designed a room, the Queen's Grill has a distinct gastronomic edge over the Princess. It is only natural that a restaurant with its own galley should offer refinements of service, choice, and style that cannot be duplicated in the larger and less specialized reaches of the Quarter Deck's main galley serving Princess, Columbia, and Tables of the World.

This apartness permeates the entire Queen's Grill surroundings, isolation arising out of its remote location. Queen's Grill diners occupy a self-sufficient corner of the ship, high up and forward, within easy reach of promenades, deck chairs, shops, casino, theater balcony, and their own bar. It has become an enclave, catering to a club whose members have no need or reason to stray anywhere else on board save for entertainment, if they care to, in the Queen's Room. It is, to all intents and purposes, a separate class. Establishment of the Princess and Queen's Grills as permanent dining rooms has brought the *Queen Elizabeth 2* full circle; she has become, sub rosa, a three-class vessel again, although not as originally conceived on the drawing boards back in the sixties. Rather than Tourist, Cabin, or First Class, now she embraces Transatlantic, First, and what I shall call Grill Class.

Although Cunard may not acknowledge this, it is only too apparent to observant passengers. The unfortunate effect has been to dilute the return on a First Class ticket. One sensible proviso on board the *France* was the absence of an extra-tariff restaurant; all First Class passengers enjoyed the same superlative cuisine in the Restaurant Chambord, preserving an identical high standard throughout. Thus an unspoken discrimination haunts First Class on board *QE2*. Regardless how stunning the service in the grills—and it is unique in all the world—life in the Columbia Restaurant has never been the same since.

Whether subdivided into three classes or two, passenger flow throughout the *Queen Elizabeth 2* is almost unrestricted, far less so than on her predecessors. Separation of the classes is officially low-key, enforced by a few removable, discreet, white-on-black knee-high FIRST CLASS PASSENGERS ONLY signs. They are found at strategic frontier points: outside the theater balcony, at the entrance to the Queen's Grill bar, in the topmost sun deck, and at the after end of the Queen's Room near the adjacent Transatlantic Class staircase. But they are largely ignored as barriers. Indeed, they are not barriers at all, merely notices. Transatlantic Class roams First Class territory unchallenged, though they are discouraged from settling in a First Class deck chair, for those are assigned by name. But there is no reason to assume that suitably dressed Transatlantic Class passengers could not, on a regular basis, establish themselves imperiously in the Queen's Grill Bar be-

The top of the ship, figuratively and
literally. Queen's Grill on board *Queen
Elizabeth 2. (Cunard photo by Robert
Alpert)*

fore lunch or dinner on day one and enjoy cocktails with fellow passengers whose cabin fare is several times theirs. (They would have to pay cash, however, for by signing a bill, they would betray their cabin location.) I once asked a longtime steward in the Queen's Grill bar how he handles Transatlantic passengers who, by either design or mistake, make themselves at home in what is patently advertised as the domain of First. His reply was enigmatic: "They don't come here often, and if they do, they don't come back." He—and I—left it at that.

In fact, the system seems to work osmotically, depending less on locks and baffles than socioterritorial phenomena. Passengers tend to make friends within their own class and tend, therefore, to remain within their own turf. On board *QE2*, they gather before meals in the bar appropriate to their dining room—Transatlantic to the Double Down or Theatre Bar, First to the Midships Bar, and Grill (my unofficial peri-class) in the Queen's Grill bar. Similarly, in the evening, they will go to their respective lounges —Transatlantic to the Double Room, First and Grill to the Queen's Room. (There is, of course, confusing protective coloration after dark due to the black-tie syndrome: passengers of any class who don dinner jackets have the run of the ship.) But, as the evening wears on, class lines blur. Gamblers from all over the vessel jam the Casino from 10:00 P.M. on while dancers will congregate either in the Theatre Bar or in what is now called the Club Lido, formerly the Q-4 Nightclub. After midnight, passengers roaming the *QE2* coexist within a nocturnal, classless society, very much the Utopia that French Line planners had envisioned for their Cabaret de l'Atlantique. But by day, crossing the Atlantic with class delineations in place, passengers' geographical imperative retains a voluntary and effective segregation.

Extraordinarily, on board a former consort, the *Norway-ex-France*, where formal class segregation no longer exists, an identical imperative obtains as well. The *Norway* is now a classless, seven-day cruise ship sailing the Caribbean out of Miami. Indoors or outdoors, subtly yet perceptibly, the passenger body subdivides organically, what a biologist might call meiosis. Take the swimming pool syndrome, for instance. *Norway* has two pools outdoors, a large one at the stern, a smaller one up between the funnels. That after pool, engulfed within a teak lido, has become a prime outdoor entertainment area, the site each noon, for instance, of an ear-splitting concert by the ship's *amplified* steel band. (Italics mine; whoever first decided to electrify steel bands has distorted a winsome island folk sound into banal vulgarity.) Boisterous pool and deck games are organized as well, attracting singles and families with small children. Two decks higher, volleyball and one-on-one basketball prevail. Those passengers in search of quiet, those who wish to read, sun, or enjoy the view, stay up between the stacks. I have completed five cruises and three crossings on board *Norway*, and on each, I have found that this Darwinian praxis recurs. The species separate according to natural passenger selection, establishing and sustaining a self-willed class system—Tourist aft, First amidships.

The process continues after dark—a more complex meiosis for passenger amusement on board the world's largest liner proliferates below decks. As on board the *Queen Elizabeth 2*, gambling is a great leveler, attracting punters from a broad spectrum. The *Norway*'s casino—called the Monte Carlo Room, natch—operates in the former Tourist Class Smoking Room, a jangling, flashing arena between Saga Theatre and North Cape Lounge. It is an inspired location, for the deck's outboard promenade has been sliced up into cabins, and the Monte Carlo Room doubles as a thoroughfare, the main passenger artery along that deck. As such, it cannot help but attract the impulsive as well as the compulsive— giggling naifs with a few quarters to burn, Sunbelt matrons clutching cupfuls of dollar tokens, and pale-skinned veterans who roost, motionless, at the tables for hours at a time, with seemingly inexhaustible rolls of bills in their back pockets. The Breughelian composite surges throughout the Monte Carlo Room during gaming hours, a shipwide blend that defies classification.

But in two public rooms aft—one new, one old, both for the accommodation of dancers—natural selection persists. Lowest down in the hull is the *Norway*'s discotheque, coyly named A Club Called Dazzles. It is as hidden from view as the casino is compellingly on display. It can be reached through two separate entrances, either by a door at the after end of Viking Deck's cabin corridor or by descent through a deckhouse kiosk on the starboard side near the after pool. The proximity of the two— noisy pool and noisier disco—is significant since exuberant passengers who enjoy the pool's jollity during the day seem to find the discotheque's raucous frenzy to their taste after dark. In turn, the upper-pool set is more likely to be found in the Club Internationale, the former First Class Smoking Room, where restraint—decorative as well as musical—is the norm. It is a serene, elegant double-height room, a traditional shipboard space with a traditional dance floor on which couples dance traditionally *en face*, timeless social choreography of the kind that their gyrating shipmates two decks down refer to, quaintly, as "touch dancing."

Sociopsychologists might dismiss these observations as oversimplified.

The Club Internationale on board the *Norway*. Its
raised midsection, designed to accommodate the North
Cape Lounge's ceiling below, creates terraced levels to
either side. Though the after glass wall from the *France*
days is gone, the room retains its elegance, ideal for
passenger gatherings and recitals. It remains, simply,
one of the prettiest rooms afloat anywhere. (*Norwegian
Caribbean Lines*)

Is Tourist necessarily "exuberant," any more than "restraint" characterizes First? Generalizations about life on board ship are dangerous, but I am persuaded, after scores of voyages, that the overriding class arbiter on board every ship is age. First Class passengers, rich enough to afford higher fares, are almost invariably older, and consequently quieter, more experienced, and often blasé. Tourist passengers, less affluent and less splendidly accommodated as a result, are younger, louder, more adventurous, and easier to please. Traditionally, Tourist Class has always been more fun: a classic North Atlantic scenario depicts well-dressed grandchildren bidding grandparents a dutiful good night before changing clothes and dashing below to the youthful zest of their contemporaries in Tourist.

If one accepts this traditional evaluation of stuffy First and giddy Tourist, then it becomes clear that the old shipboard class distinctions have survived, whether on converted Atlantic tonnage or on newbuilding designed and scheduled, at least ostensibly, for one-class cruising. The term "one-class," which can be applied to all vessels today save the *QE2* on the Atlantic, is misleading. Today's cruise ships may be one-class, but the multiple appeals they generate are not.

Though clearly defined First and Tourist Class passengers continue to sail, *they are no longer accommodated in the same hull.* In that sense, the new distinctions are more radical: just as layered decks supplanted the vertical segregation of old, now entire ships—or, indeed, entire fleets— cater to each class. There are ships for Tourist Class passengers, and there are ships for First Class passengers. I once steamed out of Fort Lauderdale on the *Royal Viking Star*, spending a week on board until we reached Barbados; there, I walked around the mooring basin and transhipped for the voyage home on board the Royal Caribbean Cruise Line's *Nordic Prince.* From afar, the blue-and-white hulls, each a Wärtsilä product, seemed interchangeable; life on board was not. The *Royal Viking Star* was as undeniably upscale as the *Nordic Prince* was accommodating humble clients. The contrast marked every facet of life on board, from the dining room walls to the color of the stairs' carpet to the staff's manners to the noise level. Perhaps most obvious was the difference in cabin size. Since RCCL ships carry twice the number of passengers of those on the Royal Viking Line, normal cabins tend to be about half the size.

Overall, the difference revolved largely around what I would call cruising's three crucial D's: Dollars, Decoration, and Duration. These are contemporary class barriers—the price, ambience, and length of a cruise. Tourist Class vessels scour the Caribbean for a fortnight at most; First Class *grandes dames* steam on global itineraries for months at a time. The respective prices and perks keep the bookings as consistently separate as the ancient socioeconomic hierarchy that existed on the Atlantic. Earlier in this chapter, we saw how shipping companies juggled names to keep abreast of changing passenger loads. It seems appropriate to do so once again. I would divide contemporary shipboard clients into two generics: Old Guard and Newpassengers. Newpassengers sail largely on newbuilding. They outnumber the Old Guard, who, incidentally, are not exclusively geriatric anymore; the days when Cunard's *Caronia* was described during its world cruise in company circles as "God's Waiting Room" are over.

But it is true that the longer the cruise, the older the clientele. Only the retired rich can afford both time and money to spend months at sea. (There are a few Old Guard devotees who cruise indefinitely on the same vessel, living permanently on board and disembarking reluctantly only during annual dry docking.) In the main, Old Guard passengers are indistinguishable from their First Class contemporaries of the species *Peregrinator transatlanticus inveteratus* who still sail the Atlantic. They are wedded to liners and seem to have sailed forever—as children with their parents, as young marrieds with their children, and, occasionally, with their grandchildren on summer cruises. They come largely from California and Florida, the two preeminent cruising states. Some forsake Sunbelt retirement to escape the worst of the summer's heat, others sail around the world each January to foil winter's cold.

The Old Guard know ships, they know service, and they know style. In one sense, they have seen it all, yet they keep on cruising year after year, sometimes even dying at sea. They spend a lot of money for their passage, and one unmistakable staple of an Old Guard vessel is a convenient shipboard office where passengers in the midst of one cruise can readily book another without having to waste a stamp. Marketing vice-presidents sometimes lament that the Old Guard will die off; when booking time for world cruises comes each fall, there is keen competition between Cunard, Royal Viking, and Holland America for Old Guard stalwarts. But I see them as hardy perennials with so many reinforcements appearing each year to fill the depleted ranks that their numbers are more likely to increase. The Old Guard will continue to be largely women: gerontological forecasts indicate that by the start of the twenty-first century, the life expectancy of women will be eighty-five, while that for men will trail at eighty-one. But overall, the actuarial Old Guard prognosis seems sound. Moreover, there is every reason to conclude that today's Newpassengers, having achieved the appropriate age and income, will become tomorrow's Old Guard. A young couple embarking on the *Starward* for their maiden sea voyage next winter may well cruise around the world on the *Nieuw Amsterdam* early in the twenty-first century.

Newpassengers are the cruise lines' lifeblood. One of the dizzying statistics bewitching shipping companies is that less than 5 percent of America's population has ever booked a cabin; so there seems unlimited scope for expansion. Most Newpassengers flock to the Caribbean, and Miami handles more of them than any port of the world. On the huge globe positioned on the *Rotterdam*'s Upper Promenade Deck, the entire Floridian peninsular has been obliterated by passengers' fingers. (So too, inexplicably, has Springfield, Illinois, remote from any coast!) Each weekend, twelve thousand passengers disembark from the white fleet tied nose to tail along Miami's Dodge Island; by sunset, twelve thousand replacements have arrived from the airport, a jostling throng sporting cruise-wear and cameras. Almost all will derive enormous satisfaction from their indolent week or fortnight afloat; research indicates that passengers enthusiastically rate cruises as the most rewarding leisure vacations available to them. I am not surprised—shipboard life is fun to start with, and the Miami companies have refined their offerings to a kind of bland perfection.

The great paradox of this booming passenger trade is that the same jets that starved Atlantic liners now feed the cruise ships that have supplanted them. No longer antagonists, ship and plane are allied in crucial partnership. If, through some extraordinary mishap, Miami and Fort Lauderdale's airports were both to close down, not a ship would sail that weekend. The same applies all the world over: the vast majority of cruise ship passengers, whether in Florida, Piraeus, Hong Kong, Hawaii, Singapore, Hamburg, or Genoa, embark from the airport and jet home at cruise's end. They fly at bargain rates, and when business is slow—always in the fall—shipping companies lure them back with free air passage. Indeed, it is worth suggesting that airplanes and ships have undergone a subtle yet pervasive role change in contemporary life. Aircraft have ascended into that presumably enviable yet risky position of the inevitable transporters. Flight is no longer a luxury but a necessity; ships and trains, on the other hand, have become preferential alternatives.

Though Newpassengers swarm on board in a single indiscriminate class, their socioeconomic origins are diverse. Not all Newpassengers are young or taking their first cruise—thousands re-book each year, even several times each year, either sampling rival companies or staying with one line. A few are rich, but most are middle or working class; still, whether sophisticated or naive, the overriding characteristic they share, in contrast to the Old Guard, is youth. One of the most successful Miami

The Newpassenger fleet's in. On Saturday, October 15, 1983, nine cruise ships tied up along Dodge Island's passenger terminal. Starting lower center, they are: *Bohème, Sun Viking, Song of Norway, Nordic Prince, Starward, Norway, Rhapsody, Festivale,* and *Caribe I.* This display of tonnage gives some indication of the new cruise market's vigor. *(The Port of Miami)*

companies, Carnival Cruise Lines, advertises its vessels as "the Fun Ships," projecting an instant Las Vegas wish/dream whose golden participants do nothing but "party," an intransitive verb that is littered throughout much of Newpassenger cruisespeak.

Life on board a Carnival ship is fast and uncomplicated. Formality of manner or clothing is discouraged, and food is as abundant as sunshine. Each ship carries a maritime as well as a ribald provenance, in the case of the *Mardi Gras* "27,250 tons of fun." The ships also carry suggestive "partying" names—*Carnivale, Festivale, Mardi Gras, Tropicale,* and *Holiday.* Brochures feature girls in T-shirts and sailor hats adorned with the motto PEOPLE LOVE US (pride or proposition?), and public rooms carry names—invariable indicators—that run the gamut from Riverboat or Copacabana Lounge to Le Cabaret Nightclub. The copy reassures inexperienced Newpassengers that "luncheon in the dining room features five courses" just as seven-course dinners will include "tempting desserts and singing waiters" in the same hectic breath. Significantly, the pictures used in Carnival publicity are usually real passengers rather than models. This is a rare practice but, for Carnival, an appropriate one: no central casting types could better deliver the company's relentless juvenile appeal. Examine an Old Guard, Royal Viking brochure: the decks and public rooms are peopled by the silver-haired, distinguished, and serene. Not so on board Carnival ships, where youth predominates. Just as significantly, there is not a blue head to be seen. The emphasis is on a frenetic week of nonstop swimming, sunning, drinking, eating, "partying," and—predictably—coupling.

But whichever market they serve, the ships sail on. Old Guard and Newpassengers still crowd the piers and decks, successors to those First, Second, Steerage, Third, Tourist Third Cabin, and Cabin passengers who crossed the Atlantic by the millions before airplanes reduced that legendary passage to a historical curiosity. In a democratic age, the old distinctions remain. Newpassengers and Old Guard may sometimes be found on board the same ship, but seldom on the same voyage. Holland America's *Rotterdam,* for instance, an old-line Atlantic thoroughbred that has completed a quarter century of elegant world cruises, occasionally offers two-day cruises to nowhere at bargain rates, but the clientele is never the same.

Less important than the respective classes, all cruise passengers share the same preoccupation with ships, the sea, and the potent mystique of shipboard. Today's Newpassengers are united less by peril and storm than bargains and suntans. In some respects, the life is very different; but in others, as we shall see, it is exactly and satisfyingly the same.

he trio of old-world stalwarts that made up the original
ucleus of Carnival Cruise Lines, known enviously
mong rival fleets as the "K-Mart of the Caribbean."
rom front to rear: *Festivale* (ex-*S/A Vaal*-ex-
ransvaal Castle), Mardi Gras (ex-*Empress of Canada),*
nd *Carnivale* (ex-*Empress of Britain).* **The distinctive**
alf-moon funnel liveries arose from an early money-
ving expedient: those on the Canadian Pacific ships
ad the same shape. *(Carnival Cruise Lines)*

We weren't as fussy in those days.

—IPHIGENE OCHS SULZBERGER

*During a recent voyage home from Java, a
fellow passenger grumbled dreadfully to me at
cocktail time because the ship's laundry had
not starched the pleats on the front of his
evening shirt in exactly parallel lines; after
which, night was made hideous for him, poor
fellow, because they had not given him enough
lemon with his caviar.*

—PASSENGER'S LETTER FROM P&O

4.

Cruises Past

They say the *Queen Mary*, moored in California's Long Beach, is haunted.
Night watchmen report bizarre nocturnal activity: oilcans placed along
Shaft Alley either move or disappear, lights flash on and off near the
original ship's morgue, and a "lady in white" sometimes floats down to the
indoor First Class pool for a swim. Those inexplicable events have only
occurred since the great Cunarder has been retired, afloat and impotent in
alien waters. Who are these restless shades? Are they spectral holdovers
of GI's who died en route to England, of German prisoners who perished
from heat exhaustion in the Red Sea, or perhaps the Italian lady passenger
who expired of fright during a severe mid-Atlantic storm before the stabilizers were put in place? Whatever the source, they are the haunted

residue of the *Queen Mary*'s three decades of service, a sea-time aggregate when the great Cunarder would sail, as Masefield had predicted at her launch, "With all the wester streaming from your hull/And all gear twanging shrilly as you race."

In this chapter, I hope to evoke other seaborne ghosts, benevolent ones, of ships rather than passengers, ships that took people on cruises, following the same itineraries we follow today but at a different pace and with contrasting attitudes. Whereas the *Mary* has been preserved—a rara avis among a vanished maritime sisterhood—the vessels of which I speak are gone. One changed names three times before her end; another was cut up in her original guise; a third burned and capsized in New York harbor; a fourth lies off the Guam roads in storm-rent fragments; and the last was consumed by fire before rolling onto her beam ends in Hong Kong. (It has always struck me odd how passenger ships, embodying such benignity during their working lives, all meet such cruel ends. Even the scrapyard is violent, more brutal than a typhoon: the spectacle of a beached vessel, listing on a mud flat while cranes tear at her innards, is an appalling sight. Steel plates protest and groan as deckhouses are wrenched from hull, trailing viscera of cabling and pipe.)

I wish here to preserve rather than destroy. And if the cruises are long since past, passengers and crew who sailed on them have, fortunately, remembered enough to flesh out clippings, photographs, and souvenirs. None of these cruises were historically noteworthy; they do not conjure up epic disaster or tragedy; there is no *Morro Castle, Antilles*, or *Prinsendam* among them. Indeed, I chose them to be as ordinary as possible. Only two have significance for the steamship historian: the *Normandie*'s Rio cruise of 1938 was one of the only two she ever made, and *Queen Elizabeth*'s of thirty years later was one of her last.

Without specific passenger or crew recall, these voyages might otherwise remain in limbo, unresurrected. Shipping companies almost never perpetuate the memory of a specific voyage; they spend much time and money publicizing them before they occur, but once under way, are preoccupied with other matters. In my library are several souvenir cruise books from prewar Cunarders that circled the globe. They are filled with descriptions and photographs of ports but contain almost nothing about what happened en route. In some cases, the ship's name goes unmentioned, not even appearing in photographs.

The best—indeed, the only—reminiscing is done by passengers and crew. I am struck, as I hope reader/passengers will be, by how similar those earlier cruises were to those we take today, voyages as fondly recalled as they were eagerly anticipated. Shipboard memories are fragile: even the most pleasurable blur and fade almost as soon as suitcases are unpacked and put away. I sailed once on the *France* for a Christmas and New Year's cruise in the Caribbean, and though I enjoyed it immensely, I have few specific memories of the cruise. They are lost in a kaleidoscope of blistering days, festive nights, and the cool splendor of those garish interiors. If now I can evoke fragments of some cruises past, I feel that I will have succeeded not only in recalling matters of interest and delight, but also in setting today's cruises into historical perspective.

Before the advent of today's mass of pleasure-bound passengers, before television, before aircraft, the world seemed infinitely larger and destinations infinitely more remote. Traveling anywhere, whether overnight to Buffalo or over much of a week to California or anywhere abroad, was an occasion. The decision to book passage for a cruise—a long sea voyage undertaken for mere idle enjoyment—entailed no less of a commitment. Just such an adventure began for over four hundred passengers who, in February 1895, embarked at an icebound New York pier on board the Red Star liner *Friesland*, sailing for a cruise to the Holy Land. They were a congenial mix of Victorian travelers with the professions heavily represented: no fewer than forty-three clergymen, thirty-five lawyers, twenty-four physicians or dentists, and four undertakers. The rest were in trade or retired; wives, widows, daughters, and spinsters made up the distaff columns of the passenger list.

Within a week of departure, one of the passengers, a Dr. Hamilton, had edited and published a newspaper on board. Significantly, he called it *The Rolly-Poly*, a choice doubtless reflecting the *Friesland*'s behavior on "That Awful Thursday" when she and her passengers suffered through eighteen hours of a North Atlantic winter storm one day out of port. The first issue—the only one that survives, perhaps the only one published—is packed with gossip and anecdotes, an imperishable record of passenger spirit on board. An analysis of the ship's passenger population revealed that of the total complement of 430, 230 were male, 200 female. "Of the women, all are wives except 78 who aspire to be. Of the latter," the editor pointed out tactfully, "there is a wide range of age and beauty." *The Rolly-Poly* announced that a ball would be held on deck (presumably clear of storm-racked waters). "Carriages," the item went on, "at 11 p.m. in the starboard scuppers." Seasickness was a subject of grim levity. A bad sailor observed that "he did not like the *Friesland*'s style of six meals a day, three down and three up." "A.B.," it was announced, "was afraid

Cruise and remembrance. An illustration from the early storm on board the *Friesland*, captioned simply "Tribute." *Left*, cover for the menu of the commemorative banquet a year later. The caption on the railside cartoon lower right is from Shakespeare's *Henry IV*: "This sickness doth infect the very lifeblood of our enterprise." (*Author's collection*)

he would die and then he was afraid that he wouldn't." The master's only comment was that, throughout the eighteen-hour storm, land had been only 3 miles distant—"straight down." One contributor to *The Rolly-Poly*, Marguerite Cook of Elgin, Illinois, wrote, "Above the hubbub of the storm, the ringing of the bells, the groaning of the sick, sounded the thumps of the small boy against the sides of the bunk above me."

Yet however physically distressing the voyage's debut, it did weld the passenger body firmly together, an amalgam that survived long after cruise's end. S. R. Stoddard of Pittsburgh (Pennsylvanians comprised the bulk of the *Friesland*'s passenger list) published privately a handsome, leatherbound volume, *The Cruise of the Friesland 1895*. It was a kind of yearbook, a journal of the cruise, complete with photographs of every port as well as every passenger. Publication coincided with the first anniversary of the New York departure, an occasion celebrated with a series of reunion banquets and receptions all over the northeast. "We, the Jersey City contingent of the *Friesland* Crusaders . . ." began one such engraved invitation. The most elaborate dinner was convened at the Monongahela House in Pittsburgh on Thursday, February 6, 1896, a year to the day after the *Friesland* had sailed from New York into stormy seas off Hatteras. The memory of that ordeal was still fresh in everybody's mind, a kind of bonding baptism they had all managed to survive and hence treasured. Chapter 2 of Stoddard's book is called, simply, "The Storm," and it commemorates one young crewman nicknamed " the midshipmite":

> Ah, then came the rolls
> That uplifted our soles,
> And all that we valued took wings;
> While the midshipmite,
> Like an angel of light,
> Brought comfort, and crackers, and things.

The lavish dinner menu that night at the Monongahela House also bore witness to continuing passenger preoccupation with the storm. After the dessert listing, a note had been amended in small print:

> ICE CREAMS IN FORMS, ASSORTED CAKES,
> SELECTED FRUITS. . . .
> A picturesque mélange—like the tour of
> the Frieslanders. Go a little slow on
> this mixture, however, or tomorrow you
> may be reminded of February 7th, 1895,
> at 12 noon, or thereabouts.

That almost quaint, commemorative urge among early cruise passengers was consistent. The *"Friesland* Crusaders" had shared hardship and pleasure, all of it to be cherished. The same spirit infused every ship that sailed on cruises in the past with an intensity that seems, regrettably, to have evaporated in the present.

The year of the first of these cruises past was 1913, a time of un-paralleled American expansion and riches, set against the ordered tempo of peace, only a year before Europe would be plunged into years of carnage. In February, a New York college girl returned midweek to her family's house on West 75th Street. The previous weekend she had selected a trunkful of summer clothes, brought out from storage closets under the eaves by those good-natured, hardworking Irish maids who, in those days, made life comfortable for so many New Yorkers.

The girl was nineteen-year-old Iphigene Ochs, only child of Adolph and Iphigene Ochs; he was the owner and publisher of the *New York Times*. Her parents were taking her out of school for four weeks of her winter semester so they could sail together on a cruise to the West Indies. (A third-year student at Barnard, she would have to make up a dropped course as a result.) They had booked—at the last minute—on board a favorite ship, the former S.S. *Deutschland*, recently fitted out exclusively for cruising and rechristened *Victoria Luise*.

On the morning of February 8, the family was driven in their Packard to the Manhattan terminus of West 23rd Street's ferry. Muffled against the cold, they crossed to Hoboken and proceeded onto the piers of the Hamburg-Amerika Linie. From the boat, they had glimpsed the *Victoria Luise*'s black stern and a peremptory column of black smoke ascending into the overcast of a midwinter, Hudson morning. At the pier barrier, Ochs presented a letter from the company; he had been issued no tickets in the proper sense, for the last-minute space offered him boasted no printed guarantees. The Ochs family would be berthed on the bridge—a gesture of extraordinary privilege. Iphigene and her mother would share Captain Martin Meyer's cabin, while Ochs would bunk in on the port side in the first officer's cabin. That the vessel's two senior officers would vacate their quarters to suit Adolph Ochs speaks volumes for the power of the press in Edwardian New York as well as HAPAG's obvious desire to accommodate the *Times*'s first family at whatever the logistical cost. Once past the pier barriers, all three trooped up the gangplank onto Main Deck. (It was properly described as a plank in those days, an open, treaded walkway with canvas-lashed railing, not the telescopic tunnels the Pas-senger Ship Terminal offers New Yorkers boarding today.)

The *Victoria Luise* at Charlotte Amalie.
Since the hull is white, this was not taken
during the 1913 Panama Canal cruise.
(Jack Shaum)

It was not the first time that the Ochs family had sailed together on the ship. In 1901, when Iphigene was only eight years old, she had crossed with her parents from New York to Hamburg on the *Deutschland*. Years later, she could recall nothing specific about her first passage on the steamer; at ninety-one, she remembered only excitement and wonder. At the time of her first passage, the *Deutschland* was not only the fastest steamer of the Hamburg-Amerika Linie, she was the fastest steamer in the world as well, the only Blue Ribband winner the company ever built. In common with all record-breakers, the *Deutschland* had been designed with a consuming preoccupation with speed. Yet speed brought its own problems; passengers endured a hard, uncomfortable ride. Moreover, the *Deutschland*'s engines were temperamental, and her eleven-year career on the North Atlantic was marred by collision and storm damage, connected with the need to keep up her bruising schedule. The appearance of a new company flagship, the *Amerika* of 1905, signaled HAPAG's abandonment of speed in favor of comfort. The *Amerika* had none of the *Deutschland*'s fine lines but was a larger, placid prototype; although the world's largest vessel for a year, she would never be—nor was she *meant* to be—the fastest. The Hamburg-Amerika Linie relinquished that honor to their Hanseatic colleagues in Bremen: the Norddeutscher Lloyd had first taken the Blue Ribband in 1897, only to lose it first to the *Deutschland* and then to Cunard's *Lusitania* in 1907.

The *Deutschland* continued in service until the fall of 1911, when she was withdrawn for a refit at her builder's yard, the Vulkan Werke of Stettin. To get the ship back up the River Oder, all her furniture was disembarked and a pair of stabilizing pontoons were riveted across the stern. Once back at her fitting-out pier, a great deal more weight was removed in the form of an entire boiler room. Then the Promenade Deck and Sun Deck were extended to the stern. When the structural work had been completed at Stettin, the vessel was moved west to Hamburg for interior finishing and the addition of 163 tons of iron ballast to replace the weight of the missing boilers. She had been transformed from greyhound to cruise ship in twelve months, her capacity reduced from a thousand transatlantic passengers to half that number carried in one cruising class.

During that period, the names of German ships in general and HAPAG ships in particular alternated between Teutonic establishment and America's republic. Chairman Albert Ballin was diplomatically attuned to the nationalistic sensibilities of his overwhelmingly American First Class clientele. Vessels named after the kaiser and his family or *Moltke* and *Blucher* sailed in congenial schedule with others christened

Captain Martin Meyer, the accommodating master of the *Victoria Luise*. The captain is still wearing blues, so the photograph was taken somewhere between New York and the Caribbean. *(The Ocean Liner Museum)*

President Grant and *President Lincoln.* Yet though his new cruise liner would spend most of her time sailing out of New York, Ballin had renamed the *Deutschland* after a popular German princess: Victoria Luise was the kaiser's only daughter. (It was, in fact, the second vessel named after her: a smaller *Prinzessin Victoria Luise* had been stranded and lost during an earthquake off Jamaica in 1906.) As it happened, Her Highness became engaged to Ernst August, the duke of Cumberland, as her second maritime namesake was nearing Cuba on its second winter cruise of 1913.

On the morning of February 8, at eleven o'clock sharp, the *Victoria Luise* slipped her moorings and, attended by a fussing of tugs, was maneuvered out into the stream; once her bows had been turned downriver, the tugs left her, and the vessel began passage under her own power past Manhattan, down toward the Narrows. The hardiest souls braved February's chill and stayed on the open, upper decks, calling and waving farewell to friends on Hoboken's pierhead. If, like the Ochs family, they were old *Deutschland* passengers, they had noticed some changes. For instance, there was a long expanse of new teak aft of the top deck's Grill Room. But passengers who ventured inside in hopes of booking a table for lunch found a Tee-haus instead, a wickered retreat full of potted palms where deck rather than dining room stewards dispensed only bouillon or tea. Its after end was open; the entrance extended through a kind of gazebo, with coconut matting on the deck similar to Cunard's popular Veranda Cafés on board *Lusitania* and *Mauretania.* In fact, that little arbor extension was situated atop the location, one deck below, of the *Deutschland's* Second Cabin Lounge skylight. Redundant on a one-class vessel, the room had been transformed into a spacious gymnasium. The Second Class Ladies' Drawing Room was now a shore excursion office, sine qua non for cruises although unknown on transatlantic ships. Nearby was a little darkroom for passenger use, a unique innovation in 1913 and seldom seen since.

But the most welcome change had occurred between the sheltered promenade decks. A new Social Hall had emerged full-blown between the Smoking Room and the original Social Hall. Finding such spatial dividends within an existing hull was an extraordinary bonus and, curiously, the reason was most clearly perceived by knowledgeable watchers on either shore who saw the *Victoria Luise's* progression down the North River. A glance at her profile revealed that coal smoke poured from only her forward funnels. The after ones were no longer functioning.

On all German four-stackers, the quartet of funnels was paired: that is, numbers 1 and 2 were grouped forward, 3 and 4 were set as a pair farther aft. The purpose was to leave a gap between 2 and 3 for a skylight above the largest public room on board, the Dining Saloon down on Main Deck. (However, it was not Main Deck anymore, but D-deck. The Germans had abrogated the traditional deck names—Boat, Promenade, Upper, and Main—in favor of more prosaic alphabetizing. It had been done in an effort to bring all the fleet into a deck nomenclature parity with the new *Imperator*-class.) The *Deutschland*'s skylight between the paired funnels remained in place on the *Victoria Luise*, providing daylight down to the Dining Saloon on Main Deck.

But though that *lichtschacht*, or lightshaft, supplied a pale north light for breakfast and luncheon, it raised havoc with the Social Hall it pierced en route. In that era, a ship's Social Hall, or lounge, was a neglected public room. When Ochs *père* disappeared into the sacrosanct male bastion of the Smoking Room, his wife and daughter had at their disposal on the *Deutschland*, at least, only that flawed Social Hall. With its center obliterated by the Dining Room's lightshaft, it remained a meager doughnut of a room. It mattered little that the company tried capitalizing on its bizarre shape by dividing it into two U-shaped facilities: forward a Music Room, complete with piano, and aft the Ladies' Parlor. Whatever the cognomen, it was disgracefully inadequate, either for lady passengers alone or for couples who planned to spend an evening together.

HAPAG solved the problem once the *Victoria Luise*'s after boiler room, no longer needed for slow-speed cruising, had been closed down forever at Stettin. A new Social Hall was placed directly under number 3 funnel, interior space formerly given over to the boiler uptakes. The funnel above, as well as number 4 farther aft, was merely decorative now, and the resultant space beneath them afforded the *Victoria Luise* a decent-size Social Hall, including a dance floor and a musicians' gallery on the forward wall. The old Social Hall, identified on deckplans as the Damen-Zimmer, still pierced by the Dining Saloon's lightshaft, remained in place, largely unused. Interestingly enough, reduced mechanical demands on an Edwardian vessel had wrought sociosexual advances for its passengers.

The Ochs family's first luncheon on the *Victoria Luise*—inevitably slow, as are first meals on board every ship of any era—was further confused because the dining tables had been reshuffled. On the *Deutschland*, the center of the room beneath the towering *lichtschacht* had been furnished with round tables, including the captain's oval centerpiece. Long institutional tables—called, euphemistically, "party tables"—were lined up along either flank. But, in the ship's cruising mode, long tables—too

Two views of the *Victoria Luise*'s new Social Hall. *Above,* in its daytime incarnation with tables suitable for tea or games. *Below,* tables and rugs cleared away for an evening of dancing. *(Hapag-Lloyd)*

many of them—were packed amidships, and round ones off to the sides. More round tables were grouped aft of the staircase, where forty-seven additional passengers could be seated in newfound space reclaimed from the vanished funnel uptakes. The new table arrangement reflected the *Victoria Luise*'s commitment to democratic one-class cruising, assuaging passenger vanity by placing as many of them as possible in the envied central portion. Yet, in effect, the change turned back the vessel's decorative clock to a time when transatlantic passengers all shared long communal tables. By 1913, in an era when fashion embraced smaller, individual tables, the *Victoria Luise*'s table arrangement seemed hopelessly anachronistic.

But one shipboard change that the Ochs family could only guess at was the increase, albeit modest, in the number of private bathrooms on board. Since the captain was the only ship's officer whose cabin boasted one, the Ochses were quite content; but the vast majority of their fellow passengers below had no such luxury. On the *Deutschland*'s Upper Deck, situated between Promenade and Main and devoted exclusively to cabins, there were only eight private bathrooms, each attached to what were called Chambres de Luxe. The rest of that deck's occupants walked the corridors in bathrobes en route to public baths or toilets. Since these facilities were located amidships, those forward had a considerable hike, more than 150 feet, before them. Moreover—and this was a hallmark of passenger/crew symbiosis in those days—male passengers shared their ablutions with ship's officers, some of whom lived cheek-by-jowl with the line's clients. The doctor, apothecary, and assistant purser were accommodated on Upper Deck's starboard side amidships. These company employees would join the passenger parade to the baths with sponge bag and clean clothes clutched in their arms. Inside cabin number 113, assigned to a passenger, was located right in the midst of the officers' enclave. (All *Deutschland* cabins, incidentally, were identified by number only; though there was a number 113, there was no cabin 13.)

Following the Stettin conversion, HAPAG hoped to convey the impression that a new scale of luxury abounded throughout the one-class *Victoria Luise*. But few additional private bathrooms had been worked into the ship, and they were attached only to the most elegant staterooms, referred to now as Luxus-Zimmer or the not quite so grand Staats-Zimmer. The problem with installing additional private bathrooms in a ship is that they consume cabin space. For instance, forward on B-deck (the old Promenade Deck), two *Victoria Luise* Staats-Zimmer had been wrought at the expense of six *Deutschland* ordinaries: Staats-Zimmer B-73—the earlier numbers now had convenient deck initial prefixes—had replaced cabins 43, 45, and 47. One deck down, cabin C-150, a curiously isolated Staats-Zimmer forward on the port side and not mirrored to starboard, had been wrought in a different fashion: old cabin 90, outside, and 148, inside, made up the new quarters, while the inside cabin had been plumbed into a bathroom. In fact, there was an improvement—there were twice as many private baths on the *Victoria Luise* as there had been on the *Deutschland*—but most cruise passengers still trudged the corridors to bathe. However, the long-distance bathers berthed forward on C-deck, the ones with the 150-foot marathon to the tub, had been accommodated with new public baths worked into a former bank of inside cabins within reach.

After that first lunch, while a few overcoated souls worked off their meal with a frigid circuit or two on deck, Mrs. Ochs and her daughter returned to their cabin to complete that inevitable first-day passenger ritual, unpacking and putting the cabin to rights. Their task was not easy: though Captain Meyer had done his best for his distinguished guests, some of his cupboards still contained uniforms. So the bulk of the Ochses' cruising clothes remained within steamer trunks, of which there were several. In contrast to contemporary shipboard deshabille, earlier passengers were as heavily caparisoned by day as by night. The bulk of yardage alone was overwhelming: the women carried dozens of long cotton skirts and dresses, shirtwaists with ruffled necks ornamented with lace jabots that the *Victoria Luise*'s hardworking stewardesses would iron by the dozen throughout the cruise. There were, as well, dozens of evening dresses and, always, hats— broadbrimmed creations, some with veils, that traveled on latticed cotton racks six to a square trunk of their own.

The gentlemen brought suits—albeit lightweight—and enough celluloid collars to match dozens of shirts. There was no laundry on board nor any Steerage women anxious to make some change by obliging First Class families. Even at the equator, throughout steaming excursions into the Panamanian and Venezuelan hinterlands, jackets and ties would be the tropical norm, with the ensemble topped by a snap-brim cap in tweed or cotton—a passenger staple to this day—and panamas or pith helmets. Once past Hatteras, black or brown leather boots gave way to white doeskin shoes or rubber-soled canvas sneakers. The flashier among them would break out black-and-white brogues, elegant and expensive footwear of a variety ensuing generations would deride as "corespondent shoes."

In no trunk belonging to the Ochs family, or, for that matter, anyone else, was there a bathing costume of any kind. There was no swimming bath on board the *Victoria Luise*, indoors or out, nor was there any expectation that, off the ship, passengers might want to cool off in the ocean. "We weren't there to swim," explained Iphigene Sulzberger with just a shade of reproof, "we were there to see things."

Indeed, that was the essential difference between those earlier tourists and the hordes that swarm throughout the Caribbean today: they were explorers, bent on education rather than recreation, who found and appreciated ports and islands as rustic curiosities. The highlight of each of the *Victoria Luise*'s four winter cruises of 1913 was a call at Colón to inspect the Panama Canal, that triumph of French inspiration and Yankee ingenuity which would be completed within a year. This was the last cruise season in which passengers from visiting ships would be able to clamber down by ladder into what David McCullough has since described as "the sucking mire of Culebra" or stroll, awestruck, over the sills and between the open gates of Gatun's incredible locks. En route and after, the *Victoria Luise* would deposit her passengers at a Baedeker of tropical ports— Havana, Kingston, Fort-de-France, and Charlotte Amalie among them— during a counterclockwise sweep of the Caribbean; but the isthmus call remained the great raison d'être, a satisfying geographical and scientific objective. It is so to this day: during ocean passage between San Francisco and New York, the same irresistible focus obtains. There is nothing afloat as rewarding as transit of the Panama Canal.

But through their four Caribbean weeks, the *Victoria Luise*'s passengers were intrigued by everything they saw everywhere, especially the life of each island's inhabitants. St. Thomas—advertised that year smugly as "America's New Island Possession"—was a foreign country rather than the gaudy marketplace it would become. The Caribbean of 1913 was as remote as the travelers who sought it out were serious. Iphigene Ochs's photograph album, carefully captioned in white ink, underscores this fact: between inevitable scenes of horseplay and deck games on board, the tone ashore is inquisitive and educational. Her lens was aimed at schoolchildren, markets, and plantations. Not one beach or restaurant is to be seen. What she has preserved is a haunting sepia glimpse of tranquil island life now vanished, deluged beneath jetports, high-rises, and the cluttering detritus of mass tourism.

First call was a two-day layover in Cuba that called for an exploration of Havana and nearby Matanzas, as well as visiting a detachment of American soldiers stationed in the countryside. Among the many tragedies of Central America's cold war is that visits to this extraordinary island are so rare. I managed one on board *Veendam* in the fall of 1980 and understood what Havana—the Paris of the Caribbean—must have been like

Ports of call. *Top,* Charlotte Amalie in 1913. The Telegraph Office in the left foreground is now Riise's Gift Shop. The building on the right side with the overhanging balcony is the St. Thomas Apothecary Shoppe and Little Europe Jewelry and Linens. Closest to the camera on the right is the Jolly Roger Tobacconist, with the same doors still in place. *Bottom, Victoria Luise* passengers survey the excavation at Culebra. *(The Ocean Liner Museum)*

in the early years of this century. Nowadays, Habaneros lead a joyless, deprived existence, and no amount of bleak, megalithic monuments to Socialist accomplishment can compensate for the tatterdemalion urban dreariness.

After a look at the hospitals and schools of San Juan, the *Victoria Luise* steamed west to Haiti. Iphigene Ochs spoke French and was besieged by Port-au-Prince's beggars; there were as many then as there are now on that tragic half-island. All tried the same disarming preamble: *"Bonjour mademoiselle vous êtes très jolie donnez-moi un sou."* The first encounter was charming, the second disillusioning, the third ignored. But her French came in handy at the palace, where the ship's touring passengers were received by the president. She chattered away with him, far more at ease than some of her companions, who, imbued with contemporary prejudices, walked abruptly out when they discovered that their host, the leader of the country, was black. His color, moreover, made any thought of entertaining him on board an impossibility. Iphigene's father hired the local HAPAG agent, also black, as a guide; the young man was delighted and, anxious to improve his English, established a correspondence with Iphigene over the ensuing months, each in the other's language, in an attempt to improve their fluency.

In Havana, the *Victoria Luise* had tied up at a dock. But off Puerto Rico and Jamaica she anchored offshore and land-bound passengers used the ship's boats. There were novel arrangements for doing so. Large steam launches—*dampfboot*—were lowered from their davits behind the bridge. As crewmen bolted the funnels upright and stoked the miniature fireboxes beneath them, passengers trooped down companionways farther aft, on both sides of the vessel, into the ship's mahogany lifeboats. When each was fully laden, with sailors in whites holding barge poles at the ready mounted fore and aft, the bosun cast off. Each boat was tied, nose to tail, into a flotilla of four and, only then, taken in tow by the *dampfboot*. In festive procession, the *Victoria Luise*'s people steamed ashore. Off-loading five hundred passengers that way was laborious and time-consuming, but the time passed quickly with a great deal of bantering and back-chat between boats. Out of the shadow of the hull or, worse, away from the open ocean breezes, each boat sprouted a multicolored awning of passenger umbrellas and parasols.

Returning to the ship, the procedure was reversed. Passengers assembled at a quay in the afternoon and embarked once again. There was no continuous shuttle between pier and vessel—the shore excursion parties made a full day of it. Then the *dampfboot* towed their crocodiles of life-

Edwardian excursion ashore. *Top,* ship's boats—three at a time and loaded with passengers—under tow behind the *dampfboot. Middle,* at the pier, passengers disembark. Note the gloves and parasols for the ladies; hats, ties, and leather shoes for the men. *Bottom,* returning to the ship, divers trail the boats, hoping for last-minute largesse. The white girdling the boats is canvas filled with cork for additional buoyancy. *(The Ocean Liner Museum)*

boats out of the harbor, out to their steamer anchored in the roads, leaving behind a dwindling chorus of pursuing divers who called repeatedly for yet another nickel or dime to be cast into the depths for them to retrieve.

Days at sea between islands were conventional—lazy, overfed, and delightful. One afternoon between Colón and La Guaira, the purser organized deck sports on A-deck aft of the cluster of cowled ventilators. All the competitions were shipboard classics, inspired nonsense that has always been part of every ocean passage, crossing or cruising. There was a spar fight, two men astride a pole slugging it out with pillows, a safety mat of several old Third Class horsehair mattresses spread across the unyielding teak below. There were ladies', gentlemen's, and mixed three-legged races and—a refinement I have never encountered—*four*-legged races, for gentlemen only, teams of three contestants lashed together with bandanas at knee and ankle. There were potato-and-spoon races for the ladies and sack races for the gentlemen, who hopped energetically along the deck waist-deep in burlap sacks sent up from the vegetable lazaret by the chief steward. Both sexes competed in a cigarette and needle race, the men threading a needle while the ladies puffed their way delicately through most of a cigarette. Other men entered what Iphigene captioned in her album as the "Dress Suitcase Race," a kind of sartorial obstacle course in which contestants were obliged to don whatever garments they found in a closed suitcase in excruciating and hilarious haste.

Spectators for the games were accommodated in special bleachers flanking the course, supplementing park benches that, normally amidships back to back, were placed temporarily along the railings. The boat deck was a popular gathering place for photographers, and one of the largest group portraits taken on board captured the more than sixty passengers who called themselves the Misfit Parade, so named because all had ordered suits made overnight by Kingston's bespoke tailors. Not one of the hastily ordered—and tailored—garments fitted at all.

The only memento that Iphigene Ochs brought home from the Caribbean was a parrot, bought in Martinique. She christened it Green Swizzle, and the feathered souvenir survived several New York winters. Neither Miss Ochs nor any of her fellow passengers brought home a tan. There was no sunning mania in those days. Shaded under hat brims, awnings, and umbrellas, the Edwardians eschewed direct sun. Tanning, Iphigene recalls of her youth, was something that happened naturally and gradually over a summer—"We had more sense than to lie out on deck." It was quite true; there were no chairs set out on the open decks of the *Victoria*

Deck sports. *Above,* the ladies' three-legged race. The chalked X on the deck was for an egg-and-spoon race. *Below,* cigarette-and-needle race. Iphigene Ochs is second from the right. *(The Ocean Liner Museum)*

Luise. They remained down in the cool shade along the promenade decks, and were used for siestas, reading, or conversation, but never for sunbathing.

Of course, there was no formal entertainment of any kind on board. Passengers made their own, deck sports by day and masquerade parties at night. During one fancy dress ball, Iphigene and her friend Edith Smith, one of the half-dozen young women on board, won first prize as a pair of black-faced beggars. The only problem was that they had to relinquish the crucial part of their disguise almost at once: none of their prospective dancing partners wanted burnt cork on their white jackets. As always, passengers gave parties; Iphigene gave a tea party up on A-deck, inviting seven couples altogether. All of the young men who came were the smart set of the ship; they called themselves The Club. One was a man whose name Iphigene never forgot—Ammi Wright Lancaster. He was a Yale man only recently graduated; four years later, he would die in France. But such a tragic end seemed ludicrously remote that warm February afternoon as, in checked cap, bow tie, and steady smile, he and fellow members of The Club posed with their hostess outside the Tee-haus on the after deck of the *Victoria Luise* as she rolled easily in the Caribbean swell, en route from St. Thomas back up to New York's winter.

The *Laconia*'s world cruise of 1922 would last three times as long as Iphigene Ochs's Caribbean adventure of 1913. The *Laconia* was a new, postwar Cunarder, built to replace a predecessor of the same name that had been sunk by a German torpedo off Ireland in 1917. (*Laconia* seems to have been a doomed name for the company. The second *Laconia* would be lost to another German submarine off the African coast twenty years later.) The vessel entered service in May of 1922 between Southampton and New York. Her profile was typical of a new generation of postwar Cunarders, a single stack instead of twin funnels atop a 20,000-ton hull. A new *Andania* and *Franconia* were also launched as replacements for wartime casualties. These were midsized company vessels with neither the impact of huge tonnage nor record-breaking speed. Often unsung and neglected, they provided the backbone of Cunard's secondary service. Of the trio, only the *Franconia*, which had been designed with world cruising in mind, would achieve notoriety. After her debut in 1923, the *Franconia* became Cunard's luxury cruise ship, the equivalent of the *Caronia* that would supplant her after World War II.

The *Laconia* entered service in 1922. Just over 600 feet long, she could carry a huge passenger load, more than the *Norway* embarks today;

A gathering at the Tee-haus. Iphigene
Ochs (extreme right) poses with her
friends after the tea party. *Right,*
Iphigene with her parrot, Green Swizzle.
(The Ocean Liner Museum)

but the bulk of those 2,200 berths were devoted to a crowded Third Class down on D- and E-decks, wretched cabins with ports seldom opened at sea because they were so close to the boot-topping. In transatlantic service, those humble passengers had at their disposal a General Room and Smoke Room—without its conventional "ing" suffix, it had an undeniably prole-tarian ring to it. It seems odd that Cunard should have incorporated so much Third Class space for a new vessel of the early twenties, hard on the heels of American disaffection with continuing mass immigration. In fact, Cunard's timing was bad; the ship had been laid down at Swan Hunter's Tyneside yard just before the congressional boom had been lowered.

She would be one of four ships circumnavigating the globe that winter: *Laconia, Resolute,* and *Empress of France* were to sail westbound while the *Samaria*, another Cunarder, a postwar arrival and sister ship to the *Laconia*, would sail eastbound. The two sisters would pass each other in the Indian Ocean. *Laconia* sailed first, in November 1922; the other three would not leave New York until January. She would be the first and, as such, would be accorded the warmest welcome of the four that winter of 1922–23. At each port, where no ships like her had called since the war, the *Laconia* would be greeted with enthusiastic delight by municipal au-thorities as well as the merchants and dealers who would sell everything— from tea sets to carpets—to dozens of avid passenger/shoppers. World cruise ships are customarily hailed as "the ships of millionaires," and the *Laconia* would prove no exception to this irresistible hyperbole. In fact, while there were a handful of very rich on the passenger list, most were perfectly ordinary middle-class Americans.

On all four world-cruise vessels, the convention was that Third Class space be closed off. Then, as now, world-cruise ships were never filled to capacity; instead, it was imperative to ensure that they were *not*. Com-panies promoting the cruise—in this case, American Express—advertised that "membership in the cruise would be restricted to 450." The words *membership* and *restricted* set the tone: marketing strategy was to sell the world cruise as a club. Simultaneously, Cunard and American Express were making it clear that the ship's world-cruise capacity would be only slightly larger than the number of First Class passengers—347—she nor-mally carried in transatlantic service. Hence, it was understood that there would be no crowding and that only the best cabins would be occupied.

But regardless of this pretension, some E-deck cabins were opened up to accommodate several minimum-fare passengers, among them a woman with whom I would cross the Atlantic on the *Queen Elizabeth 2*

R.M.S. *Laconia,* 1922. A clean foredeck, a separate bridge, a single funnel (here making more smoke than she would be allowed to in New York Harbor today), and a curiously overpowering stern deckhouse. *(William H. Miller)*

fifty-seven years later. By then, her face and nickname were famous on board Cunarders; she was known as Miss Mini-Cunard, not because of her stature but because she was notorious for wringing minimum fare out of the company.

Twenty-six years old in 1922, Carrie Wagner Schachter was a physical education instructor. Though born and brought up in Massachusetts, she lived then, as now, in New York. She was a spunky political idealist, one of the leaders of New York's Women's Suffrage Party. Dressed in a fetching white doeskin uniform, hair crammed under the brim of her cap, she had been featured in the *New York Times*'s Rotogravure section during the war. In 1922, she had to be photographed again, this time for her first passport, an outsize printed document that would be carried, quarto but loose, within green leatherette covers. It was a good likeness, according to the bearer, and shows a determined young woman, her hair cut short in the fashion of the twenties. Perhaps because of the occasional poor quality of many of those early photographs, the State Department required of its applicants a wealth of facial detail in addition. Carrie Schachter was described as: "Face—oval; Chin—round; Mouth—medium; Hair—brown; Complexion—fair; Eyes—blue"—all of which, save for the color of her eyes and hair, were easily deduced by glancing at the adjacent picture. At its top, the passport was certified as good for travel in every part of the world "including Japan"; Yokohama was on the *Laconia*'s Far Eastern itinerary.

Carrie's E-deck passage was arranged by her husband of five years, Harry Schachter. Originally a teacher of Greek and Latin, he also had business connections, having been handsomely rewarded for looking after the affairs of a friend who had been drafted into the army during the war. (As a married man, Harry had been exempt from service.) In addition to entrepreneurial ambition, he was a keen amateur tenor, and over the winter of 1922, his dream was to take voice lessons in Paris. While he was thus occupied, he planned to embark his wife on a world cruise. Implementing both dreams represented a formidable financial challenge in a household where the combined weekly incomes of classicist/tenor and gym teacher seldom exceeded $30. But Carrie's husband was a resourceful and determined man, and within a week of having seen the *Laconia* advertisement in the newspaper, he realized both ambitions by some judicious borrowing.

Carrie, exhibiting nascent skills that were to earn her later sobriquet, tackled her first steamship price structure with the same remorseless vigor that had helped to enfranchise America's women. Ignoring American Ex-

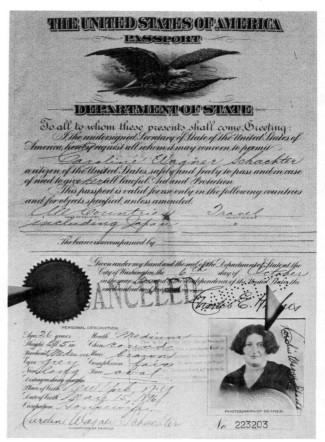

Carrie Wagner in two guises. *Left,* as a suffragette during World War I. *Right,* as world traveler. The passport opened to an imposing 17 × 12 inches. The triangular cuts are cancellation marks. An accompanying British visa was good for the United Kingdom, India, Ceylon, Gibraltar, Egypt, Straits Settlement, Hong Kong, and Palestine—all that for two pounds' worth of His Majesty's stamps. *(Carrie Wagner)*

press's lofty assertion that they offered nothing lower than a $3,000 minimum, Miss Mini-Cunard not only cut that figure in half, but obtained a 10 percent reduction as well. For $1,350, she booked a three-month passage around the world, albeit in an abysmal cabin to be shared with another passenger. (I am well aware that inflation and reduced purchasing power make a mockery of comparative dollar figures between then and now, but a passenger would be hard-pressed to book even a fortnight on the meanest ship for the same sum today.)

With her cabin paid for, Carrie Schachter's most pressing expense was a wardrobe for evenings on board. She was lucky in her friends on lower Madison Avenue; one of them, a successful clothes designer named Rose Tafel, had an atelier that provided most of the wedding dresses sold on Saks Fifth Avenue's fifth floor. When Carrie showed her her ticket, the designer shook her head slowly. "In your gym clothes," she announced darkly, "you're not going on a world cruise."

A bargain was struck. At her own expense, Carrie would supply first-rate fabrics; Rose would have her seamstresses make up dresses to her design. As a result, the pair of borrowed steamer trunks deposited on E-deck of the *Laconia* that November contained a splendid collection of evening dresses in the latest New York style. Indeed, the first Rose Tafel created a furor as Carrie Schachter made her entrance into the First Class Dining Room two nights out en route to Cuba. "You could hear spoons dropping all over the place," she remembers with a smile. What riveted the attention of her fellow passengers, both male and female, was a floor-length dress in black lace, with a bouquet of chiffon flowers at the waist that trailed streamers down over the merest suggestion of buckram panniers to either side. Passenger clothing on board ship—and especially evening dress—is a subject of inexhaustible interest and intrigue, and Carrie's first entrance established her as a fashion plate. She was not only younger than the average lady passenger on board, she was also a New Yorker rather than a midwesterner. And all of the matrons who dropped their spoons that first dressy evening were done up in contemporary flapper fashion, overage dimpled blondes with dropped waistlines and too many beads and fringes. Carrie's New York look finally caught up with the cruise at San Francisco, but until then, through the canal and along both coasts, her collaborative wardrobe was the sensation of the ship.

Regardless of her success in the public rooms, Carrie's cabin arrangement left something to be desired. Commensurate with her rock-bottom fare came cramped quarters in the bowels of the *Laconia*. It had four berths, two upper and two lower, separated by a tip-up washstand with a

inbowed with signal flags, R.M.S.
conia is pushed from Cunard's 14th
eet pier by a hard-working tug.
rrie Wagner Schachter is somewhere
ng the port promenade deck bundled
inst the November chill. *(Frank
lynard Collection)*

tank at the top that had to be filled each morning by the steward. But the space itself, however spartan, was supportable, a self-imposed exile in return for minimal outlay. What made the cabin distressing was the woman with whom it was shared. I shall call her Miss Campbell. She was a rotund, middle-aged Scots-Canadian spinster, a piano teacher from Ontario who had invested her life's savings in the cruise and was traveling, in consequence, on a very tight financial and, it turned out, emotional budget.

There were bizarre unfoldings that first evening at sea. As Carrie unpacked Rose Tafel's riches from her brace of steamer trunks, Miss Campbell disgorged clothing from a trunk that seemed, even then, a relic from another age: it was a belly-up, horsehair traveling chest from the nineteenth century, its contents dictated by frugality rather than fastidiousness. In one of the rare informative exchanges between the two women, Miss Campbell confided that she had brought only her oldest and shabbiest clothing on the principle that, once worn, it could be thrown overboard without the expense of laundering it. And this was precisely what Miss Campbell did throughout her world cruise—or at least that portion of it to which Carrie Schachter was reluctantly privy.

The shipboard social lives of the two cabinmates developed in contrasting directions. Carrie Schachter—young, popular, and amusing—made friends with everyone from Raymond Fuller, the cruise director, to a flock of male passengers, of all ages, intent on marriage. ("They wouldn't believe I was married," she protests now.) The crew took an especial liking to her; one deck steward whistled a coded signal as a caveat whenever a persistent suitor, a colonel from New Hampshire, came out on deck on the prowl. Miss Campbell made no friends at all. Instead, she alienated everyone by her habit of monopolizing the *Laconia*'s only decent piano, located in the Main Lounge, for deafening, day-long practice sessions. In her bizarre patched clothing and the gym shoes she invariably wore, day and night, she became the ship's pariah. And predictably, every rebuff on deck produced increasing tension below.

She would complain regularly to the bedroom steward—in front of Carrie—that "*she* has taken all the hot water!" When an obliging carpenter removed Carrie's lower berth to leave more room for her trunks, Miss Campbell insisted that the same be done on her behalf, even though, with her girth, a trip up a ladder to retire was not easy. Things in that squalid little E-deck cabin reached such an impasse that, by mutual consent, a line of demarcation was drawn down its center, behind which each occupant withdrew herself and her possessions, hostilely incommunicado.

The final break came on the far side of the Pacific, after the *Laconia*'s call at Yokohama. It was precipitated by a tiny Kamakura Buddha—a miniature of the great Daibutsu—that Carrie had brought back from shore as a souvenir. Miss Campbell, whose stern Scottish Presbyterian conscience forbade her even to visit temples ashore, blew up; she marched to the purser's office and demanded that she be allowed to change cabins rather than share one "with that heathen idol."

Enormously relieved, Carrie made plans to move out. But with irrational ambiguity, Miss Campbell would not hear of it: pathetic creature that she was, she presumably found the presence of her heathen shipmate preferable to the perennial loneliness of her Ontario existence. Once again, friends among the crew rallied tactfully to Carrie's aid. An engineer "found" a stubborn leak in the cabin's piping that apparently defied repair. On orders from the bridge—another subterfuge—both occupants of that unhappy accommodation were moved elsewhere. Carrie decamped happily to a single on the port side, still on E-deck. She and Miss Campbell never exchanged another word as the *Laconia* steamed toward the China Sea.

When she reached Shanghai, some of her passengers disembarked for a journey to Peking; they would rejoin the vessel at Hong Kong. That Peking trip is one of three classic overland tours offered every world-cruise passenger—the other two are crossing India by train from Calcutta to Bombay and disembarking at Suez for a glimpse of ancient Egypt. Passengers on the *Franconia*'s world cruise later in the twenties could avail themselves of a most ambitious side trip, leaving the vessel permanently at Yokohama, traversing Manchuria, Siberia, Russia, and Europe by train, and boarding any westbound Cunarder sailing back to New York from Southampton or Cherbourg. But that arduous rail journey—which, incidentally, negates half the pleasure of global circumnavigation by ship—was not offered to the *Laconia*'s passengers in 1922. Their two longest tours—Peking and India—each cost the same. After much deliberation, Carrie chose India.

It nearly killed her. Of the twenty passengers who disembarked under the charge of Raymond Fuller, two failed to reach the west coast. The party would travel by special train during their fortnight's crossing of the subcontinent. The coaches were wide-gauge and comfortable, provisioned largely from the ship: bedding, bottled water, and staples were trucked from pier to station in preparation for the departure. Each passenger was assigned an individual, rattan-walled compartment as well as a bearer who, in addition to coping with every conceivable need, slept curled up in front of the door each night, whether in train or hotel, as much a chaperone, Carrie pointed out, as a servant.

At Benares, their first major stop in the interior, an epidemic of dysentery struck the tour. The three most critically affected were two midwestern matrons and Carrie. She remembers a succession of ghastly nights, her temperature topping 105 degrees, and awful bouts of delirium and hallucination. But, regardless, each morning she staggered out of bed to join the tour, determined to miss nothing. Among other feats remarkable for one so critically ill, she managed to clamber up all five hundred steps to the top of Kutb Minar, where she was so embarrassed at having disturbed a devout Hindu in mid-worship that she retreated to the ground in fevered dismay without having enjoyed the view.

Carrie Schachter was lucky. She was young and resilient and survived her ordeal. The other two, both older women, confined to a Lucknow hospital, died before the ship sailed. Cruise passengers who reboard their vessel after even an afternoon's absence in the tropics do so with a profound sense of relief; when that India tour reached the west coast after their hair-raising hegira from Benares, the sight of the *Laconia* awaiting them in the Bombay roads was exquisite.

Carrie's recovery was slow, and she passed the hottest part of the cruise—passage through the Red Sea—recuperating quietly. She never actually slept outdoors—nor, she remembers, did any of her fellow passengers—but she did spend nights alone in a deck chair atop the Boat Deck. The sky was full of stars so clear and close that she felt she could have plucked one from the heavens merely by reaching up over her head. Sometimes in the early morning, as the deck gangs broke out hoses and holystones, she would shift her vigil to the bow, where, from the forepeak, she could gaze down to the *Laconia*'s cutwater and a pair of sharks, laden with pilot fish, traveling alongside as outriders in the bow wave.

At Luxor, the management of the Winter Palace Hotel gave a ball in honor of the visiting *Laconia* passengers. Carrie, dressed to the nines in Rose Tafel's white crepe, was asked to dance by a stranger, a distinguished, white-haired older man. Thinking him a little too old for a dancing partner, she refused, sitting down for a chat instead. He asked her, short of dancing, what she most enjoyed doing.

"Tennis," replied the gym teacher promptly, certain that he could not possibly play.

"Splendid," was his smooth rejoinder. "I have a young friend who would enjoy a game of tennis with you very much. But it must be early tomorrow morning—very early—because we are to cross the river later to look at the ruins."

Red Sea masquerade. *Laconia* passengers pose for the photographer during a fancy dress ball. Most are in some form of Indian dress, legacy of a recent Bombay call. Carrie is the toy soldier. *Below,* perhaps the largest costumed group ever seen on board a vessel. The combination of black tie and daylight serves as a clue to the location and time of year: Norwegian coast, July 23, 1914, on board the *Arcadian*. *(Carrie Wagner and George Carrington)*

Reluctantly, Carrie consented. There had been a tennis rendezvous in Manila with an American army officer from her hometown in Massachusetts who, it turned out later, had other games in mind as his driver took them back to the ship. "Very early" turned out to be 5:00 A.M.! But tennis on the hotel court in the cool of an Egyptian dawn was as delightful as her young opponent, who had been introduced to her simply as Charles. After a breakfast together on the terrace, she agreed to join both men and their party for the journey across the river to the Valley of the Tombs. Only later did Carrie realize, from the number of obsequious companions surrounding her tennis opponent as well as his imperious mother, that she had fallen in with Very Important People. After inquiring of her original contact—who served as chamberlain, he confessed—she was told that the young man was Prince Charles and that his mother was none other than Her Majesty Queen Elizabeth of the Belgians.

But even more miraculous than her inclusion in the royal party was its privileged destination: they were invited to inspect a sensational new find, the burial site of King Tutankhamen. It had been discovered the previous November while the *Laconia* was passing through Panama. Only a week before, the burial chamber itself had been breached for the first time. Carrie remembers taking her turn to step up onto an expedition case and peer through a small, exploratory hole; in the dim interior, lit by a flickering oil lamp, she could see the unopened sarcophagus, just as it had been discovered. The man who helped her down was Howard Carter; his patron and countryman, the fifth earl of Carnarvon, lay hospitalized in Cairo, already fatally ill.

She rejoined her fellow passengers at the hotel that evening, greeted by a nearly hysterical Raymond Fuller, who had been convinced that his youngest charge had survived Indian dysentery only to be abducted by a berserk dragoman. She babbled so about the marvelous tomb—which none of her fellow passengers had seen—that he feared a momentary recurrence of her Benares delirium. What tales Carrie told at the purser's table the next day as the ship steamed into the Mediterranean!

Sadly, her global circumnavigation was not completed on the *Laconia*. Waiting at Naples's American Express office was the news that her husband, back in New York, wanted a divorce. It seemed that voice lessons in Paris had been devoted less to his muse than his musical accompanist. Unable to face either New York or the faithless Harry, a distraught Carrie disembarked at Monte Carlo and entrained for Paris. She stayed there for several weeks, sailing home in the spring on board the *Aquitania*, her passage funded by the unused portion of her *Laconia* ticket. Carrie

ear after her maiden arrival, all of the
mandie's crew gather for a group
trait. Raymond Guiheneuf sits atop
ladder above the Winter Garden
dows, one o'clock from the tuba, his
at a rakish angle. *(Raymond
iheneuf)*

Schachter's world cruise was over and her world would never be quite the same again.

Now we vault effortlessly over the twenties and most of the thirties to share a *Normandie* cruise to Rio. The *Normandie* has always been a favorite of mine, and apparently the public's as well. Of all Atlantic liners, the *Titanic* and the *Normandie*—in that order—are the most consistently evoked, if for very different reasons. The White Star liner has been haloed with a tragi-romantic fantasy, subject of unending, scrupulous necropsy. Though the French ship also met a premature end, we dwell less on her demise than her extraordinary design and legacy of glamour. In 1982, for instance, the *Normandie* served as the setting of an extravagant romance novel, popular fiction peopled by women of restless sensuality in alternating conflict or sexual congress with men of enormous wealth, power, and easily distractable potency; what better location for these larger-than-life figures than the larger-than-life *Normandie?* Over the years, she continues to intrigue, remaining the quintessential ship of the thirties, a decade rampant with startling tonnage that includes *Bremen, Rex, Queen Mary,* and *Nieuw Amsterdam,* as well as a twilit decade for Edwardian steamships grown long in the funnel, *Majestic, Mauretania, Olympic,* and *France* among them.

For gross tonnage, the French say *jauge brut,* and I have always conceived a mystical onomatopoetic linkage between those expressive words and the *look* of their largest liner. Over the years, I have tried to decipher exactly what makes the *Normandie*'s profile so visually compelling. From afar, that trio of round funnels—oval, really, but dead ahead they read round—seems at first too crude for the graceful horizontals below. But after further consideration, it appears that the choice was perfect. One leafs through the eclectic sourcebook: the look is part recall of the *Empress of Britain*'s grotesquely overscale smokestacks, part motorship—the new diesel look—and part Franco-medieval, incorporating the implacable simplicity of the fortress towers at Angers. But another key lies in the nationality of the *Normandie*'s naval architect: Vladimir Yourkevitch had learned his trade at the Imperial Naval Dockyard in St. Petersburg. He was followed to France in the early twenties by another émigré, Naum Gabo, the sculptor and prophet of Russian constructivism. His movement, which would exert a powerful influence on painting as well as architecture, emphasized angularity, glorying in the stark lines of technological necessity. It seems clear that Yourkevitch's bold funnel design was influenced by the cause his fellow émigré espoused.

Moreover—and this is the secret of the *Normandie*'s timelessness—that powerful exterior is somehow perfectly attuned to below-deck chic. There is no way to encapsulate the *Normandie*'s interiors in a sentence. At Saint-Nazaire, a dozen different designers had assembled disparate components and functions into a pervasive unity, from Salle à Manger to Grill and throughout every cabin. They are all, astonishingly, of a piece, and that indefinable quality of *Normandie*-ness infuses Yourkevitch's stunning profile as well. From every prospect, she pleases, delicacy and bulk in artful compromise.

During her four years of service, from 1935 to 1939, the ship made 139 Atlantic crossings. She made only two cruises, nearly identical ones from New York to Brazil's capital city, one in the winter of 1938, the other a year later during that last year of peace. Despite the ship's durable fascination, very little has ever been recorded about either; I propose detailing the first, called by the company the "Blue Ribbon Cruise."

That cruise of 1938 not only was a significant departure from her conventional deployment, but would differ from most cruises as well. It was, first and foremost, a destination cruise. The *Victoria Luise* had had a destination as well—the wondrous canal—but it had been bracketed by a round-robin of Caribbean ports. The *Laconia*'s destination had been its port of origin, a global circuit spread between two calls at New York. But the *Normandie*'s Rio cruise was simply an *aller/retour*, a purposeful race south avoiding all but three Caribbean islands, two of which were necessary refueling stops.

During the Depression, dozens of Atlantic liners were shifted south. It made economic sense: not only could more passengers afford a week in the sun rather than a European vacation, the hard-pressed companies could also cut costs. New York to Nassau, the Caribbean's northern gateway, is a round-trip of 2,000 miles. Marine superintendents in New York could bunker their ships as though for a crossing and still have ample fuel left for a week of dawdling around the islands. None of the ships of the thirties ever went at top speed: they spent large portions of each day, or, at least, every other day, lying idly, and cheaply, at anchor. But the *Normandie*'s Rio cruise would be accomplished at flank speed. To achieve her destination in time for a four-day stay, she would steam as fast as she customarily did on the North Atlantic, her four turboelectric/generators consuming tons of oil each hour in order to have her passengers home in a little more than three weeks. The French Line was not alone that winter of 1938: the Italians and Cunard both had the same plan. *Rex* and *Aquitania* would also be transferred from their winter schedules for Rio

Opposite above, the *Empress of Britain* of 1931 in a Panama lock during a world cruise. The proportion of funnel to hull foreshadows the *Normandie*'s profile. *Opposite below*, the *Normandie*'s funnels, seen from the after starboard quarter as she sails from Pier 88, are clearly elliptical. *Left,* from ahead, the cylindrical aspect predominates. *Right,* a bow-on view from New York's West Side Highway in early 1940 shows a misleading flare to the funneltop. This is because both *Normandie* and *Queen Mary*, to the right, have covers on their stacks as they sit out the phony war stranded in port since September of the year before. *(Photographs from Everett E. Viez Collection, by Paul Hollister, and Jane Barus)*

A rare *Normandie* souvenir. Although over a thousand were minted, few have reappeared in the flea markets. Wherever they are, they remain, presumably, cherished mementos. *(Robert Forrest Collection)*

cruises. Significantly, all three vessels had nearly identical speed capabilities. (The *Aquitania* was not really in the same league as the other two but, apart from the new *Queen Mary*, was Cunard's only big ship available. The *Mauretania*, by that time mere scrap fragments at Rosyth, would have been better suited in terms of speed if not of space.) In sum, a Rio cruise was no task for small ships: only high-speed tonnage need apply.

In preparation for the cruise, the Compagnie Générale Transatlantique sent Commandant Marcel Castelneau on an aerial reconnaissance of the entire 10,500-mile route to forestall any problems connected with victualing, anchorage, and, especially, bunkering. Once he returned, the decision was taken to deliver fuel all along the cruise circuit. From Standard Oil's sales department at 26 Broadway, cables were dispatched to LAGOSHIPS, Aruba, requesting that a trio of small tankers be assigned for refueling the ship in transit. Each tanker could carry 60,000 barrels of Bunker C crude. (An oil barrel contains 42 gallons.) All three would sail from Aruba on a precise schedule, the first under way long before the *Normandie* began her last precruise westbound crossing from Le Havre in late January. She would plod all the way around the eastern bulge of Brazil south to Rio, to receive and bunker the French liner at her southernmost reach. (Standard Oil's island storage facility on Ilha Redonda would not suffice.) A second tanker would leave much later and travel only as far east as Trinidad, meeting the *Normandie* at its halfway point. The third would leave last, to rendezvous with the liner at Martinique, filling her tanks for the final run up to New York.

Why Rio? It was, quite simply, the perfect antidote to post-Depression depression and the perfect destination for midwinter wanderlust. And what a destination! Rio de Janeiro had a mythic appeal for Americans in the thirties. *Rio Rita* had started it all ten years earlier, both as a Broadway play and later as a successful talkie. Then Fred Astaire and Ginger Rogers had appeared together on screen for the first time in *Flying Down to Rio*. The film's music was infectious: couples danced—at the Copacabana, among other places—to the music of "The Carioca," the local name, incidentally, for a resident of Rio de Janeiro. The ubiquitous throb of the samba continued into the forties, capped by the filmed appearances of Carmen Miranda and her impossible fruit-salad-topped turbans. The *Normandie*'s visit would capture it all, coinciding with Carnival, that gaudy February weekend when the entire city dances itself into a frenzy.

However, there were sober ramifications to that Rio fix. In the late twenties, the *France* had sailed on a long Caribbean cruise and planners at both the Paris and New York headquarters remembered only too well

The Rio brochure for the following year, when an almost identical southern voyage was achieved by the French Line's flagship. *(Stephen Lash Collection)*

A RAYMOND-WHITCOMB CRUISE

1939

NORMANDIE TO RIO

Cosimini

how, on that occasion, the tropical excitement had been eroded by un-anticipated passenger ennui. Admittedly, the *Normandie*'s clients would be confined on board for less time than their predecessors on the older ship, but still, twenty-two days was the equivalent of five successive Atlantic crossings with weeks at a time spent at sea.

Understandably, long-cruise ships book a mixed passenger lot, divided, as was Gaul, into thirds. Some are port-happy, either curious explorers or inveterate shoppers for whom the tantalizing mother lode of Brazil's semiprecious stones is reason enough for endless voyaging. Then there is a large, fearful contingent for whom excursion ashore anywhere implies only intolerable heat, victimization, suspicious "foreign" food, or adulterated drinking water inadequately iced. Finally, there are sea-addicts, those who can sail forever, among whom, incidentally, I count myself. To my mind, ships are sea creatures, their natural habitat the open ocean, their circadian perfection disrupted by port calls. I remember crossing once from Hawaii to Japan on the *Rotterdam*: for nine unalloyed days the anchors stayed in their hawsepipes, the launches in their davits, the reassuring throb of the turbines underfoot. But I realize, too, that for every passenger like myself, there must be scores of others for whom extended ocean passage spells only confinement, a sea-trial of the worst order.

The difficulties of dealing with this disparate passenger load were compounded by the Rio cruise's complex anticipation/enjoyment curve: plotted on a time chart, it would have been shaped, appropriately but ominously, like Sugarloaf Mountain's abrupt parabola. As on every destination cruise, the upslope, outbound, would be easy: each day south would be an adventure, trail-blazing over unfurrowed waters; the weather would get warmer, and after Nassau and Trinidad, as the *Normandie* began her great circle swing around Brazil's easternmost thrust at Recife, latitude zero would be achieved with all its attendant hoopla and pageantry. The approach to and arrival at Rio would serve as a spectacular climax, followed by four hectic and exhausting days. But then, as the ship turned north, with the Carnival high subsiding, the cruise would, in effect, be over with five thousand more miles to steam. Steps would be retraced, the equator would pass without comment, and everything that had been enchanting a fortnight earlier would seem jaded and passé. That parabolic downside would infect the ship: dining room stewards would find their passengers distracted and worried about weight, smoking room stewards would sell fewer drinks and get fewer tips in consequence, deck stewards would be at a loss to alleviate meridional torpor. Disaffection would increase as the Caribbean receded in the wake, and the cold, rough passage

An earlier French flagship on a cruise. S.S. *France* off
an unnamed coast, presumably Norway, to judge by the
woman with sweater and umbrella in the doorway
beneath the illuminated nameboard. *(French Line)*

to New York would signal journey's end. Just as on a crossing, that last day at sea would be a struggle with suitcases, souvenirs, Customs declarations, tips, and all the procrastinated preoccupations of home that would loom, like Manhattan's frosted skyline, over the bows that last morning.

Unfortunately, there was no way to station tankers laden with euphoria along Brazil's interminable coastline to replenish passengers' enjoyment reserves, but every conceivable step that could titillate or amuse was taken in advance. It was reported in the press that 150,000 bottles of champagne were taken on at Le Havre specifically for the cruise. (Since this would allow 150 bottles per passenger, it seems more likely that it was merely a standard resupply of the *Normandie*'s seagoing *caves*; but it made a splendid press release.) From Paris's Hotel de la Monnaie came hundreds of blue-boxed souvenir medallions, replicas of the maiden voyage obverse with a newly minted reverse heralding the cruise. As the *Normandie* sped westbound, Gaston Magran, her *chef de cuisine*, bombarded New York with cabled victualing requirements. In *The Only Way to Cross*, I documented the notorious Rio lobster glut that resulted after a garbled transmission had requested "a gross" rather than "dozens." Among the stacks of provisions awaiting the ship as tugs eased her alongside Pier 88 on the morning of February 3 was an awesome gastronomic Rio dividend, two tons of Beluga caviar.

The venerable travel firm from Boston, Raymond-Whitcomb—they didn't add the "&" until after the war—had provided a bewildering array of special personnel and entertainment. The morning after the *Normandie* docked, a white-flanneled cruise staff boarded, headed by David Peirce, who would later marry one of the passengers. In his wake came an assistant cruise director, a treasurer, a social director, two hostesses—one senior, one junior—a bridge hostess, and a large social staff as well as a lecturer and four shore excursion people. All wore company blazers with "R-W" on the breast pockets, which, during a time-consuming foul-up on the Trinidad disembarkation, one of the passengers read as "Rush and Wait." There was a vast troupe of New York performers, from singers to dancers to jugglers and magicians, auditioned and hired especially for the cruise. All had assured their employers of an extensive repertoire, for there would be no jetted replacements supplanting them at Rio; they would work the whole cruise, there and back. Once they had been shown their cabins, they were summoned to instant rehearsal in the Grand Salon on Pont Promenade. Their first performance, accompanied by the *Normandie*'s dance orchestra, would be that evening at nine o'clock sharp, to be broadcast over a nationwide radio hookup. A special advance preview print of *Snow White and the*

Seven Dwarfs had been rushed on board from Disney's New York office. It was a film that had originally been refused by French Line officials as not being suitable for the Rio cruise; Gilbert Fuller, president of Raymond-Whitcomb, wrote them that he understood their decision, adding, "After all, it's only the *Normandie*. It would be a different story if it were the maiden cruise of the world's greatest liner." Edward Turner, one of the shore excursion staff, remembers the incident with amusement: "Snow White came on board."

So did nearly a thousand passengers. Raymond-Whitcomb had done their work nobly: every cabin offered, from a minimum inside at $395 to both huge suites overlooking the stern (eight occupants—$8,600), had been booked. The demand had been nothing short of phenomenal. A Rio cruise on not only "the largest ship ever to have crossed the equator" but also "*one* of the fastest liners in the world" (italics mine; *Queen Mary* had recently snared *Normandie*'s Blue Ribband) proved irresistible. A record number of passengers—975—had paid a record price; and the French Line crowed triumphantly to the press that the *Normandie*'s Rio junket was "A Million Dollar Cruise," the million in this case a hard figure representing the aggregate ticket sale. Moreover, it was the largest number of passengers that had ever sailed on a single cruise before, exceeding the previously held record of 850 that filled the new White Star liner *Baltic* for a Mediterranean cruise in 1902. Those who had booked were described by Monsieur Delaporte, passenger traffic manager for the company:

> While at this time I do not wish to disclose the names, the passenger list is a directory of *Who's Who* of the social leaders in the country. I believe it will be the finest list of passengers ever carried out of New York on one ship.

There was, in fact, a 976th passenger, one Alfred Donnagio, an unemployed seaman who had crept aboard in New York in hopes of obtaining work at sea. However, since French maritime law prohibits the employment of stowaways, he traveled round-trip in the solitary gloom of Third Class. (Considering the cruise's notoriety, it is surprising that he was the only one of his kind. The *Normandie* always attracted the largest numbers of illicit passengers; on one eastbound crossing the previous year, fourteen had been flushed out before arrival in Le Havre.)

There were a few Brazilian passengers on board, representatives of the Rio jewelers who had been dispatched to make the southbound leg in order to soften up passenger prospects. But the majority of those Rio-bound were Americans, and that, according to Raymond Guiheneuf and

es visiteurs sont priés de quitter le navire dès intenant!" With the ancient cry for visitors to embark still echoing through the passages, the amer-engulfed *Normandie* is about to sail from Pier for Rio. *(New York Times)*

Pierre Troadec, both Bretons who served on board as dining room stewards, was a plus. They preferred Americans to their own countrymen. Americans were less fussy and more generous, with none of that proprietary feeling about the ship that Parisians, in particular, exhibited on the North Atlantic (doubtless, conservative taxpayers who knew of the *Normandie*'s substantial governmental subsidy). Both men had been on the vessel since her maiden voyage. Guiheneuf had started his culinary career ashore as a young *aide de cuisine* at the Hotel Plaza-Athénée, followed by a stint as a waiter at the Café Royale in London: then, after military service, he had joined TRANSAT as a steward on board the *France*. Troadec started with the company when he was sixteen—first, as an *aide de cuisine* on the *Paris*, then, briefly, on the *France* for one gloomy crossing, her last voyage, during the depths of the Depression. Troadec remembers that only a single First Class passenger had booked before the vessel was laid up forever at Le Havre. In 1929, he had taken a leave of absence from the company to work in America, to improve his English as well as learn the methods of American service. At a restaurant in Newark, New Jersey, where he lasted one day, he had the most trouble with a strange new vegetable he had never heard of, called, as he mimicked uncomprehendingly, "sooookotash."

In the spring of 1935, both men were dispatched to Saint-Nazaire to join the *Normandie* as she sailed on her trials and subsequently to Le Havre into Atlantic service. For both men, it was essentially their last—and incomparable—ship. Troadec would serve briefly after the war as maître d'hôtel on the *Ile de France* while she was repatriating Canadians and their British war brides home to Halifax, but he found the standards of service, no less than the behavior of his polyglot clientele, unseemly. Madame Guiheneuf told her husband after the war that if he went to sea again, she would leave him. So both men stayed ashore, working together in New York's La Cremaillère restaurant. Both men agree that there was never anything like the *Normandie*, a maritime pinnacle that had spoiled them for service anywhere else afloat.

On board *Normandie*, Guiheneuf and Troadec joined eighty other *chefs de rang* in the First Class Dining Room. The name is peculiar to French dining rooms, equivalent to the English "steward" but with the added distinction that a *chef de rang* never leaves the dining room during the meal. His junior, or *commis*, a less experienced man, would carry trays to and from the galley but the *chef de rang* stayed watchfully on station. Troadec's first table assignment was aft of the huge statue *La Paix* (now in the "Normandie Corner" of a cemetery in Farmingdale, Long Island),

French Line steward Guiheneuf photographed at the rail of the *Champlain.*
Right, a view of the *Normandie*'s First Class *salle à manger* showing one of the
vast chandeliers that, during trials, seemed about to shake loose from the ceiling.
(Raymond Guiheneuf)

where the vessel's chronic vibration was pronounced. The enormous glass chandelier overhead rattled and shook so that he and his colleagues, together with the uneasy yard personnel and press representatives on whom they were waiting, fully expected it to fall and flatten the center table.

In 1939, Pierre Troadec was awarded one of the enviable posts as smoking room steward, considered such a lucrative sinecure that he described it as "*mon baton du maréchal.*" But on board the ship as she neared the equator that first time en route to Rio, service in the First Class Dining Room was even more coveted: it was the only air-conditioned room on the ship. (On both Rio cruises, the Grill was used as a permanent dining room rather than as an extra-tariff restaurant; clients who ate there were hotter, but they had a view.) The dining room, in fact, was sometimes too cold, not only for lady passengers in décolletage but for their dinner-jacketed companions as well. Another *chef de rang*, Bernard Pelletier, used some outrageous psychology when passengers complained of the chill. With a furtive glance at the maître d'hôtel, he instructed his *commis* conspiratorially to damp down the air-conditioning by seeming to turn a valve concealed in the base of a nearby lampstand; passengers invariably thanked him for making them warmer. But the ones who suffered most were the poor *commis* themselves, who periodically exchanged the frigid splendor of the dining room for the pantry's brutal heat below; several men developed persistent respiratory problems as a result. The air-conditioning dried the dining room air so thoroughly that when the maître d'hôtel ordered the huge bronze doors opened ceremoniously at the start of each meal, the scarlet-liveried *mousses* always got static electric shocks even though gloved in obligatory white cotton.

Every ship's dining room has its most popular seating areas, and the most sought-after in the *Normandie*'s were those tables closest to the main entrance. The eight private dining rooms flanking each side were not popular: clients assigned there usually felt cut off and requested reassignment to the larger room. Grouped at the entrance were the most favored—and demanding—passengers, known irreverently behind their backs as *les emmerdeurs*, a muttered vulgarity that kept up spirits when things were hectic. Stewarding on board ship is highly pressured, and stewards earn every penny they make. It is exhausting and exacting work that must be accomplished swiftly, deftly, and charmingly. (When Pierre Troadec was reassigned to the smoking room in 1939, the thing that pleased him even more than the perks of a percentage of drink and tobacco sales and a cut of the mileage pool was that he no longer had to handle food, or at least nothing more demanding than a tray of canapés.) Raymond Guiheneuf remembers that the largest dining room tip he ever received on board the *Normandie* was pressed discreetly into his hand at the end of that first Rio cruise: it was a hundred dollars. He accepted it with the polished grace for which French Line stewards were famous, a far easier adieu than when he had felt obliged to refuse the offer of a young French wife on an eastbound crossing who had suggested that he leave the ship, just for the summer, and come and live in the South of France with her and her aged husband.

From north to south, Brazil's coastline runs for nearly 6,000 miles. As the *Normandie* steamed along it to the southeast, toward Point Calcanhar and a course change south, it was high summer. The Winter Garden's flowers wilted and Coca-Cola ran short. Rio would be hot as well—February is its warmest month—its southern mirror latitude the equivalent of Jacksonville, Florida. The little outdoor pool on the *Normandie*'s stern was in constant and crowded use despite its odd location well down in Tourist Class country, just above the crew's abbreviated deck astern. It would have been easy for the French carpenters on board to have erected a temporary swimming pool between the funnels on Sun Deck; but for some reason, it was never done. The existing pool was never more useful than on the morning of February 12 when Neptune—a perspiring assistant cruise director in cotton wool whiskers and papier-mâché gilt crown—came over the bows and held court along its margin. Passengers who would not admit to their first equatorial crossing thronged every available after railing to watch rather than submit to his ministrations. In time-honored fashion, those who did were admitted to his domain after being interrogated, "anointed" with a variety of noisome kitchen unguents, and shaved with an outsize wooden cutthroat razor before being tipped into the pool. (Iphigene Ochs had been a willing first victim during a crossing-the-line ceremony on another vessel and had excited admiration by volunteering to go first; she admitted later that it was less bravery than forethought—she hoped to get in and out of the water fast before subsequent mustard-smeared victims joined her.)

While passengers played, the crew worked unceasingly, save for the four-day Rio layover, for two nine-day periods—the equivalent of a complete voyage to America and back without a night off in New York between crossings. Every other night, Guiheneuf was assigned to late duty in the Grill after he had finished his sitting in the main dining room. First, he was obliged to set his five tables with clean linen and silver for breakfast. This was a nearly unnecessary task; most passengers on the cruise took their first meal of the day in their cabins because the *Normandie*'s breakfast-tray

Crossing the line. The after terraces of the *Normandie* crammed with passengers watching some of their fellows submit to Neptune's ministrations in the pool. *(Stephen Lash Collection)*

delivery system was so flawless. Orders were telephoned directly from the bedroom steward's pantry to a special station in the First Class galley. Dining room *chefs de rang* on duty—and most of them were every morning —would be dispatched with a preset tray to various hot-tables and ovens before racing to a service elevator that sped them to the appropriate deck. It was *maître d'hôtel* Olivier Naffrechoux's proud boast that a breakfast tray—bearing the most complex order, a rose, and two cellophane-wrapped newspapers—would take no longer than eight minutes to be delivered from the time it had been ordered.

Guiheneuf's duty in the Grill every other night lasted from midnight until six the following morning. Grill Room service had ended by the time he reported, and the dance band would be tuning up for a late-night, six-hour gig. All the stewards would be directed by the Grill *maître d'hôtel* to set up the midnight buffet on the Grill counter forward and starboard, an extravagant feast kept replenished until three in the morning. Those extra-duty nights added to Guiheneuf's already burdensome days, their only compensation an occasional stint as relief sommelier when champagne ordered by a tipsy passenger for tipsy friends across the room might be left unconsumed. Guiheneuf used to put half-full bottles aside in a special hiding place for the musicians and cleaners, but corked ones would be smuggled down to his cabin portside forward for a furtive nightcap with friends before the empties would be tossed out into the sultry, South Atlantic dawn. Then, with a blessed reprieve from breakfast duty, he enjoyed a well-earned sleep before the rising sun cooked up the shell plating. At eleven, he would muster in the dining room to prepare for luncheon service.

But on the morning of February 16, the entire dining room staff was on duty, regardless of who had closed up the Grill Room the night previously. The entire passenger load, festooned with cameras and binoculars, engulfed both dining rooms for special early breakfast. Guanabara Bay, that enchanting, island-strewn preamble to Brazil's capital, lay through the mist over the bows. The pilot had been on board since before first light, and by seven, propeller revolutions were reduced to an almost imperceptible tremor. That was one of the few mornings when stewards at the room's after end—where, on trials, Pierre Troadec had worried about the chandelier overhead—were able to fill coffee cups and water glasses to the brim, when even the cutlery's ghostly tintinnabulation was stilled. But if the engines were *ritardando*, the human tempo on board was *agitato*; orderly sea routine, unchanged for the week since Trinidad, was disrupted by imminent landfall. Passengers and crew alike seemed apprehensive and

Rio at last. The *Normandie* at anchor in Guanabara Bay surrounded by craft from shore. *Left,* the hazy outline of Corcovado juxtaposed against a *Normandie* life ring, indisputable evidence that the French flagship had indeed arrived. *(Stephen Lash Collection)*

uneasy, Purser Villar's staff had roped off the Card Room in anticipation of a delegation of bemedaled immigration officials, and down on the port side, away from the projected tender embarkation ports to starboard, engineers were uncapping fuel pipes in preparation for Standard Oil's second tanker, which would meet them at the anchorage later that morning.

The *Normandie*'s main dining room was located amidships with no access to the shell plating or a view to either side. Distracted passengers in mid-meal kept darting topside for a scenic update, then racing back to urge on dawdling tablemates. Regrettably, there was little open deck space on board that offered a view to the front, a design shortcoming typical of vessels destined for winter service on the North Atlantic. Early-bird arrivals already packed the forward Boat Deck crescent; latecomers, unable to peer over the heads of their fellow passengers, had to settle for a stuffy vantage point one deck down behind the Winter Garden's plate glass or an oblique view from the open decks to either side. That entry into Rio's bay was heavensent for the binocular fraternity, much in evidence that morning; they had carried their glasses on deck for days with nothing to spot for their pains. Now they were the avant-garde and had long since picked out the famous Christ figure, outstretched arms already tinged with sun, perched atop Corcovado's improbable spire of distant mountain. Only the tops of other mountains could be seen, rearing up from a cushion of fog. Not until the *Normandie*'s bow had crept abreast of the fort of Santa Cruz to starboard did the morning mist miraculously evaporate, revealing an expanse of water dotted with luxuriantly forested island tops crowning steep granite cliffs that plunged vertically into the limpid bay. To port loomed the almost clichéd Pão de Açúcar, the famous Sugarloaf mountain; binoculars, redundant now, were returned to cases as the breathtaking panorama was revealed to all.

"In the South American opera," André Siegfried had written a few years earlier, "Rio de Janeiro is undoubtedly the leading tenor." It was a sentiment that the *Normandie*'s passengers, like all sea voyagers who had preceded them over that momentous threshold, echoed with varying degrees of articulation. So universal a response came from every packed deck that, at the turn of the century, the Brazilian Historical Society had published *Homanagens a Bahia do Rio de Janeiro*, a compendium of celebrated passengers' responses when confronted by that extraordinary view.

Half an hour later, within a mile or two of Rio's white ramparts, the *Normandie* dropped anchor in Guanabara Bay, destination achieved. Within an hour, the first tenders churned toward shore laden with passengers. Their first Brazilian encounter was with a cup of the strongest coffee they had ever had, so strong that even hardened crewmen, nurtured on the bitter dregs of Havrois *estaminets*, gulped ice water in its wake. Serious shoppers were ushered into ranks of stifling Buick sedans outside the pier-front's Club de Tourismo, courtesy of Rio's enterprising jewelers. Shoppers on foot fought off guides and set off along the black-and-white pebbled whorls of Avenida Rio Branco's pavement. Gamblers came ashore with luggage, taxiing to hotels near the city's four casinos; the most popular was the Casino de Copacabana because, like the ship they had temporarily abandoned, it had an air-conditioned restaurant. Rio's casinos were normally open only at night, but additional *matines* were being offered because of Carnival.

A woman with twenty-two pieces of baggage went ashore to spend her Rio visit in a local hotel. But she came back to the ship the following morning—the beds were not comfortable. Not all the traffic was shorebound; Brazilians with special boarding passes filled the outbound tenders for a look at the *Normandie*. But so many turned out to be forgeries that the visitors' program was canceled after hundreds of rioters stormed the tenders. Crewmen came ashore, after the first Rio shipboard lunch was over, in search of humbler mementos than those offered along the Visconde de Paraja. Guiheneuf still treasures to this day a souvenir tray bearing a surprisingly accurate likeness of the *Normandie*, a Brazilian flag at the masthead, tearing at flank speed across Guanabara Bay beneath a sky of inlaid butterfly wings.

But at the end of four days, the passenger consensus was that the city had not lived up to its vision from the sea. The Carnival had been essentially disappointing because no one, neither the French Line office in town, nor Raymond-Whitcomb, nor even the American Embassy, could obtain tickets to the elegant municipal balls the *Normandie* passengers felt their due. If available at all, these would have had to be purchased at least a year in advance. So passengers were restricted to the nonstop hugger-mugger of Rio's streets and restaurants, a Mafeking Night of crowds, heat, samba, and occasional harassment that palled for the visitors far earlier than for the indefatigable Cariocas. When *los Cariocas* called it quits at dawn on Ash Wednesday, first light revealed the *Normandie*'s anchorage deserted with scarcely a saudades!—Rio-ese for nostalgic farewell—cast in her wake in the manner of Hawaiian leis. She was on her way home, passage that proved predictably anticlimactic. Cruise directors reported such passenger disaffection after the ship had been fueled at Martinique that the following year Raymond-Whitcomb added another northbound call at Barbados in an attempt to alleviate end-of-cruise letdown.

Two final *Normandie* groups. A prewar crew outing to the Jersey shore. Guiheneuf (circled) sits on the extreme right of the second row. *Below,* sailing through hostile waters on the *De Grasse,* Guiheneuf (extreme left) and some of his *Normandie* shipmates, crossing back to Europe in the fall of 1939. (*Raymond Guiheneuf*)

Once in New York, the passengers off (there is no farewell more abrupt than a steward-passenger parting!) and the ship ready for eastbound departure on the morrow, Guiheneuf and his mates changed into civilian clothes for an evening at the Monte Carlo Club at 48th Street and Broadway, a favorite haunt for French crews on the town. There, Guiheneuf was reunited with his fiancée, Marie, who worked as a maid for a Manhattan family. They would be married at year's end; for their honeymoon, they enjoyed a complimentary crossing home on the *Normandie* as Tourist Class passengers, shamelessly spoiled by every steward on board.

When war broke out the following autumn, the only superliner to leave New York was the *Bremen*, her entire crew on deck, arms outstretched in a defiant Nazi salute. Outside territorial waters, the Germans evaded British cruisers by dropping a decoy lifeboat with a transmitting radio on board, then streaked home to Bremen via Murmansk. *Normandie* and *Queen Mary* stayed put. The French considered recalling the ship to Le Havre and her crew was kept confined on standby for days on end. But the final decision was to leave her at Pier 88. Her entire crew, save for a few dozen who would remain as caretakers, were mustered under the Customs letters on the deserted pier. The company issued every man a box lunch made on board and authorized a champagne toast to the ship, which was completed, Guiheneuf remembers, *à la russe*, every glass dashed to the concrete. Then fleets of chartered buses took the crew to Pennsylvania Station, the start of a horrendous three-day train journey to Halifax.

In November, the first convoy of the war steamed out of Halifax, a motley collection of cargo and passenger ships with no armed escort; in the event of attack, their captains had been ordered to disperse and run. Accommodated on the *De Grasse*, the *Normandie* crewmen survived the thirteen-day crossing—the longest they had ever known—without incident.

Three years later, in a Paris cinema during the German occupation, Monsieur and Madame Raymond Guiheneuf watched, in horror, newsreel films of the *Normandie*, with smoke pouring from her upper decks, listing at Pier 88, followed by aerial views of the capsized hull. The Germans ran the same footage for weeks on end, a propaganda effort to impress the conquered French of America's indifference toward their beloved ship. Each time Guiheneuf saw it, as did all *Normandie* crewmen throughout France, he wept uncontrollably.

And now, R.M.S. *Caronia*! She was, quite simply, the most successful dual-purpose Cunarder the company ever launched; only the *Queen Elizabeth 2* or the second *Mauretania* belongs in her league. Designed for crossing as well as cruising, her infrequent transatlantic trips were more in the nature of positioning crossings than scheduled shuttle service; as a result, she is almost never recalled in a two-class configuration. Instead, the 1949 *Caronia*, the second Cunarder to bear the name, became instantly synonymous with top-drawer, luxury cruising. No other postwar vessel was built to her demanding specifications and no other attracted the same traveling elite from both sides of the Atlantic. Her passengers were shipboard aficionados with a great deal of money, time on their hands, no particular destination in mind, and a penchant for booking with the same friends year after year on a vessel that seemed more club than cruise ship. *Caronia* inspired such passenger loyalty that on the *France*'s second world cruise, one of the most crowded parties was a nostalgic reunion of *Caronia* regulars who drank the old ship's health as she was being buffeted by legal storms in New York. And it came as no surprise at a Cunard press conference in the fall of 1983, when plans for the newly acquired *Sagafjord* and *Vistafjord* were being made public, that the company president made repeated references to the long-departed *Caronia*, buzzword for cruising par excellence.

The cruise we shall share was the *Caronia*'s spring cruise to the Mediterranean in May 1959. The ship was ten years old, still in perfect trim operationally and decoratively, poised to steam into the sixties. But that decade would be catastrophic for ships of her vintage, years that saw the final ascendancy of the jet and the lay-up of so many liners. This penultimate cruise from the past recalls the golden afternoon of the *Caronia*'s day, before the long shadows engulfed her, rather like *Normandie*, moored ineffectually at a Manhattan pier with little promise and, as it turned out, no hope.

Caronia was one of a kind, launched from John Brown's yard, building berth number 4, in October 1947, christened by then Princess Elizabeth, in her last public appearance before her wedding to Prince Philip. Even the unadorned hull was distinctive as it ground down the ways into the Clyde. She had a clipper bow, the first, Cunard proclaimed, since their *Russia* of 1867, a graceful concave swoop to the water, hinted at by the first *Queen Elizabeth*, whose central anchor bower dictated a sharply raked stem. She was short—only 715 feet overall—and, to some observers, her cruiser stern was a disappointment. The *Caronia*'s after end seemed truncated, the very opposite of the fo'c's'le's long flow, leaving the full profile unsettlingly imbalanced. Cunard may have realized this, for their standard aerial brochure view was taken from astern, diminishing the long bow perspective and favoring the stern.

R.M.S. *Caronia,* the Green Goddess, under way. The after end of the vessel is somehow a disappointment. *(Cunard)*

In her two-class mode, the *Caronia* would carry 932 passengers. Contravening conventional Atlantic apportionment, most would be First Class; Cabin Class, with only 351, was in a significant minority. The company emphasis was clearly on large cabins, the first time on any of their vessels that there were more splendid ones than spartan ones. On cruises, when no more than 650 passengers were accepted, they would be accommodated for the most part on Main and A decks. There, the cabin/bath configuration was rectangular, its long axis athwartship, the interior bathroom—almost the width of the cabin—adding insulation from passage noise. The long cabin depth created a large, hotel-like space with twin beds placed conventionally parallel and lavish storage facilities. This was the *Caronia*'s standard cruise cabin along Main and A decks, two cabins and two passageways wide from shell plating to shell plating. The central midships block contained no accommodation in First Class, given over instead to hairdressers, uptakes, or machinery spaces. (In Cabin Class, there were plenty of inside cabins and, down on B-deck, many with shared baths; however, they were closed off for cruising.) The only crowded First Class cabins were up on Sun Deck. There were thirty of them, singles and doubles, each set in a square block, their beds at right angles to each other and the bathrooms occupying an outside corner. Those Sun Deck clients had less room but they enjoyed immediate access to everything, save the dining room, lower fares, and bathrooms with a view, although it is debatable whether that was necessarily an advantage when the Sun Deck promenade lay directly outside.

One thinks of the *Caronia* as a small ship, although her gross tonnage of 34,000 tons belies it. In fact, she fitted midway into Cunard's postwar service offerings. At the top were the *Queen Mary* and *Queen Elizabeth*, express liners at over 1,000 feet and 80,000 tons, enormous and fast. Then came the two intermediates, the second *Mauretania* and the *Caronia*. And at the low end were the small ships, the new 12,000-ton *Media* and *Parthia*, for instance, traveling in tandem with old-timers like the *Franconia*.

It was a curious but unvarying convention that these small ships offered the public unremarkable and often banal interiors. Cottage chintz or provincial hotel prevailed with an occasional brick inglenook or half-timbered snuggery thrown in for good measure. Cautious, insular taste was at work, comforting middle-class echoes of creaking period rooms on the Old Guard Edwardian ships. But *Mauretania* and *Caronia* were spared this cozy predilection: their public rooms had distinct resonances of *le style paquebot* pioneered on the *Ile de France* and established full-blown on board both *Queen*s. Moreover, "big ship" standards of quality were

A DECK

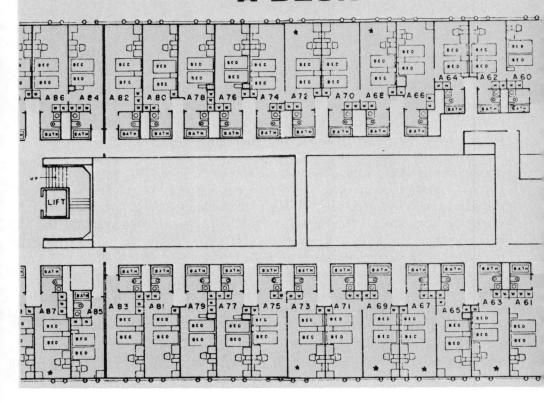

Deluxe deck plan. A slice of A-deck on
the *Caronia*. The full hull width never
accommodated more than two cabins
on these First Class decks. The stars
indicate option for a third berth.
(Cunard)

matched as well. The *Mauretania* of 1939 was a veritable prewar ship; the *Caronia*, which sailed on her maiden voyage ten years later, seemed prewar as well in taste and in the workmanship of her fittings, at extraordinary odds with the utilitarian drabness that prevailed in the United Kingdom's postwar designs. Done up like the *Queen*s, she was last British ship completed with such painstaking care. The *QE2* is a most handsome and interestingly designed ship, but she is inevitably the product of a different era and different materials, filled with convenience fabric and sheathing of a kind unimaginable in the forties.

Those *Caronia* interiors were not to my taste. The apparent watchword that filtered down from management to designers was to create a different look for a different role that would nevertheless continue to attract the leisured rich, a traditional atmosphere leavened with gaiety and adventure. Play it safe but play it loose, heady stuff for keen designers! But stylistically they floundered. Looking forward was difficult and, perhaps mercifully, they did not try to anticipate the fifties, which, as we know from its other end, turned out to be a decoratively sterile decade. They turned backward instead, offering a frozen casserole of thirties leftovers unearthed from the back of the wartime freezer, apparently a more acceptable dish for Cunard than risking postwar creative cookery.

The total effect was curious, and no better illustration can be offered than the *Caronia*'s main lounge. It was paneled in two shades of Cunard's tiger maple ordinary; each brilliantly polished column row was connected to its opposite number by a fluorescent arch, a giant, illuminated croquet hoop that vaulted over armchairs of ponderous plush—turquoise and plum predominating—many adorned with huge casual pillows in fawn satin. Underfoot, carpeting of ribbon-form checkerboard was accented with impulsive squiggles within each square. What jars so in retrospect was that not one decorative element acknowledged another, and that colors and fabrics were so indiscriminately scrambled. Throughout the vessel, an identical look prevailed: instant *Queen*s with cruise seasoning. The dining room seating was identical to that on the larger ships, as were some of the smoking room's gargantuan, multihued leather armchairs.

Cunard's obsession with glistening veneer created as much chaos as their scattershot color choices. Highly reflective surfaces are a perennial decorative hazard. New York's Trump Tower has a vast atrium, sheathed in four materials: the east wall is a waterfall and the rest is covered in hectares of apricot-colored marble with brass and mirror fasciae bracketing the escalators. All but the falling water generate unplanned and disruptive reflections. As in "trumpery tower," so, too, in those glistening lounges.

Interior views. The narrow promenade deck gives an indication of the *Caronia*'s small size. *Below,* her Main Lounge seemed all of a piece with the *Queens*'s. The portrait over the mantel is of Prince Philip and Princess Elizabeth. A peaceful room below, the ceiling reflections are chaotic. *(Cunard)*

On the *Caronia*, each fluorescent arch was duplicated only slightly less explicitly in the dropped veneer-clad headers running fore and aft, creating an infinity runoff of light-lines and cornices confusing to the eye. The volume of space overhead was haphazardly contained, definition replaced by blur.

But in truth, it is doubtful that any of the thousands of passengers who remember the *Caronia* with such consistent fondness ever scrutinized that room critically. If perhaps a little startling, it was the way steamship lounges were meant to look, sort of art deco, like the WPA post office back home or Radio City Music Hall. And that veneer radiated only good subliminal vibes; it was faultlessly maintained, it cocooned one in comfort and luxury, and it took one to nice places. In McLuhanese, the lounge was the longing; decorative nitpicking was secondary and probably nonexistent.

Cunard's exterior look was more successful and, in some respects, significantly innovative. From stem to screen bulkhead, the *Caronia*'s long forward half incorporated a series of stepped decks—loge, parterre, and mezzanine—for a capacity passenger audience intent on viewing the spectacle ahead. This was a sensible correction of a traditional Atlantic inadequacy, already mentioned in connection with the *Normandie*'s entrance into Guanabara Bay. The view forward was improved even more, for passengers and crew alike, in that the ship's only mast was situated abaft the bridge, a self-supporting tripod up on the Sports Deck. Nothing obscured the forward vista although, in truth, the change resulted from logistical rather than cosmetic evolution. A steamer's well-deck mainmast between fo'c's'le head and bridge was a tradition only because it served as the vertical element for cargo derricks in way of the forward hatch. Since the *Caronia* carried neither mail nor general cargo, the mast could be placed atop the ship, handier, incidentally, to signalmen working halyards from the bridge. The *Caronia*'s new arrangement set a trend for many fifties ships: that tight-packed summit of bridge, mast, and stack is recognizable on surviving Cunarders of the period, Sitmar's *Fairsea* and *Fairwind* among them.

The *Caronia*'s huge single funnel was located precisely amidships rather than snugged against the bridge. Complete with internal machinery, it weighed in at 125 tons. Forty-six feet high, 53 feet long, and exactly half as wide, it was larger than those on the *Queen Elizabeth*. Astonishingly, it remained in sublime proportion to the modest hull it surmounted. Cunard was very proud of that funnel, using its size as a meaningless selling point for as long as they owned the ship. It was as though they were unable to renounce their preoccupation with *Queen*-scale colossal, as though the

The *Caronia*'s single stack seen from
shore at her Venetian mooring.
(*William Archibald*)

little *Caronia* had to boast something tangibly enormous rather than settling for being "Britain's Wonder Ship," the public relations buzzword that was flashed at prospective clients. That funnel was all of a piece with *Caronia*'s "big ship" depth in the water. Her narrow, heavy hull drew a staggering 30 feet; by comparison, the admittedly beamier *Song of America*, otherwise approximately the same size, draws only 22 feet. As a result, the *Caronia* handled with difficulty in confined waters, a condition complicated by her oversized funnel, which sometimes behaved like a red-and-black spinnaker. Departing from Yokohama on her world cruise in 1958, she was caught in a lethal crosswind and driven ashore, demolishing a lighthouse and holing her bow. It was an expensive episode for the company: passengers had to be off-loaded into Japanese hotels for three weeks while the *Caronia* was patched up in dry dock. Her waterline bow plating bore the scar for the rest of her life.

The *Caronia*'s two uppermost decks were called Sports and Sun in descending order, the first time in Cunard's history that the name Boat Deck was not used. At the Sport Deck's after end was a public room called the Veranda Café, built to accommodate a hundred passengers. Running the width of the ship, it occupied the same location as the *Queens*'s Veranda Grill but offered no meals. It was merely a nightclub, and was most useful as a place where the *Caronia*'s passengers could host private parties, a practice that assumes epic proportions on world cruises. An open terrace outside, achieved by doors to either side of the bandstand, gave onto a Lido Deck set above a swimming pool. Another first for Cunard—the vessel's only pool was set permanently outdoors. That descending slope of terrace, lido, and pool, more than any other feature of the *Caronia*'s deckscape, characterized the ship's cruising course. At each corner of the enclave, the Lido Deck's bulwarks joined with four mushroom ventilators—square, abbreviated chimneys with rounded, deco tops.

Finally, if any question remained as to the *Caronia*'s warm-weather schedule, her revolutionary color belied it. It was, in fact, a last-minute inspiration: a brochure issued by the New York office in June 1948, six months prior to her maiden voyage in January of the following year, showed her in conventional company colors. But a month earlier, a young Cunard officer, by astonishing coincidence, stumbled across a top-secret rendering of the proposed color scheme. Eric Ashton-Irvine, then a first officer and destined for command of both *Caronia* and the *Mary*, was looking for a house in North Wales. He was shown over one by its owner, who happened to be an artist. In one corner of the studio drawing room, Ashton-Irvine spotted a canvas, still on its easel, of a single-funneled

Cunarder with green hull and upperworks. He remarked on it but, after he had revealed his connection with the company, noticed that his host steered clear of the easel and made no further mention of it. The company directors had sworn the painter to secrecy, and after approving his rendering, they took the decision to cover the *Caronia* entirely in shades of green.

In fact, though the company maintained there were four shades, I have never found more than three: a middling green hull, a darker green band circumscribing it, and a superstructure in a paler green. It was an almost unique departure. Prewar, only the *Franconia, Carinthia*, and four-stacked *Mauretania* had ever departed from Cunard's standard black hull livery: the former Blue Riband holder had been painted white for the West Indian cruises marking the end of her career, and the *Franconia*'s white cruising hull had been enlivened with a prescient *Caronia* touch, a green boot-topping. In our own time, Cunard's two subsidiary ships are white-hulled, and recently, a post-Falkland refit of the flagship, *Queen Elizabeth 2*, included a new color scheme as well. I had reservations about it; although putting the company colors up on the funnel was long overdue, the pale gray hull seemed a mistake. From a distance, it read white and was not flattering. The Sidney Greenstreet principle was at work: a fat man in a white suit looks fatter. The *QE2*'s light-colored hull sprawled and, worse, showed its middle age. (By 1983, she was in black again.) But the *Caronia*'s extraordinary green was inspired, a scheme extended, belatedly, to the second *Mauretania* in the sixties. At the same time, the *Caronia*'s superstructure reverted to white though, by then, "Britain's Wonder Ship" was known, worldwide, firmly and fondly as the "Green Goddess."

One of the endearing things about the Green Goddess was her immutable annual schedule, unvarying for nearly two decades. For all of December she underwent annual dry docking in Southampton, sailing after New Year's for a month-long cruise through the Caribbean to New York. There, she would pick up passengers for a three-month world cruise concluding in New York in May. A spring Mediterranean cruise would follow, then a six-week North Cape cruise, and then two consecutive Mediterranean autumn cruises, the longer second one touching at Greece, the Dardanelles, Israel, and Egypt. Before annual dry docking came round once more, the year's last passengers would disembark in late November at Southampton, guaranteed, like their predecessors on the spring Mediterranean cruise, First Class passage back to America on a *Queen* sailing of their choice.

That *Caronia* year was a Cunard constant, as reassuring a British institution as the opening of Parliament, Test Week, and the Grand National. Her largely American clientele was given every convenience: all cruises originated and all but two concluded in New York. There was no nonsense about flying to join the ship, and symptomatic of Cunard's boundless vigor of the period, the *Caronia*'s languid schedule interfaced neatly with the company's superlative express service. Steamer trunks could be shuffled from home to *Caronia* to *Queen* and home again without logistical pangs about any but gastronomic overweight. Significantly, the cruise itinerary left only two occasions throughout the year when she would be available to crossing clients on a regular Southampton/New York run. That restriction, together with a policy that no cruises, including those around the world, could be booked in segments, kept her passenger list one step removed from the general traveling public, contributing to the *Caronia*'s unique special-ship status.

A full cruise schedule meant that excursions ashore were a full-time, specialized business. The ship always carried a shore excursion staff of six, plus a port lecturer. From January through June, they were assigned from Thomas Cook and Son's New York office; American Express had the franchise for the rest of the year. The two companies, employing American staff exclusively, were quite similar. But, Thomas Cook and Son had one arcane rule forbidding their personnel from touching passengers once they were off the ship! It came from their insurance handlers, and what actuarial probability was at stake is not clear; it does seem an odd taboo for conscientious shore staff whose job was to shepherd elderly passengers—and there were a lot of them—on and off buses or up and down crumbling masonry staircases.

One of the Thomas Cook men on board the *Caronia* for the first time in 1959 was William Archibald. He was new to the company, having joined that winter. During the war, he had served in the Pacific, and after fifteen years with a New York insurance firm, he still had itchy feet. So Archibald went to work for Thomas Cook, sailing for his maiden cruise on board the *Oslofjord* to the Caribbean in the winter of 1959. His tact, dedication, and efficiency impressed his home office superiors, and he was given instant promotion for his next assignment, the *Caronia*'s spring cruise to the Mediterranean. He was made registrar, second-in-command of the staff, charged with recording and reascertaining numbers of passengers for all of the sixteen port excursions (never easy, for passengers are notoriously dilatory about options ashore) and cabling the information ahead to port agents. (Cook and American Express were the cable companies' best customers, spending thousands of dollars on cables during each cruise.)

June 18, 1959. Occupying opposite sides of
Southampton's Ocean Dock, *Caronia* and *Queen
Elizabeth* exchange loads. The smaller Cunarder has
discharged Mediterranean cruise clients, the larger is
embarking many of them for passage west to New York.
Note the crewmen clustered atop the *Caronia*'s funnel.
(William Archibald)

The *Caronia*'s shore excursion staff sailed as passengers, booked in regular cabins and eating—albeit at their own table—in one of the two regular dining rooms. (These were called Sandringham and Balmoral and were nearly identical, though, throughout the *Caronia*'s British life, there was an overwhelming passenger predilection for what had been designated originally as the First Class room. It made no difference that the captain alternated scrupulously between the two nor that menus and service were identical; old *Caronia* hands and not-so-old parvenus wrote months ahead, anxiously requesting a Balmoral table.) Archibald, who would become an old *Caronia* hand in the years to follow, was usually booked into cabin 103, next door to cruise director Vaughan Rickard. (Rickard was also an American, even though an employee of Cunard, not Thomas Cook. It was an odd convention: the majority of today's cruise directors are British and always on British ships.) On the other side, his cabin was adjacent to the shore excursion office, to which he would report, each morning at nine, in suit and tie. In that respect, Archibald and his colleagues were not passengers; they kept office hours and office dress every day the ship was at sea. The *Caronia*'s shore excursion office was located aft on Main Deck, in what was otherwise the port half of the Raleigh Room, the Cabin Class smoking room used for that purpose for only a fortnight each year. Regardless, the room was partitioned temporarily during cruises and its starboard half, as well as the aft-facing Raleigh Bar, served as the *Caronia*'s serious drinkers' bar, equivalent to the bar in the Cabaret de l'Atlantique on the later *France*. So flimsy was the plywood separating office from bar that Archibald, as were all newly arrived staff on board, was immediately cautioned by his superior to say nothing indiscreet about passengers or, for that matter, about anything because the morning's Bloody Marys were being consumed within earshot to starboard.

(The *Caronia*, in fact, played host to some of the hardest drinkers afloat. But one of them, at least, was not quite as far gone as the cruise staff thought. Vaughan Rickard remembers one old *Caronia* regular who drank double brandies steadily all day. She would start after breakfast in the Observation Bar, then stagger aft to the Raleigh Bar, then, in the afternoon, reappear in the Observation Bar. Once, as the ship was steaming through the Andaman Sea, she squinted briefly out into the blinding glare and confided to the barman, "There's something out there." He smiled patronizingly. "There's nothing out there, madam." After a few moments' silence, the woman insisted again that she saw something floating out in the water. To humor her, the barman telephoned the bridge. It turned out that there *was* something out there and only the brandy drinker had spotted

Later on in his career with Thomas Cook, William
Archibald—adopting the consistent solemnity with
which many Asians face the camera—accepts a plaque
on behalf of the Japan Travel Bureau during a world
cruise in 1963. Plaques, dozens of them, are
acquisitional hazards for cruise ships. *(William
Archibald)*

it: a life raft that had been adrift for three weeks with some Malayan crewmen near death from thirst.)

At least Bill Archibald's working days were spent within sight of ocean and sky. I always think it odd when naval architects confine regular shipboard workers to inside offices: on the stretched Royal Viking ships, office and shore staff, pursers, shopkeepers, and even the hotel manager spend their working days closeted along a closed, midships passage. The *Caronia*'s shore excursion staff looked out through plate-glass windows at one of the three stretches of Cabin Class Promenade Deck that were wrapped, one above the other, around the *Caronia*'s stern.

In one respect, those secluded decks were extremely useful, particularly when the *Caronia* sailed with an elderly passenger load. There is an old Mediterranean bromide: "See Naples and die." That is just what one passenger did that spring, and Archibald, who knew the widow, was invited to attend her late husband's funeral. It was a small gathering, the widow, Archibald, Captain MacLean, the master-at-arms, and two seamen. Those haunting little ceremonies were never announced to the ship at large and took place at dawn, long before the Raleigh Bar crowd had stirred. The ship stopped off Elba and the master read a brief service for burial at sea; the deceased, shrouded in canvas with a weight at his feet, disembarked from his favorite vessel for the last time. At once, the officer of the watch, who could just see the splash by craning far out over the bridge wing, signaled for engine revolutions and entered the exact time and location of the funeral into the ship's log. (Years later, after a *Caronia* passenger, traveling with a much younger female companion, had been duly buried at sea, his wife cabled within the week requesting that her husband's body be kept on board and disembarked in New York. Wisely, the master referred the entire matter to Cunard's North American manager in New York.)

But that isolated grief was the only incident of its kind marring the otherwise cheerful tranquility of the *Caronia*'s Mediterranean circuit. After a benign six-day crossing from New York, the *Caronia* steamed along her projected itinerary, to Madeira first, then passage through the Strait of Gibraltar (a call was scheduled there for the return leg), and on to Spain, Majorca, and Malta. At nearly all her ports, because of her huge draft, the *Caronia*'s shore tenders were used. They were excellent sea boats, 45-foot cabined vessels with a broad teak-grated margin surrounding their deckhouses. Each could accommodate sixty passengers; they were as carefully made as the *Caronia* and had been launched into the Clyde one at a time from a small-boat yard in nearby Renfrew while their mother ship was being fitted out. That morning off Palma, they were lowered, three a side,

Secured in its davits, one of the *Caronia*'s
superb shore tenders. *(William Archibald)*

suspended from their midships davits, the largest ever installed on any ship until the *Norway*.

The early-morning thump of boat against plating and the unholy racket of the winches are traditional harbingers of arrival in port. It is a time when outswung davits presage diversion rather than disaster, a time, too, when touch-up crews go over the side in bosun's chairs and the sacrosanct disc of sky within a cabin porthole suddenly includes a man with a paintbrush, as countless passengers fresh from a pre-excursion bath can attest. Shorebound passengers on the *Caronia* were no less restless than their predecessors on board *Normandie*, victims of the same uneasy distress infecting herds of cattle within olfactory range of the abattoir. They worry a lot: they worry about what to wear; they worry about how much and what kind of money to take; they worry about cameras and lenses; they worry about tardy wives, husbands, or companions. Old or disabled passengers worry about coping with the transfer from ship to launch to pier.

First ashore were Bill Archibald and the rest of the cruise staff, clipboards at the ready, marshaling buses and guides for the passenger hordes at their heels. That first impact had all the pressured suspense of a latter-day blast-off at Cape Canaveral: buses had to be launched into programmed tour orbit on precise schedules, their countdowns in constant jeopardy at the hands of querulous passengers who, though often seemingly unable to follow the simplest instructions, were nevertheless ruthlessly explicit about which end of the bus they preferred and who might share their seat. (At cruise's end in Lisbon, the last great tour port, the dynamics of seating priorities would change, incorporating requests that they not sit next to or, in extreme cases, not even share the same bus with certain newfound enemies.)

For the elderly or infirm, a long tour was demanding, and they were comforted by the presence of ship's medical personnel, either doctors or nursing sisters, who accompanied the more arduous ones. No less than five ship's officers came as well; as a matter of Thomas Cook policy, they were given complimentary tickets, ostensibly as a treat but in actuality assuring the excursion manager that there would be capable hands along in the event of an emergency. According to Archibald's cabled instructions, two chauffeured cars awaited the *Caronia* at each port, one for the shore excursion manager, the other for the captain or, if he were being entertained by the ship's agent, one of his senior officers.

There was only momentary respite after the last bus had lumbered off the pier. Then Archibald and the agent would crisscross every tour route throughout the day, especially when lunch breaks had been planned. Local tour operators seldom abused the company; they were often Thomas Cook agents themselves. Moreover, the ship called so regularly at these ports each year that the Mediterranean tour paths had been worn smooth, like cathedral steps, by *Caronia* pilgrims. Although Archibald's responsibility ended theoretically once the passengers had clambered off their buses, he never rested until every misplaced camera or purse had been retrieved from the overhead racks and the last launch had been safely resecured in its davits.

Bus tours crammed with a day of concentrated sightseeing offer mixed blessings. But they do guarantee nervous passengers that the captain is obliged to await their return: occupants of a bus delayed by a flat tire atop a mountain pass were advised by their guide that the *Caronia* would not leave without them. Drivers of Andalusian jitneys could offer their independently booked clients no such assurance. In Spain, just such a fate overtook two of the *Caronia*'s VIP passengers, two Maryland state senators. They arrived at Malaga's pier hot, disheveled, and incredulous to see their ship—and there is no more cataclysmic vision—steaming majestically out of the harbor. There followed some frantic bargaining with a local boatman and a heart-stopping scramble up a Jacob's ladder to an open port in the shell plating. The episode served as an object lesson to the large passenger gallery assembled on the *Caronia*'s upper decks. No one ever missed a sailing again, at least on that cruise. Ships must and do adhere to the sailing time posted prominently inside the debarkation port. In fact, passengers are advised to be on board half an hour before then. Strict departures are predicated on complex, interlocking factors, including subsequent itinerary, fuel consumption, stevedores' hours, pilotage regulations ad infinitum. Though cruise planners built time buffers into the *Caronia*'s Mediterranean schedule to insure against adverse weather conditions, captains were loath to use them if for no other reason than to keep potential laggards on independent outings on the qui vive.

The *Caronia* stopped overnight in several ports: one night in Malaga (with inland Granada as the preferred objective) and two each in Venice, Naples, and Lisbon. Vaughan Rickard remembers that Naples was, consistently, the cruise's least favorite stop. Despite the Amalfi Drive, Pompeii, Capri, Herculaneum, and even the bay itself, passengers near the pier were so pestered by urchins and touts selling black market trinkets that they disliked the port regardless. The unquestioned favorite was Venice, Queen of the Adriatic, a layover so enchanting that it was always the highlight of every *Caronia* Mediterranean cruise. Prewar ships had anchored out in the Lagoon, enabling their passengers to cross to shore, if they wished, by that

Enthusiastic but inaccurate residents of Malta welcome the "M.V." *Caronia*; she was steam rather than motor driven. *Below,* the *Caronia* off Villefranche. *(William Archibald)*

most romantic conveyance, a gondola, disembarking in the center of things at the Piazzetta steps. But by the fifties, Venetian authorities had dredged a deep-water berth alongside the Arsenal. Venice was indeed the archetypal Mediterranean call, a jewel in a diadem of ports rimming the ancient sea, where visits ashore offer generous portions of antiquity, food, and charm— a shore ethos so sadly lacking in the Caribbean or on Mexico's west coast. It was an itinerary that especially suited the elegant *Caronia*.

A popular dividend of the Venice stopover was that passengers could enjoy a long overland weekend in Florence before rejoining the westbound *Caronia* at Naples. Those who did missed the only maritime drama of the cruise, a time when Cunard's time buffers would be called into play. After steaming around the heel of Italy's boot, the ship made two Sicilian calls, both in the same day. After a dawn arrival at Catania, a day-long tour was arranged paralleling the ship's waterborne route north to Messina. Lunch was taken on the terrace of Taormina's Hotel San Domenico, where, over coffee, passengers could see the Green Goddess steaming past toward its afternoon rendezvous.

When Bill Archibald and his charges arrived in Messina, there was the *Caronia* again, far offshore but, ominously, making no headway though her anchors were patently not in the water. Clouds of black smoke from the funnel indicated trouble of some kind, confirmed only too soon by the local Thomas Cook agent: the *Caronia*, he had been signaled, was aground —temporarily, it turned out—offshore too far to ferry passengers on board. Archibald was severely tested that evening, keeping busloads of exhausted clients amused and entertained. All saw more of Messina and its nightlife than they ever cared to see again before the ship floated free and welcomed those *in extenso* tour passengers back on board.

Archibald stayed on at Thomas Cook and remembered that he never saw more unhappy passengers than the year following; those passengers were not stranded ashore, they were stranded *afloat*. It was on the *Gripsholm*'s first Greek Island cruise and he was in charge, shepherding a very elegant and select passenger load, including Hilmer Lundbeck, the company's president. Among the most eagerly awaited ports of call was a visit to the centuries-old monasteries at Mount Athos. But someone at Swedish-American Line had goofed: not only were women barred from the monasteries, they were not even permitted ashore. Only men were welcomed, and when they returned to the *Gripsholm* at the end of a fascinating day, they faced the feminist wrath of the cruise's lady passengers—then, as now, in the majority—who had spent a fruitless day at anchor, confined on

oored alongside Venice's Arsenale, the
ronia disgorges passengers for
other day's sightseeing. The
mpanile glistens in the background.
'illiam Archibald)

board. The business of shore excursions, Bill Archibald found out, is not all gravy.

Alas, the *Caronia*'s last years were grim. She was disposed of during Cunard's blood-letting in the sixties, sold for $3 million to a Greek owner. He changed her name to *Caribia*; it was a cheap conversion to implement— only two letters at each bow and across the stern had to be replaced. On a subsequent Caribbean sailing, a boiler explosion killed one man and seriously injured another, leaving the vessel without electrical power in mid-ocean. She limped back to New York only to be struck by her crew because of what they claimed to be appalling working conditions. For a year, she lay at anchor down near the Verrazano-Narrows Bridge. When her owners moved her upriver to moor in the middle of the slip south of Pier 84, the Department of Ports and Terminals slapped a ticket on her for parking illegally. It was delivered by a police launch, written on a regular automobile summons slip: "BOAT: S.S. *Caribia* YEAR: 1949 MAKE: John Brown Hull COLOR: White."

Time was running out, but the ship stayed on for years, ironically a burden at the same port she had patronized so loyally in Cunard's original service. In 1974, she was sold to the scrapyards of Taiwan. After an auction of her furniture and fittings, the hulk left her Brooklyn berth for the last time, behind the seagoing tug *Hamburg* at the end of a mile-long towing cable. But she never reached Formosa—a Pacific storm parted the *Hamburg*'s tow off Guam and the *Caribia*-ex-*Caronia* ended her life pounded to bits by mountainous seas. Many of her fittings can be found to this day as part of the decoration of a lower Fifth Avenue restaurant in New York called One Fifth: although they seem fragmented and strange in their new tile-floored setting, their solidity and workmanship are still remarkable.

Thus far, the ships of these cruises past have had something in common: they were all relatively new, vessels in their prime, whether new to cruising or not. To ring down the curtain on that era, we need embark on one last sea journey from a time that seems, to me, at least, not the past at all but, in terms of our subject, light years away. The ship in question was the first *Queen Elizabeth*, overtaken by the war in 1939 and pressed into harried wartime service as a trooper. She did not return to peacetime sailing until 1946. By the time her first civilian passenger—the seven-year-old daughter of an American businessman living in Britain—had embarked that October, about a third of her anticipated life span had passed. By the time we join her, it was all but over. April 1968 saw her last cruise to the Caribbean, her last sailing from New York, and her last scheduled crossing

R.M.S. "CARONIA"   CUNARD LINE

GREAT WORLD CRUISE

Mr. & Mrs. Bernard Christopher Wren
Need your help celebrating Oriental Night
If you come in costume -
you'll add to the light !
i the Verandah Cafe

R.M.S. "CARONIA"

GREAT WORLD CRUISE

CUNARD LINE

R.M.S. "CARONIA"
GREAT WORLD CRUISE 1965

THE RADIO OFFICERS
cordially invite you
to their Wardroom
for a
"CHERRY BLOSSOM" EVENING
from 7.00 p.m.
on Tuesday, April 6th, 1965

—o—

Dress: KIMONOS (Optional)

R.M.S. "CARONIA"   CUNARD LINE

GREAT WORLD CRUISE

Please join us for Cocktails
on Wednesday, April 28th
at seven o'clock
in the Verandah Café

THE MUIR'S AND THE RENOUF'S
RTS and SHIFTS

R.M.S. "CARONIA"
GREAT WORLD CRUISE   CUNARD LINE

Hawaiian Party . . .

Marquis Albert
& Marquise Virginia Leriget de la Plante
and Lady Price
est the pleasure of your company
to Cocktails
day, April 19th, 1965
Verand-

R.M.S CARONIA   CUNARD LINE
GREAT WORLD CRUISE

Itsy Bitsy O'Oliver
and Elizabeth McGreenberger
would be happy to have you join them
St. PATRICK's NIGHT
" COCKTAIL DANCE
erandah Cafe

SUNDAY, APRIL 21st, 1963
6.30 p.m. to 8.30 p.m.   Tour **DRINKING SPECIAL**

Name........**BILL ARCHIBALD and STAFF**

Coach....**R.M.S. "CARONIA"**   Cmpt.   **Port Side**

Hotel....**CRUISE OFFICE**   Place....**Main Deck Aft**

PLEASE ACCEPT THIS AS YOUR INVITATION

mnants of distant frivolity. Perhaps the most evocative
ronia legacy, some of the thousands of special
itations turned out by the print shop on board
ring the vessel's golden years. They hint at stilled
ghter, forgotten gaieties, and scores of epic sunsets
the *Caronia* drifted languidly around the world.
illiam Archibald)

of the Atlantic. The following spring, she would tie up for a two-year stay in Florida's Port Everglades, moored in a specially dredged backwater as a failed exhibition piece, in touch with but hopelessly remote from the stirrings of a vigorous new Caribbean steamship life for which she had never really qualified.

Jack Shaum had been in love with ships since he was eight years old. His mother, a nurse at Baltimore's Marine Hospital, had cared for a patient who was captain of a night boat traveling between Baltimore and Norfolk. Mother and son were given a complimentary passage, and the thrill of that long night on the water, the delight of their simple overnight cabin, and, overwhelming for an eight-year-old, the captain's friendship on the bridge, left an indelible impression on the young passenger-by-chance. Two years later, after he had read and reread *A Night to Remember*, Walter Lord's gripping account of the *Titanic* disaster, he was hooked: Jack Shaum's bewitching memory of that nocturnal Chesapeake Bay passage had been augmented into a consuming passion for all ocean liners.

Ten years later, after a tour of duty with the marines, he worked as a reporter with the *Baltimore News-American*. He saved enough from his wages for passage on a liner. Though he could not afford a crossing—that would entail a return fare as well—he could just manage a short cruise. But if the cruise were short, the ship he chose was not: the *Queen Elizabeth* was one of the four largest ever built. Jack Shaum mailed Cunard's New York office a check and received in return a passage ticket guaranteeing him a single inside cabin for a five-day Easter cruise on the *Elizabeth* from New York to Nassau and back. His cabin was number C-244, a number only one less than the dollar price of his fare.

Neither Jack nor his family had ever seen a proper liner before, so they all entrained for New York early one Thursday morning in April, a family outing to see their son safely and ceremoniously onto the *Queen Elizabeth*. On board, they trooped down to his C-deck cabin, where, crowded onto its berth and single chair, they toasted the departing passenger with warm champagne. Someone had sent a fruit basket that, glistening in amber cellophane, lent the cabin just the right touch. After a tour of the ship, the first warning gong sounded; passenger and visitors separated at the gangway, promising each other a final wave above as the ship pulled out. Jack's family had even brought streamers and confetti from a Baltimore Woolworth's.

But things went awry. Jack, responding to a cabin request that he book his table in the Windsor Restaurant—cabin C-244's occupant was entitled to a seat in the *Elizabeth*'s Tourist Class dining room—got embroiled in a

...ar the end. The venerable *Queen Elizabeth,* out of
...ne, out of place, and out of sorts, anchored off
...ssau on one of her last forays to the Caribbean. She
...ght well have been photographed beneath a palm leaf
...m the same tree seen in the *Nieuw Amsterdam*'s
...ture in Chapter 1. *(Everett E. Viez Collection)*

queue and arrived on deck to find the ship sliding past the Battery. His family, mystified by his nonappearance at the rail, had thrown their streamers anyway, then headed for Pennsylvania Station and home.

The Windsor Restaurant was inside, and that Jack Shaum could not even tell that his ship was under way in New York harbor proved the first of several disappointments he encountered in the days to follow.

In truth, they were small disappointments, things to which his 1,600 fellow passengers probably paid little heed. But they had booked on a cruise: Jack Shaum, in a sense, was embarked on a pilgrimage. Deprived of his crossing, he hoped that five days to the Bahamas and back on the giant Cunarder might serve as a gratifying facsimile. But, as he found out on Friday morning, his first full day at sea, the *Queen Elizabeth*'s motion was all wrong; to be more accurate, there was none at all. He felt as removed from movement through the water in his cabin as he had when queued up in the dining room in New York harbor. It was not like being at sea. Even outdoors after breakfast, with a brisk sea breeze scouring the decks, the *Elizabeth* seemed placid, only half-committed to the business of passage. Moving at a sedate 18 knots over calm seas, the ship showed none of the ocean struggle its keenest passenger had envisioned, no surge and shudder of hull against wave.

There was lack of commitment as well in the *Elizabeth*'s sorry maintenance. She was showing her age badly. What had appeared huge and puissant from Pier 92 seemed, on board, to have been abandoned to decline. Rust was everywhere—scarring railing and deck fitting, streaking the colors on both funnels. She made inordinate amounts of smoke. "Thick enough to walk back to New York on," commented Chief Staff Engineer Willy Farmer, at whose table Jack sat. The same neglect extended below decks as well. Carpeting was faded and stained, the rubberoid linoleum of the passageways was worn, and an air of genteel decay had fallen over every public room.

I had last traveled home on the *Queen Elizabeth* from France the previous summer and so could share that assessment. Yet my westbound passage had been a crossing, its shipboard ambience part of a familiar North Atlantic ritual that Cunard had mastered long ago. Jack Shaum's Bahama cruise was alien to the *Queen*, and a mood of spurious southern jollity had been superimposed on the ship's inbred northern persona. In 1966, she had been given what was presumed to be the definitive refurbishment for tropical waters. An outdoor pool and Lido Deck were installed above the stern, larger than but similar to the *Caronia*'s. Two Tourist Class public rooms—the smoking room and lounge—had been redecorated in

With most of her passengers ashore, the *Queen Elizabeth*'s new on-deck pool remains underutilized on a warm-weather cruise. Farthest aft, the crew deck is busy while passenger lidos above are deserted. A surreal banqueting table, complete with a dozen chairs and white cloth, has been set in the center of one. Far to the right, the aft-facing shelters for deck-sports spectators are still in place, legacy of Atlantic winds. (Cunard)

Kon-Tiki basic and were identified on cruises only as the Club Room and Caribbean Room. A temperamental air-conditioning system blew fitful gusts throughout the ship. But, in sum, it was no more than a desperate face-lift; no amount of cosmetic patching could disguise the fact that those cavernous paneled interiors had never been conceived with the tropics in mind.

There was, too, the problem of light. On the North Atlantic, the sun goes down almost imperceptibly, usually buried in a bank of horizon cumulus. In the Caribbean, unfailingly long sunsets throw slanting, flat light into promenades and public rooms, affording the kind of scrutiny that no one, especially an aged dowager, should be subjected to after a certain age. No amount of cruise folderol, whether artificial palms or draped fishnet, made any difference. The tropics jarred everywhere on board. Jack Shaum summed it up best when he related how, throughout the string concert on the stage of the Main Lounge during Friday afternoon teatime, there could be heard the insistent, percussive jangle of cha-cha lessons in the adjacent Midships Bar.

Despite the shortcomings, however, Jack enjoyed himself immensely. He explored every room, passage, and deck on board. He visited the engine room, thanks to his table host, and even had a luncheon drink with Commodore Marr and Staff Captain Law. He went ashore both days in Nassau, but returned for dinner on board Saturday night and an Easter Bonnet parade that cruise director Harold Grimes had organized for passengers who preferred not having to endure the steel bands and limbo ashore. On Sunday, he attended divine services in the Main Lounge, conducted by the captain, and was happiest, later that day, when the anchors came up and the ship turned her bows back to sea. There was a patch of dirty weather off Hatteras during the passage back to New York, but not as dirty as he had hoped to enjoy. Most of his last evening was spent out on deck, the night pitch black around him with only the faint twinkle of an anonymous masthead beacon away off in the dark to port.

On the train home to Baltimore, he felt that his cruise had been a success in many ways: he had finally sailed on a liner, he had been to sea, and he was one of the millions of passengers who had sampled an extraordinary class of ship. His addiction to ocean liners would continue unabated after that first exposure. In 1981, he and a fellow historian, William Flayhart, would publish their definitive work on four-stackers, entitled *Majesty at Sea*.

To this day, Jack recalls one final postscript to that first cruise. As he and his fellow passengers sailed into Nassau by tender, they saw several

assenger and master: Jack Shaum
ıakes the hand of Commodore Geoffrey
arr at a reception on board. *(Jack*
ıaum)

The new breed at Nassau. A typical day at the
Caribbean port. *From top to bottom, Flavia* (upper
left) ; *Emerald Seas* with *New Bahama Star* behind
(upper right) ; *Oceanic*; *Oronsay*; and, being nudged to
her mooring, the *Maxim Gorky*. The wedge ships
have arrived. *(Everett E. Viez Collection)*

ships tied up at George V dock, vessels small enough to have negotiated the harbor and discharged their passengers directly onto the pier. One ship excited amused comment, a curious white creation with a golden sunburst logo on either flank. To those Cunard passengers, her profile seemed bizarre. Superstructure the width of the hull crowded fore and aft; severely raked twin funnels astern were linked to a kind of greenhouse mast base forward, giving her top hamper the look of a seagoing Luna Park. It was the first ship of a new company, the *Sunward* of Norwegian Caribbean Lines, the largest vessel ever built in Norway. She was so successful that a consort, the *Starward*, would be joining her by Christmas.

They were the advance guard of the new Caribbean conquerors, an impending Viking invasion as far-reaching as the Nordic longboats that had pillaged European coastlines centuries earlier. Symbolically, *Sunward* had taken Nassau by storm, just as her sisters would take other island ports in the years ahead, leaving haughty old tonnage lying helplessly at anchor beyond the Hog Island Light. Cruising was on the cusp that Easter of 1968, and the Nassau encounter dramatized it. The Atlantic was dying, the Caribbean burgeoning. The wedge ship, crammed with Newpassengers, had arrived. Cruises past were over, cruises present were beginning.

*Over all the movements of the
traveller, the weather exercises
its despotic sway.*

—BAEDEKER, GUIDE TO
NORTHERN ITALY

*. . . a warm bath of extraordinary
workmanship wherein one may swim
and have a prospect at the same
time of the sea.*

—PLINY THE ELDER,
THE PHILOSOPHY OF THE BATH

5.
Tropical Rig

Most of today's cruise dollars are earned in temperate or tropical waters.
For every northern summer excursion to Scandinavia, the Baltic, Alaska,
or the Saint Lawrence, dozens of permanent itineraries ply the Caribbean,
Mediterranean, Black Sea, South Pacific, and what is popularly—if gener-
ously—called Mexico's Riviera. Ships on world cruises venture no further
north than Yokohama and achieve their extreme and almost identical
southern latitudes at Cape Town and Sydney, although a few press on to
New Zealand. But the norm is warm: semitropical seas are picturesque,
weather is predictably good, and passengers can book with the assurance
that their vessel's keel will remain relatively even.

Mid-Atlantic, high summer. Passengers take tea under shelter at the forward end of the *Queen Elizabeth 2*'s Sports deck. Brisk weather sends Dennis Dawson (right) and his fellow deck stewards scurrying with pads and blankets. Dawson is founder of a select *QE2* Sports deck organization, the No Character Club, of which my wife and I are proud to be members. *Left,* the back of the card is inscribed, "He has brains, breeding, money, and position, everything except the main qualification —Character." *(Author's collection)*

This predilection for sunny, hence calm, seas dictates the look of today's newbuilding as well as the pattern of shipboard life. Contemporary ships must thrive in the hot sun, their design configuration keyed not to maintaining schedules against hostile seas but to providing sufficient open space for swimming and sunbathing. For decades, naval architects and crews of vessels obliged to pass near or across latitude zero waged an unending campaign against the twin equatorial adversaries: high heat and humidity. The battles were fought with traditional and often ineffectual weapons until after World War II, when there occurred the first of two great technological cruising breakthroughs: the second, already cited, was the arrival of the jet aircraft that carry passengers to and from their ships; the first and even more significant was air-conditioning. No other shipboard refinement has so established cruising's present mode. Air-conditioning is no longer a luxury; it is a necessity and such an integral part of every company's perquisites that brochures no longer advertise it. Passengers expect it, and the only time they do not take it for granted is, understandably, when it fails, when chilled air inside a sealed hull begins cooking up.

But before Carrier's name and equipment appeared in engine rooms all over the world, sustained hot weather at sea and, especially, in port made life on board uncomfortable. Traditionally, builders' specifications for ships referred to "heating and *ventilating*" (italics mine), never cooling. What were called thermotanks stored sea air for circulation throughout the ship, and it was propelled, by either normal draft or electric fans, into every cabin and public room, issuing through punka louvers. (The word *punka* has hot-weather significance: a punka fan was one of those manually operated, stiffened panels of material swung by servants from the ceilings of Indian interiors. The air that issued from cabin punka louvers in the Indian Ocean was little different from the air stirred by a punka on the subcontinent, *agitated* but not *cooled*.)

Vessels plying the North Atlantic were seldom troubled by heat, save during summer turnarounds in New York, Boston, or Montreal. Midocean air is invariably cold. I remember crossing on the *Queen Elizabeth 2* a few years ago while America's northeast baked in a record heat wave; only twenty-four hours from New York, we could sit outdoors only in the most sheltered deck chairs, swathed in Cunard's reliable, blue-and-red steamer rugs, managing only a scant hour before the intense cold made even holding a book impossible. But steamships sailing to Australia, for instance, ran a gauntlet of appalling heat before achieving their destination. Recalls Basil Greenhill, historian as well as passenger, "You became

omenade deck, circa 1905, vessel unknown.
ssengers off the Norwegian coast enjoy shelter and
ashine. Judging by the clothing worn, the weather is
ol though dry; canvas awnings on top are rolled up
t the railing is still lashed to keep out damp or
eezes. *(Author's collection)*

gradually accustomed to the heat in the eastern Mediterranean, more accustomed in the Suez Canal, and very accustomed in the Red Sea." But did passengers on the earliest ships ever really get accustomed to the heat? Consider this excerpt from *A White Star Journal*, published aboard the vessel *White Star* for Saturday, May 12, 1855:

> The heat has been dreadful. . . . Our ladies . . . have had headaches and fainting fits. . . . It is for the men to suffer to the extent of absurdity and to show grotesque appearances. They wander about, with great beads of perspiration bedewing their faces, seeking vainly for cool places, and employing their time in compounding strange drinks.
>
> Dinner time used to be our happiest time, but the tropics have rather taken the fun out of it. Pea-soup, at three in the afternoon, in the atmosphere of a brick kiln, and partaken of in the inside of a steam boiler in the course of construction, is not an agreeable picture, but it is very like what we endure at dinner time; with the addition of a brass band working its passage out, ceaselessly braying at our very ears: "Pop Goes the Weasel" or "Annie Laurie."
>
> But the sufferings by day are nothing to what we endure at night. As bedtime draws near, lower-deck passengers may be seen carrying their beds about the deck, vainly looking for a quiet place where they may lay them down in the fresh air, such as it is. In the saloon berths, it has been found hardly possible to sleep; and many of the ladies and gentlemen have been obliged to try and get a little sleep out on the mess-room floor.

Before the advent of air-conditioning—well into the twentieth century—the only remedies for heat east of Suez were traditional ones. The simplest was shade, and it had, for different reasons, been built into passenger vessels since 1870, when White Star's *Oceanic* offered her passengers the first open-air alternatives. Her midships deckhouse had its roof extended to the ship's sides, where it was supported on a row of stanchions extending up from the railing. Thus was created not only the Atlantic's first outdoor covered walkway but an exhilarating choice for passengers as well. Formerly, they had only gone "on deck"; now, they could choose one of two weather decks, either the shelter deck—the vessel's covered main deck—or, one flight above, a revolutionary new top deck that had been christened, boldly, the hurricane deck.

Amusingly enough, the etymology of the word *hurricane* offers two derivations—one maritime, the other not; either may have influenced the White Star Line in their choice. A "hurricane house" was the original term for a crow's nest. In addition, there exists an interesting eighteenth-century origin wherein *hurricane* describes "a confused meeting of Company of both sexes on a Sunday." Taken together, the two describe to perfection the brisk and breezy sociability of passengers thronging the *Oceanic*'s topmost deck on a mid-Atlantic if not necessarily Sabbath morning. It is a refreshingly pungent deck name, the kind that would send contemporary public relations people running for shelter; today's top decks are almost exclusively Sun or Sports decks, never hurricane decks.

Between every stanchion on the *Oceanic*'s shelter deck were horizontally rolled canvas awnings that could be lowered and lashed, if necessary, to the bottom railing, providing complete, if gloomy, protection for passengers determined on fresh air during foul weather. It was an expedience that spelled the end of the shelter deck almost before it began. First to go was the term, originally part of the naval architect's glossary, replaced almost at once by the steamer publicist's "promenade deck," a more pretentious euphemism reassuring passengers that a promenade at sea could be as effortless, extensive, and pleasant as one ashore in a park or along a boulevard. As the years passed, promenade decks on larger ships, though higher above the water than those on earlier hulls, were made even more secure: railings were replaced by solid bulwarks and permanent plate glass supplanted canvas awnings.

The exact crossover can be pinpointed to 1912 with the construction of the *Titanic*, second of the *Olympic*-class White Star liners. Whereas the *Olympic*'s promenade deck had been open along its side to the elements, it was decided that the *Titanic*'s would have windows along its forward portion to protect First Class passengers during winter crossings. That supplementary glazing served little purpose during the vessel's first—and only—crossing, since the weather up to her encounter with the iceberg had been calm. But it did serve notice that the open shelter deck was, at least for North Atlantic vessels, on the way out. During ensuing decades, promenade decks became interior spaces, less walkways than porches, galleries, or even conservatories. On the *Olympic*, part of the promenade deck was given over to a café, the original teak underfoot replaced with gutta-percha tiling. Only two years later, portions of the *Aquitania*'s promenade deck were permanently enclosed as Garden Lounges. This gentrification of promenade decks meant that by the twenties, a traditional fixture from the past could be dispensed with: the long strip of coco-matting laid as a dry pathway over damp teak. It disappeared simply because it was no longer needed. By then, promenade decks were dry, indoor rooms that were swept or vacuumed rather than scoured with sand-

Gentrification sets in. By 1913, as here on HAPAG's *Imperator,* promenade decks on the larger steamers had been permanently glazed along most of their length, insulated from the worst of the weather and on the road to parity with public rooms. *Below,* ultimate absorption. On board the *Queen Elizabeth 2,* what in former days might have served as an encircling promenade has become an extension of the interior. *(Hapag-Lloyd and Cunard)*

stone; they were never wet. The sea was in sight but at bay on the far side of substantial fenestration. (Before we leave the *Olympic*-class ships, it should be pointed out that each had what were called shelter decks two down from the promenade, a deck open to the elements only fore and aft in the wells but occupied solidly amidships by banks of cabins the full width of the hull.)

The shelter or promenade deck remained open on hot-weather ships. Enclosing the extended deckhouse box would have offset the advantages offered by leaving them open: while North Atlantic shelter decks protected passengers against damp, Far Eastern shelter decks thwarted the pitiless midday sun. (We talk of bitter cold but never bitter heat; it seems an adjective appropriate to the scorching discomfort of the tropics.) And though the vertical awnings between stanchions were dispensed with, they had their horizontal counterparts all over the weather decks above, forward and aft, even on the wings of the bridge. East of Suez, Far Eastern ships blossomed with canvas awnings held up by a network of wooden or steel supports. They were sensible and invaluable devices that vanished with the advent of air-conditioning and the mania for sunbathing. Moreover, profile aesthetics originating in the thirties ordained clean-swept decks; awning supports were seen as clutter that the new fashion would not tolerate. Now, interestingly, awnings have reappeared: the *Veendam* had a large tented awning over the stern, aft of the pool, *Sea Goddess* passengers lunch in the shade of canvas, and on the *Song of America*, food is served beneath a double awning aft of the funnel. Awnings on board the Orient Line's *Oronsay* of 1925 were invaluable once, when the ship's propellers were damaged in the Suez Canal: sails rigged out of awnings were instrumental in helping the vessel reach port.

The great benefit of the awning is its horizontal shade combined with an absence of vertical obstructing wall, a perfect and inexpensive shipboard cooling device; awnings not only cool passengers, they also cool the decks and cabins beneath them. On the Nederland Royal Mail Line's *Johan Van Oldenbarnevelt* as well as the *Dempo* of the Rotterdam Lloyd Line, upper-deck First Class cabins had large windows set back from the edge of the vessel so that sloping canvas awnings, similar to those used on land-based casements during the summer, could be hung against the sun. Below, the principle of the awning's openness was extended to all decks: ports and scuttles and, where possible, doors were left open so that prevailing sea breezes or merely the breeze from the vessel's progress through the water eddied throughout the ship. Cabins on P&O ships, like rooms in Far Eastern hotels, had alternate doors, a conventionally solid outer one as well as a pierced ancillary inside, its upper and lower panels louvered to circulate air either from the passage into the cabin or, if the wind were abeam, from the open port in the cabin into the passage. The cabin door ajar remained a familiar fixture even on Atlantic liners: the *France* of 1962, even though totally air-conditioned, had a special lockable latch that would secure the cabin doors in a 6-inch open position.

On many vessels, sailing as well as steam, fresh air was circulated below deck by wind chutes—large, open-mouthed canvas sails rigged over hatches that, turned toward prevailing winds, delivered fresh, moving air to interior spaces. One correspondent wrote:

> I was in a German prison ship in the war in the tropics when we were down in the fore hold and a canvas wind ventilator worked like a charm and was much better than—say—the *Empress of Australia* in which it was once my misfortune to return from Manila, a ship built, in fairness, for the North Atlantic run.

Shipping companies offered the same device for individual cabins: detachable metal wind scoops that projected out through the port. Shaped like hearthside coal scuttles, their cutaway side was turned into the wind, diverting whatever breeze there was into the cabin; reversed, they would draw air out of the port. These were standard perks on hot-weather ships. It was a curious fact that on board the legendary *Caronia*, before she was completely air-conditioned in the fifties, there were never enough of those cabin wind scoops to go around. Experienced passengers wise enough to book a table in the (First Class) Balmoral dining room reserved a wind scoop in advance as well. The crew must have appropriated more than their fair share, but those crewmen with cabins close to the waterline grew wary of leaving wind scoops in place: if the vessel rolled, wind scoops became water scoops that, thrust only momentarily beneath the surface because of the rotation of the hull, deluged a cabin and adjacent passageway in seconds. When the *Caronia* had first come into service, Cunard hoped that her light-colored hull as well as a heavy insulation of asbestos would keep her cool. This proved wildly overoptimistic, and Bill Archibald recalls that she was, succinctly, "a hot ship," particularly when tied up in Mediterranean or Far Eastern ports.

Before there was electricity on board ships, manual punka fans hung over each table in the dining saloon, kept in hypnotic motion by white-jacketed lascars in the corners. The first ship on the Australian run to be electrified was the *Orient* of 1879; her brochures advertised REFRIGERATION in large letters. Yet, although better provision storage and unlimited ice

Waging the battle against humidity in the thirties. Her signal flags wilting in the early-morning breezeless glare, the westbound S.S. *Kroonland* awaits her first Panama lift at the bottom of Gatun's triple flight of locks. Wind scoops sprout the length of the hull. Crewmen have rigged an awning over the fo'c's'le to protect line-handlers from the worst of the heat. Awnings cover the bridge as well. *Left,* anchored off St. Croix in 1936, the S.S. *Nerissa* has swung bow into the prevailing wind, ensuring that a breeze will circulate through those forward cabins equipped with wind scoops. *(Courtesy of the Steamship Historical Society Collection, University of Baltimore Library and photograph by Everett E. Viez)*

were assured, the new energy source on board did little to comfort the passengers. Gradually, electric punka fans—the kind energy-conscious Americans have recently hung from their ceilings—appeared in the public rooms. Unfortunately, they were not installed as standard cabin equipment. For decades to follow, Far Eastern pursers made a tidy income for the company by renting cabin fans—stir-about fans, they were called—for one guinea the entire outbound passage. Those passengers without them had to rely on forced air from the punka louvers, systems that became less efficient in the tropics not only because the air entering the system was already hot and moist but also because dense, warm air does not circulate easily. A woman who sailed back and forth to India between the wars remembers that all the punka louvers did was "to move hot air about, never replenish it."

Of course, one's location in the ship was supremely important. There cannot be a passenger alive unfamiliar with POSH—Port Out, Starboard Home—the coveted acronym with which Far Eastern booking agents would initial cabin requests of their favored clients. It had nothing to do with scenery, only heat. The shaded side of a ship is several degrees cooler than its sunny counterpart. Hull plates are notorious heat collectors: during construction, a vessel's flanks are measured at night because a side measured in sunlight will read longer than its shaded opposite number. Those berthed on the sunny starboard side sailing to the Far East might have been more comfortable in an inside cabin, perhaps deprived of a porthole but at least insulated from the heat absorbed by the shell plating. Each day past Suez, the hull absorbed heat from the sun, heat that accumulated and spread by convection through every plate, stanchion, and pipe. Even on an air-conditioned vessel, after a few tropical days only tepid water issues from cold-water faucets, and increased oil consumption in the engine room reflects the expense of cooling the hull.

But in the old days, despite awnings, fans, punka louvers, and open ports throughout the vessel, conditions below were trying. Though they submitted each evening to the black-tie ritual of a stifling dining saloon, passengers often slept on deck in cots provided by the company. Robert Arnott, master of the *Queen Elizabeth 2*, recalls serving as a young officer on board the second *Mauretania*, which, like the *Caronia*, had no air-conditioning as we know it today:

> Some of the public rooms had the air coming through the punka louvers chilled through a thermotank system. That was all; no cabins or crew accommodations were cooled. Mind you, it was still pretty warm! Each cabin had a reciprocating electric fan to stir up the

almost comical cross section of
tilating devices—cowls, mushroom
s, and blowers—marshaled like a
-tag army on the after decks of the
*ann van Oldenbarnevelt. (Photograph
Paul Hollister)*

warm air! Depending on weather conditions, certain portholes and shell doors were allowed to be open to maintain a circulation of air. For those passengers, particularly the ones on the lower decks whose portholes couldn't be opened, there were dormitories at the after end of the enclosed promenade deck—one side male, the other side female. There were just a large number of camp beds which passengers booked like deck chairs.

In those days, there was no alternative so passengers just had to grin and bear it!

I think Bob was right: it was just accepted as the way things were. I asked Iphigene Ochs Sulzberger how she and her fellow passengers coped with Panama's heat and humidity; she could recall no special discomfort. "It was winter and we all wore cotton clothes." Others demurred. One man who cruised around the world on the *Belgenland*, in 1929, wrote, "People just expected to be hot. . . . We were pretty constantly hot from the time we sailed from Hong Kong until we reached Suez. . . ." Another passenger adopted a stoical stance, suggesting that "passengers just expected a warm voyage, put it out of their minds, dressed for it, and enjoyed it." Basil Greenhill suggests, in retrospect:

Nobody expected air-conditioning, you were completely conditioned to be extremely hot, there was no air-conditioning in your living quarters in the countries in which you were stationed either, nor in the cars or trains in which you traveled. . . . Believe me, even in the good first-class cabins we traveled in, it got extremely hot. You lived on deck during the day and looked forward to the cool of the night and the night breezes. Quite often people slept on deck and you were in the swimming pool a great deal.

When the four-funneled *Mauretania* first sailed to the West Indies, the stewards' starched jackets wilted in the Caribbean humidity. The buffet luncheon on deck—now a cruise ship standard—originated in an attempt to seek relief from the stifling François I dining room; the velour upholstery was a nightmare for every passenger. When the *Aquitania* went south for the first time, passengers grew accustomed to seeing cabin passageways full of sweat-drenched pillows being aired dry before the next sweltering night.

It is scarcely surprising that the first ship's public rooms to be air-conditioned were dining rooms. By the mid-thirties, the *Normandie, Nieuw Amsterdam,* and *America* all had cooled dining saloons, as did the Pacific's Matson liners and the *Orion* and *Orcades* of the Orient Line.

These last two sisterships are of particular significance for other reasons as well. When the *Orion* was commissioned in 1935, she created as great a sensation as the *Ile de France* had the previous decade. Whereas the French Line implemented a decorative "steamship style," the Orient Line was adapting a ship's interior design for the Far East's hot weather. Some of the adaptation was mechanical: in addition to her air-conditioned dining room, her most luxurious cabins (called flats instead of suites) were experimentally air-cooled as well. But in addition to awnings, fans, and punka louvers, most of the ship was cooled by an innovative design scheme.

The interiors were the work of Brian O'Rorke, originally from New Zealand. He had been engaged as the vessel's sole "lay" architect (distinguished from his naval colleagues) and was hailed as the first ever commissioned single-handedly to design and decorate an entire vessel. In fact, he was the third: Johann Poppe had been so designated by the North German Lloyd during the last decade of the nineteenth century, as had Charles Mewès for the Hamburg-Amerika Linie before World War I. But O'Rorke was certainly the first Britisher so charged, which was all the more remarkable because of his youth—he was only thirty-two when engaged—and his complete lack of naval experience. His most imporant work up to his employment with the Orient Line had been the Mayor Gallery in London's Cork Street. Nevertheless, on the strength of that as well as his avant-garde promise, Colin Anderson, one of the young directors of the Orient Line, hired him to design the *Orion*.

Anderson presented O'Rorke with a manifesto, or brief, a document containing not so much what he should achieve but what he ought to eschew. Excerpts from its list of taboos give us an insight into the decorative shipboard precepts that were apparently inescapable on Far Eastern tonnage, sometimes described as upholsterart. O'Rorke was advised to avoid curtains ("unless they had a real use"), wall-to-wall carpeting, fireplaces, "squeak and chatter decoration," and any surface requiring extensive upkeep or cleaning. Passengers on the *Orion*, it was stated, would spend five weeks on board rather than seven days, as on the Atlantic, and the directors of the company were anxious to create new interiors that would be as inviting, restful, and cool as possible. In 1933, the young architect set to work.

Critics visiting his completed ship were unanimous in their praise. *Country Life* called the *Orion* "the first British liner to be fitted out and furnished in a straightforward modern manner . . . free from whimsicalities." "A landmark in the evolution of the modern liner" trumpeted *The Architectural Review*. The prestigious *Journal of the Royal Institute of British Architects* declared that "O'Rorke has aimed at and succeeded in giving a ship-like character to the whole." Orient Line publicity about their new ship was self-satisfied, citing the *Orion* as "the reflection of the age."

Regrettably, history has somehow neglected O'Rorke's considerable achievement. Though large for the Far East, *Orion* was mid-sized by North Atlantic standards, and she was not especially fast. Moreover, O'Rorke's first ship sailed on the wrong side of the globe: the preeminence of Atlantic liners as high-visibility benchmarks has remained a historical fact of life for all architects, naval or lay. Finally, his pioneering deck treatment would become redundant almost before it could be imitated. But O'Rorke's timing was impeccable: the *Queen Mary*'s late entry into service, caused by severe economic headwinds, ensured that *Orion* would emerge as the first really modern liner produced by British yards.

It would be safe to say that this "landmark in the evolution of the modern liner" was not particularly impressive from a distance. The *Orion*'s profile was remarkable only in the context of Orient Line vessels that had sailed before her. Where they had carried twin funnels, she boasted only one, capped, as were those of her predecessors, with a black Admiralty cowl. Though she was, in fact, the largest liner ever launched for the Australian run, she seemed, despite her 23,371 tons, a small ship. Perhaps it had to do with the single funnel, perhaps it was her plethora of deck gear. Fore and aft were stolid quartets of king posts, emphasizing her cargo-handling capabilities; they gave her a freighterlike, workhorse look, at variance with contemporary liner pretensions. Down under, she was known affectionately as the "Big Tug." Yet the open weather decks lining the deckhouse, as well as the pierced hull plating near the stern, underscored her passenger-carrying role. Apart from the *Orion*'s single funnel, the only other radical change visible from over the water was the "corn color," as it was described, of her hull.

Only on board could the *Orion*'s unorthodoxy and O'Rorke's genius be fully perceived. He had grouped the First Class public rooms forward on B-deck, surrounded by an extraordinarily wide shelter deck. The *Orion*'s promenades were a full 20 feet deep where the deckhouse was narrowest, 16 feet elsewhere. Deep promenade decks were not uncommon in huge vessels; the *Aquitania* and *Ile de France* could accommodate two successive ranks of deck chairs while still providing a railside passageway for strollers. But 20-foot promenade decks on a ship with an 84-foot beam

Orient Line's *Orion* of 1935. Scarcely prepossessing
on outside, the ship represented a stunning
breakthrough in interior design and decoration for
warm-weather sailing before complete air conditioning.
As with the *Bremen* and *Europa* before her, her funnel
had to be lengthened to keep smoke off the passenger
decks. (*Author's collection*)

were remarkable. The main lounge was furthest forward, surrounded by openable windows on three sides. They were curtained in Allan Walton's abstract fabric, clear indication that O'Rorke, despite the company's manifesto, was mindful of glare from the late-afternoon tropical sun. Just behind the lounge were galleries, a U-shaped suite of narrow rooms nestled around the funnel casing. It was the space directly aft that was so innovative. Though *The Architectural Review* called it "the Ballroom," the architect had labeled it on his deckplan, tentatively and ingenuously, "dancing space." Certainly O'Rorke was closer to the truth; what he had contrived bore little resemblance to the gilded fustiness of Mewès's domed Louis XVI halls on board *Berengaria* and *Majestic*.

That dancing space was no more than a section of raised deck, floored with teak rather than parquet. Unadorned stanchions supported a naked steel ceiling; its only ornamentation were round electric globes and plain clerestory windows. Furniture was restricted to rattan tables and chairs and an upright piano cocooned within a special weatherproof case. A traditionalist blundering into the dancing space might have thought himself abruptly transported back to one of those general rooms provided for immigrant passengers years earlier. Even *The Architectural Review* balked, temporizing that it seemed "a little underdone." Yet whatever the initial response, it seemed clear that O'Rorke had crossed a kind of nautical Rubicon, linking the rigid formalism of "interior" with the clean functionalism of "exterior."

Accordion-folding glass doors tracked athwartship served as the gallery's after wall. Once folded back out of sight, gallery was united with dancing space. Moreover, the row of glass panels separating dancing space from promenade deck to either side could also be removed: they were hinged at the top and, swung inboard through a ninety-degree arc, could be secured parallel to the deckhead. The labor of raising or lowering these panels was considerable; no machinery or hoisting mechanism had been provided. It was beyond the capability of passengers or stewards, clearly the province of deckhands. Once opened, presumably east of Suez, they remained open. Passenger life on board the *Orion* flowed effortlessly outdoors and back, the very reverse of the hyperprotection built into North Atlantic promenade decks, in which passengers were barricaded against the elements. Similarly, the café farther aft had also been equipped with sliding glass doors so that the interior bar could, at will, become an intrinsic part of the courtyard of the deck surrounding the swimming pool.

These public rooms with removable walls were not merely variations of the old Veranda Cafés that had graced after ends of Atlantic prome-

O'Rorke's innovative "dancing space." The *Orion*'s indoor/outdoor continuum with half of its glazing up and half down. Notice that the teak decking is repeated indoors, uniting promenade and public room. *(Architectural Review)*

nades—those had been primarily outdoor shelters that were deserted after dark. O'Rorke's indoor/outdoor crossovers had specific roles within the *Orion*'s sociogeographical schedule both day and night. And though there was nothing new about dancing on deck aboard Far Eastern ships, extraordinary was the designed interchange between outdoor deck and interior public room.

In those rooms with no immediate deck access, O'Rorke's design scheme breathed fresh decorative air as well. The main lounge was a spare, modern chamber, cool and uncluttered. Plain white columns, devoid of bases or capitals, rose from an uncarpeted floor. Small, understated rugs of abstract design were the work of Marion Dorn. The furniture was simple and clean-lined. There, as everywhere throughout the vessel, O'Rorke made no attempt to conceal or disguise punka louvers; instead, they were chrome-plated, incorporated frankly into deckheads wherever necessary. Save in the main staircase, wood paneling was given a matt finish, avoiding the reflective chaos that would reign on both *Queen*s and the *Caronia*. Typifying O'Rorke's admirable restraint was that only in the children's playrooms did he succumb to ship's wheels, knotted ropes, and decorative portholes; there was no spurious maritime kitsch anywhere else. The only elegant exceptions were charming crystal sea-horse light fixtures, the work of his wife, Juliet, in the First Class dining room.

Perhaps not since Walter Gropius sheathed the Fagus Werk with steel and glass curtain walls in 1911 had an architect so influenced an engineered original. Poppe and Mewès, after all, had served up a réchauffé of period rooms for the German fleets; O'Rorke was creating anew. Yet as it happened, his interesting experimentation would be nullified by technology. In the ensuing decades, shipwide air-conditioning became standard on tropical and temperate ships alike, vitiating development or refinement of the open deck planning O'Rorke had espoused on the *Orion*. Though the Lido Bar on board *Norway*, for instance, lies next to the outdoor pool on Lido Deck, permanent glazing divides them; access between the two is restricted to port and starboard entrances. So, too, the shelter deck has come full thermal circle. Cooled air now circulates throughout every interior space. Cabin ports are hermetically sealed and promenade decks are enclosed or dispensed with. The *France*'s promenade has become the *Norway*'s air-conditioned mall, a cooled interior.

Though air-conditioning is a splendid technological luxury and an unparalleled boon to tropical travelers, something indefinable was removed from shipboard when it became commonplace. Not the least of these vanished delights was the design ingenuity that O'Rorke first implemented in 1935 on the *Orion*. Evocative nautical features are found in his commissions ashore. The restoration of a country house near Devon's Ashcombe Town, completed during the *Orion/Orcades* period of the late thirties, had "main lounge" columns in the drawing room and, upstairs, bedrooms that owed much of their compact ingenuity to ships' cabins. Another of his works, a beach house on the Kentish coast, included window and terrace arrangements similar to promenade deck repeats and exposed steel columns supporting a terraced deck; the spare white components recalled with little effort the neat, functional simplicity of his dancing space. The *Orion* sailed until 1963, and among architects both naval and lay, she was often referred to, simply, as the *O'Rorke*.

The only curious blind spot in O'Rorke's completed commission for the Orient Line were the outdoor pools for First and Tourist Class. They were as alike as two peas in a pod, conventional, rectangular depressions tightly enclosed in railing, very ordinary and vastly inferior in concept and execution to his other innovations on board. The only new features about them were splash baffles built in at either end. Since outdoor pools are higher up in a hull than those indoors, sea motion is amplified and more water splashes about in rough weather. (It should be noted at once that this slopping over is governed by waves alone and bears no relation to the kind of water in the pool. As the *Rotterdam* labored through a sunny but turbulent Pacific off Hawaii, a lady passenger once inquired of a crewman if the pool water were salt or fresh. When advised it was salt, she commented, "No wonder it's so rough.")

Those outdoor *Orion* pools made their debut a quarter century after the first shipboard swimming pool had appeared in the bowels of the *Olympic* in 1911. (An even earlier fixture on board a White Star ship had been a plunge bath, part of the *Adriatic*'s Turkish bath complex; we shall deal with the word *plunge* momentarily.) The term "Olympic-size" had a contrasting connotation in those days. The pool on the *Olympic* was very cramped, being only slightly smaller than the chamber containing it, and as penned in as O'Rorke's would be on the *Orion*'s open deck. A full-sized ship's railing flanked each long side, and the whole affair was so tightly thrust against the starboard shell plating that only a scant walkway remained beneath the portholes. To port, a row of changing cubicles duplicated the crowding, hard against the casing coming up from number 5 boiler room below. The pool lacked the most rudimentary facilities that we have come to expect; there was room for swimming and changing but nothing else. On a vessel notorious for lavish provision of space, the pool compartment had almost none. The reason lay not in a space shortage on

Architect and clients on the site. Brian O'Rorke (far right) stands on the deck of the completed *Orion*. Next to him is Sir Colin Anderson, the young director of the company who took a chance on an untried architect with such signal success. *(Juliet O'Rorke)*

F-deck but in contemporary attitudes about bathing in general. Swimming was refreshing, swimming was exercise, swimming built character, but swimming was not for relaxation, and a pool, whether afloat or ashore, had no need of marginal embellishment. So, in accord with Edwardian perception, the *Olympic*'s simple, rectangular pool was perfectly adequate. After all, *The Shipbuilder* had advised its readers that it was "fitted out exactly as would be an up-to-date swimming bath ashore."

Three-quarters of a century later, shipboard pools and their occupants have changed dramatically. Today's Newpassengers have returned to swimming as the ancients first conceived it, if not quite as decadent, then at least concerned with pleasure rather than prowess. The earliest pools were not mere swimming holes. Both the great bath at Mohenjo-Daro, in present-day Pakistan, and the lake-size spreads of Egypt's pharaohs had surrounds that included kiosks, pavilions, and pleasure houses. The Greeks favored warm-water bathing: history's first natural hot-spring pool, or *kolymbethra*, was located at Thermopylae. But it was the Romans who, guaranteed abundant water by their city's aqueducts, established a social focus at their baths. The largest flourished under the emperors Diocletian and Caracalla, enormous indoor complexes accommodating thousands at a time. Bathing was only part of the ritual: clients could exercise, read, gossip, attend lectures, be massaged and cleaned, or sweat away to their hearts' content. Having dripped in the *caldarium* or *sudatorium*, they would partially cool off in the *tepidarium* before braving the unwarmed waters of the natatorium. The enterprise ran as much on slave power as on the enthusiastic support of the regime. The unabashed hedonism of lolling about in warm water seems a primal indulgence, doubtless acquired *in utero*, where all mankind awaits birth nestled in soothing, amniotic suspension.

The Victorians rejected that admirable Roman prototype; antiquity's only surviving contribution to the cast-iron municipal bath was the ethic of the Spartans and a frigid natatorium. Lolling was out as water temperatures were kept ruthlessly low. In England, a dour establishment brought bathing to the masses once more, but at a horrendous price. Cloaked in grim competitiveness, pool routine was formalized. Starting blocks lined the narrow ends, racing lanes were inlaid in compelling black tile beneath the surface, and bleachers thronged pool margins. Below, a warren of subterranean passages herded incoming bathers through turnstiles, changing rooms, obligatory showers, and foot baths. Clients emerged shivering in a dank, echoing pool enclosure where the only choices were into the

Far from the sun, male passengers sport in the *Imperator*'s pool, the most monumental and handsomest indoor bath ever installed on board a ship. Mewès's "Pompeiian" scale suffers when the space is photographed with occupants. *Right,* an early convertible pool. Bathers—mixed by then—enjoy the semi-open-air *Schwimmbad* on the *Reliance* in 1926. *(Hapag-Lloyd and National Archives)*

chemically treated depths or back to the changing rooms. The institutional swimming bath was off on its own Dotheboys Hall kick.

The plunge bath, a sinister term first coined in a Marylebone Gardens public pool in the 1880s, became a British institution. Conceived in plebeian surroundings, it evolved into an upper-class symbol of male social acceptability with which public school boys were saddled long after their proletarian countrymen had settled for less harrowing—or Harrow-like—ordeals. "Plunge" said it all: abrupt immersion in icy water, presumed as bracing for the spirit as the body, somehow uplifting. When dawn breaks over the United Kingdom, the right stuff plunge into cold baths; those effeminate few who grope for the hot tap are, clearly, the wrong stuff. This was the state of swimming-bath mentality ashore when the White Star Line elected to install their pool on board the *Olympic*.

Other shipping companies followed suit, and rival shipboard pools proliferated. But with the exception of Mewès's Pompeiian Baths on board the *Imperator*-class vessels, most adhered to the *Olympic* mold, essentially confining and bleak. The *Pearl of Scandinavia*, one of the most recently renovated cruise ships, has an indoor pool that, although awash with fluorescent lighting, seems very little improved over the White Star prototype. Perhaps it has to do with the location of indoor pools in the hull—in the cellar, so to speak, so low that the main staircase seldom achieves them, far from daylight, and cheek-by-jowl with noisy machinery spaces. Only when pools emerged into the fresh air was the original Roman concept resurrected. Not surprisingly, the Italians led the way; at the same time that Brian O'Rorke ordained his pedestrian municipal baths for the *Orion*, the enterprising Italians set about installing imaginative shipboard pools *in divo*.

These would not be the cruise expedients of canvas and wood perched temporarily atop hatch covers. My grandmother recalled a passage home from Egypt on the *Adriatic* when, through the open window of her stateroom forward on Bridge Deck, she overheard the following conversation around the pool:

FIRST MAN (in the pool): Hey, George, come on in!
SECOND MAN (on deck): I better not, my throat's still sore.
FIRST MAN: Come on, just gargle with the salt water, it'll do it good.

She decided to postpone her swim until Cape Cod. Later during that passage, as the *Adriatic* left the Mediterranean, the temporary deck pool was dismantled; bathers repaired below to the plunge bath. One of them,

The first indoor shipboard pool ever.
Drained and deserted, the *Adriatic*'s
celebrated plunge bath. Directly above
the far ladder is the steel shower stall that
proved so confining to one of my
grandmother's fellow passengers.
(Harland & Wolff)

a very heavyset woman, lathered with soap and squeezed into the narrow entry to a steel shower stall. Once rinsed off, she was unable to emerge; she remained imprisoned until a bath stewardess handed her a cake of soap so that, relathered, she could slip out!

Permanent on-deck pools were almost nonexistent on liners confined to the North Atlantic, television re-creations notwithstanding. Exteriors for an episode of the television version of *Brideshead Revisited* were filmed at sea on board *Queen Elizabeth 2*, evocatively recapturing Charles Ryder and Lady Julia Flyte's celebrated midocean affair of the thirties. But there was one memorable gaffe: during a scene showing the lovers on deck, shrouded in steamer rugs, the director indiscriminately included the First Class pool throughout the shot, hopelessly compromising the historical authenticity his designers had imparted so well elsewhere, particularly in the splendid, studio-constructed cabin interiors. But then, British television has never been strong on basic transatlantic research; as Walter Lord pointed out in the illustrated edition of *A Night to Remember*, poor Lady Marjorie of *Upstairs, Downstairs* sailed to her death on R.M.S. *Titanic* booked into a nonexistent "cabin 6"!

The only cold-weather vessel to have an outdoor pool in the years between the wars was, as noted in Chapter 4, the *Normandie*. It was located on the stern, the lowest of those descending terraces that were such a splendid architectural feature of the ship. The pool's out-of-the-way location betrayed it as a novelty, an afterthought with no suitable surrounding, designed for Tourist Class or crew. Its only sustained use came during the *Normandie*'s two Rio cruises and over wartime summers while the vessel was tied up at Pier 88 on Manhattan's west side.

But permanent on-deck installations did appear on sunny routes. The first was on the after end of the 1926 *Roma*; on the *Augustus* that came into service the following year, the pool was located just aft of the second funnel. Both were for First Class only. The S.S. *Arandora Star* was the first cruise ship ever to have a permanent outdoor pool placed in the after well-deck when she was redesigned exclusively for cruising in 1929. Grace Lines's four *Santa* ships had outdoor pools; so did the *Resolute* and *Reliance*, the German cruise ships. But it was on two record-breakers, *Rex* and *Conte di Savoia*, that the Italians pulled out all the stops.

It was clear that, before the Genoese or Triestine naval architects set pencil to paper, they had absorbed three great truths about swimming pools. The first was that the Edwardians' plunge bath ethic could be supplanted by sybaritic indolence. The second was that for adults, pools exert powerful yet complex attractions. Of those drawn to them, few swim:

On board the fictional S.S. *Constantia,*
Jeremy Irons and Diana Quick huddle in
steamer rugs, betrayed by the *QE2*'s
First Class swimming pool. *(London
Express)*

instead, they doze, read, sunbathe, rest, eat, drink, or gossip—a resurgence, if you will, of the Caracallian ethos. Some undress, others stay fully clothed; as many wish shade as care for sun. Some enter the water but merely soak. (On board Home Lines's *Oceanic*, it was discovered that the children's wading pool was invariably monopolized by their elders as a dank conversation pit. As a result, on their *Atlantic* to follow, the company created a large shallow pool for adults, and the margins of all cruise ships' pools today are surrounded by a low bench/dike, creating a wet area periodically awash with pool water displaced by the ship's motion.) If not actually swimming in the pool, all passengers share a compulsion to be near it.

Having absorbed these first two truths, the Italians coped with the third: commitment to *gran' lusso* shipboard swimming devoured deck space. More than a pool was involved; there would have to be an even larger lido. "Lido" is, appropriately, an Italian original, the name of the area encompassing the beaches surrounding Venice's lagoon. It has insinuated itself into our language, overwhelmingly on board cruise ships, as a space for sunning, showering, drinking, and eating as well as swimming.

Those huge *Rex* and *Conte di Savoia* lidos not only were groundbreakers, they would influence all successive shipboard pools as well. They were possible because of warm weather on the transatlantic route between New York and the Mediterranean. Life on board both ships was spent predominantly outdoors, most nearly duplicating the sun-drenched lallygagging that Newpassengers associate with shipboard today. I sailed to Algeciras on the American Export Line's *Constitution* in 1962 and well remember the novelty of sunny—if windy!— al fresco lunches around the pool, in stark contrast to conventional steamer midday meals consumed deep within the hull.

The *Rex* sailed first, a vast spread of lido dominating her after decks. The First Class pool ran fore-and-aft, its rounded ends delineated within a decorative grill rather than hemmed in with ship's railing. To either side and aft of the pool was an extensive piazza, dense with umbrellas, deck chairs, and even some of those hooded wicker sentry boxes so popular on Continental beaches from the Lido to Silt. If there was, as yet, no formal poolside catering, a remarkable rearrangement of deck priorities had been established: no longer a space for a stroll or a game of deck tennis, the *Rex*'s lido was a fixed, outdoor seating area in the tradition of an Alpine sun terrace. It was the forerunner of dozens of today's lidos on which passengers themselves—and their towels, chaises, and umbrellas —are as much a part of superstructure dressing as lifeboats, ventilators,

Models ape passengers on board the
latest *Nieuw Amsterdam*. Lolling is in,
swimming is out, in the pool complexes
of today's cruise ships. *(Holland America
Line)*

nly half empty and devoid of passengers
Genoa, the *Rex*'s *piscina di prima
asse,* a capacious bathing pool set,
nsibly, in an equally capacious lido.
ight, as it appeared at sea, the same lido
ronged with bathers et al. *(Italian Line)*

and funnels. The focus, as always, was the pool itself, both the First Class one described in the case of the *Rex* and another for Special Class, a smaller facility located one deck down toward the stern on the *Ponte dei Salone*.

Only the top two classes on the Italian flagship had outdoor pools; there was simply not enough room within those conventional Atlantic silhouettes to triplicate—let alone quadruplicate—identical facilities for all. The *Conte di Savoia*'s lido was forward, up between the funnels, the same location as on the *Augustus* and *Roma*. The pool was at the center of two banks of terraced steps that served for spectators or sunbathers without actually reaching the water; visually, though, they gave the effect of majestic marble staircases descending into an ancient natatorium. Railings surrounding the water were discreet, with no broad varnished handrail as on the *Orion*; hence, they were almost invisible. The *Conte di Savoia*'s pool was ringed with equipment for games: a diving board aft, a slide forward, and, bridging it midway along its length, a sturdy, horizontal pole—at least 10 inches in diameter—for exercises or aquatic gymnastics. Umbrella-shaded tables and chairs lined either side of the pool and one level higher was a participatory gallery: peripheral margins of the deck above served as walkways surrounding all four sides of the pool, connected to its margins by decorative staircases topped with flags. Spectators above could watch the pool inboard or the horizon to either side. The Italians had designed a multilevel, intrafunnel amphitheater, as significant for cruise ships to come as had been the *Oceanic*'s hurricane deck sixty years earlier.

Direct and flourishing descendants of that *Conte di Savoia* prototype are found today on board ships of the Royal Caribbean Cruise Line. Since RCCL's fleet remains almost exclusively in the Caribbean, the company has never installed retractable Magrodomes; their pools remain open to perennial blue skies. And whereas other companies have offered *Rex*-style pools aft of the superstructure as well as *Conte di Savoia*–style upper deck pools, RCCL, save for a crew pool at the stern, has confined their passengers' swimming area to an incredible upper deck, as ambitious as it is successful. Of the company's first three vessels, two were returned to Finland for lengthening; but it is the fourth, the *Song of America*, the same vessel that I saw under construction at Helsinki in 1981, that embodies the latest Wärtsilä refinement. The Finnish naval architects had enormous reserves of top-deck space at their disposal, for the *Song of America* is longer and beamier than her trio of predecessors; the two verticals encompassing the horizontal summit—mast and funnel—are

220   LINERS TO THE SUN

The *Conte di Savoia*'s heroic midships pool.
The ventilators bracketing the forward stack have a pleasing
art deco look, and the railings down each flight of steps
down to the water are skeletal—without mahogany tops—
so that they almost disappear. Clearly, this pool
foreshadows the Royal Caribbean Cruise Line's
top-deck installations of half a century later. *(Italian
Line)*

nearly 300 feet apart. It is as well they are: a huge, one-class passenger load has to be accommodated poolside at the same time. The amphitheater contains two pools separated by an expanse of varnished deck that serves as a dance floor after dark. There are outdoor bars at either end of each level and, as there was on the *Conte di Savoia*, an encircling upper promenade providing vantage points for spectator/sunbathers as well as shaded seating for lunching below.

Aft, there is a second balcony, if you will, a unique profile feature. Wärtsilä called it, originally, a funnel pavilion, but RCCL, allying Nordic and monarchic associations, preferred Viking Crown Lounge. No other ship in the world offers anything like them, and they have become invaluable, corporate eye-catchers for RCCL. Seen from below or glimpsed in a brochure photograph, Viking Crown Lounges appear as tethered flying saucers floating serenely above the vessel. Most passengers clamber up for a look at least once during their cruise. The first three of these elevated bars were appendages, semicircular lookouts facing aft. Designed primarily for evening use, they were achieved by outside staircases that, when ascended by lady passengers, allowed stiff breezes to disarray hair or, worse, blow skirts up as in a carnival fun house. Moreover, a premium was charged for Crown Lounge drinks even though they arrived in a throwaway plastic glass: no water for a dishwasher had been piped up that high.

But the *Song of America*'s Viking Crown Lounge, completely encircling the smokestack, boasts interior access by stair or elevator as well as plumbing galore. The glare of the earlier lounges, their ceilings sheathed in highly reflective material, has been reduced, though the noise level has not—even in broad daylight an amplified combo batters away. One hundred and fifty passengers can be accommodated at circular tables facing aft or on alcove sofas to either side, their backs against the casing. Sadly, the exhilarating, forward prospect has been furnished with the most banal seating: a score of bar stools are crammed along the glass. But at least those barflies, customarily denied a vista other than bottles or televised football, are rewarded with a splendid panorama below. It satisfies all the criteria of a public square in the classic tradition—formal, appealing, and capacious, an acre of ingenious, carpeted sun bowl. Extraordinarily, that greensward never seems crowded even though more than a thousand passengers could, conceivably, gather there at one time. However vast, it is not monotonous, its varying terraced levels deftly integrated. Compass deck wings to either side—sun walks, they are called—overlook pool and sea. Throughout mornings and afternoons, hundreds of passengers are absorbed by the space, roasting in the sun, dozing in the shade, or dabbling contentedly in one of two seagoing *tepidaria*, neither one of which bears the slightest resemblance to a plunge bath. Lunch is within easy reach beneath a shaded awning aft of the funnel and can be brought amidships beneath one of the sun walks. It is, quite simply, a superbly designed shipboard space, possible only for the tropics and one that also works, surprisingly, after dark. My first contact with Wärtsilä's ultimate upper deck was on board the *Nordic Prince* during a midnight buffet as the ship sailed from Barbados. One's attention was divided, precisely as the designers had intended, between preparations for departure at the adjacent pier and festivities inboard.

The only false note is the artificial green underfoot. Though it makes for a pleasing aerial view, Astroturf has its drawbacks. It is, admittedly, nonskid, inexpensive, and cool to bare feet, imparting a kind of putting-green patina to the upper decks of many warm-weather vessels, the *Norway* and *Scandinavia* among them. Yet on several counts, the material is unsatisfactory: it retains litter and water, repeated overnight soakings and daylight bleachings promote discoloration, and pale pathways appear where traffic is heaviest. Once so scarred, unlike conventional decking, it cannot be sanded and refinished. (It is especially surprising to find it in such quantity on board RCCL vessels, for their wooden decks are, without question, the most superbly maintained of any in the world. Made of Douglas fir rather than teak, they are varnished, and I am told that a specialist refinishing crew travels on endless circuit from one RCCL ship to another, keeping those glistening decks pristine. They have one disadvantage: when wet, they are slippery, which accounts for the liberal use of black friction strips laid down near all entrances indoors.)

Almost invariably, tropical rig spawns white-painted hulls: only marginally cooler, they *look* cooler. Companies often band their hulls with blue or red racing stripes, although these are expensive items to repaint. On large ships, pale hulls can be aesthetically inadvisable. I have already commented on the *QE2's* abortive gray, post-Falkland coat. Somehow, the *Michelangelo* and *Raffaello* made it work, perhaps because they remained spotless; masters of New York and Genoa tugs used to drape their bows with clean white canvas before nudging Italian Line flagships in and out of port. Most Caribbean piers are fronted with surplus black truck tires, and each white hull that docks there inevitably sails with an unsightly row of smudgy circular imprints just above the boot-topping. Holland America has done well with dark blue: from a distance, their hulls look black, providing a nice link with their North Atlantic past. Norwegian Caribbean Lines made the wise decision not to bring their huge *Norway-*

Genesis of the Crown Lounge. Under
construction at Wärtsilä, one of the
earliest prototypes—facing aft only—c
the first three RCCL ships. Its exterior
stairway proved bothersome to female
passengers ascending at night. *Left,* on
the *Song of America,* an amplified
Crown Lounge surrounds the funnel
completely, its tinted glass reminiscent
a "big brother" Darth Vader. *Opposite
top,* the view from inside. *Opposite
bottom,* looking back aft from the
bridge, the spread of terrace and pools
(the second is out of sight beyond the
dance floor) provides ample and
well-designed space for hundreds of
Caribbean passengers. *(Wärtsilä's
Helsinki Shipyard and Royal Caribbea
Cruise Line)*

ex-*France* into color compatibility with their other white hulls. Instead, they chose royal blue, its final electric hue determined only after weeks of experimentation at HAPAG-Lloyd's Bremerhaven yard. Choosing an appropriate Caribbean shade by northern winter light was challenging, a kind of chromatic crapshoot. It looked odd in the North Sea but works well in the Caribbean.

Tropical rig has influenced the interior palette as well. Since most of today's ships are fitted out in northern yards, cabin and public room mock-ups are evaluated by incandescent or fluorescent light rather than the relentless sun that will illuminate their progeny for life. Perhaps for this reason, newbuilding interiors are ablaze with color, some of it ill-advised. If one characteristic distinguishes old public rooms from new, it is polychromatic overindulgence. Bright shipboard colors expertly juxtaposed can be exciting: the *QE2*'s embarkation lobby, with its lime green sofa rising out of black carpet beneath silver-gray concentric rings above, is stunning, a splendid passenger introduction to the vessel. But too often on some newbuilding, no overall design rationale has been established. Lounges, lobbies, and stairwells within visual touch compete rather than complement. There is a prevailing school of lounge decorators that favors yellow and orange highlighted with Miami gold and rust. More recently, one finds the spectrum's mauve bands exploited for effect—magenta, plum, and violet predominate, sometimes leavened with pink, that most dangerous choice. Lacking most sorely is dignity.

These efflorescences spring from attempts to pander to an archetypal passenger/consumer. Though foreign-built and foreign-owned, cruise ships sail with American passenger loads, a marketing constant dating back to the twenties. In consequence, owners encourage their designers to adhere closely to what they, the owners, perceive as America's decorative ideal. At stake is the approval of a specific passenger composite that I once found delineated in a Wärtsilä memorandum: a middle-aged, middle-western American housewife. (Presumably, in line with her other centrist characteristics, she is middle class as well, though socioeconomic value judgments of this kind are rare in Scandinavia.) She is the cruise lines' mythic client-at-large, queen of America's demographic Reno/Trenton heartland, the prototypical passenger to please. And it is in an attempt to define the elusive parameters of her taste that today's public rooms are awash with Sunbelt glitz.

No vessel is immune from this disease. Within the shipping fraternity, it has a name. In the spring of 1984, the Sitmar ship *Fairsea*—a converted Cunarder launched as the *Carinthia*—went into Newport News for a public

versize and overbright. The mural on
ard *Song of America* indicating the
trance to the Can-Can Lounge.
uthor's collection)

room overhaul. It was more than a cosmetic renovation: the promenade deck lounges, casino, library, and grill were rearranged. Corridor traffic flow was improved, the casino was enlarged for live gambling, and second-sitting passengers were provided with more waiting space before their after-dinner entertainment. Several months before the scheduled work, I sailed on two consecutive cruises on board *Fairsea* and, during the first, was fortunate enough to share a dining table with one of the company's naval architects. When I asked him how the new rooms would be decorated, he replied that he had not seen any renderings, only that they were to be "Americanized." Though a Dutchman employed by an Italian company founded by a Russian and headquartered in Monaco, he conjured up, with one nationalistic buzzword, the *Fairsea*'s third decorative reincarnation.

The first had been born with the ship at John Brown's yard on the Clyde, Cunard's postwar Atlantic blend of chintz and Chippendale. When Sitmar bought her for cruising in 1970, shipyard workers at Trieste gutted the hull and installed completely new Italian interiors. (They did not expunge all traces of *Carinthia*; to this day, cinema levels on board are marked DRESS CIRCLE and STALLS and, for some extraordinary reason, the dining rooms are still called Grosvenor and Dorchester.) But the new Olivetti-modern interiors carried both *Fairsea* and *Fairwind*—her identical sister, the former *Sylvania*—through the seventies.

Then a new consort, the *Fairsky*, appeared. Built in and for the eighties, she was a product of the same French yard that had built Home Lines's *Atlantic* three years earlier. Tropically rigged, she would replace *Fairsea* on Sitmar's lucrative summer service in Alaska; henceforth, the older vessel would remain in tropical waters, and so, in the spring of 1984, she was sent to Newport News for "Americanization." (It was only coincidentally an American yard. Ships can be "Americanized" anywhere in the world; even the labor and materials were imported wholesale from Italy.)

Admittedly, after twelve years in operation, the *Fairsea*'s public rooms were in need of attention. Fabrics and carpeting, muted to begin with, were shopworn. Every public room was renovated, save the library. It had been a favorite of the owner, Boris Vlasov, and his designers were instructed to leave its decoration and furnishings intact. It is certainly a comfortable room, full of sleep-inducing chairs, but unfortunately bereft of writing desks. There is no provision for writing letters anywhere on board *Fairsea*, not even in the cabins; on my cruises, letter writers battled with bridge players for possession of the card room's four tables.

The other public room one wishes Vlasov had spared was the Grill, the little restaurant off Harry's Bar, one of the most successful spaces I have ever seen on board any vessel and a facility unique to Sitmar. The Grill served small and extremely well-made pizzas at noon and during the evening. The room was paneled and a dozen tables, complete with cloths and flowers, were spread along the room's three levels, all with a view through the promenade deck windows to port. Though popular, it was never overcrowded and fulfilled its function admirably. At Newport News, a replacement appeared in its stead but without the charm of the original.

It was on board *Fairsea* that I discovered an amazing decorative fact of life—the paradoxical effect of interior tropical rig. My two back-to-back cruises carried me through climatic extremes, from Alaska to Panama. One wet overcast day, when rain-sodden clouds hung low over Ketchikan's wooden slopes, I went ashore to visit the newly arrived *Pacific Princess*. The on-board contrast was remarkable. Her interior tropical rig was a marvelous antidote to the murk outside, her public rooms as bright and cheerful on that gloomy day as the *Fairsea*'s were cheerlessly subdued. But, a fortnight later, anchored off Cabo San Lucas, those same under-stated Milanese interiors provided blessed relief from the brilliance out-doors—the cerulean glare of Baja sky, the water's glitter, and the sere ocher of hills surrounding the bay.

A great truth dawned: I suddenly realized that newbuilding designers have it all wrong. Ships confined to tropical itineraries do not require exotic interiors; there is color enough on deck without gilding the lily indoors. Tropical rig need not—indeed, *should* not—prevail in public rooms and cabins. So roll up that citrus chenille, uproot all giant cacti, defoliate those parrot-filled palms, unseat your rum-barrel barstools, pluck away coconut-frond thatching, short-circuit the steel drums, and release every yellow bird in sight! Tropical appurtenances should be encouraged only on ships confined to the north; vessels bound for West Indian or South Pacific islands have no reason to install wholesale facsimiles on board.

On world-class vessels, at least, designers have seen the light. I first encountered the latest *Europa* fitting out at Bremen, too early to determine her public-room flavor. But when she visited New York in the fall of 1983, a brief tour convinced me that HAPAG-Lloyd had grasped the right end of the decorative divining rod. The Club Belvedere, overlooking the bridge, one of those crescent-shaped observation lounges, is finished elegantly in beige and white. The *Europa* lounge aft boasts a sepia palette, sofas, chairs, and tables of a traditional design and look that would have seemed

Fairsea before "Americanization." Teatime in the South Sea Lounge amidst decoration from a past decade. Although shabby, after a dozen years in service, those interiors had the advantage of restraint. *Below,* anchored in Ketchikan, the Sitmar ship seen from the decks of the newer and positively glowing *Pacific Princess. (Author's collection)*

at home on board her namesake of the thirties. Her Clipper Bar is decorated with historical paintings and ephemera. Though the *Europa* spends time in the Greek Islands and South Pacific, her interiors do not sport a tropical rig, and she is all the better for it. Just as her public rooms are not "Americanized," neither is her passenger list: the *Europa* carries German travelers almost exclusively. But Holland America's *Nieuw Amsterdam* caters largely to Americans. She is a pleasing hybrid, sane, traditional, yet refreshing. Her high-tech lines enclose a restful interior where decorative peace prevails. She is filled with history, the detail authentic, the touch deft. Only occasionally have the designers strayed off course; but if the Peartree Club is too purple and green, the Crow's Nest and Lido remain sensibly restrained.

One of travel's delights is the opportunity to glimpse cultures and styles other than one's own. That used to happen not only abroad but also on board the vessels that took us there. Today, however, the ships of only three companies have retained their own distinctive nationality: the *Europa, Queen Elizabeth 2,* and Holland America's surviving triumvirate *Rotterdam, Nieuw Amsterdam,* and *Noordam;* the rest, sadly, have all been "Americanized." The Norwegians seem to have capitulated with only a token struggle. Ships of the Royal Caribbean Cruise Line bear the scars. The Miami management has prevailed over the owners' Norwegian-ness, feeling, perhaps justifiably, that it is better equipped to gauge American popular taste.

The minutes of a meeting held in Oslo's owners' club, the *Shippingklubben,* in February 1981 point up this Nordic-American dilemma. On the agenda was an evaluation of decorative guidelines for the company's fourth vessel, *Song of America.* Of the fourteen men present, only one was American; the rest were Scandinavian.

> During the subsequent discussion, MS [Moritz Skaugen, an owner] pointed out that the ship, in spite of her name and American musicals selected, should have decorations in suitable places around the ship which stressed the Norwegian aspect of our operation. SBE [Sigvart Erikesen, Oslo's RCCL general manager] referred to the Harris study, where the Norwegian maritime reputation was listed as one of the major reasons for booking an RCCL ship. AW [Anders Wilhelmsen, another owner] felt that folklore motives with Hardanger fiddle were out but accepted Norwegian marine decoration such as Leif Erikson, etc. Americans' Norwegian heritage was also referred to and accepted as a decorative element on the ship. [Migration by ship and settling in U.S.]

In the same discussion Showboat motive was suggested used at the end of the corridors instead of the Viking ship presently in use on the other ships.

The underlying disparity of choice is clear: Hardanger fiddle versus riverboat kitsch.

On other ships of the line, the company's attempt to wed pop appeal with ancient cliché is uneasy at best. Designers were apparently instructed to embrace the past. But these are not scrupulous re-creations: one finds no Palladian lounge, no François I dining saloons, no Jacobean smoking rooms. They are bland retreads of nineteenth-century maritime interiors, as though *Ile de France* and *Orion* had never sailed.

A glimpse of the H.M.S. Pinafore Dining Room on board RCCL's *Sun Viking* serves as a case in point. Turquoise Naugahyde upholstery battles it out with white Austrian shades shrouding windows to either side. The subdued carpet turns out to be woven to resemble teak decking, splined and pegged. An enormous ship's wheel dominates one end of the dining room, the other is walled with a mural of square-riggers. The decorative brightwork that Brian O'Rorke hoped to banish from public rooms has resurfaced: the mural is fenced in brass, and electrified oil lamps wink from the walls. Varnished oval columns, girdled in white hemp, have been tricked up as spars while deckhead and bulkhead are united by artfully scrolled knees.

This broadside of nautical eclecticism is overwhelming, a kind of mischievous, maritime travesty. By the same token, might not Warren and Wetmore's New York Yacht Club, with its stone-framed galleon windows and 'tween-deck dining room beams, be similarly criticized? Not quite. The Yacht Club's salvation, apart from its exquisite detailing, is its site. Whereas one accepts maritime resonances in a structure firmly aground in Manhattan schist, spurious duplication of sailing ship features within a diesel-driven room at sea breaks sensibility's back. There is talk around Wärtsilä's design ateliers of a fifth, bigger RCCL vessel, code-named *Song of the World*. One hopes that the Norwegians will be better represented below decks. Most ironic about the Wärtsilä design choices for RCCL is that, above deck, those very successful open-air pools represent contemporary Scandinavian taste at its best, while below, Formicoco predominates. Saddest of all, Newpassengers are welcomed on board by reproductions of the romantic make-believe of the shopping centers and malls they ought to have left behind.

But enough: tropical rig, exterior and interior, is here to stay. Other shipboard conundrums require unraveling and thence we shall proceed. The largest proportion of cubic footage on board every cruise ship is devoted to private rather than public rooms. Beyond lobby and lounge, far from pool and promenade, below stairs or elevator, along die-straight passageways, down alleyway cul-de-sacs to port and starboard, lie hundreds of anonymous doors, individual holds housing human cargo. These are the cabins, each a sanctum sanctorum; let us examine why they are the way they are and what goes on inside.

*Along quiet little streets in
which are hidden the rows of snug
domains, so neat and excellent, in
which fans whirr silently to cool
the highly sensitive occupant, and
bath taps twinkle and glazing gleams. . . .*

—E. P. LEIGH-BENNETT,
HISTORY OF A HOUSE FLAG

*Sorry no cabin changes
available. Ship is booked to
capacity.*

—SIGN PERMANENTLY
AFFIXED TO PURSER'S DESK
ON BOARD *S.S. Rotterdam,*
REGARDLESS OF LOAD

6.
Cabin Fever

The cabin is every passenger's castle. Whether sunworshipper, shopper, jogger, or dancer, whether recluse, honeymooner, reader, or invalid, cruise passengers share one overwhelming commonality about their time on board: most of it will be spent within that unique shipboard abode, the compact space that is a cabin. On the thrust stage of the theater of cruising, the cabin is the players' retreat, their inviolable inner below. Moreover, it is a soothing space, secure and private yet united by porthole with the changing seas and skies outside.

Quiz a random sample of passengers after a cruise: when asked what they best recall, all will be most articulate about their cabins, more so than about itinerary, dining companions, entertainment, or excursions. And just as the memory of a cabin endures long after the cruise, so it exists in the imagination long before the cruise even begins. Ships' cabins are the only traveling accommodations assigned specifically the moment passage is booked: a passenger ticket carries with it the guarantee of a chosen space reserved, a contract wherein the company assures its clients of a shipboard headquarters that will be theirs for the duration of the voyage.

No other passengers enjoy such territorial prearrangements with their carriers. Bus or train travelers seldom know where they will end up, the location most often a last-minute resolution achieved by eminent domain. Those who fly are confined within one large, collective cabin, occupying nearly identical seats assigned just before take-off. But a ship's passenger has preempted his or her on-board turf months ahead: the brochure, with its plan or picture, assumes the role of voyage talisman, treasured against the day of embarkation. Even though the promised cabin is no more than one of a row of identically colored smudges along any of several decks, its location—adjacency to shell plating reigns supreme in its importance—size, and contents are evaluated endlessly. Intriguing shipboard glyphs—the minuscule symbols for berth, closet, sofa, or tub—must be scrutinized. The moment that cabin letter/numeral has been assigned, a proprietary bond links it to the prospective occupant. It is the voyage's encoded lodestar, adorning each luggage label, heralded in corridor signs, and finally, distinguishing the cabin entrance itself. In a compelling way, once that door is opened for the first time, one enters and is already at home.

Significantly, despite what may be seen as the cabin's alien nauticality, even inexperienced Newpassengers find themselves instantly and familiarly comfortable. And the cruise lines' archetypal client—that midwestern matron conjured up in the preceding chapter—assumes her most formidable guise as cabin chatelaine. She knows nothing about naval architecture, less about navigation, and remains vague about what pleases her in the way of food, entertainment, or excursion; but in the matter of curtains, mattresses, closets, shelves, bureaus, showers, and scrupulous housekeeping, she is expert *sans pareil*. After only a week's stay on board, she becomes devastatingly familiar with every cabin fixture and faucet, and an awkward closet or wayward drawer will rankle long after the euphoria of a tropical sunset has vanished.

Shipping companies, well aware of their future clients' scrutiny, hope with each new vessel to have created the perfect cabin. Once its design has been accepted on paper, a full-scale mock-up is erected at the yard, fitted out with the proposed furniture, carpeting, upholstery, and curtains. A bathroom—complete save for actual water—is attached to these ghost

The "inner below." The author's wife at
home, cabin 730, *Nordic Prince.*
(Author's collection)

cabins and electric "sunlight" floods in through the ports. Outside, a length of prototypical passageway has been contrived so that the visiting ship-owner can approach and ponder at length this most critical of his vessel's interior spaces. Photographed cabin mock-ups are invaluable for his public relations people during that barren visual wasteland between keel-laying, launch, and delivery, when there is nothing to share with the press save those fanciful public-room renderings so exaggerated and distorted as to be meaningless.

Obviously, large cabins command higher tariffs and Old Guard ships offer roomier "standard" quarters than Newpassenger tonnage, where a high passenger density restricts spatial largesse. For instance, Royal Viking and Royal Caribbean have Wärtsilä hulls of nearly identical dimensions, but whereas *Royal Viking Star* accommodates only seven hundred passengers, *Song of America* absorbs twice that number. On more than one line, the cabin-as-kennel philosophy is allied—unwisely, as far as I am concerned—with hard-nosed business practice. Passengers idling in roomy cabins, marketing strategists opine, are not spending money (i.e., drinking in the bars and public rooms or buying gewgaws in the shops). Hence, claustrophobic quarters will propel passengers out into spacious, as well as income-producing, areas of the vessel.

In fact, passengers do not behave this way at all. I discovered long ago that on board every ship, regardless of cabin pretensions, from five to seven in the late afternoon, during that languid interval between sun and soirée, public rooms are deserted. Passengers are resting, reading, or bathing in their cabins, withdrawn contentedly into their inner below. That potent cabin mystique always wins out.

I sailed for a week on board the *Nordic Prince* booked into cabin 730, one of a hundred identical category-D, standard outside staterooms on Main Deck. When first surveyed, the space allotted for two passengers, their beds, belongings, bureaus, and bath, was jarring. Admittedly, the cabin did have a large window (two subsidiary passenger decks make do with ports), which, ironically, served largely to emphasize the dimensional paucity of the area it illuminated. The window's length was only marginally shorter than the combined widths of the two berths (running athwartship) and table placed directly under it. Of necessity, unpacking became a systaltic ordeal and placing an emptied suitcase beneath the berth required acrobatic ingenuity. Seated on our beds *en face*, my wife and I had to interlock our knees with care in the trough—there is no other word to describe it—separating us. Nevertheless, in short order, we learned to live comfortably and happily in cabin 730.

Cabins have always exercised this magic. In a previous chapter, I suggested that Atlantic ships were most clearly distinguished from land-based hotels because they accommodated a broad social spectrum within one hull. Despite cruising's single class, another distinction exists to the present: floor space is restricted, ceilings are lower, bathrooms are crowded, and beds are smaller and closer together. Conversely, the cabin also offers compensation: it is ingenious, pleasing, and, somehow, immensely cozy. On newbuilding in particular, cabins are even smaller. With miniaturization has come increased complexity, and every cabin nowadays is wired for air-conditioning, temperature controls, outlets for electrical shavers and hair-dryers, television or radio controls, telephone and public address speaker —a far cry from half a century ago, when passenger mechanical dalliance was restricted to opening a port or fiddling with a fan or punka louver.

Predictably, cruise lines are proudest of their top accommodations. Public relations firms hired to court the press invariably hasten travel writers to the hushed confines of the upper decks to tour a sample suite. These are scarcely cabins—they are more like hotel penthouses, elaborate spreads complete with private balconies and every conceivable luxury. The service is as lavish as the acreage: Royal Viking stewardesses assigned to look after these extravagant quarters are advised in training manuals that their clients should be given "anything they want," largesse that, presumably, falls short of droit du seigneur. A company's preoccupation with its most splendid offerings is understandable. Flying the luxury flag not only lures prospective clients away from competitors but impresses the groundlings as well. Even if those treated to a brochure glimpse of these suites never book one, their existence on board feeds a kind of vicarious tribal snobbism, most especially on a carrier where the price of every fellow passenger's ticket is common knowledge.

In truth, there is no shipboard accommodation that guarantees nirvana; every cabin has its share of surprises. On two different vessels of the Holland America Line, I found that upper as well as lower categories had as many quirks as perks. For a Panama Canal transit aboard *Veendam*, I was assigned cabin 618, the largest and most splendid on board. When the ship had been the *Argentina* of the Moore-McCormack Line, cabin 618 had housed the ship's surgeon. When the Dutch took over, they refurbished the space, reserving it as a possible haven in which one of the Dutch royals might freshen up during a state visit. But the small hours revealed why the Americans had assigned cabin 618 to a ship's officer: it lay directly beneath the galley, and for much of the night, a penetrating lullaby serenaded its occupants as early-morning cooks dragged containers and cases across the steel deck overhead. Conversely, when honeymooning on board *Rotterdam*, my wife and I occupied cabin 735, which was down very far aft on B-deck in a modest section of the ship called Broadway because so many of the ship's entertainers were accommodated there. We were so close to the waterline that during an October gale off Hatteras the porthole approximated the view through a washing machine door. But regardless of the weather, that little cabin came equipped with demonic stereo: from aft came the threshing of propellers, from below, the unceasing reverberations of the engine room. Most puzzling, like some surreal dream fragment, was a recurring siren, as though a berserk policeman were racing amongst the turbines in a squad car. The captain solved the mystery one night at dinner when he informed us that what we heard was the ring of the duty engineer's telephone, which was amplified thus to cut through the racket.

Most interesting to me are median-range cabins, where one can see what the average passenger's cruise dollar buys. I propose to examine in depth those of a ship on which I have never sailed but which I saw under construction: newbuilding 234 of the Aalborg Werft A/S, better known to the public as the *Tropicale*. Though I had missed seeing her huge single funnel hoisted aboard that early morning, I had inspected her cabins, both in mock-up and undecorated steel, at length. *Tropicale* is the first new ship ordered by Carnival Cruise Lines; three more would join her in service in the years to follow, vessels replacing the aging *Mardi Gras*, *Carnivale*, and *Festivale*, which, though popular, would see the end of their operational lives by the end of the century.

The *Tropicale* flaunts a profile as modern as those of her fleetmates are dated. They were all built for other companies in the fifties and sixties, conventional tonnage of the period with a large, single stack amidships on the order of the *Caronia*. But the *Tropicale*'s funnel is aft, a branching structure à la *France*. Though its side vents are, visually, too abruptly truncated, it has an aerodynamic refinement, a round scoop vent facing forward that adds slipstream impetus in dispelling stack gas far out to either side and over the stern. It works well; at Aalborg, one of the welders working on the stack's top section reported to me that his torch flame was continually blown out by air currents passing through the funnel even as it lay at rest on the pier.

She is just as modern below decks. Of her 511 cabins, 12 are deluxe, 314 are outside, and 185 are inside. Each of the dozen suites includes a hidden third berth. All inside cabins can absorb either a third or fourth passenger if necessary. (It is thus that cruise lines can publicize an enviable superfluity of passengers, identified in the trade as "over 100 percent

Good public rooms do not good profiles make. In an early model of the *Tropicale,* the line of oversize ports just forward of the logo are level. *Below,* on the actual vessel, they appear to tumble. Why? Because they follow the descending interior terraces of the Tropicana Lounge on Empress deck forward, with an asymmetrical 5-4-5 porthole sequence.

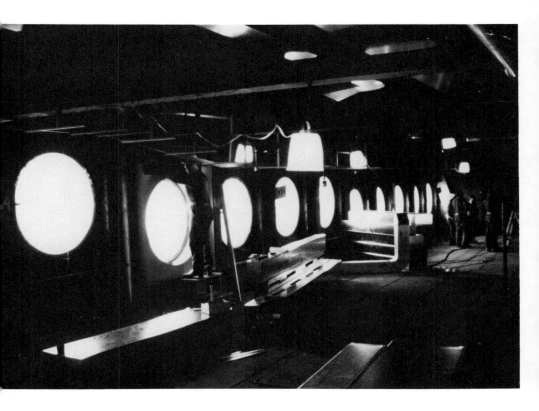

Sensible within, the effect without is disquieting: serial rows along a ship's flank should adhere to the horizontal. Alas, the look persists. *Below,* on the *Holiday,* seen during her fitting-out in 1984, again just forward of the logo, the outsize ports are lozenge-shaped but they still tumble. *(Carnival Cruise Lines and author's collection)*

Typical cabin arrangement forward on *Tropicale*'s
Main Deck. Note that as the hull narrows, the cabin
walls do not curve with the shell plating but continue
their modular integrity. *(Aalborg Werft)*

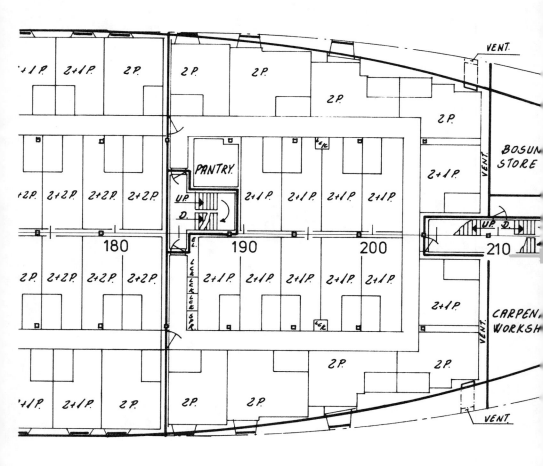

capacity." That mathematical impossibility serves as indication that optional bunks, customarily folded out of sight into the bulkhead, are occupied for especially inexpensive or popular cruises.) The *Tropicale* has no single cabins whatsoever: just as America is geared, logistically and emotionally, to couples, so the Newpassenger archetype is the twosome. On board all five vessels of the Norwegian Caribbean Lines—including the vast *Norway* —there are only six single cabins, all of them on the little *Southward*. On the other hand, Old Guard ships, which cater to large numbers of widows, have several dozen single cabins each, though the exact number is difficult to determine; some Royal Viking one-berth cabins, for instance, are frequently assigned to entertainers. But single passengers traveling alone in the Caribbean on Newpassenger tonnage either have to bunk in with friends (or strangers) or pay a rate-and-a-half for the privilege of occupying a double cabin alone.

As though underscoring newbuilding's focus on couples, it is only inferior cabins—small and inside—that absorb additional occupants; most of those on the outside accommodate two only. These *Tropicale* outside doubles are surprisingly large considering the vessel spends its year booking Newpassengers on one- or two-week itineraries only. Old Guard Royal Viking outside ordinaries encompass approximately 160 square feet; so, incredibly, do outside ordinaries on board *Tropicale*. The cabin width, fore-and-aft, is 9 feet 10 inches, and the depth, from corridor to shell plating, is 16½ feet. That 160-square-foot rectangle includes, of course, a bathroom occupying an inside corner. It is a small one, but the choice of compact bathroom space is deliberate. In an area where square inches are crucial, designers are convinced that passengers will happily endure a crowded shave or shampoo in return for more lavish floor space between berths. By way of historical comparison, a deluxe cabin on board *Gallia*, Cunard's last iron screw steamer of 1879, boasted 70 square feet; but floor space was amplified by the fact that nineteenth-century oceangoing deluxe shamelessly offered upper and lower berths.

All bathrooms on board the *Tropicale*, save the dozen attached to the suites, are the same size. They were ordered, quite literally, from a catalogue —in this case, the broad range of choices offered by the H. W. Metallbau company in Germany. It is symptomatic of today's irregular newbuilding that surges of multiple plumbing repeats—there are 621 passenger and crew bathrooms on board *Tropicale*—cannot be produced on demand by an ancillary work force of journeymen plumbers such as used to be recruited with ease along the banks of the Elbe, Loire, Clyde, or Tyne. Nowadays, shipyards turn to expensive but reliable specialist houses for

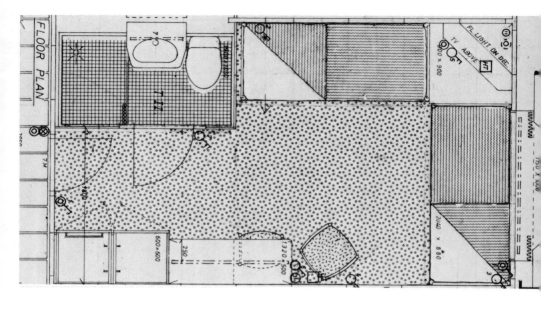

Shipyard plans of a *Tropicale* outside *(above)* and inside ordinary. Note the arrangement of the prefabricated bathroom. *(Aalborg Werft)*

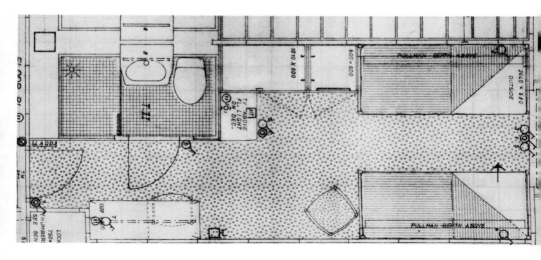

their plumbing needs; several European firms manufacture a complete range of cabin bathrooms. Those on the *Tropicale* could have been ordered in a variety of sizes—all 3½ feet deep in three choices of width, from 6 feet to over 8 feet wide.

Aalborg's naval architects chose the median size—3½ feet deep and 6½ feet wide. Across the long wall facing the door are toilet, sink, and shower, from left to right. The bathrooms arrive at the yard in sealed crates. Inside, they are spotless, complete with fixtures, tiling, towel rails, shower curtain rods, mirrors, shelves, and even soap dishes, awaiting only water, soap, and occupants to make them functional. They are kept locked during fitting out to prevent shipyard workers from fouling them. Since there are waste pipes housed underneath the bathrooms, their floors must stand at least 6 inches above the steel deck; regrettably, with the traditional sill between tiled bathroom and carpeted cabin now a substantial riser, use of cabin bathrooms on all newbuilding is difficult, if not impossible, for those confined to wheelchairs.

Shipboard sewage is termed "black" or "gray": black from the toilets, gray from sinks, showers, dishwashers, or laundry. But regardless of which holding tank stores these alternate waste categories before discharge over the side at sea, the original water supply is, in all cases, fresh only. Saltwater is no longer piped onto passenger decks, and that time-honored taste-test for cabin leaks—salt or fresh—is now unnecessary. Today's shipboard toilets are flushed with fresh water operating through a new vacuum system, replacing Sir Thomas Crapper's traditional elevated tank. Passengers derive a mixed blessing: no tank crowds their bathroom walls nor, when in port, does noxious harbor water reek from the toilet bowl. However, a passenger's first exposure to the new system is startling since vacuum toilets flush as abruptly and noisily as a slammed door.

The *Tropicale*'s prefabricated cabin bathrooms are compactly engineered, 23 feet square. Readers unable to envision square feet may prefer an instantly comprehensible unit of measurement: the standard bathmat, 2 feet by 3 feet, contains 6 square feet. Thus, the *Tropicale* bathroom is the size of four bathmats, laid as a rectangle, including the shower. Bathtubs on board have nearly vanished. Only the top dozen suites come equipped with them. At least they are standard size: the prefabricated bathrooms on *Norway* have token tubs, about the size of a generous perambulator. Passengers sailing on NCL's flagship bathe more comfortably in the original French bathrooms with tubs of Atlantic rather than Caribbean dimension.

Bathrooms in boxes. During the *Norway*'s conversion at Bremerhaven, the old Tourist Class promenade from the *France* days was cut up into cabins. Here, before partitions were installed, bathrooms await alignment and hooking up. *Below,* an aerial view of one of Metallbau's superior bathrooms with a Jacuzzi-ed tub and more room than the *Tropicale*'s modest units. *(Norwegian Caribbean Line and H.W. Metallbau)*

There is one universal shortcoming about the prefab bathrooms, and that is the curious arrangement of the towel rails. They are hung, Uffizi fashion, one directly above the other, ideal for neatly folded dry towels but hopeless for airing wet towels. The old-fashioned thermos pitcher in its circular bracket has been phased out, replaced by a mean little ice bucket in the cabin that sweats. On *Scandinavia*, the French prefab bathrooms included a slotted cutout in the sink fascia to dispense tissues. Unfortunately, the slot was cut to European-size tissue boxes rather than the larger American box with which the ship had to be stocked during her brief New York stay. Back on the Oslo/Copenhagen run, all was well; but as *Stardancer* out of Seattle, the problem recurs.

Unchanged is the cabin's outer door, which has certain fixed requirements. It must have a raised sill beneath it to prevent flooding in either direction and yet space enough between that sill and the bottom of the door to slip messages, newspapers, and invitations into the cabin; cabin sills are, universally, shipboard mailboxes. The enlarged aperture serves an additional, though accidental, use: the light it admits from the passageway provides an unerring guide to the bathroom when the cabin is dark.

Though cabin doors nowadays are kept locked, such was not the case on board ships of the Atlantic ferry. Some years ago, a fraudulent American maritime antiques dealer offered for sale a cabin key purported to have come from the *Titanic*, with a numbered tag attached as proof. Fortunately, he was ignorant of the fact that, earlier in this century, passengers were never issued cabin keys. Stewards locked cabin doors in port; since one of their number was always on duty in the pantry, stewards opened doors for newly embarked passengers on request. Once at sea, cabins remained unlocked.

On board several new ships, a new kind of security system has been instituted: instead of a key, as one would normally think of it, the passenger is issued a perforated plastic wafer, the size of a credit card, into which a random selection of holes has been punched. If a passenger inadvertently carries the card ashore at cruise's end, it can be replaced by another bearing a changed code. Although an enterprising idea, because of the lock's stiff mechanism the card is often bent when pushed into place. On Sun Line ships, passengers lock their cabins and hang the key in plain sight on a board opposite the pantry: that way, stewards can tell at a glance who is in and who is out. The same system was once in use on board Sitmar ships, but the racks are empty now, and the keys are carried in passengers' pockets or purses. In actuality, there is very little thievery on board cruise ships, and what little there is cannot be traced to stewards or stewardesses; the villains are usually nonservice crewmen or, more likely, visitors from ashore.

No shipbuilder has yet devised the perfect indicator to advise stewards whether a cabin is occupied or not. *Sagafjord* and *Vistafjord* have a discreet red/green disc in the escutcheon plate above each lock, so small that it is often ignored. French stewards had an ingenious expedient of their own: they improvised a little flag, a double fold of metal foil wrapped around the shank of a pin that was stuck into the upper corner of each cabin door frame. In the morning, while delivering newspapers or schedules, stewards would lean each flag against the door; once the passenger emerged, the telltale flag dropped. Cunard stewards on board *Queen Elizabeth 2* follow the same principle by wedging scraps of paper between door and frame; its only disadvantage is that, by cruise's end, the hall carpeting around each cabin door is littered with paper scraps as yet unretrieved from each morning's use.

Opposite the bathroom, the far side of the cabin entrance is given over to a second obligatory space intruder: the closet. Indeed, the little entranceway offers a fine confusion of interlocking doors, enough for a restoration comedy. They all open within the same taxed threshold: the outer door must open inward—if it swung out into the corridor, passersby might be injured—as must closet doors. Bathroom doors also swing into the cabin, although the Metallbau firm offers clients four options: hinges inboard or outboard, doors swinging in or out. The *Tropicale*'s closets are 2 feet square, an arbitrarily designed response to the perennial question of how much clothing Newpassengers will bring on board for their cruise. Invariably, passengers will have flown to the port, effectively curtailing luggage volume common in the old days. Each *Tropicale* passenger is provided with 2 feet of hanging space. Old Guard ships are more generous with closets, the *QE2* most generous of all. But smaller need not be worse. Indeed, it surprises me that shipboard closet interiors, where such innovative ingenuity is required, tend to be unimaginative. Frequently, the closet's top shelf is given over to the storage of life jackets, though on board *Tropicale* these cabin necessities are stored neatly out of sight in a special corner table. Whereas lady passengers need a full closet height for long dresses, their husbands would be better served by a hanging rod placed waist high, leaving shelves above accessible for shoes or loose clothing. And whatever a vessel's closet provisions, exterior hooks, scattered about the cabin walls, remain at a premium since all passengers have a variety of hangables—bathrobes, binoculars, scuba gear, raincoats, hats, cameras, ad infinitum.

Whenever I board, my first requests to the cabin steward are, invariably, another pillow and more hangers. The latter seem to be in chronic short supply on every vessel. Hangers are either pinched by departing passengers or, more likely, inadequately dispensed by housekeepers. Some companies, Cunard and Sitmar among them, equip their closets with permanently mounted rings attached to the rod; the detachable hangers are useless on conventional rods at home. The French Line tried discouraging hanger theft by equipping their closets with extra-thin chrome rods; thus, their plastic hangers could be extruded with very small hooks, too small for use on a normal rod. The ship most often short of hangers was undoubtedly the *United States*. During an inspection of the moribund vessel at Norfolk by representatives of the company restoring her to service, an engineer opened a cabin ceiling panel only to be deluged by a shower of coat hangers. A former steward among the party cleared up the mystery. At the end of each crossing, chief steward's inspection always revealed quantities of missing hangers; written off as pilfered by passengers, they were replaced from stores. In fact, the retired steward revealed, the missing hangers had been—temporarily—concealed in the deckheads of empty cabins against anticipated demands by incoming passengers. Presumably, stewards who could produce extra hangers at short notice received larger tips at voyage's end.

Past bathroom and closet into the body of the *Tropicale*'s standard outside, 100 square feet (sixteen bathmats) of floor space remains. Half of it is taken up by bureaus, a chair, and two berths at right angles to each other—one beneath the paired windows parallel to the ship's side, the other along the forward wall. They are separated in the corner by the life jacket storage unit. Bridging the same corner, on the wall above, is a diagonal shelf bearing the cabin's closed-circuit television set. Cabin dimensions and furniture are so contrived that the athwartship bed can be turned ninety degrees and set parallel to its mate, creating, according to the company's Design Narrative Synopsis, a "full king-size bed." A bogus claim, in fact: the resulting resting place is nothing more than twin beds placed side by side.

To my knowledge, only P&O's *Royal Princess* and Sea Goddess Cruises have devised a successful convertible single-to-double bed configuration. Land-based motels get around the problem by offering clients twin beds but shipboard space is too precious for this solution. On *Queen Elizabeth 2*, double mattresses with appropriate linen can be ordered, though the price paid for this limited service is the unsightly parking of unused double mattresses at the bottom of staircase lobbies; paradoxically,

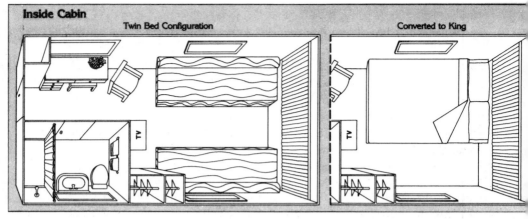

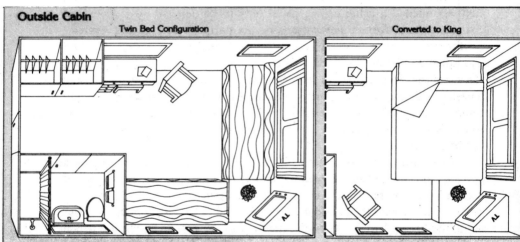

Bird's-eye view for Newpassengers. A picture worth a thousand words, showing prospective passengers just what to expect. *Below,* a cabin mock-up at Aalborg. Shipyard designers have "dressed" the cabin with belongings so that it seems an occupied space. *(Carnival Cruise Lines and Aalborg Werft)*

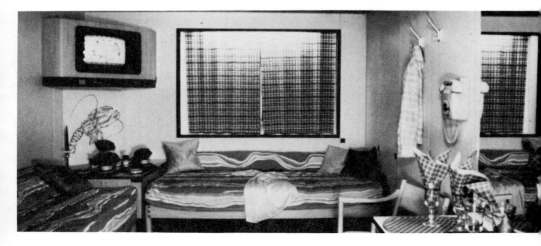

there is a shortage of short-term storage space on board even the largest liners. Occasionally, companies will provide double beds on command. There was once a passenger on board the *Sagafjord* bound from San Francisco through the Panama Canal. An older man, he had invited a much younger lady friend to join him for the cruise. Booked at the last minute into a standard cabin, he was distressed to find that its two berths were immovably anchored at opposite ends of the room. As he was one of a congenial party of seven as well as *un ami de maison*, an aggrieved complaint to the hotel manager resulted in a telex being dispatched to the ship's Los Angeles agent. As the *Sagafjord* approached the Wilmington piers, waiting dockside was an enormous, baby-blue king-size mattress and box spring. Within an hour after it came on board, obliging ship's carpenters had completely rebuilt the man's cabin, juggling its fixed furniture so that, for the remainder of the cruise, the gentleman and his roommate were happily ensconced in a double bed.

Before leaving the subject of cabin berths, there is an irresistible story, doubtless apocryphal, about a lady passenger on the *France* who found her cabin bed too hard. Trying to communicate the problem to her steward in schoolgirl French, she reduced the man to tears of barely suppressed mirth by informing him that she could not sleep properly *sans deux matelots* (without two sailors); the word she needed, of course, was *matelas* for mattress. Similarly unsure of her Gallic syntax was a matron chatting with the captain of the *Flandre: "Je préfère* Flandre *parce qu'il y a un pissoir pour mes enfants."* She had meant to say *piscine* for pool.

Tropicale's moving beds are complemented by provision of what is, to my knowledge, a unique reading light, that critical adjunct to "the compleat cabin." Rather than a decorative wall fixture hung above the berth, Aalborg has reading lights recessed into the ceiling: three are provided, accounting for both positions of the cabin's movable bed. These deckhead installations are ideal, with framing irises that direct a square of light onto the pillows below *and nowhere else.* To be practical, cabin reading lights should not disturb a sleeping partner, a proviso as vital as it is largely ignored.

A kind of awful cabin gentility is at work here, an ambition that should be discouraged. Old Guard companies suffer from an affectation that, by day, cabins should not remain as sleeping chambers, but must, instead, become diminutive living rooms. In the old days, when almost every cabin had a sink in the corner, this could not be done and no one tried. Honest bunks or berths are nowadays disguised as sofas, with floor-length, tailored bedspreads and retractable backs that conceal pillows. One disadvantage of this bed-sitter mentality is that reading lights are chosen less for efficiency than decorative clout. Thus, Royal Viking reading lights are overgenerous brass-and-globe structures the size of hatboxes; they not only flood the pillow below with light, but the entire cabin as well. Reading lamps on board *QE2* are fluorescent bulbs housed in a cutaway tube that only just restricts spill onto neighboring pillows. Norwegian American uses a more sensible anodized brass bullet. Holland America's cone-shaped reading lamps aboard *Rotterdam* would be splendidly practical were it not that sometimes extremely long tubular bulbs are employed, projecting a glaring filament well past the end of the shade. Sitmar, apart from the *Tropicale*, offers one of the few sane arrangements, a low-wattage lamp housed inside a lensed receptacle, facing into the berth and away from the opposite corner. Sadly, the rest of their cabin lighting is frantic, overwatted fluorescent fixtures that bounce off the all-white formica walls with the subtlety of a Florentine pizzeria.

I dwell on passengers as insomniacs with reason: most embark after a plane ride, so their cruise routine is often complicated by jet lag. Then again, rough weather can cause sleeplessness, as does, for some people, the novelty of a strange bed. Second to a good book is the cabin's alternate soporific: closed-circuit television. Most newbuilding incorporates individual television sets for every passenger. Every Royal Viking cabin has been wired for television, but sets have been installed only in the most expensive ones, tangible perquisites offered in return for higher fares. On the *Norway, Scandinavia, Nieuw Amsterdam, Noordam, Tropicale,* and *Fairsky*, television is included in passenger cabins of every category. Television for passengers is, I suppose, inevitable, like every other shipboard luxury—the provision afloat of that which is commonplace ashore. In addition to screening films, Norwegian Caribbean Lines use their television network to acquaint passengers with shipboard geography and activities: all day, a character generator repeats a crawl of the day's events. As a cunning means of ensuring passenger viewing, the audio of that channel is the cabin's only music source as well. Yet, regardless, each evening stewards still slip a mimeographed program under the cabin door—the Orwellian eye has not, as yet, completely supplanted the printed word.

Unfortunately, television in the cabin has had the effect of diminishing the quality of movies on board. The *Tropicale*, for instance, boasts no cinema at all. On the *Norway*, films are occasionally screened, but on the massive, single-reel 16-mm units popularized on aircraft, a sorry substitute for the 35-mm equipment that the French originally had installed in the ship's Saga Theatre. Sometimes, films are screened in the North Cape Lounge instead, although sightlines there present additional problems: centrally located members of the audience are guaranteed a full view of the screen, while those to either side must contend with *allées* of ship's stanchions.

Though cabin-screened movies are conceived as a passenger luxury and convenience, too often they are scheduled either very early in the day or too late at night, never in prime time, so to speak, hence avoiding conflict with the cruise director's public room entertainment. (Once again, the wisdom is that passengers sitting passively in their cabins do not buy drinks; those watching cabaret will.) For my taste, a film in a ship's theater is a splendid way to end one's day at sea. As on dry land, theatrically screened films are unquestionably superior to those broadcast over a little box. Technically, the picture and sound quality is better; even more important, though, the presentation is a shared, social experience rather than an isolated vigil confined to the cabin. The ultimate cabin movie has only recently been inaugurated. On board the yacht-size vessels of Sea Goddess Cruises, each of the fifty-eight cabins has been equipped with its own videotape player. Since the ship's library carries a selection of film cassettes, passengers can screen films of their own choosing at a time pleasing to them. Although this was a pioneering—and expensive—innovation of the mid-eighties, my suspicion is that on board the next generation of cruise ships, cabin viodeotape players will become increasingly common, if only in the top-drawer accommodations.

One of the consistent ironies of bargain space on board ship is that multiple occupancy cabins are inevitably the smallest. The *Tropicale*'s inside ordinaries are narrower than their outside counterparts by a foot and a half; small wonder that the residual floor space is cramped, reducing a potential quartet of occupants to the kind of deferential dressing choreography once practiced exclusively by polar explorers confined to conical tents. Moreover, the walls are narrowed even further by the thickness of two pullmanlike berths hinged against the upper walls. There are only two

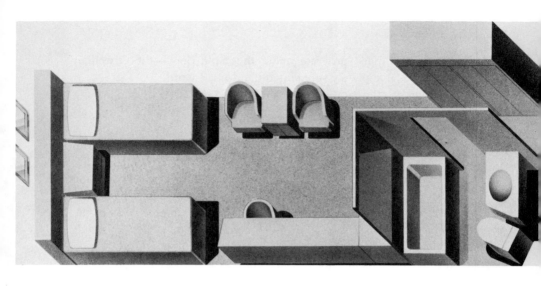

State-of-the-art Old Guard, mid-eighties. An outside double on board *Nieuw Amsterdam*. Holland America has retained its traditional chintz, not only on the beds but on the curtain separating sleeping and sitting areas as well. Both *Nieuw Amsterdam* and *Noordam*, identical save for one additional cabin on the latter, have obviously been designed with long-range or world cruising as an eventual option. *Facing page,* state-of-the-art Newpassenger, mid-eighties. An outside ordinary on *Song of America*. The berths are at right angles: one folds up into the wall by day, the other doubles as a sofa. The little table bearing a fruit bowl nests ingeniously beneath the dressing table at night. Especially practical and convenient is the cutout closet handle seen on the extreme left of the upper view. *(Holland America Line and Royal Caribbean Cruise Line)*

closets for four occupants, although one of them is double-sized. On the wall behind the head of all four berths is a framed expanse of fabric, what Carnival calls "large draped recessed light boxes to give the illusion of a window." For late sleepers, it is the perfect solution, a "window" that admits no daylight whatsoever.

Yet for most, that loss of touch with the outdoors is what stigmatizes the inside cabin, outweighing its obvious economy. A singer on board the *Rotterdam* once lamented that in her inside cabin, she never knew where she was when she woke up. She and, indeed, most ships' entertainers keep late hours and, if they have no porthole, remain suspended like spelunkers within troglodytic isolation.

Parents traveling by sea with their families often book inside cabins for the children. A couple I met on a ship once had done just that while sailing for Europe on the *Bremen* before the war. Their four children shared an inside cabin adjacent to but not abutting their outside double. Having ushered her offspring into their quarters the first night out, the mother made a wise decision never to visit the space again. Four-berth insides often assume the dense intimacy of wartime troop compartments, and stewards assigned to them earn every penny of their salary and tips keeping things in order. But this mother had an informer: the youngest of her children—a seven-year-old—would report each day after breakfast on events of the previous night. One morning he remarked innocently that his older brother, seventeen, "had thrown up all night because he was seasick." Since the ocean had been dead calm for the entire crossing, this inadvertent intelligence confirmed parental suspicion that their oldest child had consumed more nine-cent beers that he could handle. Perhaps it is best to draw a discreet veil over the trauma of adolescent overindulgence from an upper berth.

The strangest story about life in an inside cabin was told to me by James and Jackie McVicar, an English couple who worked as a dance team first on the *France*, then, after 1974, on Sitmar ships. On a Caribbean cruise, a frail old man was booked into the inside cabin adjoining theirs. The first evening, when the McVicars retired, they noticed a DO NOT DISTURB sign on his doorknob. It stayed there throughout the following day. Before dinner, they asked their steward, who was responsible for both cabins, if he had seen their reclusive neighbor; the steward replied that he had not, nor had he made up his cabin. After dinner, the sign was still ominously in place, and James finally telephoned the cabin. To his relief, the man answered immediately.

"Are you all right?" inquired James.

"I'm hungry." There was a pause. "Could you tell me what time it is?" James told him the time as well as the day.

"Well, in that case, I'll get up. You see, I've been waiting for it to get light." As a first-time passenger, the poor man had not realized that his inside cabin lacked a porthole. (There was an amusing postscript. James felt sorry for the man and, as the ship neared St. Thomas, decided to take him on a shore excursion. "You be ready to go ashore at ten o'clock," he spelled out carefully. When he entered the cabin the next morning, he found the man fully packed, a suitcase in each hand, ready to disembark permanently. He had thought, it turned out, that "going ashore" meant that his cruise was over.)

An inside cabin occupied by a quartet of strangers spells opportunity for some. On several Matson Line ships in the Pacific, pursers grew wise to Amy, a shrewd young passenger who always booked the cheapest fare in a four-berth inside cabin, shared with strangers similarly inclined. On the first night, her behavior was consistent: she would stay up late, returning to the cabin in the small hours, when she would stumble over suitcases before turning on all the lights, treating her newfound friends to a lengthy shower —with song—before clambering noisily into her upper berth. It was a fine-tuned performance, guaranteed to antagonize. The next morning, a trio of outraged cabinmates would troop to the purser's office, demanding in vociferous unison that the obstreperous Amy be removed. She would be, forthwith, always to a single or two-berth cabin elsewhere. Mission accomplished: superior digs for inferior fare. Amy's only mistake was repeating the ploy too many times on ships of the same line.

Of course, essential to the success of her particular ruse was that the ship *not* be full. And even with empty cabins at their disposal, pursers are loath to move passengers: it is a nuisance to the office as well as the housekeeping department. Some companies forbid it altogether: displayed prominently at the bureau on board *Queen Elizabeth 2, Norway,* and *Rotterdam* are notices never removed, even on empty sailings, advising passengers that no cabin may be changed. Yet sometimes passengers have legitimate reasons to do so—noisy neighbors, a disagreeable steward, sparse closet space, too much light, not enough light, cabin too stuffy, cabin too chilly—pursers are familiar with a full range of grievances. On board the *Stella Polaris* years ago, Purser Allan always kept an empty cabin on tap. The first passengers with legitimate problems were moved into it. The next complainers were moved into the newly emptied cabin and so on; the game

Four Jills in a jam. Vacuous publicity from Canadian Pacific, circa 1959. As unlikely a quartet as ever laughed off life in a four-berth inside. They apparently embarked in their nightclothes, for the closet is nearly empty. Models smile throughout their voyage; passenger smiles would have vanished after the first few days. *(Canadian Pacific)*

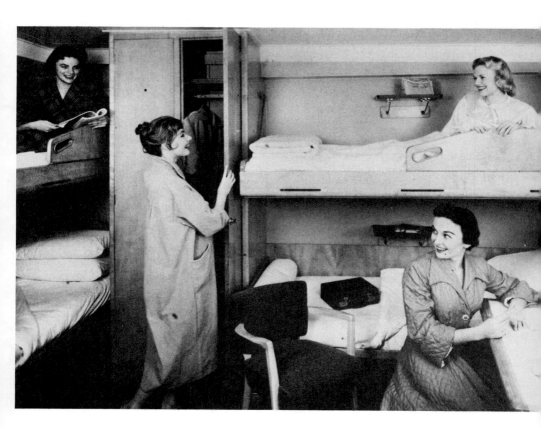

of musical cabins petered out in midpassage and, interestingly, none of the complainers ever complained about their new quarters. That clever purser had probably divined a significant aspect of the passenger psyche: the move —indeed, *any* move—seems to assuage all unrest.

I have traveled in an inside cabin only once, on the *Norway*'s maiden voyage to New York in the spring of 1980. During that memorable crossing, the criterion of cabin desirability was less its number of portholes than the reliability of its plumbing; our inside cabin was our third of the crossing. (On the first leg, Kristiansand to Southampton, one fellow passenger informed me that he had shaved, perforce, exclusively with Perrier.) In that respect, cabin N-101 was admirable. On the same crossing, friends and tablemates Justin and Gloria Scott were accommodated in an inside cabin also on Norway Deck, farther forward on the opposite side of the ship. Though ostensibly inside, cabin N-84, it turned out, had a unique outside aspect: some anonymous *France* predecessor, either steward or client, had drilled a discreet peephole through the back of their closet into adjacent cabin N-86. Through it, one could see both portholes and had, hence, a means of divining the probable weather outside. Whether the original voyeur was in quest of meteorological or pulchritudinous reward will, unfortunately, never be known. I wonder whether that hole is still there.

A curtain keeping daylight at bay is only one of the baffles surrounding a cabin. There are soundproofing barriers as well, for the most part steel wall panels separated by 2 inches of rock-wool insulation, enough to exclude some, but not all, noises from abutting neighbors. The most consistently penetrating sound from one cabin to another is the closing of a bureau drawer. For some extraordinary reason, naval architects have never installed a cushioning device to dampen that disruption. Worse, since cabin bureaus are the same height as a berth, the slammed top drawer zeroes in acoustically on a supine passenger next door.

Apart from those drawers and, more recently, the thump of the vacuum toilet, the next most aggravating auricular incursion comes from neighboring loudspeakers, either electronic or human. Though that 2-inch insulation is an industry-wide standard, it is too easily pierced by passengers' raised voices. A fabric wall-covering might help, though on board *Queen Elizabeth 2*, during one recent crossing, even this did not muffle an intriguing female neighbor of ours—whom I never met in the passageway—with the most deliciously infectious giggle imaginable. Yet I have also suffered voices raised in anger or drunken squabbles continuing far into the night, intrusive but, invariably, not quite intelligible. I once met a doctor/

passenger who told me that he never sails without his stethoscope on the theory that, if combatant neighbors are determined to keep him awake, he might as well enjoy the drama to the full by eavesdropping efficiently. One is reminded of Wendy Smolen's "Lament from 6B":

> The people in 6A are arguing again
> It's coming through my bathroom wall
> I wish they'd be louder
> And clearer
> Or else not fight at all.

Next door to us once on a Royal Viking ship were a most unlikely pair—two L.O.L.'s (Little Old Ladies, to use a shipboard abbreviation familiar to cruise staff worldwide), sisters who were constant, doting companions all over the ship. But inside their cabin, we discovered, the Grandma Moses affability was dropped, and their perpetual nagging and bickering came right through the wall.

As it turns out, the *Tropicale*'s soundproofing is just as inadequate. One passenger told me that while telephoning a friend two cabins away, she could hear the response live through an intervening empty cabin as well as she could over the phone. Then again, not all disturbances come through the walls. On one new ship, a couple freshly arrived on board were trying out their cabin's gadgets, including the rock channel. Within a very short time there was a banging on their wall; lightheartedly, they banged back. Within moments, a frail octogenarian widow appeared at their door, asking that they turn down their music. They did so, but within moments she was back, begging them almost in tears to turn down the radio even further. They turned it off completely in the interests of amicability. Yet again, the woman complained, and it was only when they accompanied her back to her cabin that they discovered that the offending music came from her own loudspeaker, presumably left playing at full volume by the steward who had cleaned the cabin.

Passengers booked into the *Tropicale*'s cabins have at their disposal three channels of recorded music, one classical and two of that mindless musical pap described popularly as "easy listening." Worse, the stuff oozes nonstop throughout public rooms on nearly every cruise ship, even the dining room, as well as outdoors onto every weather deck. It is insidious stuff, monodic banality on a sociological par with television laugh tracks, plastic flowers, smile buttons, and "have-a-nice-day." This unctuous tidal wave floods, unbidden, throughout the twentieth century's megascape, the auditory mildew of our time. It has so insinuated itself into Middle

America's auricular subconscious that generations to come will perceive it as an essential component of every public space and, indeed, of daily life itself.

The intent of easy listening is, presumably, to soothe, though when it is triggered over the telephone by a corporate hold button, my unerring response is to hang up in fury. In the cabin, easy listening can be terminated —easily—by turning a knob, the only source on board, incidentally, where passengers enjoy this advantage. Musical alternatives include one's own tapes played on a recorder or a stab at the classical channel. But sadly, even that option, though superior, is studded with pitfalls. It would seem so easy to broadcast, say, all nine of Beethoven's symphonies or play through performances of Verdi's operas for an orgy of uninterrupted listening at sea. But the cruise lines' musical consultants, programming that elusive generic, "classical," invariably play it safe. Heard most often is a parade of chestnuts—blandthologies from the Boston Pops or snippets of "the classics" from those pirated albums peddled on daytime television. The most adventurous selections are tone poems: *Till Eulenspiegel* is a perennial Royal Viking favorite, while *Sheherazade* used to play twice daily on board *Veendam*. Too often, the man charged with rotating the four-hour tapes neglects his job, and the same cycle unspools for days on end. The most bizarre classical tape broadcast repeatedly in *Rotterdam* cabins is an assemblage—there is no other word for it—wherein piano sonatas segue abruptly into the middle of symphonies, only to be interrupted in midmovement yet again by fragments of an aria. It plays for all the world as though some demented programmer had sliced original tapes into random fragments, then reassembled them in haste in the dark. On Sitmar ships, where the classical programming is the most successful I have found, curious aberrations persist. A mellifluous announcer reads lengthy program notes in anticipation of Beethoven's Ninth Symphony, then restricts its performance to the first three movements; the missing fourth was played days later buried in a subsequent tape without a word of explanation.

Finally, turning from the polemic to the practical, what gives every cabin its endearing cachet is a perquisite endemic to all, a steward. The saddest change on contemporary newbuilding is that a hotel mentality restricts his availability; for large portions of days at sea, none is in sight. Of course, one can be reached by telephone, but he will arrive tardy and impersonal, *a* steward rather than *the* steward. (That passenger/steward symbiosis works both ways: just as clients rejoice in "their" steward, so a steward responds to "his" passengers.) Then, too, newbuilding breakfast trays arrive from an anonymous central galley, ordered by multiple-choice menus hung on cabin doorknobs the previous night. (These are favorite targets of late-night passenger vandals, children or adults, who, having closed the last bar, swap cabin breakfast requests as they weave home.) Today's stewards' pantries are less watch stations than utilitarian storage closets. Only on Cunard's Atlantic holdout, *QE2*, do ancient standards obtain. Scattered along the present *Elizabeth*'s passages are curtained doorways concealing tiled caves that twinkle with toast racks, coffee jugs, and teapots, exuding each morning an evocative fragrance of toast and hot urns. There, stewards and stewardesses on first duty exchange chatter of home and ship, awaiting the pleasure of awakening passengers, "summoned," as was John Betjeman, "by bells."

On board *Queen Elizabeth 2*, at least, traditional call buttons remain in place and, even more important, in operation. Starting in 1871, when the Atlantic's first call system was installed on the White Star's *Oceanic,* the call button has been a part of every cabin's decoration. ("A touch on the ivory disk commands the instant notice of the attendant.") That single button then evolved into twin buttons, one each to summon a company servant of either sex, set atop a felt-based ormolu box tethered to the baseboard by wire sheathed in woven silk. In the cabin bathroom, a duplicate set was mounted within reach of the tub. One of the most famous ships' bathroom call buttons was that in the Imperial Suite on board R.M.S. *Franconia* during the last war. Winston Churchill lived on the ship during the Yalta Conference, and Cunard carpenters constructed a special wooden "desk" that straddled the tub so that the prime minister could work as he bathed. He spent so much time at his watery desk that periodically, he would depress the call button with his toe, summoning a steward to replenish the hot water in his cooling tub as he churned out reams of those notorious dispatches. Another special fixture of that *Franconia* suite was a plumber's candle that burned each night in a saucerful of water placed next to Churchill's bed; its purpose was not as a night-light but a means of igniting a nocturnal cigar.

With the advent of seagoing plastic on the *Queen Mary* in 1936, call buttons were extruded with a likeness of a steward or stewardess incised on top. On the *QE2*, the buttons are color-coded red or green; and whereas rival merchant marines adhere to red port and green starboard running lights in universal agreement, they have always differed as to which color should determine the gender of the attendant summoned. Cunard opted for green stewards and red stewardesses; the French and Dutch preferred the opposite. For many years, cabin summonses were anonymous: a push of the button activated an annunciator board within the pantry only. A telltale drop or dangling numeral would alert the steward to proceed to the appropriate cabin. Then the annunciators vanished, replaced by red and green signal lights hung above each cabin entry; a buzz or bell in the pantry sent the duty steward's head popping out into the passageway like a cuckoo clock chiming the quarter, searching for the source of the summons. Those lights have been removed along the *Rotterdam*'s passageways; only wooden blanks, bleak as tombstones, remain to remind seasoned travelers of how things have changed. Curiously, on board *Norway*, the company has left in place the original French corridor signals, the margins of their red and green plastic globes still surviving a rising tide of corridor wall repainting. They are ignored by Newpassengers, for whom the moribund system has as little significance as the auxiliary ice-water taps in their cabin bathrooms, which are scrupulously polished by stewards each day but have been arid since the fall of 1974.

As a general rule today, Old Guard vessels, which book preponderant numbers of widows, employ cabin stewardesses exclusively; Newpassengers in the Caribbean will find stewards making up their cabins. Sun Line, like Cunard, still has cabin attendants of both sexes. Cabin stewardesses are found on board Norwegian-crewed ships because of an archaic and stubborn masculine prejudice: whereas males will cheerfully grease a bearing in the engine room, tote a trayful of dirty dishes out to the pantry, or even pass a teapot in the lounge, they will have no part of cleaning a tub or a toilet. It is considered beneath the dignity of Scandinavian men, and hence, on all top-drawer Norwegian ships, stewardesses prevail.

The routine of Royal Viking stewardesses has been standardized in a training manual prepared by Flora/Elkind Associates, a San Francisco consultant to the company. Each day, all over the world, from 7:30 A.M. until 1:30 that afternoon, stewardesses on each of the company's trio of ships, from Black Sea to South China Sea, begin an identical ritual. Each stewardess is assigned up to a dozen cabins that are to be cleaned twice daily, once in the morning and again that night. The morning makeup is the most laborious, especially every third day, when the *piccolos*, the most junior crew members on board, wheel trolleys of fresh linen down the corridors, hanging fresh sheets for each cabin over the hand railings. The stewardesses wear ill-fitting white cotton lab coats for their morning work, their passkeys suspended around their necks on a piece of string. Some, new to the rigors of the job, are advised to wear protective gloves, not only to clean bathroom porcelain but to make beds as well.

Each cabin, it is recommended, should take no longer than twenty minutes. First chore, after ascertaining that the cabin is empty and removing the breakfast tray, is to turn on all the lights—burned-out bulbs are spotted this way—and leave a cairn of cleaning equipment, a mop, pail, or vacuum cleaner, visible in the open outer door so that passengers anxious to find the stewardess for any reason will know where to look. Some steward tricks are as old as passenger vessels, among them the practice, when making up a berth, of twisting the corner of each bottom sheet tightly under the mattress to ensure a drum-tight surface that lasts. Royal Viking stewardesses actually knot the corners together. Leaning in to make up sofa beds against a wall is made easier by resting one's head against the sofa back, leaving both hands free. Since the obligatory rubber nonskid bathroom mat is prone to mildew, stewardesses are taught to dry it by wrapping it momentarily within a dirty bathmat. Tub and sink drains are scoured daily, as is the round air-conditioning vent, a notorious dust collector. Stewardesses are advised in their manual to be vigilant about dust: "What would you look for if you were the housekeeper?" (This is a common post on board Norwegian and Dutch ships, less so on British and French; Dutch housekeepers are male, Norwegian ones are female.) The only personal touch the stewardess may leave in the cabin—once again by direction of the ubiquitous San Francisco manual—is to fold the little extra mohair blanket "in your own creative design." In between cabin chores, stewardesses must wash down their pantries once each fortnight and always "before every American port," a caveat in anticipation of surprise visits by inspectors from the United States Public Health Service.

When the stewardesses come back on duty at six-thirty in the evening, they are clad in a pleasing rust-colored Nordic dress, with lacing across a white blouse and a Norwegian peasant apron in a contrasting color, the same rig in which they greet newly embarked passengers. This second cabin session is less arduous, a time to clear up glasses, empty ashtrays and wastepaper baskets, turn down beds, draw curtains, and lay out passengers' nightclothes. Between morning and evening chores, stewardesses are off duty save for one of their number who stays on call during the afternoon, answering requests for tea trays in the cabin. Cabin tea has always been popular, as witness the plight of one novice stewardess on board the *Queen Mary*'s maiden voyage in 1936. A couple rang to order tea; by the time she had returned to the pantry and prepared it, she had forgotten the number of the ordering cabin. So she tried a process of elimination, knocking on random doors with tray in hand, inquiring if the occupants had ordered tea. None had but all admitted they would like some. The poor woman had to make up and relinquish seven trays before the eighth knock unearthed the original couple. "You certainly took long enough," grumbled the wife. The

264   LINERS TO THE SUN

stewardess, relieved to have finished her marathon, merely apologized and left.

During a westbound crossing on the *Royal Viking Sky* in the summer of 1984, I asked our Norwegian stewardess how long she had been working for the company.

"Since two days ago," she replied cheerfully.

Her name was Gry Henriksen and she was the older of two sisters, daughters of an engineer who, though working ashore now, had originally sailed on board a tanker. Throughout her childhood, Gry had fantasized about sailing around the world on a ship and now, at nineteen and a half, was realizing that dream. Her last job before joining Royal Viking had been as an *au pair* in England. She looked typically Scandinavian: tall, thin, and muscular, with short, corn-yellow hair that, as she worked, spilled repeatedly across her face. She had had no formal training for her job as stewardess for eleven lower-deck cabins and admitted that she was learning as she went along.

I asked if I might watch her make up our cabin to see how she coped; she agreed. It was clean linen day and she turned first to our two berths, stripping the sheets and blankets. Gry told me that making twenty-two beds each day, smoothing sheets and bedspreads, was hard on her fingertips. Once the beds were made, she dusted everywhere—"anything that shines," one of her friends had advised her—so she tackled the chrome chair legs as well as the assorted clutter that passengers leave on every table, bureau, and desktop. In the bathroom, she scrubbed the floor on her hands and knees and wiped down the mirror, shelf, and ceiling with a damp facecloth.

Long before she had finished, I realized that her job involved intensely hard physical labor. Royal Viking berths have innerspring mattresses that are stiff and awkward. Gry had, literally, to wrestle with them, using arms, knees, and hips to keep them from flying across the room as she bent on the new linen. The corners of the old sheets were so tightly knotted underneath that Gry finally loosened them with her teeth. Although the entire cabin-cleaning process is presumed to require only twenty minutes, half an hour had passed before Gry was finished. I was partly to blame, for she was distracted as we talked. She knew that as the weeks passed, she would become faster. Even the business of returning to the corridor supply trolley would become more efficient; in fact, her training manual had ordained a step-by-step, time-study routine that she had not yet mastered. Her days, she admitted, were exhausting. She slept each afternoon before coming back on duty in the evening, and never stayed up as late as her more experienced colleagues. Crews on board ship keep long

Gry Henriksen's morning at sea. The
first of a dozen cabin berths to be made
up with fresh linen. The stewardess's day
is long and demanding. (*Author's
collection*)

hours, relaxing only late at night. Crew movies, for instance, cannot be shown in the theater until the regular passenger screenings have ended, which means they don't finish before the early hours of the morning; Gry had not seen one since she left England.

Her conscientious, cheerful demeanor reflects the attitude of all good cabin staff. "Never say no" is the cardinal rule, one that is scrupulously observed for the most part, though sometimes it is not easy. Occupants of the inner below can be tiresome, as we shall see. But stewards and stewardesses who are well trained and conscientious make cruising the pleasure that crossing used to be. Some are better than others. Newpassenger tonnage carries what is called a Caribbean crew, an industry catchword indicating a polyglot of nationalities serving on one vessel. More than three dozen countries are represented on board *Norway*, for instance, so many that the flag of the United Nations flies from the main truck by special permission of the secretary general.

Caribbean stewards come from all over the world; those from the Far East cope with idiomatic English disarmingly. A friend of mine sailing to the Bahamas on board *Scandinavia* was greeted by her steward, his face wreathed in a gold-toothed Korean smile, in singsong redundancy: "Good morning, my name is Mr. Lee. You can call me Mr. Lee." His grasp of idiomatic English was no less suspect than that of the Norwegian staff of the *Royal Viking Star* when the ship first entered service in the early seventies. They identified their offices with English abbreviations, the ambiguity of which did not emerge until pointed out by American passengers. The hotel manager's door, for instance, had been inscribed, proudly, HOT. MAN.; next door was PURSER'S ASS.

The last cabin we shall visit is low down in the hull of the *Sagafjord*. In the fall of 1981, it was assigned to a married couple, on board not just for an idyllic fortnight but for months of travel and hard work. Passengers are not the only cabin occupants on board; crew members retire to their own inner below as well. And whatever delights cruising holds for passengers, there are fewer for those who toil behind the scenes.

"Ships!" exclaimed an elderly
seaman in clean shore togs. "Ships! . . .
Ships are all right, it's the men
in 'em."

—JOSEPH CONRAD, THE
MIRROR OF THE SEA

The moral was not to make chums
with sailors though who I've made a
chum of is the purser who's different
on account he leads a very cynical
life with a gramophone in his cabin
and as many cocktails as he likes and
welsh rabbits sometimes and I said
but do you pay for all these drinks
but he said no that's all right.

—EVELYN WAUGH, CRUISE

7.
Backstage

Cabin 562 on board Norwegian American Cruises's *Sagafjord* is furnished identically to all minimum-category inside doubles on board save for its upper and lower berths. Just as transatlantic bunks were upgraded to brass beds in the Edwardian era, so vertical passenger berthing on board older passenger vessels has been supplanted by twin beds; elderly or infirm passengers are neither expected nor inclined to clamber up a ladder to retire. But along the length of *Sagafjord*'s B-deck, which houses crew exclusively, archaic uppers and lowers abound. In the fall of 1981, cabin 562 was crammed with belongings. It was home to a young, newly married couple whom I shall call Jim and Diane Boyd—their only home save for Jim's bedroom at his parents' house in Florida.

Since the *Sagafjord* roams as far north as the Gulf of Alaska, the range and bulk of clothing with which the Boyds traveled overwhelmed their modest cabin closet; a complete climatological spectrum of dress, from parkas to bathing suits to the uniforms they wore on board, was stacked neatly on their upper cabin berth, enclosed within curtains stitched by Diane. The Boyds slept in the cabin's lower single berth, which they'd converted, willy-nilly, into a double: a plywood shelf extended from the original bunk's edge, its narrow mattress supplemented by a stack of deck-chair pads "borrowed" from passenger chaise longues surrounding Veranda Deck's outdoor pool. Though that jerry-built extension meant more room for sleeping, it depleted the already scant floor space remaining. All bureau tops and shelves—more than adequate for a transient occupant—were crowded with the conventional detritus of civilization that, ashore, would easily have filled a studio apartment: pictures, souvenirs, ornaments, tape-recorders, radios, books, and records.

Yet cabin 562 was as ingeniously arranged as it was spotlessly clean. Diane Boyd had made the matching curtains and slipcover for their single upholstered chair; her husband, by mutual consent, assumed the daily burden of making the bunk and keeping floor and adjoining bathroom clean. *Sagafjord*'s senior officers and staff have stewards to look after their cabins; those below the maritime salt must shift for themselves, an economical advantage in that they are not obliged to tip a crew steward as must their senior shipmates. But Jim and Diane agree that even had stewards been available, their preference was to look after their own quarters, not only for reasons of privacy—at a premium on crew decks everywhere—but also because only they could cope with so many possessions in so restricted a space. The reason Jim cleaned the cabin and looked after the laundry was that his wife spent her days cleaning passenger cabins; relieving her of the care of yet another in her off-hours seemed only fair.

Diane did not start her life at sea as a stewardess. British-born, she is a tall, attractive brunette, a London beautician who had applied for an overseas shipboard assignment with a London firm supplying cruise ships. The company recruits hairdressers, manicurists, and masseuses for a variety of cruise lines, not only Norwegian American but Royal Viking, Sitmar, and RCCL as well. Company personnel sail as staff on their franchised vessels, and there is no shortage of candidates to fill the two-hundred-odd posts available. With England in a recession, suffering from crippling inflation as well as its legendary bleak weather, the travel, adventure, and sunshine that cruise ship work offers have potent appeal, offsetting the admittedly meager compensation. In addition to her round-trip airfare, Diane was paid a weekly salary of $24, plus 10 percent of the business she generated and all of her tips. As a result, her take-home pay seldom exceeded $100 a week. Conversely, she had no living expenses whatsoever, save what she chose to spend at ports of call.

Though there is no shortage of first-time applicants, the company has a harder time re-signing their employees after their first six-month contract has expired. Once on board, the Londoners see that their stewardess shipmates make several times their wage, averaging $25 a week from each of a dozen cabins. Nor is the life of the young women who work in the concessioned shops on board RCCL ships much fun, hedged in as it is with regulations and penalties. Each must buy her own uniforms at $90 apiece, and if she wishes to appear in the public rooms, she is required to change into a long black skirt. She can sit only at a specific table, far in the back of the entertainment lounge. If three complaints are made about her by customers in the shop, she is dismissed. During their two-hour lunch break, the concession staff cannot eat at the passenger buffet on deck, but must sit in the chilly reaches of the dining room, waited on by stewards who have been assigned to those nontipping tables because they, in turn, have received complaints from previous passengers; hence, they receive indifferent service. They are paid very little apart from their commissions and are given only $25 a month for drinks. In an attempt to restrict on-board lateral transfers, the company inserts a conditional clause in their employment contracts, prohibiting the applicants from working for the shipping line in a different capacity for nine months following expiration of their original contracts.

Diane, who is as honest as she is engaging, abided by her agreement. During her first six months at sea on board *Vistafjord*, she fell in love with Jim Boyd. A pleasant, blond American college drop-out, he worked as a utility boy. (There are relatively few Americans working on foreign-flag cruise ships; despite an overwhelmingly American passenger load, most of the Norwegian American stewards are European—Italians, Austrians, or Swiss—and the stewardesses are Scandinavian, although there are increasing numbers of Italians and English, many of them ex-hairdressers from London.) Before he came on board, Jim had worked on chartered yachts out of Florida.

In due course, he and Diane were married. They left the sea and went north to Michigan, where Jim re-enrolled in college. But they hated the cold winter weather and, within a year, were back in Florida, staying with Jim's parents. One day when the *Sagafjord* came into Fort Lauderdale, they went on board for a nostalgic visit and, subsequently, reapplied to Norwegian American Cruises. Diane was taken on as a stewardess, while Jim was hired as a utility boy again, a lower-paying job. His first day's job was helping a carpenter carry some sheets of Formica on deck; one of them slipped, gashing his wrist badly. When he went down to the hospital to be bandaged up, the chief stewardess overheard his American accent and immediately promoted him to be in charge of the *Sagafjord*'s indoor pool. She needed an English-speaking attendant who could accommodate passengers telephoning for massage appointments. Jim's other duties included filling and draining the pool each day, keeping the place clean, and supplying fresh ice water and towels, as well as supervising the adjoining gymnasium.

He worked from eight in the morning until eight at night, confined indoors, as remote from daylight as cabin 562, his schedule at odds with his wife's. She started work at 6:00 A.M. (During that two-hour grace period conferred by their disparate schedules, he put the cabin to rights.) She was in charge of half a dozen very grand penthouse suites seven decks above Jim's pool, accommodations so spacious and comfortable, she reported ruefully, that her passengers stayed put for much of the morning, leaving her waiting to finish up. The only compensation for this inconvenience was that after 1:00 P.M., she started earning overtime. During her afternoon break, Jim was still on duty at the pool; only during the evening could they share any leisure time together.

Of the two, Diane was the better paid, and when I talked with them in 1981, they planned to stay on board only long enough to save for and buy their own charter yacht in the Caribbean. In that sense, they seemed more transient than their fellow crew members who were aboard for the foreseeable future. And the Boyds remained at a distance from the rest of the crew because they were not part of what Jim, from the security of his connubial vantage point, referred to as "the combined circus and zoo of B-deck," an enclave so sexually liberated that, as he put it, "musical bunks" were the norm.

Though cabin 562's enviable domesticity serves as an intriguing introduction to a cruise ship's backstage, its occupants were, in fact, atypical. The Boyds were young, childless, and, most significantly, together. Their older shipmates, grown beyond B-deck's jejune hugger-mugger, were less fortunate. Spouses and children are remote from their daily lives, their marriages a series of respites between interminable periods at sea. Alfred Lunt once told me that actors should never marry or, at least, never bear children; perhaps the same should apply to cruise ship personnel. Tradi-

Sagafjord crew members are fortunate:
the forward cargo hatch contains a
swimming pool for their use on deck.
Most cruise ships have no swimming
facilities for off-duty personnel. *(Author's
collection)*

tionally, life at sea is predicated on extended absences from home. But the reality of those absences, for the sailor, his wife, and children, can be distressingly harsh.

Recently, I stood at the boat deck railing of a Royal Viking ship sailing from Bergen. A ship's officer stood next to me while down on the pier, clutching the hands of their two very small children, was his wife. He had had a bonus day at home because of his ship's North Cape cruise schedule. Those last exchanges between pier and ship were all the more poignant for what was unspoken; real anguish lay beneath the blown kisses, waves, and smiles. The wife, her face grim, put on a brave show, urging her uncomprehending children—for whom cranes and bollards held far more fascination—to wave farewell yet again to their father. The officer stayed at the rail until a corner of the shed obscured the pier, then turned away abruptly. He would not see his family again for six months.

The old days were different. While the Atlantic ferry sailed, European ships crossed westbound and eastbound continuously. Common to and cherished by every man on board, from captain to stoker, was the anticipation following each voyage to America of spending one or more nights at home, whether in Liverpool, Southampton, Bergen, Bremerhaven, Rotterdam, Le Havre, or Genoa. That biweekly reunion was as intrinsic a part of the year-round sea routine as boarding the pilot or annual dry docking. Another emotional lifeline was a culture and country of origin shared with all their shipmates, so that whatever the distance from home, a national commonality sustained them.

But things changed drastically in the seventies. Holland America ships abandoned the North Atlantic. Dutch crewmen precipitated the crisis, in effect signing their own death warrant by escalating wage demands to a point where the company would have to either capitulate and go under—as the Swedish-American Line had done—or survive by defying the union. In September 1971, it chose the latter, exiling itself to the tropics. Ships that had been built, maintained, and crewed out of Rotterdam were reregistered in Willemstadt: Holland America Line became Holland America Cruises. When the *Rotterdam* sailed from her home port of the same name for the last time in 1972, defiant stewards on the dock knotted their uniform jackets into long strings of bunting; sympathetic crane operators hauled them up into the air, fluttering blackleg banners.

Though Dutch officers remained in command, cheap labor had been recruited from the independent remnants of the Far Eastern Dutch Empire, trained at a special school in Bandung and signed onto the lower decks. The first contingents were greenhorns: they were terrified of loud machinery of any kind and steered clear of the galley dishwashers. They had no idea how to operate the cabin vacuum cleaners. The first time that the *Rotterdam* sailed with Indonesian crews, Maître d'Hôtel Dirk Zeller came down to dinner before the first sitting to find his neophyte stewards cowering beneath the dining room tables. Even though they had been broken in by waiting on the families of crew members while tied up at the Wilhelminakade, the prospect of real passengers was apparently terrifying. Even their clothes felt alien and uncomfortable: some of the new stewards discarded their new black shoes in favor of socks only. One man even painted his bare feet navy blue before he was ordered re-shod.

But they learned, admirably, and Indonesian crewmen are a beloved and endearing component of Holland America's service. They endure long separation from their families because they earn so much more at sea than they can in their homeland, where the average annual income is less than fifty dollars. Stewards on board *Rotterdam, Nieuw Amsterdam*, and *Noordam* are rich men by Indonesian standards. But because of their presence on board, no ship of the line has returned to Holland since 1971. Years after the fact, Rotterdam's sympathetic dockworkers may have relented but no one at Holland America Line—the company has recently resumed its original name—is anxious to put matters to the test.

Shortly after the Holland America revolution, the French Line not only relinquished the route, they went out of the passenger business altogether. In September 1974, the *France* sailed westbound for the last time under the tricolor. During the crossing, cabled exchanges flew between union representatives on board and company headquarters at 6, rue Auber. The outcome was as bleak as it was predictable: the ship would be taken out of service and her crew discharged. This was not merely union-busting; it represented a basic governmental retrenchment. Giscard d'Estaing was not going to continue subsidizing American crossings with French taxpayers' francs. An era had ended. The *France* was the company's last remaining passenger vessel, and her retirement rang down the curtain on more than a century of legendary TRANSAT service between Le Havre and New York.

The news discomfitted the traveling public, but the impact on board, especially to the stewards, was devastating. Whereas deck and engine room shipmates might transfer to tankers or cargo ships, the stewards' particular skills were suddenly and tragically redundant. As the ship steamed up to Pier 88 for the last time, dining room stewards serving that last inbound breakfast—as funereal as any condemned man's—were numb, many of them in tears. In future, they would either practice their

ykjavik recreation. Costumed crew
m the *Royal Viking Sea* disembark
 a mock Super Bowl in Iceland.
nding the moment during a one-day
pover for an entire team to be off-duty
one time is never easy. *(Author's
lection)*

craft ashore in Norman restaurants or apply for duty on board French-speaking vessels of the Paquet Line on permanent Caribbean itineraries. Overnight, the balanced structure of their ship-and-shore lives had been destroyed, that transatlantic pendulum stilled. Sea duty for them would never be the same again.

Some of Britain's seamen and stewards still have their home port links, but only in the summer months. For the rest of the year, Cunard's flagship sails far from Southampton, as do P&O Cruises's *Canberra* and *Oriana*, following the sun in competition with growing fleets of new rivals. Envisioned from afar, steaming toward the horizon, cruise ships seem the equivalent of that traditional chimera, the desert island, alluring and idyllic. Yet those stationed on board find that desert island remote, isolated, and unreal. Far from home, they voyage endlessly, modern-day Flying Dutchmen, sailing under a curse of economic expediency in quest of the tourist dollar.

Nowhere is this sense of national dislocation more prevalent than in Florida, where Norwegian officers from over a dozen cruise ships spend the bulk of their lives, six months at a time. Their vessels steam continually on a circuit of too-familiar Caribbean ports with only a few hours' turnaround to mark the end of one cycle and the start of another. That cruise carousel spins ceaselessly, year-in, year-out. There are few overnight stops, so that the ships' crews are, in a very real sense, shipbound for their entire tour of duty. And particularly for Norwegians, who, of all nationalities, share the fiercest love of homeland, the exile is distressing. Norway's national anthem begins: *"Ja, vi esker dette landet, Som det stiger frem"*; these and the lines that follow translate into ponderous English, revealing nevertheless the Norwegian's specific attachment to homeland:

> Yes, we love with fond devotion
> This our land that looms
> Rugged, storm-scarred over the ocean
> With her thousand homes.

The focus is not on flag or crown but on Norway's seagirt coast, approached by sea. It is, geographically as well as emotionally, a far cry from the flat, sunbaked gaudery of southern Florida. A Norwegian captain once remarked from the bridge of his ship as he gestured over the side, "That's my favorite view of Miami." He was pointing at the final marker buoy at the end of Government Cut, the port's deep-water channel out to sea.

The Norwegian officers' wives either stay in Norway or relocate to Florida in hopes that even a few weekly or biweekly hours together may preserve attenuated familial links. Exiled like their husbands, they are determined, nevertheless, to sustain their children's Nordic heritage. Each May 17, in a recreation ground spread alongside Miami's piers, the city's seagoing Norwegian colony gathers for an Independence Day picnic. As at any American Fourth of July celebration, there are songs, speeches, barrels of beer, and, inevitably, a parade. A dory is rigged and fitted out as a Viking longship with a brightly colored square sail, its thwarts lined with painted cardboard shields. Mounted on a wheeled trailer, it is towed by car around the cinder track, followed by a crowd of mothers and children in ethnic finery, pink-faced in Florida's warm spring sun. But the only "land that looms" over those facsimile bows is the futuristic concrete roof of Dodge Island's passenger terminal. And, typically, unless Norway's Independence Day happens to fall on a weekend, husbands and fathers are absent, compelled by their unremitting schedule to miss one of the year's classic family outings, for which, among other reasons, their wives have come to live in Florida. Christmas and children's birthdays are annual casualties as well.

For the wives who remain in Norway, there are, besides their husbands' home leaves, occasional reprieves from loneliness when they are allowed to sail with their husbands on cruises. Yet even those shared voyages, enviable in prospect, can have corrosive aftereffects. Arne Baekkelund, who served as hotel manager on Royal Viking ships for years and now heads Sea Goddess Cruises's hotel operations in Miami, described an all-too-typical scenario. He prefaced it with the observation that officers on board ships, those not concerned with passenger amusement, lead routine and unexciting lives. The difference between wardroom and public room on a passenger vessel is marked.

One perceives this symbolically from afar. Across the water, at night, a cruise ship's hull and superstructure appear as two conjoined but separate entities. Aft of the bridge, the ship is ablaze with light, rows of ports below, glittering bands of public-room windows and floodlighting above, every rail garlanded with light: the ship's after end floats on a sea of twinkling reflection. But nothing save running lights relieves the anonymous mask of the foredecks. All is black, illumination ruthlessly concealed; passengers whose cabins face over the bows are obliged to draw shades and curtains each dusk so as not to interfere with night vision from the bridge. These contrasting aspects of the same vessel—one festive, the other almost

A cherished celebration in an alien
setting. Wives and children of Miami's
Norwegian colony parade around Dodge
Island's cinder track on May 17.
(Author's collection)

furtive—characterize the differing life-styles on board: whatever the gaiety aft, forward the ship's routine is shrouded, as uneventful and mono-chromatic as the blacked-out bridge screen. Ship's officers are encouraged to spend time in the public rooms but, apart from the young bachelor officers, the senior men do so only perfunctorily. The cabaret tends to be repetitive and being on good company behavior to amuse indifferent passengers becomes tedious.

Then, Baekkelund hypothesizes, the officer's wife arrives on board. At once, she and her husband are seen everywhere. On his own, he seldom visits the pool, lounge, or discotheque; now, for her sake, he fits into his schedule as much of the vessel's built-in diversion as he can. It is demand-ing. Though his wife is on holiday, he is not, and must sandwich weeks of hectic after-hours fun between regular working days. Yet, however ex-hausted, he is determined to give his wife the best possible cruise, com-pensating while he can for the deprivation she suffers most of the year.

The rub comes long after she has flown home. Back in Norway, her tan fading during doleful winter months, she thinks back to her time on board, nostalgically and, increasingly, resentfully: why, she wonders, should she struggle at home, coping with housekeeping and children by herself while her husband is having all that fun on board? Needless to say, he is probably *not* having fun on board but has instead resumed his prosaic routine, the frenetic gaiety of his wife's visit long past. However, the damage has been done. "That," concludes Baekkelund, "is why so many of those shipboard marriages go bad." Another officer suggests that the failure rate for officers' marriages is as high as 60 percent. Ragnar Nilsen, in command of the *Norway* periodically, admits that whenever his wife joins him for a cruise, he purposely "bores her to death!"

Not surprisingly, there is a strong affinity between the wives. Often, on Holland America ships, I have seen Dutch women passing their days in adjoining deck chairs or sitting alienated among passengers at teatime, awaiting the moment when their husbands—who are sharing their frus-trating holiday—come off duty. And if extended absences are hard on wives, they are even harder on the children of these stressful marriages. Sons in particular need a full-time father within reach rather than as an occasional visitor.

Flemming Wandahl is a Dane serving in the *Sagafjord's* dining room. He started his seagoing career in 1978 when, because of the oil crisis, the Copenhagen Hotel, where he worked, went out of business. He could find no other job in Denmark and decided that his only salvation, apart from the—unacceptable—possibility of welfare, was to sign with Norwegian

Lounge scene, midafternoon. Cruise staff and performers rehearse for an evening performance in the Bergen Lounge on board *Royal Viking Star*. Leaning on the piano in a white shirt is Peter Hovenden-Longley, the urbane Royal Viking cruise director. *(Author's collection)*

American Cruises. He and his wife, Rut, as well as their two sons, Hendrik and Thomas—then ten and eight—shared in this disruptive and challenging family decision.

Once on board, Wandahl did phenomenally well. Beginning as a waiter, he achieved the title head waiter within three months; two months later he was promoted to chief assistant steward. But he and his family still missed each other terribly. When I sailed with Flemming in 1981, he admitted ruefully to anyone who would listen that "my two sons still call me Daddy." Making things work out was possible only because of Flemming and Rut's dedication and the surprising resiliency of their two children, who weathered adolescence with no father at home and, for one summer, when Rut took a job on board *Sagafjord* as a cabin stewardess, no mother either. More recently, she and, sometimes, the two boys have been allowed to sail as passengers on long cruises with Flemming as he works. But the early years were difficult: payments had to be kept up on their house—not easy on Flemming's starting salary—and Rut, alone at home in Aalsgaarde, had to persevere despite rumors among family and neighbors that her marriage was over, that her husband's departure for sea was, in fact, a trial separation. Not long ago, Flemming wrote:

> This, my life at sea, could only be made possible with my family's understanding. Never would I decide upon anything without first having asked Rut and the boys' opinion and permission. We still have the same agreement as in 1978 when I first started here. The minute my family decides that they want me to stop sailing I will do so— no question about that. My family is my life, they mean the world to me. I just love my job and I am very proud of it. I am also aware how fortunate I am to get to see the world and get paid for it. . . . At this point, neither of us have any plans about giving up this life-style. We all four think that this has given us so much which we could never achieve if I had had a job in Denmark.

The Wandahl family survived a difficult situation well.

Crew members described thus far are peripheral players in the ship's spectacle, darting onstage for production numbers and scenery shifts, but for the most part remaining out of sight behind the proscenium. Though stewards share a certain intimacy with their passengers, it does not extend beyond working hours; so, too, ships' officers remain detached from the company's clients if they choose. But centerstage and relentlessly limelit is a group of players with run-of-the-cruise contracts, seldom out of sight of their restless passenger audience. These are the cruise directors and their staffs, faced with the task of keeping the pump of passenger enthusiasm in continuous prime.

Provision of these specialist teams most distinguishes ships that cruise rather than cross. In the old days, passengers amused themeleves under the remote if watchful eye of the purser. But when voyages became vacations, passengers were entertained with cabaret and someone had to coordinate the show. Enter the cruise director. Over the years, his part has been padded. No longer merely master of revels after dark, he is now the cruise's full-time compère/confessor, a shipboard institution without which Newpassenger life in particular would grind to a halt. More than any other crew member, he is the company's man-on-the-spot, responsible for anything that happens—or does *not* happen—throughout the cruise.

Many passengers have no need of him. They can find their way about the vessel, stake out a corner on deck, look after themselves after dark, and make their way ashore—and back—with ease. But passengers embark in bewildering variety: some have never been on board ship before, some have never been anywhere before, some have traveled on rival lines and are checking out the competition. A few are determined to confound the company whenever possible. In common, all have invested in an exotic vacation afloat. It is with this amorphous throng, full of unpredictable expectations and antagonisms, that the cruise director must cope. It is not easy, nor, after a couple of months, much fun; once again, beneath the desert island's illusory exterior, the reality is sobering.

Old Guard ship lines hire cruise directors who are almost exclusively British. On seven- or fourteen-day Newpassenger vessels sailing out of Miami, they tend to be American. On European-based ships, they are multilingual: Sun Line cruise directors in the eastern Mediterranean must be fluent in English, French, German, and Greek. Very few cruise directors are female, despite the example on television's preposterous *Love Boat* series. But women rank high on the cruise directing staff, assigned to the important role of hostess. A ship's hostess bears no relation to her harried airborne counterpart but serves, literally, to assist the captain, who, in turn, is considered host of the ship. It is at his side, during the obligatory captain's cocktail party inaugurating each cruise, that the hostess stands, murmuring hundreds of names into his ear as, glassy-eyed, he pumps every passenger hand on board.

Though time-consuming, that is, in a sense, her least demanding chore. Requiring more stamina are daily sessions with every cruise-load's problem passengers, elderly widows, spinsters, and loners, the L.O.L.'s— Little Old Ladies—who do not swim, sun, play bridge, read, or have any

Potato-and-spoon race on board *Aquitania* en route to Rio in 1938. In front of a lethargic passenger audience, cruise director Rider (lower picture, center, wearing ascot) kept the pace up and the losers happy. *(Joseph Rider)*

apparent recreational resources of their own. They are found on every ship, sitting alone in empty public rooms or lobbies, clutching handbags and staring into space. Some may have booked in hopes that the camaraderie eluding them at home would materialize on board. (Statistics are against them: unattached males of the right age are rare on contemporary passenger manifests.) It is the hostess's job to involve these hard-core uninvolved with something, filling what might otherwise become barren, empty days at sea. She organizes sessions at which grandchildren's pictures are compared; she—or a specialist in handicrafts—offers instruction in chocolate box découpage, needlepoint in primitive colors, raffia bracelets, or boxes made from seashells and ice-cream sticks; if she can find an indulgent ship's officer, she will have him visit her ladies in a corner of the lounge; she conducts them on tours of the provision room or galley. But mostly, she talks; "chatting up the passengers" is the mainstay of her demanding job, sympathizing with a litany of complaints about aches and pains, lost bifocals, unsatisfactory accommodations, or intolerable tablemates.

Curiously, though she spends hours dispensing comfort and cheer to the L.O.L.'s, the hostess is frequently abused in return, the target of malice never directed at male colleagues but for which she is deemed fair game. It is not clear what prompts these unprovoked outbursts but, invariably, they come with the hostess's territory on every ship. I once sat at a large dining room table with the ship's hostess and half a dozen elderly, female passengers. I happened to know, from mutual friends, that she was married to the cruise director, intelligence never revealed to her tableful of ladies; she was scrupulous about using her maiden name and avoiding her husband's company in public. I wondered if this resolution to maintain separate identities resulted from a company regulation but, when queried, she confided that her secrecy was dictated not by rules but, rather, by passenger response. In the past, when her marriage had been common knowledge, more than one lady passenger had commented to her face that marriage was her primary qualification for the job. The same hostess, I also noticed, consistently arranged her hair atop her head in an elaborate chignon, even at luncheon. When I suggested that it made her seem older, she agreed, pointing out that part of her protective coloring was to narrow the age gap between herself and her tablemates, leaving less leverage for mother/daughter reproof. On another ship, the hostess told me that, invariably, her clothes provoked critical comment. By day, hostesses wear a company uniform, but at night, when they don the evening's choice from what has to be an extensive wardrobe of evening dresses, the L.O.L.'s' knives come out. Everything about the hostess's appearance—from fabric to cut of her dress, including makeup and jewelry—arouses articulated envy or scorn. Such random passenger sniping prompted the hostess to refer to her days on board as "life in the trenches."

Other members of the cruise staff endure their share of passenger torment. Dance teams cope with it all the time. Every ship has a dance team, almost always a British couple who are contracted to perform at occasional evening cabarets as well as give passengers a daily, complimentary dance lesson. Every morning, on almost every cruise ship, after the yoga instructor has relinquished the main lounge, the dance team and their tape recorder take over. Although a few couples appear, most of their passenger pupils are single women who, once the pattern of steps has been established, must dance with each other during practice sessions to follow. Often, to fill the perennial male void, assistant cruise directors have standing orders to attend.

The dance team supplements their wages by giving private lessons, and it is during these encounters, conducted each afternoon in a shuttered nightclub, that lonely or frustrated lady passengers prove troublesome. For a few, the prospect of having a handsome young partner all to themselves is too much and, just as physicians examining female patients are obliged to keep a nurse in attendance, so the husbands of dance teams keep their wives as chaperones in the same room. One man revealed that for certain insistent widows, he must change his traditional dance grip so that his right arm, instead of enfolding his partner, serves as a barrier between them. On one occasion, it was his wife who paid for his resistance. On the cruise's last morning, she was standing at a crowded railing when one of her husband's most rapacious partners crowded in beside her. Rather than provoke a complaint, the wife withdrew to a less crowded vantage point: the widow followed and stood close to her, even though there was plenty of room to either side, and sank her teeth into the dancer's arm.

During long cruises, Old Guard vessels recruit what are called social hosts—half a dozen men temporarily attached to the cruise staff. All of them perform double duty on board: one gives language lessons, another art classes, another golf instruction. But whatever their secondary talent, an overriding and irreplaceable chore is partnering unattached lady passengers. With a ready supply of small talk and inexhaustible enthusiasm for dancing, they are on call whenever an orchestra plays, seeing to it that women alone in the public rooms are not neglected. There are no social hosts on Newpassenger tonnage, where the couple quotient is satisfactory; but Old Guard ships book quantities of widows, so extra men are essential.

Social hosting is a gender switch on that American phenomenon of the twenties, the taxi dance halls conjured up by that famous flapper lament, "Ten Cents a Dance." Financially, social hosts do better, though not by much. They are paid as much as $150 a week, though some companies, Royal Cruise Lines among them, manage to attract social hosts with only the offer of a free ride in addition to airfare to embarkation ports and a cabin by themselves. Some companies throw in free laundry, many defray shipboard tips. Bramson Entertainment Bureau of New York, the world's largest supplier of shipboard performers, recruits social hosts for a variety of companies. Their ideal candidate is an older man—nearer the age of his prospective partners—though they occasionally book social hosts still in their thirties. Retired men often volunteer for the post, filling enforced leisure with travel that they would never be able to afford under normal circumstances. One social host who was a great success on one world cruise was booked for the following year but neglected to tell his employers that he had undergone triple bypass surgery; he could not keep up the pace and had to be flown home. And sometimes, even stout hearts quail. The manager of the *Queen Elizabeth 2*'s branch of Barclay's Bank, upon reaching his company's compulsory retirement age, consented to remain on board as a social host. Though considered indefatigable on the dance floor, he lasted for only one world cruise.

Beyond the physical demands, it is a job that palls with repetition. On long cruises, small talk long since expended, these couples of convenience waltz dispassionately around the floor, each partner's face a mask. But widows and spinsters obviously prefer the system to sitting alone and each year new cadres of social hosts arrive on board. I used to know one, whom I shall call Bill; he sailed regularly on the *Rotterdam*'s world cruises. One year, after I noticed that he was not wearing his customary daytime uniform, one of the cruise staff told me that, on this cruise, Bill was "passengering." He had renounced multiple social obligations to serve instead as exclusive escort to a Sunbelt widow whom he had met the previous year, a woman who was, if not old enough to be his mother, certainly well beyond his years. We talked about his new position, one that seemed ideal for both parties. No sexual intimacy weighted their relationship. His own cabin was adjacent to his employer's, and before lunch and dinner each day, he would escort her to the bar for a drink before leading her on his arm into the dining room, where, incidentally, he was the hit of her all-

Dancing around the world. Social hosts
take up the slack for first-sitting
passengers on board *Rotterdam* during
cocktail hour in the Queen's Lounge.
(Author's collection)

female table. After dinner, he would squire her up to the lounge for dancing and the evening's entertainment. After that, once she had adjourned to the casino, he was free to do as he wished. At ports of call, he was always on tap, accompanying her ashore as guide and factotum. He was provided with pocket money and his bar bills were paid. At voyage's end, he anticipated receiving a handsome tip. (He did.) It seemed an eminently practical solution, one that might make sense for any number of lonely widows who could afford it.

On occasion, social hosts do not complete the course. Recently, six were embarked on a vessel at the start of a world cruise. One got sick, left the ship in the Far East, and reached home only to die of a heart attack. Another was fired for chronic drinking. Two more, who had become favorites of a rich lady passenger, jumped ship with her in Acapulco for an extended Mexican toot. Only two of the original six were left in harness, and they had to dance their feet off all the way around Central America. With mordant gallows humor, one of them divided his clientele into two categories: ballerinas—the most indefatigable—and the Wilis, after that supernatural corps de ballet from *Giselle*.

Some women traveling alone manage an entrée onto the dance floor via ingenuity rather than waiting for an overworked social host. One always booked a seat at the doctor's table, where she was sure to have firsthand word of any incapacitated wives whose husbands would need a dancing partner that evening. Another ingenious woman, a retired schoolteacher, Ella May Fyfe, had some cards printed up before she embarked, little blue rectangles with her name at the center and, beneath, the legend: "World Traveler, Dancing a Specialty." She still uses them to great and gratifying effect.

No one on board, with the possible exception of the captain and chief engineer, carries a more taxing work load than the cruise director. On well-run vessels, he and the captain are good friends; if they are not, they should be, because their combined concerns—one maritime, the other social—for the ship's human cargo demand close cooperation. A captain can serve a cruise director's purpose admirably, most invaluably as ultimate arbiter.

Beset by perseverating passengers, a cruise director can always defer to the captain. The master of a vessel, whether cruise ship or coal barge, can refuse anything with impunity—his word is law. Moreover, he remains aloof from passengers save during fixed ceremonials—the captain's dinner is one—requiring his presence. A captain's apartness from passengers and subordinates alike is advisable. "There's such divinity," as Claudius said, "doth hedge a king." The captain can remove himself to the splendid sanctity of the bridge without question. But a cruise director cannot. He is, in effect, the company's full-time representative on board, officer of the day every day, all day, and much of the night.

There is not a waking moment on board, from dawn jogging to late-night dancing, that does not fall within the purview of the cruise director. In between, there are cabaret performances, lectures, bingo, horse racing, port talks, shore excursions, talent shows, masquerades, boat drills, children's parties, deck sports, tournaments—whether shuffleboard, deck tennis, or backgammon—and the unceasing demands of passengers of every idiosyncratic quirk. The cruise director must keep everything, and everyone, humming, preferably the same pleasing tune. It can be demanding work for months on end. I once asked a Caribbean cruise director how he planned to spend his forthcoming leave. He replied that he was counting the minutes before he could disembark, climb into his car, and "drive as far from the ship, the sea, and passengers" as he could.

That hostess was correct about "life in the trenches." A cruise director at sea is akin to a battalion commander in the front lines, combating tenacious hordes that threaten to overwhelm his position. At the same time, as is every field commander, he is beholden to brigade headquarters far in the rear—perhaps on the other side of the globe—remote superiors who dispatch occasional reinforcements, not all of them seasoned campaigners by any means, and demand incessant situation reports. The cruise director finds himself isolated on two sides—from the passengers he is meant to amuse and from the home office that has hired him. Entertainers, many of whom he does not know and whom he has had no choice in selecting, arrive on board at various ports that, in turn, he has had no choice in selecting either. More than one cruise director has opined that ports on a company's itinerary are selected at random by a man at headquarters equipped with a blindfold and a pin. Yet whatever the entertainment, whatever the itinerary, whatever the passenger displeasure, the cruise director is there to cope with them all.

One classic home office/cruise ship brouhaha symbolizes the difficulties of shore-to-ship meddling. A line's entertainment director once decided that the extrawide masking tape used on board to contrive temporary prosceniums in the lounge was too wide and hence too expensive. A cabled directive went out to the fleet ordaining adoption of a narrower width. Every cruise director telexed back objections; the company man elaborated, unleashing yet again a torrent of complaint. The head man finally won out, but his economies in narrowing the masking tape had been obliterated, for years to come, by the cost of those cabled dialogues overseas.

Cruise staffs inevitably are bonded by frontline camaraderie. The staff know each other well—sometimes too well—and know, moreover, what will happen each day of their lives for months in advance. Ship, ports, and itinerary are grindingly familiar; there are no surprises. And the great shipboard certainty is that each embarkation day, hundreds of novice passengers with nothing but time and a desire for diversion will swarm on board to make demands. Many are newcomers, bewildered, gauche, or defensive, never as slim, tanned, or knowledgeable as the cruise staff that is supposed to befriend them. Too often, the staff perceives them less as guests of the company then as intruders into an otherwise well-oiled routine. The task of sorting them out, answering their questions, teaching them the geography of the ship, setting the tempo of their days at sea or in port, is time-consuming, a rite of passage dominating the beginning of each cruise. As the voyage progresses, that passenger-care quotient subsides. It is revealing, on any ship, to monitor the noise level in the dining room each evening, increasing as it does from the first night's hesitant buzz to a crescendo of chatter by cruise's end. Dining room managers aboard *Queen Elizabeth 2* are instructed, each successive evening, to lower lighting levels in the dining room, diminishing illumination cross-curved against decibels. By the same token, the necessity for staff support is similarly reduced as the passenger organism begins generating its own momentum.

But it is not an easy process. Some passengers never settle down, and troublemakers can plague every cruise. On embarkation day, the cruise director and his staff stand just inside the shell plating, dressed in their best, faces frozen in company smiles. They greet incoming passengers, pose with them for the obligatory boarding photograph, and pass them along to the cabin stewards, who will guide them below. It is a busy time, but not so busy that one cruise director I know cannot spot the difficult ones. "You can see 'em coming for miles, the minute they step onto the gangplank," he reports. According to him, there are lady passengers of a certain age with sullen mouths whom he has learned to treat with extreme caution. He is also attuned to hectoring or abusive men and, always, drunkards of either sex—passengers who stagger along the deck even when the vessel is moored securely to the pier.

Drunks, of course, create perennial problems everywhere, nowhere more irritatingly than on board ship. The loud and aggressive varieties are especially disruptive in the lounges. One drunkard on the *France* derived his greatest pleasure from haranguing the assistant pursers, who, in those days, introduced the entertainers. The French Line was scrupulous in training its crew members of every rank to accommodate the behavior or appearance of their clients. I remember once watching with awe the mute impassivity of two young *mousses*—the red-liveried bellboys—whose duty it was to open and close the dining room doors at the top of the dining room staircase; no flicker of surprise or amazement marred their composure, however surreptitiously, as bizarrely dressed cruise passengers paraded by them en route to lunch. But the drunk in the Salon Fontaine-bleau had to be dealt with and was, summarily. Before a roomful of passengers, the purser delivered so withering a reproof that the man desisted and stumbled out. It was a rare confrontational occasion on board that exquisitely run vessel.

If they are to be plagued by dipsomaniacs, cruise directors prefer extreme cases, those who can legitimately be passed along to the supervision of the master-at-arms or the surgeon. The sometimes-tipsy passenger is much more unpredictable than the falling-down drunk; if rebuked, he has a way of sobering up the following morning and putting indignant pen to paper for a letter of complaint to company headquarters. Matson Line ships crossing the Pacific always had their share of alcoholic passengers and used to circulate a "dry list," names of those to whom bartenders and sommeliers could dispense only the softest of drinks. But determined topers circumvent those restrictions with ease, either buying their own bottles ashore or bribing crewmen handsomely to keep them supplied at sea. On some ships, drunks achieve a kind of awful celebrity. There is one lady passenger who, inadvertently late one night, was elected an honorary member of a certain ship's wardroom. She remembered the honor quite clearly the next morning and now, whenever on board, monopolizes what is, in effect, the officers' private club each night, escorted—or carried—down to her cabin in the small hours by one or more of her fellow members.

But not all heavy drinkers on board are passengers: some can be found among the crew. Most do not let drink interfere with their onstage duties, but those that do are remembered. There was an Australian sommelier on one Royal Viking ship who was flown home to Sydney from a port of call in midcruise. He had been popular with his passengers, who, when they inquired of his offense, were told that he "had had trouble with his elbow." "Trouble with his elbow," it developed, had been a weakness for strong drink during working hours, culminating in a reprehensible episode in the lounge one afternoon. A rota of dining room stewards, the sommelier among them, serve tea there each day. On board was a lame passenger who had with him one of those swivel chairs mounted on an electrically driven platform, which he would drive into the lounge before transferring to a chair for tea. Leaving the unattended toy within the tipsy sommelier's range was a mistake; he mounted it and raced at top speed up and down the aisles of the lounge, pulling cloths off tables as he went, scattering stewards, passengers, and trays with hilarious abandon before being apprehended and unhorsed by a posse of assistant hotel managers summoned from below.

But boozers apart, each cruise has its share of difficult passengers. They come in all sizes. Children booked on board a Royal Viking cruise one summer inconvenienced an entire passageway by stuffing cabin door locks with toothpicks late one night. Elsewhere, nocturnal colleagues were busy collecting potted palms from every deck foyer and putting them into the elevators: passengers closing up the nightclub early the next morning were nonplussed when summoned elevators resembled stuffed hothouses. Another child on board was a junior pyromaniac who enjoyed starting fires in wastebaskets at the bottom of stairwells.

Ship's medical personnel are always privy to what might be described as the passengers' soft underbelly. Janet Olczak, who was a nurse on board the *Norway* during the ship's conversion, maiden voyage, and early Miami service, had her own rule of thumb when summoned to cope with emergencies on board: "Below the waist, a broken leg; above the waist, a heart attack." Often, she would respond to urgent calls from the ship's discotheque only to minister to a supine geriatric felled by too much drink. One extraordinary late-night call came from a priest who, while cleaning a licensed pistol, had shot himself; Janet always wondered why the priest felt he needed a gun on board and how he managed to shoot himself on the underside of his left buttock in the course of oiling the weapon. But in truth, ship's medicos have learned to be cautious because their passenger load is larded with potential invalids. Clients who have planned and paid for a cruise months in advance are loath to cancel because of last-minute medical crises. Hence, there are dozens of medical time bombs on board: behind the façade of outward well-being lurk any number of bleeders, arthritics, epileptics, cardiacs, tumids, or hypertensives. Some passengers have been known to check themselves out of hospitals to sail on time.

World-cruise surgeons are surfeited with borderline patients. Only in extremis do elderly passengers produce the medical histories prepared by sympathetic hometown physicians; usually, those reports make appalling reading, betraying vulnerability of a high order. Many afflicted on the far side of the globe, either in midocean or within reach of marginal hospital facilities ashore, should patently have been allowed no further from home than a neighboring town. The *Rotterdam*'s senior doctor once made a cabin call in the midst of a world cruise. He entered a large suite. Parked in the foyer were two walkers; next to them was a pair of wheelchairs. Both cabin occupants were tucked up in bed, one a woman well past ninety, the other—a companion—in her late eighties. Traveling with them was a middle-aged nephew—the nonagenarian's ultimate beneficiary—who "looked in on" his charges only once each day. The two women remained below for the entire cruise, almost oblivious of whether their vessel was in port or at sea. But at least they stayed put and made no clamor to be included on shore excursions. Surgeons must often refuse, despite fierce objections, certification to elderly passengers clearly unable to withstand the rigors of a taxing, overland trek to Peking, for instance. Both those cabin-bound ladies survived the cruise, and the doctor admitted later that it made more sense for them to be traveling by sea rather than vegetating somewhere in a retirement home ashore. The same doctor recalled another trio: two sisters who were traveling with their grandfather. He was confined to a wheelchair, but they saw to it that he was not confined to his cabin, and each evening, though he was almost completely aphasic, they dressed him in black tie and wheeled him into the Ocean Bar for a drink before taking him and his chair down to the dining room. He was, apparently, enormously rich and his grandchildren saw to it that neither he nor they lacked anything during their three months on board.

There are some passengers who arrive on board in perfect health, but make it their business to seek compensation for injuries—real or contrived—sustained during the cruise. America's judicial system is succumbing to what Chief Justice Burger has called "an orgy of litigation," and some cruise passengers are adding to the load. One man, stuck in a malfunctioning elevator for twenty minutes, settled out of court for $5,000 and a free cruise. A wife who slipped in her cabin bathtub sued the company for $1.2 million, including $300,000 for loss of consortium with her husband. Some "bathtub slippers," as they are identified in actuarial casebooks, are not very clever. A woman who slipped in the tub on board ship argued that no adhesive friction strips had been applied to its bottom. They were found, balled up in Kleenex, in the bathroom's wastepaper basket. A septuagenarian widow with acknowledged bad eyesight fell down a ship's staircase while dressed in a hula costume; she broke both ankles and a wrist and tried collecting damages from the shipping line for "allowing masquerade parties on board." A woman who fell while boarding a tender to go ashore sued the company for negligence, claiming severe concussion. She made two mistakes: first, staying ashore and shopping happily for the day, and second, remaining silent for weeks after she had returned home. I am well acquainted with this last case because I was foreman of the jury that decided against her.

Not all conniving passengers stoop to injury in an attempt to claim damages. Some do so with cumulative complaints, a Chinese water torture litany of discontent. A hostess on board a Sitmar ship noticed that one of her lady passengers seemed unhappy on principle, displeased with her bridge partners as well as the quality of the prizes she received. (These are the assorted trinkets—bookmarks, scarves, and souvenir pens—that all companies dish out as premiums to their clients.) At daily staff meetings, it emerged that the same woman also found endless fault in the dining room, dissatisfied with tablemates, stewards, and the food. The purser reported that she was at his desk at least once daily, fretting about her accommodation. A telexed inquiry to company headquarters revealed that the year before, on another ship of the line, the same passenger had complained so relentlessly that she had been given a free cruise in compensation. Her attempt to repeat the scam was aborted after a curt session in the purser's office.

A justifiably litigious grievance was initiated by the father of an adolescent girl who filed a charge of statutory rape against a cruise director. Ostensibly discussing the details of a forthcoming "sweet sixteen party" in the young woman's cabin, the couple was discovered in flagrante delicto by her outraged papa. The cruise director was flown home, and the case dragged on for years. This incident hardly typifies the subject it raises: sexual dalliance between passengers and crew, which is discreet but widespread, and is nowhere more prevalent than on one- or two-week Newpassenger cruises.

Though unattached Newpassengers may be young or unsophisticated, most are conditioned to believe that a cruise should encompass what their parents might have characterized as "a little romance." But in this era of sexual permissiveness, romance is short-order, as brief and uncomplicated as a stop at a fast-food franchise. On board ship especially, lovers "pass in the night" just as ephemerally and poignantly as Longfellow's converging vessels. Moreover, susceptible passengers are already halfway there. They are booked on a voyage of adventure and novelty, journeying to a remote, magical kingdom. Embarked, they relish their quasi-anonymity no less than the seductive tropicality: a mood of insouciance takes hold, stopping well short of promiscuity but relaxing hometown strictures. And there is no more likely liaison on board than one between lady passengers and ship's officers. "The uniform used to do it," mused a retired hotel manager once. "They seemed *mad* about the uniform."

In point of fact, most initial contacts are made—specifically and literally—out of uniform. Around the pool of every Newpassenger cruise ship during the first day at sea will be a group of observant males. They are the ship's junior officers, mostly bachelors but, it must be admitted, occasionally married. They are clad in bathing suits, indistinguishable from male passengers except for their tans, which betray them as habitual shipboard occupants. But that day they are less concerned with enriching their bronzed patina than their ensuing week at sea. Clustered near the deck entrances, they search for an attractive female prospect. Once she is spotted—preferably alone—she will be presented with a surprise drink, delivered free-of-charge by a well-briefed steward who will indicate, with an ingenuous smile, her distant but attentive benefactor. Contact thus established, the rest follows easily: if the drink's recipient is as enterprising as its donor, a relationship crystallizes at once. A cruise director once complained that Norwegian officers tend to be tight-fisted while drinking in bars ashore; but on board, at least during those crucial, first-day pool encounters, their generosity seems unbounded.

The legendary amatory success of the ship's officer derives less from his appearance than an essential territorial prerogative. Single women tend to travel in pairs, sharing a cabin: logistically as well as emotionally, they are discouraged from entertaining visitors of the opposite sex. A dislodged cabinmate, however obliging the first time, may soon feel slighted; moreover, she remains a sobering link to hometown morality. Crew members who share cabin space and wish privacy while receiving visitors hang a specially coded DO NOT DISTURB sign on the outer doorknob to alert unwanted roommates. A drummer on board a Royal Cruise Lines vessel had the misfortune to be bunked in with a sexually adventurous roommate, and got very little sleep in his own berth. Resourceful passengers will sometimes reshuffle obliging friends on a permanent basis, shipboard accommodation of a high order: two Sun Line passengers who became lovers on a cruise rearranged the occupants of no less than three adjacent cabins so that they could have one to themselves.

But the ship's officer has his own quarters, discreetly backstage, beyond the ken of the passenger audience. He has, thus, an inescapable edge over male passenger rivals in addition to whatever the mystical, sartorial appeal of his tropical whites. Lady passengers who pass a night in officer country see it, inevitably, as a cachet, a forgivable conquest without stigma attached: no scarlet letters are embroidered on contemporary shipboard

T-shirts. There was a not atypical incident very early one morning atop the upper decks of the *Rotterdam*. Normally, the narrow deck flanking the officers' quarters is deserted at that hour, but on this particular morning, the ship was entering Rio's fabled Guanabara Bay and almost the entire passenger complement crowded every railed vantage point. The door from the officers' passageway opened and a young woman stepped out daintily into the dawn, still in evening dress, carrying a purse in one hand and sandals in the other. When she saw the assembled gallery, she retired in confusion. After a moment, she reemerged, braving the scrutiny of hundreds of eyes and even some sporadic applause to walk gaily back to passenger country.

It was not always so. Indeed, on board the vessels of one company cruising out of Miami in the early seventies, the owners, some of whom were Spanish, enforced a rigid sexual apartheid. Passenger/crew liaisons were forbidden, as were those between male and female crew members. Stewardesses, singers, and hostesses were housed along cloistered passageways, like college sorority rows of a sanitized MGM musical in the fifties. The mingling of sexes within crew cabins was grounds for dismissal. Enforcing this regulation on board one ship of the line was a staff captain—traditionally charged on every ship with crew discipline—who stalked crew passageways in search of transgressors. Outside the cabin of an entertainer newly arrived on board, he distinctly heard two separate voices—male and female—through the door. Summoning the master-at-arms, he confronted the occupant forthwith, an astonished and uncomprehending ventriloquist who had been rehearsing for his performance the following evening. The duenna/staff captain, attempting to save a very red face, searched the cabin regardless.

I remember once, when I was a passenger on board the *Queen Elizabeth 2* in the Caribbean, that a bar steward in one of the public rooms struck up a discreet relationship with an attractive lady passenger. They were not young; he was a senior man and she was, in her mid-fifties, the type of single passenger who might otherwise have had an isolated cruise. On board, throughout his tours of duty, she would sit patiently in the dim light at one of his tables, nursing what I presume to have been a succession of complimentary drinks and talking quietly with him whenever he was free. She was rooted there for most of the days and evenings at sea. Only ashore, in hotel swimming pools, could the two be openly affectionate. (Caribbean hotel managements discourage cruise passengers; they do not rent rooms, they spend little money for lunch, and they are gone by nightfall. Regardless, passengers and crew alike always manage to infiltrate hotel lidos from beach or boulevard.) At every port of call on that cruise, the steward and his lady friend were much in evidence. Dressed in bathing suits, they seemed no different from any middle-aged couple enjoying a vacation at a resort hotel save for two incriminating pieces of evidence: the steward's forearms, covered with the luxuriant, tattooed stigmata of long service in Britain's merchant navy service, gave the game away to at least one keen shipboard observer. This was in the early seventies, and it has not been lost on me that, as the cruise market has broadened, elaborately tattooed swimmers are no longer exclusively crew members.

Passenger/officer affairs produce interesting ramifications, some comic but most not. On one Greek ship, crew members were always delighted when their staff captain's advances to lady passengers were reciprocated because it meant that he was no longer "on their case" so diligently. A passenger who spent most of her cruise in the cabin of a bachelor Sun Line officer met him a week later on an Athens sidewalk accompanied by his wife and children, a not uncommon denouement for many shipboard scenarios of this kind. Some women fall hopelessly for their officer suitors, a love that is seldom reciprocated after cruise's end. Though officers occasionally do meet their future wives as passengers, those happy endings are in the minority. The postvoyage emotional differential is significant; the departing lady passenger has been one of consecutive dozens, a carousel of cruise conquests. The officer, that evocative, sun-bronzed deity waving farewell from the bridge wing high above the turmoil of debarkation, fills, in retrospect, a compelling niche at the center of a cherished cruise façade. Perfumed letters to the ship from faraway towns are frequent legacies of these cruise trysts, a threnody of lingering, unrequited entreaty that seldom arouses a sympathetic response.

Yet though the shipboard affair may be endemic to most cruise ships, not all lady passengers traveling alone are, by any means, interested or ensnared. A recent fellow passenger of mine—a high school teacher from Texas named Jane—is tired of maritime lotharios. An attractive divorcee, she sails on at least one cruise each year and, much as she adores the life on board, finds the sexual pressures as onerous as the general irresponsibility. "Nobody seems to care about anything but fun, sex, and what they have bought." Males, both crew and passengers, urge her to "be romantic" and remind her continually that "this is a cruise" and that she should "take advantage of every opportunity." As an academic, she is less curious about the prowess of her fellow passengers than the seas and ports to which the ship is carrying her. She books religiously on every shore excursion, despite her admirers' protestations that she will be too tired for what they describe with unassailable optimism as "the festivities of the evening." She concluded a letter to me with the assessment: "I realize that I am not your typical tourist." On the contrary, I think she is, refreshingly so, and hope that her future sailing will be less aggravated by sexual opportunists.

Love afloat notwithstanding, the extremes of passenger behavior are challenging, keeping a ship's backstage crew perpetually on its collective toes. A woman in distress appealed to the purser one day at sea, saying that her husband was behaving irrationally, even writing her threatening notes. The purser assigned her to an empty cabin, located where he hoped her deranged husband could not find her. But, with the cunning of the insane, he did, ambushing and assaulting her brutally in the passageway as soon as she emerged the following morning; both were put ashore at the next available port. There was a very rich woman, the widow of an admiral, who once sailed on the *Queen Mary* to the Mediterranean. She always arrived at Southampton's Ocean Terminal in a chauffeur-driven Rolls, sweeping grandly on board with a fortune in matched luggage. But salt air precipitated bizarre changes in mood. She never slept and the ship's wildest passengers were drawn irresistibly to her like moths to a flame, carousing each night in her cabin. Inevitably, sleepless neighbors telephoned the purser's office and night stewards would be dispatched to intervene, though not without risk: one peacemaking crewman was ejected bodily into the passageway with a bleeding nose and half his jacket torn off.

Stewardesses on a vessel passing through the Panama Canal were alternately intrigued and repelled by a young German couple occupying the most expensive suite on board. The couple apparently used neither shower nor tub; fresh towels hung daily in the bathroom were never touched. Either they never bathed or confined makeshift ablutions to the swimming pools. Diane Boyd, the *Sagafjord* stewardess we have already met, once looked after two couples occupying adjacent suites high up in the ship. Bound home from Alaska that summer, the husband of the first couple bought his wife a new mink jacket in Victoria; she, in turn, presented her old one to the stewardess, in addition to a sizable tip. Immediately next door was a different pair, clearly very odd types. Within days of sailing from San Francisco, the hostile wife accused the stewardess of stealing from her, reviling her whenever their paths crossed. On the last morning—just after she had been presented with the mink jacket next door—the stewardess was tipped, hastily and almost surreptitiously, by the husband. Only after they had disembarked did the stewardess find that the wife had left a remembrance of her own in the cabin: walls and doors

298

298   LINERS TO THE SUN

were smeared with makeup and every mirrored surface bore obscene, vindictive graffiti scrawled in eyebrow pencil.

Here, after this final, baffling glimpse of contrasting passenger psyches, we shall tiptoe out the stage door, leaving shipboard's backstage denizens to the privacy of their own floating cosmos. Whatever sea delights they share with the passenger load, their inward, private existence is testing. In the wings, behind the scenes, and in dressing rooms, that backstage life seems twilit, only occasional surges of color relieving the monochrome. The cruise ship sonata, if there is one, seems a plaintive melody, picked out on the black keys.

Years ago, on board the *Queen Elizabeth 2*, the cruise director was housed in a cabin forward on the starboard side of One Deck. Walling off his length of corridor was a door marked CREW ONLY. On the other side of the door, read as one regained passenger country, was another sign: ESCAPE. For those abandoning ship, presumably it indicated the proximity of the main staircase 100 feet aft. But every time I saw that sign, it occurred to me that, coincidentally, it served to indicate a symbolic bolt-hole, respite from a demanding and sometimes deadly schedule, week in and week out, for years on end.

It was midnight—Norm was asleep.
I had been reading in bed and put my
book down when I smelled smoke.

—VIVIAN QUILLINAN, *Prinsendam*
PASSENGER ON HER FIRST CRUISE

8.
Dark Nights

Despite their bulk, passenger liners are almost as vulnerable to damage as the human cargo they carry. As miniature models, they are tested exhaustively in a tank, pitting their design characteristics against miniature waves in artificially induced torment. This testing is an essential prerequisite for all newbuilding, and vessels beset by storm almost always prevail. Most shipboard emergencies arise internally, and can occur even in the calmest of waters. Fires or groundings may happen at any time, as can mechanical failures of circuitry, plumbing, navigation, or propulsion.

Passengers and crew can fail as well, interrupting the cruise just as unpredictably as a shattered bearing or balky circuit-breaker. This chapter, then, concerns random shipboard emergencies and disasters, dark nights when things elemental, mechanical, or human go wrong, turning events from their anticipated course.

Our first encounter is with a rogue wave, produced by an underwater disruption of the seafloor hundreds of miles away. The wave collided with the *Rotterdam* off the coast of North Africa in January 1976 as she lay outside the port of Casablanca; Captain Cornelius van Herk was on the bridge. The ship had arrived early on the first leg of the world cruise from Fort Lauderdale. The second officer had just concluded a conversation with the pilot station ashore over the radio; it had been agreed that the *Rotterdam* would wait outside the breakwater for an hour and would pick up the pilot inside because of weather conditions prevailing. There was a stiff breeze blowing onshore, winds that qualified on the Beaufort Scale of 1 through 12 as Force 5, "a fresh breeze with winds between 17 and 21 knots," with "waves more pronounced and longer form, more white horses, and some spray."

Van Herk reduced his engine speed to conserve fuel while he waited. He ordered the ship's stabilizers, which had been deployed, back inside the hull because, at slow speed, they are ineffectual in dampening roll. Shortly afterward, both Captain van Herk and his chief officer, Mr. Post-humus, heard an unusual and extraordinary roaring noise. Both turned to starboard and saw, bearing down on the ship, a huge wave. Van Herk later estimated its height at 100 feet, completely white and breaking at its crest, a crest over his head, even though he stood 70 feet above the surface of the ocean. Moving at awesome speed, the wall of water smashed directly against the *Rotterdam*'s starboard flank. The impact was staggering. Immediately, the vessel experienced a swift, plunging roll to port, later estimated at anywhere from forty degrees (by van Herk) to seventy degrees (by passengers below). No one can ever be sure either way. Bridge clinometers, those free-swinging pendulums suspended on the wheelhouse's after wall, do not, as a rule, record terminal extremes. Whenever such an abrupt list occurs, the effect is usually so riveting that observing the movement of the clinometer is seldom uppermost in the minds of those in command, who are more concerned with hanging on for dear life to prevent themselves from tumbling down against the side of the bridge.

The wall of water that assaulted the ship that morning has been christened by oceanographers with the Japanese composite word *tsunami* (*tsu* means port, *nami* means wave), a predictable elision for a country whose shores and harbors are periodically devastated by seismic waves resulting from earthquakes, eruptions, or landslides many miles away below the surface. Tsunamis are most perilous near shore. Had the *Rotter-*

dam encountered the same wave in midocean, no one on board, from Captain van Herk on down, would have noticed its passing, for, in deep water, the tsunami's height is seldom more than a yard. Moreover, it travels incredibly fast, at approximately 340 knots. When the wave reaches shoal water, however, its height increases phenomenally. There is a continental shelf off the Moroccan coast, the underwater, sloping foothills, so to speak, of the hinterland's Atlas Mountains. A mile off Casablanca's Grande Jettée, where Holland America's flagship was awaiting entry into port, the water is only 12 fathoms deep. Interestingly enough, the first indication that those on shore would have of the tsunami's approach would be an abnormally large recession of water seaward, a fleeting harbinger of catastrophic flooding to follow.

The sudden, violent angle the *Rotterdam* assumed immediately after the impact was like nothing her captain or crew had experienced during the vessel's years of service since 1959. Captain van Herk's immediate concern was to bring his vessel's bows around to the west. The first of a tsunami's wave series is not necessarily the worst: often, the fifth or sixth will be even higher. It was essential to turn the ship ninety degrees, pointing her in the direction of attack rather than submitting to subsequent broadsides. Working port engine ahead and starboard astern, with his rudder hard over, the captain managed to turn the still oscillating *Rotterdam* into the west. Had he lost electrical power as a result of that first impact, there is every reason to suspect that the ship might have recovered from the first terrible blow only to be driven helplessly onto the Grande Jettée or the Towne Reef, which was within sight only a mile and a half over the heaving stern. So the ship was saved from capsize or being driven onto the coast. But the on-board effect of even that single, momentous roll was devastating.

The most damaging characteristic of the *Rotterdam*'s sudden heave to port—whether forty degrees or seventy degrees—was a whiplash effect. As the ship rolled, dozens of deck chairs went overboard, flipped over the side of the ship; those along the starboard promenade were hurled against the public-room windows, some of which shattered, and several Promenade Deck windows caved in under the weight of water. (Among my collection of steamship artifacts is a fragment of that shattered safety glass, almost opaque with fracture lines, retrieved from the Promenade Deck after the *Rotterdam*'s Casablanca roll.) Deck chairs farther aft were flung into the sagging cargo net covering the drained open-air pool; the *Rotterdam*'s recovery from the roll was just as abrupt as the initial response.

Rotterdam deck chairs, before and after. This is the way the Upper Promenade deck would have looked moments before the tsunami hit. *Left,* crewmen fish chairs out of the *Rotterdam*'s netted on-deck pool following the roll. *(Author's collection and Holland America Line)*

Petrus van den Bemt, the *Rotterdam*'s chief housekeeper, had been unable to sleep that night and was one of the few hotel officers up that early. When the wave struck, he was standing in the main square on Lower Promenade Deck aft of the staircase talking with a pair of Indonesian stewards. When the ship heeled, he grabbed a nearby stanchion with one hand and the collar of one of the stewards with the other; he managed to secure the second man between his knees with a scissors grip. All around him was the clatter of breaking glass and china as the display shelves of the Lynbaan, the *Rotterdam*'s shopping complex, burst through their plate-glass windows. Window displays on board ship are just as ambitious as those ashore: breakables and fragile items are anchored down with a sticky, puttylike substance that New York theatrical prop men call "morticians' wax." But that impact tore everything loose and entire shelf-loads were wrenched from their brass fittings, cascading out onto the portside carpeting.

It was just as well that van den Bemt and the stewards had not been forward of the staircase. One of the most formidable projectiles thundering athwartship across the *Rotterdam* that morning demolished the casino doorway. Weighing several hundred pounds, it was an electric mechanical roulette machine the size of two large bass drums stacked one atop the other. Parked but not anchored just inside the entrance, it was set in diabolical motion by the violent list, bursting through the casino's locked steel-and-glass door and cannonading across the square before crashing against the port wall. The paneling there still bears the scars. It would have killed anyone in its path. One deck higher, aft in the Ritz Carlton, the grand piano from the bandstand was found wedged beneath the staircase on the opposite side of the ship. It had pursued the same lethal orbit as the roulette machine and, again, no one on the dance floor or sitting at a table in its path would have survived.

Indeed, the miracle was that of any time for a tidal wave to have struck the vessel, between 5:00 A.M. and 6:00 A.M. was the best moment. The Tropic Bar had closed two hours earlier and every passenger was asleep. If the impact had come at any other time of day or night—when people were sunbathing in deck chairs, trying their luck in the casino, lining up for breakfast in the Lido Restaurant, or dancing in either the Main Lounge or Ritz Carlton—the carnage would have been appalling. As it was, there were fractures aplenty but no fatalities.

But even passengers asleep in their cabins were in for a rude awakening. One was Eleanor Britten, a New York travel agent who had a party of clients on board. Eleanor has sailed the oceans of the world for decades. She had been vaguely aware, since early that morning, of the ship's

304

sea-motion, but when the great upheaval came, she was only half-conscious. She remembers wondering, groggily, at the sudden flare of early-morning light in her cabin, then seeing the porthole curtains standing straight out from the wall, as did a dress hanging in the corner. These visual impossibilities confused her for a split second before she realized that she was being pressed uncomfortably against the restraining board flanking what had become, alarmingly, the down side of her berth. She cried out in pain as the cabin bureau toppled onto her shoulder, a blow as painful as it was fortuitously beneficial: with one abrupt, punishing crack, it cured the bursitis that had been plaguing her for years. As the *Rotterdam* recovered and began its reverse roll to starboard, Eleanor Britten remained imprisoned by that overturned bureau. With time to reflect, she was mystified to find her bed awash in what seemed a gruel of golf balls and mud. Only later, after stewards, forcing an entry through an adjoining cabin rather than her blocked entrance, had freed her from a tangle of bedclothes, furniture, and belongings, did it all make sense: the golf balls were a cache of plastic creamer containers stored in her ice bucket and the mud was scattered mulch and vermiculite showered into the melted ice from up-turned plants that had been brought on board by well-wishers in Florida.

All over the ship, passengers were imprisoned in their cabins. Teams of crewmen and stewards worked their way along every passageway, trying and entering each door, more often than not releasing entombed occupants from a welter of dislodged cabin furniture. There were several broken arms and legs; every doctor on board was dragooned into service by the ship's hard-pressed surgeons, helping to set bones and soothing bruised or sprained limbs. Every working space on the ship was a shambles: the purser's and shore excursion offices were ankle-deep in papers and over-turned desks, the galley, storerooms, and bakery a wasteland of broken eggs, fruit, and flour. A carpet of glass and china shards adorned both dining rooms. In the casino, the cash-drawer had burst on impact, scattering currency and slot machine tokens throughout the interior.

Captain van Herk decided not to call at Casablanca at all: Morocco was aborted in favor of the cruise's next port, Villefranche. During the ensuing two days at sea, passengers recuperating from their dawn excitement exchanged war stories: "Where were you when the wave hit?" punctuated every conversation. Perhaps the most amusing story was told by an elderly couple sleeping in parallel twin berths when the cabin turned on edge. The husband was hurled, still asleep, into his wife's arms—"The first time," he reported to all who would listen, "I've been in Emily's bed for years!"

Milton and Bea Bronston, the *Rotterdam*'s bridge experts, were awakened down in cabin 617. Bea always places the cabin's Gideon Bible on top of the cabinet separating the beds to leave more drawer space. The wave hit, toppling the volume squarely onto her sleeping husband's head. "For the first time," he remembers ruefully, "I got religion, all of a sudden." Bea staggered out of bed, intent on picking up her vitamin bottles, which were rolling about on the floor. But her husband told her to get back in bed, that no vitamins were worth getting killed for.

It seemed a common instinct to start picking up the pieces at once or, in the case of Bill Kephart, in another cabin on that world cruise, to get dressed. But putting on trousers while the cabin floor was at such unpredictable angles was impossible, and his wife, Ann, in turn, recommended that he get back into bed. But a woman in a cabin adjoining the Kepharts' was injured very badly as she lay in her berth. Both legs were seriously hurt and she was flown to an Israeli hospital in Haifa, where doctors managed to avoid the possibility of amputation. She rejoined the vessel a fortnight later.

Another tsunami disrupted the cruise of the *Bergensfjord* when she was circumnavigating South America in the early sixties. Late one night, those on board felt as though the vessel's keel had struck a submerged reef; a tremendous jolt had sent the ship toppling to port. The encounter was, in fact, the first of several shock waves that for some reason—perhaps shifted cargo—sustained the list for several hours. Many of the passengers were still up and about. In the Main Lounge, dancers disentangling themselves from the heap in which they had been tumbled against the port wall were serenaded for several minutes by a bizarre electronic chorus, spontaneous *musique concrète* from the room's loudspeakers, which reflected the drubbing absorbed by the system's amplifiers. All passengers were ordered into their life jackets before it was verified that the hull was intact and that the *Bergensfjord*, despite her continuing list, was in no danger of foundering.

One or two passengers experienced minor heart palpitations, occasioned less by the first shock than an uneasy aftermath of hastening up to the lifeboats. Several passengers ran on the flat as well, caught in the wrong cabin at the moment of crisis and hurrying discreetly back to their own quarters to retrieve valuables and life belts before mustering on deck. A few passengers, their hearts in perfect order, were terrified nonetheless. Two sisters lamented loudly throughout the night, swearing in chorus that they would never sail in a ship again if they survived the disaster. (The

LINERS TO THE SUN

Bergensfjord's hostess subsequently encountered one of them on another ship, none the worse for wear.)

Stories that made the rounds of the smoking room the following day included one classic. A woman traveling alone had been annoyed ever since boarding by a loose screw in the paneling next to her closet: its sharp edge was forever catching the fabric of her clothing as she brushed past it. She kept forgetting to tell the steward about it and one night, before retiring, decided to take matters into her own hands. Using the round end of a nail file, she tried tightening the screw, but with no success; so she loosened it instead. Slowly but with increasing ease, she unscrewed it until, triumphantly, she was able to pull it from the wall. At that precise instant, the *Bergensfjord* reacted to the underwater tremor, lurching hideously to port. For the rest of the night, the terrified woman was convinced that it had been her meddling with the vessel's infrastructure that had triggered the emergency.

The fear of those two sisters during that dark night's list is understandable. A continuing slope on board a ship, even of only a few degrees, is unsettling. Sometimes, ships tied up at Charlotte Amalie's pier are listed purposely to port by the chief engineer in order to avoid grounding the starboard bilge keel in the accumulated silt next to the pier. The effect on board is disturbing. Once, during a crossing I made on board the *Queen Elizabeth 2*, a persistent gale from out of the northeast actually helped drive the vessel westward, with substantial fuel savings. The entire flank of the Cunarder behaved like a sail; ballast tanks and stabilizers were set to sustain a five-degree list for much of the day. It made everything on board awkward for the passengers, from eating to climbing stairs to dressing for dinner.

It was during that crossing, in fact, that the late Willy Farmer, *Queen Elizabeth 2*'s chief engineer, reminisced about *his* darkest night on board, early in the spring of 1974. It was April Fools' Day, and when Willy was first aroused from sleep in his cabin, he hoped that his caller might be pulling his leg. But the duty engineer was all business, reporting on the telephone that "the boilers were out." It was that plural, Willy remembers— boilers with an *s*—that filled him with dread. The *Queen Elizabeth 2* has three boilers: two are customarily in service, a third serves as backup. "With one boiler out, I could have coped," he said. "But two meant we were in trouble." He found out shortly thereafter that all three were useless.

An oil feeder pipe in the engine room had fractured without triggering the alarm that should have alerted duty engineers. Fuel had contaminated the ultrapure water circulating through the ship's boiler tubing before the system could be shut down. The *QE2*'s great heart had stopped beating: lights all over the vessel flickered out, and when standby generators roared into life, only bleak emergency circuits came on. Air-conditioning quit as well, and passengers awoke to an uncomfortable mugginess building up below decks. The engineers tried valiantly to raise steam in the ship's third boiler, and passengers felt the almost human shudder that resulted. For half an hour, the *Queen Elizabeth 2* limped along at reduced speed, but by dawn, Farmer and Captain Peter Jackson agreed that, to avoid further abuse of the system, the turbines should not be pressed. The *Queen Elizabeth 2*, en route to a seven-day cruise in the Caribbean, lay dead in the water between New York and St. Thomas, with 1,648 passengers and 940 crew on board.

As I would find out on board another vessel six years later, a passenger ship without electricity is uncomfortable, especially in semitropical waters. There is no light, no cooking, no cooling, and, almost worst of all, no water; pools are empty, toilets do not flush, all cabins and public rooms become stifling. Passengers were in no immediate danger; the *Queen Elizabeth 2* was adrift in the midst of the ocean with no reefs or shoals closer than Bermuda, 280 miles to the northeast. Throughout the first day, the mood on board was adventurous: passengers joked, enjoyed warm drinks from free bars, and made light of improvised buffets of canned meats and salads.

That Tuesday afternoon, thirty-six hours after the first sign of trouble, Victor Matthews, chairman of Trafalgar, Cunard's parent company, sent a message to all on board, admitting the unlikelihood of restoring power at sea. "The odds of immediate success are not favorable," he predicted. Another sultry day passed on the immobilized liner, less amusing than the last. The cruise's dietary regime became monotonous; after twenty-four hours without power, quantities of perishables in danger of going bad had been thrown over the side. Tap water became cloudy.

Plans for the off-loading of *QE2*'s passengers were put in operation. Every vessel in distress has its maritime helpmate somewhere over the horizon—the *Titanic* had her *Carpathia*, the *Andrea Doria* her *Ile de France, Morro Castle* her *Monarch of Bermuda*—and that April of 1974 the *Queen Elizabeth 2* had *Sea Venture*, one of two ships of the Norwegian-owned Flagship Cruise Lines, now the *Pacific Princess*. She was a 20,000-ton motorship, only three years in service, a Bermuda government contract ship on weekly tourist visits between New York and the island. When Cunard's call for assistance came, she was tied up alongside Front Street in Hamilton in the midst of a three-day stopover.

Top, encounter in midocean. *Sea Venture* passengers crowd the rails for a glimpse of the stricken Cunarder. *Bottom,* the shuttle under way. Although three of the *QE2*'s starboard boats are hanging below their davits, none were used in the transfer. *(Bermuda News Bureau)*

Captain Torbjorn Hauge's passengers were in the middle of lunch when the decision was made to go to the Cunarder's rescue. The announcement he made was brief, ending tersely: "Please get some clothes and get off the ship." Three hundred agreed to remain ashore in Bermuda, leaving more room for the *Queen*'s vast passenger load to be housed on board. Those electing to do so were given $50 spending money apiece as well as a hotel room, no simple matter during the height of the island's spring season. Shortly after 1:00 P.M. on the third of April, *Sea Venture* slipped her cables and, once clear of the channel, steamed at 21 knots to the southwest and the stricken Cunarder. Passengers exploring the island on tours or by motorized bicycle arrived back at Front Street to an empty berth. Couples sunning on remote beaches near the Bermuda ship channel were horrified to see the *Sea Venture*'s unmistakable silhouette vanishing over the horizon without them.

The two vessels made contact at three o'clock the following morning, the *Sea Venture* with every light ablaze; Captain Hauge remembered how strange the British ship looked, drifting silently with all but emergency lighting extinguished. He stood 1,000 feet off until first light, then lowered his boats to the water. Since, without sufficient electricity, the *Queen Elizabeth 2* could not retrieve any of her boats, only the *Sea Venture*'s four tenders would be used to transfer Cunard's passengers. The first load carried over to the *Queen* included five boiler technicians who had flown out from England in time to board the *Sea Venture*, as well as extra diesel fuel to replenish supplies for the *QE2*'s emergency generators, which had been drumming ceaselessly ever since the breakdown seventy-two hours earlier. Before any Cunard passengers were embarked on the rescue ship, boatloads of life preservers were ferried across, augmenting supplies on board *Sea Venture* in anticipation of a passenger load in excess of any that her designers had ever dreamed she would carry. While this preparatory work went on, crewmen at both ends of the tender run greased the sides of each ship's temporary landing stage so that tenders rising and falling in the 2- to 3-foot swells would slide rather than chafe. Empty tenders leaving the *Sea Venture* carried replenishments of icy beer for the Britishers working to disembark their passengers.

Transferring them took all day. Each *Sea Venture* tender could embark seventy and had to make six round trips. The process was laborious: Eric Mason, the *QE2*'s energetic fitness instructor, remembers that men on duty at the staging had to be relieved every half hour. Evacuated passengers were allowed two suitcases apiece; one exceeded his allotment with an enormous green teddy bear. Elderly passengers found the trek down to

Five deck difficult—no elevators were working; an additional descent by companionway down to the water and into a heaving tender was no easier. The process had to be repeated in reverse order at the other end of the run. Miraculously, the weather held and the seas stayed relatively calm, making the ferrying task almost anticlimactic in the eyes of the two relieved captains. At dusk, as the last tender chugged clear of the giant black hull, crews lining the Cunarder's railing roared choruses of "Auld Lang Syne," "Tipperary," "Land of Hope and Glory," and finally "God Save the Queen." Those on the decks of the *Sea Venture* wept as the two ships parted.

On board the *Sea Venture*, facilities were taxed. By doubling up, crewmen freed some lower deck cabins and every passenger accommodation housed at least four on extra berths and mattresses. Even so, not all newly embarked passengers had a bed. One seventy-one-year-old woman would enchant officials back in Hamilton with the remark, "We let the older people sleep in the rooms and we slept on the floor." Those bedded down in the main lounge got little rest, for the chief steward mounted an all-night buffet for the hungry new arrivals. Steward Romano Silviera remembers only that all the *QE2* passengers were relieved and grateful. Hank Stram, coach of the Kansas City Chiefs, summed it up for the debarking passengers when he said of Cunard, "It was very obvious that they were a class company." Twenty-three members of a Bayside, Long Island, yacht club presented Captain Hauge with an improvised commemorative plaque: they all signed a *Sea Venture* linen napkin. He has kept it to the present.

When the rescue ship entered Hamilton Harbor on the afternoon of April 5, cannons boomed in salute, a steel band played the "Hallelujah Chorus," and signal flags above the harbormaster's office spelled out WELL DONE, SEA VENTURE. Before they disembarked from his ship, the rescued passengers besieged Captain Hauge on the bridge, asking him to pose for pictures, hugging him, and wishing him well. He had been without sleep for two days. "Never mind," he was heard to say, "we'll sleep when we are old." Once they went ashore, passengers were bused to two chartered 747's that were standing by to ferry them back to New York; company officials estimated the breakdown had cost them $2 million. Once the ship had been cleared, the *Sea Venture*'s original passengers reboarded for their return to New York.

Willy Farmer's ordeal was nearly over. A pair of seagoing Moran tugs dispatched from New York towed the *Queen Elizabeth 2* to Bermuda, a thirty-hour marathon delayed near its end as the weather, which had held so providentially throughout the rescue, deteriorated: 12-foot seas prevented the tugs from reaching a safe anchorage for several hours. Once

Top, Torbjorn Hauge, master of the *Sea Venture*, keeps his vessel close by but clear of the *Queen Elizabeth 2*. *Bottom*, back at Hamilton, he poses with rescued passengers. Note the *"QE2"* scrawled above *Sea Venture* souvenir hats. *(Flagship Cruises)*

QE2 was safely anchored offshore—she is too large to tie up in Hamilton —thirty of her three thousand boiler tubes were replaced. On April 16, she sailed back to Southampton.

Several Saturdays later, tied up at adjacent berths in New York harbor, *Sea Venture* and *Queen Elizabeth 2* were reunited. The two masters, Hauge and Jackson, exchanged greetings in person. I asked Captain Hauge some years afterward how Cunard had rewarded him. He replied that they had not, and his unruffled acceptance of what might seem to nonseamen an oversight only underscores an immutable law of the sea: vessel, passengers, and crew in need are assisted by whichever ship is closest and best equipped to help, irrespective of size or circumstance.

I remember one of my first crossings on *Queen Elizabeth 2* eastbound to Southampton in the early seventies, when a distress call from a Grand Banks fishing boat obliged the Cunarder to make an extended northern detour to take on board a fisherman who had hurt his back. Rendezvous was made late at night in the fog and, on this occasion as well, the sea was calm. The injured man was brought on board by a *QE2* tender. Having responded, *Queen Elizabeth 2* resumed course and raced through the night to make up for lost time, necessitating considerable expenditure for additional fuel. A more complex late-night emergency involved a dangerously ill crewman on the ore-carrier *British Tyne Bridge* in July 1974. Bleeding from a perforated ulcer, he was transferred to the diverted Swedish-American Line's *Gripsholm* steaming westbound across the North Atlantic on a positioning cruise. The patient was admitted to the ship's hospital for intensive care and, ultimately, surgery. But he was in danger of succumbing to shock and a radio distress call went out from the Swedish master to the U.S. Coast Guard's AMVER—Automated Mutual-Assistance Vessel Rescue system—for a quantity of RH-positive blood. It was loaded onto an aircraft in Virginia that flew east, refueling in Bermuda. Contact was made with the vessel, and on the evening of July 22, after an operation had been successfully concluded on board, three precious containers of blood were parachuted into the sea alongside the cruise ship; they were retrieved by crewmen waiting in an inflatable rubber raft and rushed on board. The crewman's recovery was complete, and he flew home to England as soon as the *Gripsholm* docked in New York.

Six years after coming to the aid of the *QE2*, Captain Hauge knew a dark night of his own when, near midnight, also en route to St. Thomas, his vessel lost power at sea in August 1980. This time he was in command of the giant *Norway*-ex-*France*, carrying her tenth load of passengers out of Miami. I was on board on that occasion, an episode to be recounted more fully in an ensuing chapter. On the bridge, it was an ironic inversion of roles: Hauge, the rescuing captain of the *Sea Venture*, had become victim of the *Norway*'s breakdown. In this instance, passengers were not evacuated. The trouble was not in the boilers but in the electrical system. A disastrous short-circuit triggered consecutive interlocking failures of an oil valve, switchboard, and generator that plunged all cabins and public rooms into stygian gloom. Normal catering was impossible and the denial of that essential cruise ship triad—light, water, and air-conditioning—lasted for twenty-four hours as the *Norway* drifted in the Caribbean north of the Caicos Islands and Cuba. Emergency generators produced enough ice to cool the fruit juice, soft drinks, beer, and wine that were dispensed free in every bar though hard liquor was, understandably, taboo for the duration. That "Black Tuesday" was a tense, steamy, irritating day; our formerly luxurious vessel suddenly an overheated, oppressive vehicle stuck in summer traffic, packed with restless, soured travelers.

Passengers everywhere have had their share of nocturnal despair, none more appallingly than ten from the *Sagafjord* who, having completed their independent tour of China's hinterland, arrived at a Canton pier to re-embark. Though well in advance of the vessel's scheduled sailing time, they found the dock deserted; the only evidence, at once promising yet chilling, was a discarded Norwegian American baggage label. That discovery was followed by another: a sharp-eyed ex-navy man among the party spied, through his binoculars, the light-festooned stern of the *Sagafjord* just disappearing around a bend in the Pearl River.

At once, this extraordinary man took charge. He galvanized his fellows and, together, they stormed the harbormaster's office. In forceful sign language, he demanded that the officials communicate with the ship. The radio operator, as lethargic as his interlocutor was persistent, was unable to do so; the passenger shoved him aside unceremoniously and succeeded in making contact with the *Sagafjord*'s bridge. The master apologized for his precipitous departure, explaining that the falling tide had made it imperative to be downriver ahead of schedule. He promised to slow down but could not return.

The next requirement was a serviceable chase boat. The passengers found one among a flotilla at an adjacent pier. A bargain was struck with its owner, and the *Sagafjord* party transferred luggage via a bucket brigade across a series of noisome, rafted vessels. The skipper cast off and sped in pursuit of the elusive cruise ship.

Although none of that anxious boatload knew it at the time, their most ardent—if unintentional—ally was a stubborn Chinese immigration official still on board the *Sagafjord*. He refused to leave with the river pilot until ten missing passports—at that moment in the luggage of the pursuing river boat—had been accounted for and returned to the purser's office. When the returning passengers finally clambered gratefully aboard, they were greeted by the grinning Chinese apparatchik in the purser's square. Their delight in rejoining their vessel was made that much greater by the delivery, to each of their cabins, of a bottle of extremely good champagne.

Whether champagne or, more likely, too many pints of beer, it was drink that hampered a boatload of *Oriana* passengers from getting ashore for an evening in Piraeus in the early seventies. Once cast off from the anchored vessel, it became apparent that the coxswain commanding their tender was a drunken incompetent. As they approached the landing stage, the weaving tender collided with an anchored sailboat in its path. After some ineffectual maneuvering, the coxswain succeeded in hopelessly fouling his propeller in the mooring. A tenderful of frightened and annoyed passengers remained where they were for three hours, prevented from communicating their plight to passing small craft by an impenetrable Greco-Anglo language barrier. Finally, a search vessel dispatched by the officer of the watch on the *Oriana* arrived to tow them back to the ship. The drunken crewman was dismissed on the spot, but very few of his boatload tried another trip to shore.

Another fouled propeller initiated a long dark night for most of the *Kungsholm*'s passengers off the northern coast of Wales in May 1968. Passengers ashore for the day in Llandudno were recalled by radioed dispatch from the captain; a storm was brewing and they were ordered to reboard at once. Carrying them back to the ship was the *St. Trillo*, a shore-based tender that embarked all four hundred shore excursionists. One of them was Stanley Page, an American from Carmel, California, and his account of the ordeal that followed tells the story with an immediacy and vividness that cannot be improved upon:

A line thrown from the *St. Trillo* to the *Kungsholm* fouled the propeller of the *St. Trillo* causing us to drift off into a night of rain, wind, heavy seas and terror for the 400 aboard. A lifeboat dispatched from the shore tried, without success, to pass a tow line—this went on for six hours; meantime, cold, wet, violently seasick passengers crowded the one small lounge below decks or stayed on the open decks for fear of being trapped below, while we drifted helplessly close to the rocky shore. Disaster becomes a common leveler and the passengers who had spent cruise days perusing the New York Social Register looking for "the right people" cradled other passengers in their arms, joined together in misery and fright. All aboard, including myself, would have given up all their worldly goods to get off the *St. Trillo* that night. Finally, they got a line aboard and the slicker-clad, courageous Welsh lifeboat crew towed us to the dock in Llandudno where we were met by dozens of people who escorted us to hotels for the night; meanwhile, "our" *Kungsholm* had deserted us by sailing off to a safe haven, Liverpool; a move to avert possible disaster to her. Llandudno is a summer resort and hotels do not open till June, but that night those wonderful Welsh people opened their hotels, gave us drinks, put hot water bottles in our beds and gave us ham and eggs at midnight; quite a job to accomplish on short notice.

The next morning, we were bused to Liverpool where the *Kungsholm* was waiting for us, band playing, lunch ready and the captain acting as though nothing had happened—that is a Swedish specialty. Once, en route from Panama to Tahiti, the *Kungsholm* "went dead" for 3 to 4 hours at 3 A.M. with all lights out due to generator failure, some passengers showing up on deck in their night clothes and life jackets. The next summer when I mentioned this to the same captain, he looked me in the eye and said: "It never happened." All's well that ends well—after we sailed from Liverpool, the passengers collected almost $10,000, which was sent to the lifeboat crew; really a small amount compared to what could have been collected aboard the *St. Trillo* while the rescue operation was at its height during that night of terror and misery!

I am familiar with Stanley Page's reference to the Scandinavian officer's business-as-usual façade when faced with calamities. Once on board *Sagafjord*, off Mexico's west coast, all the lights went out just before midnight. A yachtsman/passenger asked one of the officers on deck why the vessel was dead in the water as well as being blacked out.

"The ship is *not* dead in the water," snapped the officer. "We are still moving at ten knots."

"Extraordinary," observed the passenger. "There's a piece of driftwood alongside making exactly the same speed."

Caught in an obvious lie, the officer hurried away. His prevarication was doubtless encouraged by his superiors: losing power or headway in midocean is as much an embarrassment as a possible cause for fright among more susceptible passengers. But conversely, lying to passengers undermines confidence. How much to tell is a fine line that ship's captains and officers must tread, usually on short notice.

Some ship's officers can be faulted for foolhardiness. During the *Rotterdam*'s 1982 world cruise, two Dutch officers spent a riotous night on the town in Pattaya, the Thai port serving seagoing tourists bound inland for Bangkok. At 3:00 A.M., they waited on the pontoon landing stage for the single tender that seemed their only means of returning to the ship. It was a glorious tropical night, and to cool off as they waited, the two men jumped into the waist-deep water. Immensely refreshed and buoyed by Dutch courage, they decided that the most direct and pleasant means of reboarding would be to swim. So they set out for their ship, which lay at anchor 2 miles across the warm waters of the Gulf of Thailand. Those on the dock—who had failed in their efforts to discourage them—communicated their concern to the officer of the watch on board. Emergency boat crews were mustered for a fruitless search of the waters between ship and shore in the still dark night.

Neither swimmer achieved his objective. As soon as they had cleared the point, both were immediately swept off course by the powerful current that scours Pattaya's coastline toward the southwest. Although separated, each could see the lights and hear the engines of the search boats crisscrossing the waters beyond both their reach and the sound of their voices. As it happened, both men were extremely lucky. By dawn, one managed to crawl ashore on a beach far down the coast. His arms were covered with a virulent red rash, legacy of his passage through a flotilla of stinging jellyfish. By great good luck, his companion had been swept by the current against an offshore net buoy, where he was found, at first light, by the crew of a fishing boat coming out to check the night's catch. They returned him to the *Rotterdam*'s companionway. The officer in hospital ashore rejoined his ship by air farther along its global itinerary.

It was a senseless prank. Nothing is more unattainable and remote than a cruise ship at sea seen from the water level. I have never had to swim out to my ship, but I did once disembark from the *Norway* on the pilot boat outside Government Cut off Miami. It was unseasonably rough, with turbulent seas that, unfelt on board the world's largest liner, had the pilot boat pitching and tossing like an angry bull. As we sped away, the towering stance of that great blue hull, capped by a glittering halo of light, was imperishable, most especially from that unique vantage point low down on the water.

It was the same vantage point shared by those two foolhardy swimmers, as well as those unfortunate passengers who choose to end their lives at sea. According to cruise ship veterans, daylight jumpers are mere grandstanders; most suicides are achieved after dark. Those tortured souls hurl themselves into the darkest nights, a decision requiring fully as much bravery as desperation. There is an interesting phenomenon connected with

America's most potent lure for suicides, San Francisco's Golden Gate Bridge. Hundreds have jumped from its central span, and in consequence, elaborate safety precautions—barriers, fences, and nets—have been installed over the years in an attempt to lower the appalling annual toll. But those safeguards are restricted to the bridge's *eastern* flank only, the side facing the lights across the bay. Suicide seems to be spurred by a compelling yet somehow cautionary bravura, apparently tempered by regret up to the end; a terminal longing for life is embodied in the jump toward the life-representing phantasmagoria of San Francisco and Oakland inland. Almost no one jumps from the bridge's ocean side, presumably because the sea prospect in that direction is so forbidding. Similarly, passengers who clamber over a railing or exit through a door in the shell plating must commit to the same comfortless black; only in the water do they manage a tenuous, final vision of life, their illuminated ship drawing away into the night.

There is a spot in the Pacific, midway between San Francisco and the Hawaiian Islands, that holds as specific a notoriety for suicidal passengers as does the Golden Gate for their landbound equivalents. Halfway between two parallel undersea fracture zones—the Murray to the north, the Moloki to the south—is an area where passengers on ships traveling a regular steamship route are as far from land as it is possible to be on the globe's surface, not only from terra firma over every horizon but also from the sea bottom 3½ miles down. Though it is a relatively obscure geographical curiosity, would-be suicides apparently know it well. Matson Line vessels, which sailed regularly westbound from San Francisco until the late sixties, consistently attracted the most suicides.

The pattern of disappearance and subsequent discovery within reach of that deep-water midpoint became familiar. First to notice missing passengers were table companions; unless the weather was rough, continued absence from the dining room was as rare as it was significant. Cabin stewardesses were often the last to know, for a berth repeatedly undisturbed could indicate an assignation down the corridor. But there was another cabin warning that pursers came to recognize: stewardesses were alerted to report passengers carrying very little luggage. Just as professional gamblers on board ship carried almost no baggage in order to disembark on the run, so those intent on going over the side two days out of San Francisco seldom brought more than a weekend's worth of clothing. One man who jumped from the *Mariposa* never even unpacked the single suitcase he had brought on board apparently to establish passenger credibility. When opened, it was found to contain only a random selection of shabby winter clothing. Suicides afraid of heights used to jump through door ports low down the shell plating, leaving their clothes folded neatly just inside the exit. (It was to forestall this dangerous safety violation that companies rigged telltale signal lights on the bridge that would indicate any unauthorized opening of port doors at sea.) This preoccupation with neatness is fascinating. A woman on her honeymoon on board the second *Mauretania* jumped from an upper deck. It was her evening shoes, filled carefully with all her jewelry, including her wedding ring, that confirmed her intent to the master-at-arms. Another man on the *Queen Elizabeth* jumped late at night from the railing, leaving behind his passport, shoes, and wallet in a tidy pile.

But not all seagoing suicides are surreptitious. A man apparently enjoying an open-air party on the stern of a ship in the Caribbean said his good nights, then climbed the railing, and was gone. His abrupt departure was cloaked in mystery: he was traveling alone and none of his fellow passengers knew what had prompted his decision.

In the late forties, there was a tragic episode on board the brand-new *Caronia*, arising out of bitter disappointment and loneliness. A spinster schoolteacher from America's Midwest had invested all her savings in a blue mink stole and a world cruise, determined to snare a husband. Only weeks into the voyage, it was apparent that her search was fruitless. Russell Southern, who lives now in Bermuda, served as an officer on board *Caronia* during this period and recalls that it was not the kind of ship that encouraged conquests of any sort:

> The average age of the passengers was well over sixty. To us young enthusiastic bachelor officers, it was disaster!!! Thank God for lady Assistant Pursers, nursing sisters, etc. . . .

So too, alas, for the retired schoolteacher. One Saturday night, in a flood of tears, she implored a female assistant cruise director to introduce her to one of the few bachelors among the passengers; as tactfully and sympathetically as possible, the woman assured the distraught teacher that there were just no available or interested men on board. The following noon, immediately after divine services, the poor woman climbed over the railing and dropped into the sea. She went over the side wearing her mink, and horrified passengers saw it floating on the surface long after its owner had disappeared. Stewards on board another cruise ship still recall a row between a man and his wife, chronic smoking-room habituées. They were perennial quarrelers, lapsing each noon into a monotone of constant, boozy squabbling. But one day, something apparently snapped: goaded beyond recall, the woman jumped from her chair, raced on deck, and, in broad daylight, hurled herself shrieking over the side. Her body was eventually recovered. Every master keeps prominently displayed on the bridge a chart of the maneuvers required in the event of anyone falling overboard, an exacting figure-eight sequence of helm changes that turns the vessel precisely onto a reciprocating course.

Just such a course change became necessary on board a southbound Union Castle liner several days out of Cape Town when an understandably agitated passenger telephoned the bridge to report that his wife—who had not exhibited any suicidal tendencies—was no longer on board. She had failed to keep a daily teatime rendezvous and was neither on deck nor in their cabin, the cinema, or any of the public rooms or lavatories. The vessel was turned about and, after an hour, the missing woman was found, treading water in midocean. She had somehow fallen overboard and remained on the surface in shark-infested waters for nearly two hours. She was brought on board in a lifeboat, miraculously suffering no ill-effects from her prolonged immersion.

A less fortunate Union Castle lady passenger was traveling on the *Durban Castle* in the opposite direction. Eileen "Gay" Gibson, an actress who had just completed a theatrical engagement in South Africa, was on her way home to England in October 1947. On the night of the seventeenth, after an evening's dancing, she was escorted to her cabin—number 126, a small outside on B or Shade Deck—by two friends who bade her good night at 11:30.

At 3:00 A.M., shortly after passengers in adjacent cabins reported that they had been wakened by a struggle in 126, a senior night watchman, a man named Murray, was called to the cabin by lights on his annunciator board: both red and green were flashing, an unusual summons at any hour. When he arrived, the door was opened by James Camb, a handsome young deck steward who had, some days earlier, struck up a bantering relationship with Miss Gibson; he fancied himself a ladies' man, even though it was common knowledge on board that he had a wife and young daughter back in England. Now, through the half-opened door of Gay Gibson's cabin at three in the morning, he told Murray, "It is all right." Murray left, assuming that Camb had made good on his boast of a passenger conquest. But he was uneasy and, ten minutes later, returned to cabin 126, only to find the door locked. There was no answer to his knock.

The next morning, following her usual custom, cabin stewardess **Field** went to wake Miss Gibson; she found the bunk empty and the porthole ajar. The black dress that Miss Gibson had worn the night before was on its hanger, though the stewardess noticed at once that a strap on one of Miss Gibson's gold shoes had been broken. She made the bed and tidied the cabin, waiting for Miss Gibson to reappear. When she did not, she called the chief steward, who had the vessel searched. The captain was notified and the *Durban Castle* was turned about. For two hours, Captain Arthur Patey searched her wake; nothing was found.

Later in the day, when Camb reported to the surgeon for examination, he was found to have scratch marks on his arm and neck. He insisted they were from a rash as well as the friction of an extremely rough towel. He was confined to his quarters and, when the ship reached Southampton, arrested. Camb went on trial at the Winchester Assizes in March 1948 for what the press immediately dubbed the Porthole Murder. In his defense, Camb said that Miss Gibson had seduced him, and that while they were making love, she had died of natural causes. He had panicked, he told the court, and put her body out through the porthole. The actual porthole in question had been erected in the court, a grisly re-creation of the murdered woman's cabin. The jury found him guilty, and James Camb was sentenced to life imprisonment.

There have been some startlingly penurious aftermaths involving the companions of passengers who have killed themselves at sea. One recent widow, whose husband had gone over the side of one of the smaller ships of Norwegian Caribbean Lines, remarked to the purser that "the stupid old fool left no note," an omission, she complained, that would complicate settlement of his estate for years to come. Another suicide, witnessed by several RCCL passengers on deck one night, prompted the deceased's traveling companion to inquire of the purser how he should enter a claim for redemption of the unused portion of his late friend's ticket.

Passengers are not the only shipboard suicides. An executive chef went over the side of the *Queen Elizabeth 2* in the Caribbean one night, and in January 1969, on board a former *Fairsea*, the captain killed himself. An engine room fire had shut down everything on board; without power or light, the ship lay dead in the water. Emergency measures were successful: carbon dioxide extinguished the fire and, within a few days, a seagoing tug arrived from Valparaiso to take the ship in tow. But though the passengers and crew survived the crisis, tragically, their captain did not. Overwhelmed by worry and fatigue, he shot himself. It was the staff captain who took over the remainder of a complex but successful salvage operation. The Chilean tug broke down as well but, within a day, the disabled *Fairsea* and her inoperative rescuer were, in turn, taken in tow by the *Louise Lykes*, a transport en route home from Vietnam. The little flotilla reached Balboa, where the passengers were flown home; all of them had adapted without rancor to picnic meals and sleeping on deck.

I cannot abandon this lugubrious subject without touching on one personally observed potential suicidal episode. Some years ago, during a long cruise on board a ship that shall remain nameless, I had been asked by the company to deliver some lectures for the entertainment of my fellow passengers. One of them, who sat at an adjacent table in the dining room, was a gray-haired woman in her late fifties who was traveling alone. Her age belied her condition; she looked hugely pregnant, her lower abdomen protruding to the dimension of a basketball. In fact, she wore maternity clothes, but apart from that grossly distended belly, seemed unnaturally thin. Obviously, I decided, she suffered from an inoperable tumor.

After my final lecture, the woman came up and spoke to me, saying how much her late husband would have enjoyed them as well. She went on to tell me that he had died at sea *on that very ship in those very waters* several years earlier. An instant scenario flashed through my mind: in that same heartbreaking locale where she had lost her husband, the widow planned to end her own life before the tumor did it for her. That night, our last on board, would be her last on earth. Patently, there was nothing I, as a perfect stranger, could do to stop her; actually, I felt her decision was a gallant solution that made very real sense.

So much for life imitating art: when we disembarked the following morning, she was on the pier. After she had sorted out her luggage, she waved at me cheerfully and boarded a taxi for the airport and home!

Without question, the most terrifying maritime emergency is fire, a plague that has ravaged ships both wooden and steel for centuries. It is an ever-present danger, one that can engulf a ship at a pier no less devastatingly than at sea. A roll call of gutted hulks—*Morro Castle, Yarmouth Castle, Paris, Atlantique, Normandie, Seawise University, Antilles, Cunard Ambassador, Angelina Lauro, Prinsendam, Scandinavian Sea*—bears witness to the mortal potential of an on-board conflagration.

Though I have never experienced a fire on a ship, I confess to unbridled paranoia whenever the faintest suspicion of one arises. One morning on board a vessel in the Caribbean, I was typing in the empty card room when I noticed the unmistakable reek of scorched or burning plastic, a pungent, ominous smell that floated through the card room for several uneasy minutes, long enough to convince me that it should be reported. I went down to the purser's desk and notified the attendant in charge before returning to the card room, fully expecting an officer or firewatch to appear momentarily. Astonishingly, none did. After fifteen minutes had passed, the smell receded, and though I had returned yet again to the purser's office, no one in authority ever appeared. It seemed an extraordinary lapse on an otherwise impeccably run vessel.

Everett Viez, several of whose photographs appear in this work, cruised on board the *Sagafjord* in June 1981. As the vessel approached Fort Lauderdale on the last leg of her voyage, a fire broke out in the laundry room on C-deck, detected just after 11:00 P.M. Viez writes:

> About 11:15, the general alarm was sounded, and of course a "standby" distress call sent to a Coast Guard cutter and two other vessels in the vicinity. Everyone remained at their boat stations, life-jacketed, until about midnight when the fire was finally extinguished. This was indeed fortunate, for at the time we were somewhere between Cape Hatteras and Morehead City, North Carolina, and the sea was boiling. Not the kind of night for abandoning ship! The crew, every one of them, performed in an exemplary manner; so did the passengers who were mostly in the high age brackets. Doubt if the news media got in on this one, for no "abandon ship" or full S.O.S. was necessary. The ship resumed its voyage about 12:30 A.M. but no one really got much sleep that night. It was a very smoky fire and the pungent odor remained in some parts of the ship for the remainder of the voyage. The laundry room and everything in it was totally destroyed; and replacement machinery, linen supplies, etc., were awaiting the ship when she docked at Port Everglades, along with drums of detergent to wash down the elevator shafts, etc. And that's the saga of the *Sagafjord*!

I cite the *Sagafjord*'s fire at sea because it was, in sense, a classic, textbook case where a vessel's crew and equipment worked according to plan: a small local fire was contained and extinguished. Two years earlier, during a March weekend in 1979, crewmen on board the Costa charter *Angelina Lauro* were less efficient. The ship was making its weekly call at St. Thomas, the last full day of a seven-day cruise originating out of San Juan. The *Angelina Lauro* was secured at the West Indian Dock Company's berth number 4, the last berth at the long pier inside the harbor at Charlotte Amalie where most visiting cruise ships are moored. Directly ahead of her, also moored starboard side to the quay, was the *Cunard Countess*. Most of the Costa ship's 669 passengers, as well as her captain, staff captain, and many crew members, were ashore. By midafternoon, they were returning to the ship by taxi, in anticipation of that evening's scheduled sailing to Puerto Rico and cruise's end the following day.

But the cruise would end sooner than that. Shortly after 3:00 P.M., someone in the crew galley, forward on the port side of B-deck, left a deep-fat fryer at its highest temperature level untended. Within a few minutes, the overheated oil ignited, sending flames up into an overhead, hooded vent. The trunk or, in effect, chimney, from that vent turned horizontally almost at once, leading across the ceiling of the Continental Dining Room aft, an acceptable breach in what the Coast Guard describes as "a vertical fire zone boundary." The flames spread along the aluminum duct, passing failed or melted dampers, igniting the flammable materials above the ceiling panels.

There was an inexplicably long delay in reporting the fire, a universal failing at conflagrations either ashore or afloat. Over half an hour passed between the time someone smelled smoke and the sounding of an official alarm by the second officer on the bridge. In the interim, crewmen battled the flames independently and, as it turned out, ineffectually. In addition to the potentially disastrous situation of a fire raging out of control in the B-deck dining room, returning passengers, ignorant of any danger, continued to board the vessel via the passenger gangway leading into the A-deck foyer directly above it.

The Virgin Island Fire Department arrived at the pier and hooked up their hydrant-powered hoses; water pressure from the ship's pumps was already failing. It was more than an hour after the first official alarm—an hour and a half after detection of the smoke—that the last passengers were evacuated from the ship. That they could step ashore rather than endure a lifeboat evacuation was the only extraordinarily lucky fluke of the day: normally, the *Angelina Lauro* anchored in the Inner Harbor, ferrying her passengers ashore by tender. As it was, there were no fatalities and no serious injuries. The most endangered fire victim was a civilian defense volunteer from the island who had to be rescued from an elevator stuck between decks. To the very end, passengers struggled to disembark via their gangway directly above the worst of the fire, rather than go aft to the available crew gangway on B-deck.

Though every life was saved, the *Angelina Lauro* was a total loss. She burned throughout the night, listing so badly to port that those on the pier were afraid the mooring lines might snap. But the ship righted herself slightly once water was drained off the upper decks, and she finally grounded on the harbor bottom next to the pier. The evacuated passengers were divided among three adjoining cruise ships to be ferried back overnight to San Juan and the airport for flights home. Coast Guard and local fire authorities continued fighting the fire for another three days before it was finally put out. The *Angelina Lauro* remained grounded next to the pier

LINERS TO THE SUN

for four months, scarcely a cheering sight for that spring's cruise visitors to St. Thomas. She was eventually taken in tow for the Far East by the tug *Nippon Maru*; though destined for the scrapyards, she never made it, going, instead, to the bottom somewhere in the Pacific.

The timing of the fire that destroyed the ship was actually fortuitous. It might just as easily have occurred a few hours later while the ship was at sea en route for Puerto Rico. The same providential timing characterized the fire that broke out on board the *Cunard Ambassador* in September 1974. She was empty, deadloading from Miami to New Orleans, on her way to pick up a load of passengers, when, at 7:15 in the morning, a fire broke out in her engine room. At the time, she was close to land, 39 miles southwest of Key West in the Straits of Florida. Two hundred and fifty-six of her crew took to the boats, leaving fifty-two of their shipmates on board to battle the flames. But they were forced to abandon ship as well twelve hours later when emergency power was lost. Two Coast Guard cutters— *Vigilant* and *Steadfast*—stood by the derelict, and by the time tugs arrived to tow the still-smoldering hull into Key West, she was listing at seventeen degrees.

The *Cunard Ambassador* was never reconditioned for passengers, though she was restored for service as a cattle boat sailing in Australian waters. But she seemed jinxed, burning again in the mid-eighties. At the time she was being built in Rotterdam in 1972, another ship the same size was under construction in a neighboring yard: Holland America's newest passenger ship, the little *Prinsendam*, was laid down at the De Merwede Yard at Hardinxveld; by coincidence, both would be destroyed by fire, six years apart. In fact, *Prinsendam* suffered her first severe fire during fitting out, when a welder's torch ignited a blaze that set back her delivery schedule by six months. She finally sailed with her first passenger load from Rotterdam in a blizzard in November 1973, the last Holland America vessel to depart from the company's historic passenger terminal, the Wilhelminakade.

There followed the longest maiden voyage ever undertaken by a passenger ship: 14,431 miles from Rotterdam to Singapore. (Perhaps the next longest was that of the *Kenya Castle* in 1952, when she circumnavigated the African continent with her first load of passengers.) This was only one of a series of distinctions about the new ship. She was the first vessel to be christened *Prinsendam*, uncommon for a company that customarily recycles identical ships' names: for instance, since Holland America Line was founded in 1873, there have been no less than five *Rotterdam*s. Distinctive, too, was that the *Prinsendam* had been laid down by the company as a specialist vessel—one of a kind, a latter-day Dutch *Caronia*, if

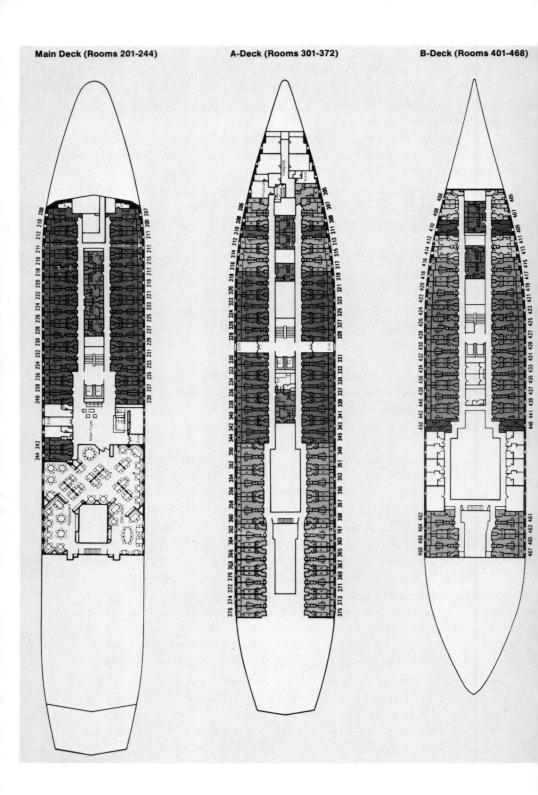

Main Deck (Rooms 201-244) **A-Deck (Rooms 301-372)** **B-Deck (Rooms 401-468)**

(Holland America Line)

Promenade Deck

Bridge Deck (Rooms 151-172)

Sun Deck (Rooms 101-116)

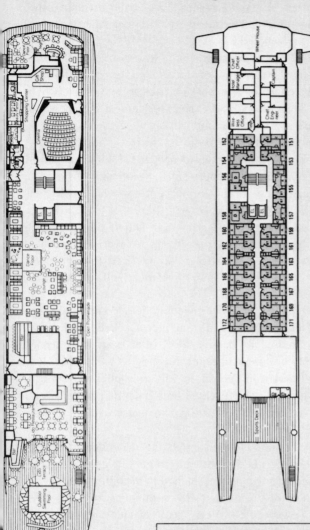

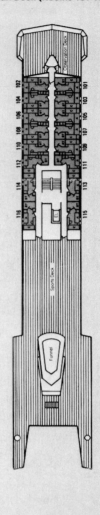

Prinsendam Technical Particulars

Length overall 130 M or 427 ft.
Breadth . . . . 19 M or 62 ft.
Draft . . . . 5.7 M or 19 ft.
Cruising Speed . . . . . 19 knots
Gross Register . . . . . 9000 tons

The vessel is fully air conditioned and stabilizer equipped. All rooms are equipped with private facilities and telephones. The *M.S. Prinsendam* is registered in the Netherlands Antilles.

Deck
dge Deck
menade Deck
eck
eck

you will. The ship had originally been tailored exclusively for cruising year-round through the reaches of Holland's former Far Eastern empire, the Indonesian Archipelago; her employment during the summer Alaska season was a later amendment to her schedule.

Most distinctive of all, *Prinsendam* was small. At 9,000 tons, she was only 427 feet overall, two-thirds the length of the *Statendam*. To match her dimension to an Atlantic predecessor, we must go back to the 1880s, when ships like the White Star sisters *Runic* and *Cufic* were almost her identical length. But there the similarity stops: Atlantic tonnage of the period was built for rough-weather stability with a deep draft—30 feet—and a narrow hull. With their length-to-beam ratios of ten-to-one, the White Star ships were only 42 feet wide. The *Prinsendam* had a substantial beam of 62 feet, a width that permitted a shallow draft—only 19 feet—and made her ideal for navigating between Indonesian ports of call.

Despite the *Prinsendam*'s diminutive size—her Dutch officers nick-named her "the cork"—she carried 375 passengers in average comfort. (Once she had sunk, press reports irresistibly characterized the vessel as "luxurious"; in fact, she was no more so than any other Holland America ship devoted to Old Guard passengers.) By providing the ship with a squared-off transom counter, the De Merwede builders could make an efficient use of her broad, boxy hull. The Promenade Deck housed every public room, including the cinema and beauty salon, in an extra-wide deck-house structure that left only a narrow open promenade to either side, too shallow for even a single athwartship deckchair. The only public room not on that deck was the dining room, which seated only half the passengers at one time, necessitating two consecutive sittings on every cruise; it was located one level down, on Main Deck.

But it was precisely her dollhouse dimensions that so endeared her to those she was designed to attract. Old Guard passengers in general prefer small ships. When Royal Viking's trio were stretched to accommodate seven hundred instead of five hundred, many of the company's regulars dis-approved. Then, too, they resent the Las Vegas scale of entertainment that larger vessels mount to attract Newpassengers. On a vessel the size of the *Prinsendam*, passengers would get to know each other, the crew, the ship, and even her machinery very well, some more so than they wished. When a party of entertainers boarded the vessel for the first time during her last Alaskan cruise season in June 1981, she was so crowded that, for an additional $100 a week, they were berthed temporarily in the ship's hospital, right up forward on A-deck. None of them had ever sailed on a ship before, and though they got used to the pronounced pitching that far forward, it was the racket of the *Prinsendam*'s single bow-thruster—located directly below the hospital—that came as a nightmare shock at six o'clock in the morning as the ship was being maneuvered into the pier at Ketchikan, its first port. The stabilizers, too, were hard by passenger spaces and their corrective thrust and shudder were familiar rough-weather concomitants the length of B-deck. Small-ship passengers share a kind of mechanical intimacy with every piece of machinery on board.

But *Prinsendam* was a good and dependable sea boat. One of those sailing on her maiden voyage was Arthur Hartley, an Englishman who played the piano in the little Prinsen Club forward under the bridge. Hartley had worked formerly on Union Castle ships, and he wrote me about "this quite amazing little ship":

> Even in Biscay, she seemed to just bury her sleek prow into the green water and say "Well, here I am, now see what you can do to test me!"
>
> She proved to be marvelously seaworthy, and soon showed that not only did her stabilizers deal nicely with the rolling, but her general squat design plus the bulbous bow took care of the pitching. She pitches beautifully with none of the sudden tugging that you so often get!
>
> Personally, I believe that her length-to-breadth ratio and lack of unnecessary height have much to do with riding performance, and when seen from dead ahead or astern, our ship presents a really comfortable appearance. Having her superstructure built well forward, they have taken full advantage of cubic space for the passenger facilities. Her unusual (for a passenger ship) flat stern helps this, and the after deck space just goes right to the very fantail itself! She may not have the most streamlined look in the world, in fact, you could even call her chunky, I suppose, but she is doing her job very well and everyone is so happy with her, both crew and passengers.

The *Prinsendam*'s profile was astonishingly advanced, considering that 1973 was the year of her debut. With the bulk of her superstructure forward, paired kingposts atop stepped decks aft provided continuity with the *Rotterdam*'s twin stacks, though her single orange funnel was sited further aft than the *Statendam*'s of 1957. Her paint scheme was interesting: white superstructure predominated over a narrow dark hull line, emphasizing a low-built, seaworthy stance. The cruise ship explosion was just beginning in the early seventies and, in an attempt to attract Newpassengers to a new kind of vacation, experimental wedge ships were steaming the length of the Caribbean. In contrast to some of those seagoing Edsels, the

The *Prinsendam*'s last Alaskan season. The ship at rest in front of the Margerie Glacier. One of her boats is out foraging for an ice fragment to bring back on board. *Below,* Lynn Stafford and Sally Woodson, entertainers on board, pose with a life ring in Glacier Bay. *(Lynn Stafford)*

little Holland America ship was presciently distinctive, with spare, clean, high-tech lines that would flower, a decade later, into the mid-eighties sisterhood of *Nieuw Amsterdam/Noordam*. It is one of the sad facts of word association when dealing with maritime catastrophe that the ignominy of her fiery end eclipses the *Prinsendam*'s innovative look. Mention of the name evokes only memories of disaster when, in fact, she should be recalled as well for her advanced good looks and ingenuity.

On Tuesday afternoon, September 30, 1980, over three hundred passengers boarded the blue-and-white vessel at Vancouver. One of them, "B. K." Stephenson, was seen off by his son and daughter-in-law; he bought them a drink in the Prinsen Club and was astonished to see a large cockroach scuttle across their table, a rare sight on board the usually immaculate Dutch ships. Later, as they left the pier, his daughter-in-law told her husband that she had an awful premonition that something was going to happen to the *Prinsendam*. "B.K.," meanwhile, was down in the dining room, arguing with Willem Dansberg, the maître d'hôtel, about getting a seat at the second sitting, as requested; Dansberg wanted to put him on the first but Stephenson insisted and finally got his way.

He and his fellow passengers were to see more than the Alaskan sights their predecessors had enjoyed that summer: the *Prinsendam* was being repositioned for her winter's Indonesian cruise program and was headed for the Far East. With Captain Cornelius Wabeke in command, the ship sailed up the Inland Passage, calling at Ketchikan, Juneau, and the splendid isolation of Glacier Bay one last time before heading west into the Gulf of Alaska. Her next port would be Yokohama, nine sea days across the northern Pacific.

Ever since *Prinsendam* had cleared the mainland that Friday, October 3, the weather had been rough. Ropes were strung across the open lobbies to help passengers get across the expanse of space. Cruise Director Gene Reid had scheduled two shows that evening, but the featured singer, Richard Ianni, felt almost too seasick to perform. Some Dramamine made him feel better. Afterward, passengers either sampled what is called, on Holland America ships, the show buffet—an especially elaborate spread in the Lido Restaurant—or went down to their cabins to bed. Near midnight, the weather cleared and a bright moon lit up the calming sea.

An hour later, just before one o'clock the following morning, October 4, a fuel pipe in the engine room ruptured, jetting diesel oil over an adjacent, super-heated pipe. A flash fire broke out. Crewmen fought it with hoses and fire extinguishers. One officer ran to cut off the fuel supply to the affected Werkspor Diesel, another telephoned Captain Wabeke. Ten minutes later, a series of explosions reverberated throughout the lower decks.

Passengers Irving and Isabella Brax, whose cabin was on the port side aft, were among the few passengers roused by the noise. But in the main, it was acrid smoke, seeping along A- and B-deck corridors, that alerted passengers still awake that something on board *Prinsendam* had gone disastrously wrong.

Vivian Quillinan, who had been reading in bed, went out into the A-deck passageway, saw smoke, and woke her husband. (They had decided to celebrate their golden wedding anniversary by embarking on their first cruise.) Together, they hurried to the main staircase, where an officer told them that there was "a small fire in the engine room" and suggested that they go up to the lounge until the smoke cleared; they did, clad in bathrobes and slippers. Other passengers, similarly dressed, were already on the stairs; some held damp cloths across their faces against the smoke.

Gene Reid had been typing a daily program change in his cabin and thought, at first, that the burning smell was his electric typewriter. After he saw smoke in the passage, he telephoned the bridge. Captain Wabeke answered and told him to come up to make an announcement to the passengers. Reid did so, asking first if he should say anything about warm clothing or life jackets; the master said no, merely tell passengers bothered by the smoke to assemble in the lounge for drinks. Either Captain Wabeke purposely played down the emergency or he honestly believed that the blaze would be easily contained.

Jack and Beatrice Malon, magicians from New York who had been booked as entertainers for the cruise, had seen Richard Ianni's show in the lounge before retiring. They were awakened by a telephone call from Roger Ray, another entertainer, who told them that the *Prinsendam* was dead in the water. As Jack got out of bed to look out the porthole, Beatrice saw smoke seeping under the bathroom door. Their cabin was directly over the engine room. They hastened to the Promenade Deck.

Helena Grenot, one of the half-dozen singer/dancers on board, had been seasick for so long that she was determined to be on hand for that night's midnight buffet. As she emerged from her cabin dressed in sweater and blue jeans, she ran into two of the ship's Dutch engineers. She knew one of them, and he asked her to fetch a nurse from the hospital. As Helena was on her way forward, the ship's alarm bells rang for the first time.

Either because of the Dramamine or because the sea had quieted down, Richard Ianni felt better. He had gone down to his cabin on A-deck after the show to change out of his dinner jacket into something warmer, planning to watch the northern lights out on deck. In his cabin bathroom, he saw tendrils of smoke curling from the air-conditioning vent. When he opened the cabin door, he found the same two engineers in the corridor—they had just left Miss Grenot—one with a respirator on, the other almost overcome by smoke. They came into his cabin to let the sick man lie down. Just then, the alarm bells went off. Ianni remembered being on board another cruise ship in the Caribbean that had lost power and the half-day party that had ensued, with drinks on the house and neither vessel nor her people in any danger. Despite the smoke and the sight of the gasping officer, he recalls thinking that the same kind of carnival night lay ahead. He left his cabin at the same time as the officers, taking neither life jacket nor valuables with him.

Next door, two entertainers, Regina O'Malley and Maida Meyer, were first awakened when the *Prinsendam*'s engines stopped. Moments later, there was a knock at the door; it was Terry Allan, the ship's photographer, urging both women to go up top with wet towels over their faces. When they tried turning on their cabin faucet, no water came out. So Regina went up wearing, as she described it, "a nightgown and a hairclip." She was barefoot and even forgot her glasses, an extraordinary omission for one so nearsighted.

Passenger Muriel Marvinney had set her alarm before going to sleep at midnight and remembers thinking, when it rang, how short the night had seemed. But the clanging bell was the alarm activated by a closing fire door outside her cabin. When she stepped out to investigate, the officer who lived across the passageway advised her to put on warm clothing and take her life jacket up to the lounge. She and her roommate, Agnes Lillard, dressed hurriedly. Muriel went up wearing only one shoe; the other's lace was so stubbornly knotted that she decided to untangle it after she was up in the lounge away from the smoke.

Ed and Patricia Halliday dressed warmly as well, though they had to do so in the dark. Just after one, the cabin's electrical circuits in their part of the *Prinsendam* went dead. When passenger William Powell heard Gene Reid's announcement, he muttered to himself: "Damn, there goes the trip."

In increasing numbers, the *Prinsendam*'s passengers assembled throughout the Promenade Deck public rooms. Stragglers who had slept through alarm bells and announcements were roused by stewards with passkeys urging them topside; one woman was still in curlers. The mood was cheerful and resigned, the smoky fire seen only as a nuisance, a minor disruption that would soon be over.

The sea had calmed down. Those venturing out onto the Lido Terrace aft found the moonlit sky clear, intermittently awash with a glowing green panorama of northern lights. Nevertheless, it was cold. Passengers in the lounge had opened the shuttered bar and were passing around warming jiggers of brandy. A few in their nightclothes improvised shawls out of the traditional Dutch chintz curtains. Forward, Captain Wabeke's wife, assisted by "B. K." Stephenson, opened the shop and passed out its entire stock of sweaters and jackets. Many of them were adorned, presciently, it seemed, with the logo PRINSENDAM ADVENTURE. (Once a passenger/shopper, always a passenger/shopper: shop manager Mary O'Hagan reported that more than one shivering matron, recipient of an invaluable, life-saving sweater, returned moments later to ask if there were anything in a different color or a slightly more flattering fit!) Two decks of cabins—the most expensive on board—were up above on Bridge and Sun decks; blankets and life jackets from those cabins, safely above the fire line, were distributed among the neediest. But Regina O'Malley, the singer who was still wearing only her nightgown, recalls that some passengers with several blankets refused to give up even one. She had drawn a sweater from the shop but had surrendered it to a shivering Indonesian steward. A passenger had given her a pair of shoes; for some unaccountable reason, that passenger had grabbed an extra pair when she left her cabin. They were too big for Regina but they were warmer than bare feet.

Richard Ianni was one of the few who made it back down to their cabins. Most who tried were thwarted by closed fire doors or impenetrable smoke. Ianni was after additional clothing, not for himself but for some elderly passengers still in their bathrobes. He gathered up some warm woolen shirts, his life jacket, a Swiss army knife, and, providentially, a pair of gloves. A singer friend who had preceded him on the Alaska run had advised him that gloves were a necessity, even in summer. Now he was one of the few on board who had them; they would serve him and his fellow castaways well later that day. He raced back up to the Promenade Deck the same way he had come down, his face masked by a wet towel. Even so, the heat and fumes along A-deck's passageway scorched the inside of his nostrils painfully.

Far below the carpeted passenger decks, failing electrical power rendered the pumps inoperable. Engineers then tried stifling the flames by filling the engine room with carbon dioxide. But they were too late. The fire moved relentlessly upward, spreading to the lowest public room on Main Deck. The dining room was U-shaped, made so because the *Prinsendam*'s single funnel uptake pierced its center; intense heat from that central core—connected directly to the inferno below—had already ignited the dining room. The lounge, one deck higher, was soon no better. When Captain Wabeke had ordered its fire doors opened to admit chilled passengers from the open decks, it was impossible to enter.

Shortly thereafter, all Promenade Deck public rooms became untenable: Lido, Lounge, Cinema, and Prinsen Club were written off as choking passengers, their eyes smarting, trooped outdoors onto the weather decks. One of the last crewmen in the lounge saw that the composition filler between the planks of the portside dance floor was bubbling and liquor bottles shelved behind the bar, lined up in rows next to the superheated sheathing around the funnel casing, were exploding like cherry bombs.

On deck, the funnel had blistered, its portside plating buckled and caved in. Most passengers congregated at the stern, sheltered by the afterdeck overhang. The ship's entertainers performed an impromptu concert; once they had exhausted their repertoire of show tunes, they switched to Christmas carols. Just then, the loudspeakers announced that lifeboats were being lowered to the Promenade Deck—their loading position—"as a precaution," the captain put it. Shortly thereafter, the lounge caught fire and the order "Abandon ship" came from the speakers. *Prinsendam* passengers, surging to either side of the Promenade Deck in the predawn darkness, were to cross a shipboard Rubicon achieved by very few: entering a ship's lifeboat at sea rather than in port, for rescue rather than for a ride ashore. The after lifeboats, those nearest the fire, were loaded and lowered first to get them away from the smoke, flames, and intense heat of the burning dining room one deck below. The forward boats went last.

Holland America's lifeboat drills are among the most conscientious I know. Attendance is taken scrupulously at each station by the ship's officer serving as boat commander, and routinely, lifeboats are lowered to the rail on either side so that passengers may see inside them. Crewmen operate the Fleming gear—the T-bar rocker arms replacing oars—that, pushed back and forth, set the boat's propeller into rotation. Yet regardless, lifeboat drill on board every ship seems, from a passenger's point of view, perfunctory, an obligatory precaution endured within hours of boarding that turns into a kind of social gathering. The ship's photographer is on hand, clicking his way down each side of the Boat Deck, amassing a portfolio of life-jacketed passenger group photographs to be posted and

A Coast Guard helicopter hovers over
the derelict *Prinsendam* long after the
last passenger has been evacuated.
Opposite, two views of the burned-out
vessel before she went to the bottom. The
hull and superstructure are scarred by
fire rash. *(Official U.S. Coast Guard
photos)*

sold the following day. Now, the *Prinsendam*'s cautionary rehearsal had become drama rather than drill. As the Promenade Deck railings were swung open, anxious, elderly, or frail passengers pressed forward to clamber—in some cases, agonizingly slowly—across the gulf from ship to boat. For them, it was a step into the unknown, an evacuation down the side of a ship into a brisk sea at night with no emergency lights working.

Every passenger account stresses the crowding in the *Prinsendam*'s lifeboats. One wonders why. Of the 520 souls on board when Captain Wabeke ordered the ship abandoned, forty would remain behind to fight the fire and another twenty-five would go over the side in four covered, inflatable life rafts. The balance should have had at their disposal a total of eight boats. The *Prinsendam* was equipped with two enclosed shore tenders, each accommodating fifty-five. Lifeboats 1 and 2, hung just aft of the bridge, and also motor driven, could carry forty-four apiece. The four remaining boats, numbers 3 through 6, were larger, driven by Fleming gear and capable of taking ninety-nine people each. Even though the starboard tender, fouled in its davit falls, would never be lowered, the seven boats remaining offered a combined capacity of 539, room for far more than the 455 who were anxious to board them. But the fact is that a lifeboat, even one loaded only to its rated capacity, is, simply, very crowded.

Then, too, loading was chaotic. Ideally, ships' evacuation plans are predicated on the hypothesis that passengers will proceed directly from their cabins, half the passenger load climbing to the odd-numbered boat stations to port while their starboard-berthed shipmates report to the opposite side. But after several hours of aimless milling about on the *Prinsendam*'s Promenade Deck, a sense of disorientation had taken over. There was confusion about or impatience with prearranged station assignments. Lifeboat number 3, for instance, amidships on the port side, was one of the first to load. It went down the side carrying 105, six more than its rated capacity. On the starboard side, boat number 4 was so overloaded and imbalanced before descent that it began tipping in the davits, threatening to dump its occupants down the side of the shell plating. Dozens were ordered out before it was finally let go carrying eighty-five. There was no room for passengers to move or operate the Fleming gear; all they could do was remain where they sat or stood, wedged in place. In boat number 6, Beatrice Malon said she never sat down throughout her hours afloat. Mrs. Walter Clapp observed to reporters later, "It was not really like the unsinkable Molly Brown," a reference to the redoubtable Denver heroine who had taken charge of one of the *Titanic*'s lifeboats.

Loading elderly passengers took a long time, and although there were instances of some stewards and orchestra members pushing ahead of them, other ship's personnel waited their turn. One was Regina O'Malley, who sat on the railing as boat 6 was being loaded. She had, in fact, every reason to disembark hurriedly: a lounge window had just shattered. (Fortunately for all those passengers packed onto the vessel's narrow Promenade Deck, those windows that burst did so *inward*, the glass pulled inboard by consumed oxygen inside rather than blown outward.) Then too, the deck under her once-again bare feet was agonizingly hot. She had discarded her gift of oversized shoes for fear they might hinder her if she had to swim, and so she sat perched on the railing, her bare feet tucked beneath her, watching the rubberoid grout between deck planks bubbling from the heat of the steel just below.

Just as consistent as complaints about crowding was universal fear, among survivors of every age, during that journey down to the water. Muriel Marvinney, in boat 4, wrote later that her boat had fallen down the side "in one heart-stopping drop of 70 *feet*" (italics mine). Another passenger asserted that his boat had been lowered for 30 feet, then "fell the remaining 20 feet" to the water, a combined distance of 50 feet. Both accounts suffer from exaggeration. Hotel Manager Dirk Zeller recalls that the actual distance from the *Prinsendam*'s Promenade Deck to the surface of the ocean was no more than twenty feet. He suggests that the still-rough sea may have contributed to the exaggerated sense of distance as lifeboats landed one moment on the crest and another in the trough of waves. But at whatever speed that vertical journey was achieved, it was climaxed in every case by severe difficulty in releasing the blocks once the boat was safely afloat. As crewmen struggled with the balky latches, the rising sea repeatedly dashed the filled boats against the unyielding hull they sought to quit. Passengers in boat 4, still attached to the falls, drifted forward so that boat 2, until checked in its descent, was being lowered directly on top of them. (It was, in fact, the urgently flashed lights of a rescue helicopter above that alerted crews at the davits that they should cease lowering until the water below was clear.) The parallels with the same problems of debarkation on board the *Titanic* sixty-eight years earlier are chilling.

By 6:30, all boats had left the burning ship. The only consolation carried away by passengers and crew was that help was on the way. Helicopters had buzzed the *Prinsendam* repeatedly as the boats were being loaded, and earlier, Captain Wabeke had comforted passengers with the news of an approaching ship: the *Williamsburg*, an enormous tanker loaded at Valdez the previous day and bound for Galveston, was already on a reciprocal course and headed in their direction. So on board each boat, in each heart, was at least a central, reassuring kernel of hope. It would be cherished as the lifeboats drifted apart over the gray, mounting seas. There were rations and water on board, though an army man who sampled the food likened it to "moldy K rations." Some passengers found and ate emergency sugar wafers for energy, leading later newspaper accounts to report with ludicrous inaccuracy that *Prinsendam* passengers were served ice cream in the lifeboats. In fact, few were hungry: the severe sea motion made almost everyone sick. Initially, those sitting along the sides tried to be delicate, murmuring a polite "Excuse me" before turning and vomiting discreetly over the side. But those packed amidships threw up where they sat, wet, cold, and miserable. Helena Grenot's dentist told her later that the enamel on facing surfaces of her teeth had been worn down by monumental bouts of shivering. Ed and Pat Halliday, jammed in opposite ends of overcrowded boat 3, could only call out to each other as the interminable day progressed. Vivian Quillinan sat with her bare feet awash in seawater at the bottom of the boat; her husband, Norman, shod in half-slippers, fared no better. "B. K." Stephenson, in boat number 4, managed a wry smile when Willem, the maître d'hôtel with whom he had argued about a table and who was now commander of the boat, said, "Mr. Stephenson, you can be in the *third* sitting if you want!"

Survivors who opted for the covered life rafts stayed no drier. Audrey Goral joined a score of crewmen in one of the inflatables about to be lowered over the side; when they reached the surface, seawater came flooding in through the open entry ports at either end. There was no way to bail and so they had no choice but to sit all day in 6 inches of water. Cruise Director Gene Reid, along with eleven staff and crew, was in another inflatable that had a visible leak in its floor panel. All day, occupants took turns stemming the inflow with their thumbs. A woman who suggested that they use the repair kit read only the first line of the directions: "Make sure all surfaces to be glued are completely dry. . . ."

A curious phenomenon manifested itself in every boat. Despite the cold and discomfort, Richard Ianni experienced an overriding sense of disbelief: "Is this *really* happening? Am I really adrift in a lifeboat?" In boat 6, Regina O'Malley repeated to herself over and over, an *obbligato* to her chattering teeth: "I am in a movie, this can only be a movie." Helena Grenot, too, was convinced she had been cast "in a grade-Z movie." Malon, the magician, also felt he was "making a movie." In truth, that abrupt transition—from cosseted passenger to shivering castaway—had overwhelmed their senses. The protective mental response was withdrawal, a removal of self from troubling reality. Psychiatrists call it psychic denial, doubtless the source of those convincing cinematic scenarios.

But reality obtruded nonetheless. Vivian Quillinan confesses that she and her immediate neighbors, all in their seventies, "gave up" several times, only to be sustained repeatedly by a surprising and blessed resiliency. Everyone just held on, awaiting rescue. There was neither panic nor tears. A few tried singing "Oh, What a Beautiful Morning!" as the sun came up but most songs died after a desultory chorus. Conversation was as fragmentary as the singing. The only continuous group effort was prayer, both in private and in vociferous unison.

The first passengers were plucked from the sea in early afternoon by helicopters hovering miraculously overhead. Baskets were lowered at the end of a hoisting cable. Positioning these on the heaving boats was difficult. Richard Ianni's gloves proved a godsend as he took charge of seizing and securing the lowered basket before survivors could clamber inside. The ride aloft, albeit tantamount to rescue, was terrifying, and helicopter crewmen repeatedly had to pry fingers loose from the baskets' rims once the occupants had been winched safely inboard.

The survivors in boat 6 were nearly lost by a combination of logistical oversight and deteriorating visibility. They were not found until after midnight. Literally moments after the last passenger had been hoisted aboard the Coast Guard cutter *Boutwell*, the empty lifeboat, after having been dashed repeatedly against the rescuing ship's side while it was off-loaded, split down the middle and disintegrated.

First priority on board the ships or stations ashore were quantities of hot soup, hot showers, and rest in a berth. Ashore, in addition to clothing, replacing eyeglasses involuntarily abandoned in the cabins also took precedence, and there was a run on magnifying glasses in local stores at every rescue port.

Dressed in a motley array of makeshift clothing, the *Prinsendam* passengers flew to Seattle, where, after being issued tickets and $65 spending money each, they went home. Muriel Marvinney and Agnes Lillard arrived home in Short Hills, New Jersey, and were immediately presented by relatives with twin blue T-shirts, already bearing the legend I SURVIVED THE PRINSENDAM. The Quillinans reached Sacramento and were interviewed in front of television cameras already set up in their living room. Jack and Beatrice Malon arrived home to a different welcome: their Queens, New York, apartment had been ransacked by thieves, so, in that fall of 1981, both their seagoing quarters and their home base had been violated.

Photographed from a helicopter,
passengers in one of the *Prinsendam*'s
lifeboats hold on to the rescue basket
before another load is winched up to
safety. *(Official U.S. Coast Guard photo)*

The *Prinsendam* was a total loss. Even though the stubborn conflagration was never completely extinguished, there had been hopes that the gutted hull might be saved. But she continued a fatal list to starboard. The line of dining room ports, blown out by the inferno inside, sank below the waterline. The list increased until finally the port stabilizer was completely exposed. A week after her mortal agony had begun, the line from the towing tug was slipped and the *Prinsendam* disappeared beneath the waves, plunging to the bottom a mile and a half below.

If "fire" and "foundering" are two inevitable *Prinsendam* word associations, "miracle" is another. Every single soul from the ship had been saved within twenty-four hours, the largest air/sea rescue in maritime history. There was not one fatality. It is symptomatic of thirty-day cruises that the median passenger age would be advanced, that many would be infirm, that some would not be able to walk. None seemed likely to survive consecutive traumata of an anxious night aboard a burning ship, a day in open boats threatened by hypothermia, or even a dizzying aerial ascent above a storm-tossed ocean; but all of them did. In retrospect, their age was seen as abetting their survival. "If we had been dealing with people of thirty-five or under, there would have been panic," suggested Captain Donald Hudson, the air force surgeon airlifted to the *Williamsburg* to monitor the condition of hundreds of geriatric patients streaming in from the helicopter pad. "These older people had things in perspective. Their lives were straightened out. The wisdom of years really paid off." Those words are an inspiring testament to the gallant and indomitable *Prinsendam* passengers who survived their darkest night on board any ship.

Before leaving this grim subject, it is worth concluding with two tales, one a ghost story set on another Dutch ship—which one, I have never been able to discover; perhaps it was the *Rotterdam*. In any case, I have heard the account from too many different sources to discount it entirely. The incident involves a passenger, an American surgeon, and several superstitious Indonesian crewmen. The passenger died of natural causes on a long cruise and his body was placed in the ship's morgue. The surgeon needed some physical details to fill in the death certificate and went down to the morgue to complete the form; then he was unable to open the door from the inside. Rather than summon assistance, his frantic knockings convinced crewmen that the dead man's spirit was trying to escape. They pointedly ignored the noises for the rest of the night. The doctor spent a long, dark night before he was released, shortly after dawn, by a puzzled but relieved colleague.

The second incident also belongs in the "things that go bump in the night" category. It occurred during an eastbound crossing of the *Queen Elizabeth 2* shortly after her return from service in the Falklands; some of her interior fittings had suffered from abuse by the departed military. Bill and Ann Kephart, the same couple encountered on board *Rotterdam* during her 1976 roll, were asleep in berths one above the other. Ann was in the upper because Bill's arthritis made the climb up and down difficult. Near midnight, the upper bunk suddenly dropped from its wall brackets almost but not quite on top of the lower. A night steward answered the Kepharts' summons and moved them at once to a vacant cabin nearby. When their regular steward came on duty in the morning, he tracked them down; his first question to the middle-aged couple was, "What on earth were you both doing in that upper bunk?"

On to Cruises Present!

*In the First Class, the company contracts
to give each adult passenger a separate
berth, to provide all food and do the
cooking. But passengers are liable
to be rejected if, upon examination, they
are found to be lunatics, idiots, dumb,
blind, maimed, infirm or above the age
of sixty years.*

— WHITE STAR BROCHURE, *1871*

*I was greatly surprised to see so many
elderly people—I might almost say so
many venerable people. A glance at the
long lines of heads was apt to make one
think it was* all *gray. But it was not.
There was a tolerably fair sprinkling of
young folks, and another fair sprinkling
of gentlemen and ladies who were
non-committal as to age, being neither
actually old or absolutely young.*

— MARK TWAIN, THE INNOCENTS ABROAD

9.
Cruises Present

We embark now on a second quintet of cruises. Whereas "Cruises Past"
evoked yesterday's shipboard, the emphasis in this chapter is on today's,
which, unrecorded, might vanish with the same finality. Reportage has
been enriched by firsthand observation; each voyage took place in the
eighties, each embarked my wife, Mary, and myself as passengers. Selections of cruise and vessel are arbitrary; geographical diversity no less than
Old Guard/Newpassenger balance has been maintained.

    With few exceptions, the focus remains on board. Most passenger/
diarists invariably wax lyrical about their vessel in early entries, only to be
diverted at the first port of call, their ship life eclipsed by sights ashore.
They may be forgiven because, in a sense, only the itinerary regiments

Sailing day, January 9, 1984. The author
and his wife on board S.S. *Rotterdam* as
she leaves her New York berth. Surely
the pleasantest day of any cruise, with the
bulk of it to follow. *(Barry Winiker)*

those languid days; surely there is no catchphrase more apropos than "If this is Tuesday, it must be Belgium," a cliché that, like so many of its kind, is relentlessly on target.

What follows is neither journal nor commonplace book; days at sea slip past easily, blurring even more than they do ashore, with little to distinguish them from those before or after. Moreover, what amuses or compels one traveler may not do the same for another. But it is hoped that passenger/readers booked for this second selection will find much that is familiar and worth recalling. All five cruises were ordinary save the first, which featured a bizarre Caribbean episode aboard a vessel just restored to service; the second involved a Far Eastern circumnavigational segment, the third a Panamanian transit, the fourth an Alaskan quest, while the last—cruise and crossing combined—brought us home to New York from Scandinavia.

One of today's cruising realities is that sailings from New York's North River piers—only minutes from my door—have become increasingly rare. Yet a flight to Miami seems as nothing compared to the exhausting air marathons needed to join a vessel in Hong Kong or Bombay. Miami is, literally, the world's busiest cruise port, and it was there that I flew in August 1980 to board the *Norway*. A circle of sorts was closed: twelve years earlier, I had first encountered the same vessel as the *France*, first sailed the Caribbean, and, indeed, first embarked for a cruise rather than a crossing.

The ship had been awaiting execution of what seemed an inevitable death sentence, having been tied up at the Quai de l'Oubli—"the pier of the forgotten"—in Le Havre since her withdrawal from Atlantic service in September 1974. The oil crisis and OPEC had done her in, as the price of fuel—Bunker C crude—escalated catastrophically. Though some die-hard *France* aficionados felt that ticket prices, however steep, would not discourage First Class patronage, it was clear that without a solid underpinning of Tourist Class income, the ship could not survive. As it was, Giscard d'Estaing's government had been subsidizing the *France* to the tune of $20 million annually by the time she was withdrawn.

Then in 1977, after three years on death row, a reprieve—of sorts—seemed at hand. In ironic dispensation of the same petrodollars whose amassing had crippled the ship, Akram Ojjeh, a Saudi Arabian financier, bought the *France* for $22 million. He planned on transforming the vessel into a floating hotel and casino off the Florida coast. He also bought part of the contents of New York's Wildenstein Gallery to refurnish her interiors, but the scheme fell through. The *France*'s future remained obscure,

The long wait. *Above,* on December 19, 1974, the year she was withdrawn from service, *France* left the Le Havre ocean terminal under tow through the brand-new François I lock. All perishables had been off-loaded. *Below,* moored in the central maritime canal the following spring. A skeleton crew of firemen patrolled around the clock and, each winter, a boiler was fired to dispel damp. *Opposite top,* she left her mooring only twice, once inadvertently when a northeaster broke her momentarily loose and, here, for routine maintenance in dry dock number 7. Apart from the rust on her hull, she looks in excellent condition. *Opposite bottom,* reprieve. In August 1979, with crewmen on the fo'c's'le deck, the vessel, renamed *Norway,* is taken in tow by tugs. *(Porte Autonome du Havre: Robert Graham Collection and Guy Mercier Collection)*

with only those of her crew still living in Le Havre keeping an uneasy vigil over their beloved ship. Léon Tardy-Panit, the *chef de patisserie*, had transferred to the *Queen Elizabeth 2*; whenever he came home on leave, he was so heartsick that, though the *France* was visible from his windows, he made a point of never looking at her.

But the cruise boom in the late seventies proved her ultimate salvation. At the end of "Cruises Past," Jack Shaum, carried ashore by tender from the aging *Queen Elizabeth*, spied an early wedge ship, the *Sunward*, tied up at Nassau's dock. She was the forerunner of a phenomenally successful quartet of ships owned by Norwegian Caribbean Lines. The parent company of NCL was Klosters Rederi of Oslo. Knut Kloster, son of the founder, faced a seemingly limitless demand for additional cabin space, so he decided to renovate the *France* for the Caribbean.

After buying the ship from her Saudi owner, he rechristened her *Norway* and had her towed to HAPAG-Lloyd's Bremerhaven yard for conversion. Correcting an original warm-weather shortcoming, two outdoor pools were installed; lido decks were enlarged, new cabins were fitted, and two-class public rooms were brought into one-class decorative parity. Since *Norway* would never adhere to *France*'s bruising transatlantic schedule, the outboard pair of four propellers was removed. Twin-screwed, she consumed half as much oil as she had previously, her propulsion scaled down for a short, sedate Caribbean itinerary. With her outboard tail-shafts pulled, the *Norway*'s forward engine room remained inoperative. Both funnels were retained nevertheless, their TRANSAT horizontal black-over-red repainted in NCL's blue-and-white in a elaborate swooping contour that effectively diminished funnel *hauteur*. The black hull was refinished in vibrant royal blue.

Moored alongside Miami's Dodge Island in 1980, the *Norway* towered above the passenger terminal, her 1,000-foot-plus bulk consuming space normally required by a pair of her consorts. We boarded through ports at either end of the hull, denied access to the traditional embarkation lobby amidships by the placement of Miami's gangways. Throughout, the interiors were as vibrantly colorful as her hull, the previous winter's inspiration of New York interior designer Angelo Donghia. Second only to questions about the future of the *United States*, I am most often asked how the *Norway*'s interiors compare with their French predecessors. To my mind, they have been vastly improved. Ocean liner interior designers are faced with challenging commissions, having to allow for and accommodate the changing tastes of three ensuing decades, the projected life span of the

New name, new life. The S.S. *Norway*
at Bremerhaven on a March day in 1980
when steam was raised for the first time.
She was also sporting new funnel colors.
(Author's collection)

vessel they are helping to create. The French had opted for late-fifties low-tech: tapestries and anodized aluminum or brass murals sheathed the walls, angular abstract chairs with steel spider legs crowded the monochromatic carpeting, and a relentless fluorescent wash illuminated them all. The effect was at once harsh, metallic, and cold. When she first reached New York in the winter of 1962, a correspondent for the magazine *Interiors* came on board and pronounced the *France*, ambiguously, "the St. Moritz of the Atlantic," presumably more a sociological than decorative evaluation.

The miracle that Donghia wrought was to have successfully juxtaposed some new furniture, fittings, and fabric against inescapable *France* structural holdovers: warmth—so sorely lacking before—pervades the present ship. That the capacity of each public room would have to be increased for Caribbean service was inevitable; to have done so while enriching them was a decorative tour de force. Donghia's *Norway* touch was nowhere more deft than in the Club Internationale, formerly the First Class Smoking Room and, apart from the dining room, the only double-height ceiling on board. Discreet chair groupings are congenial, each table's center a twinkling beacon of light. The steel-and-enamel columnar ornamentation has gone, replaced by a cool serenity of white fluting. Garlanded statuary in niches to either side adds exactly the right touch of giddy extravagance. Underfoot, as throughout every public room, passageway, stairwell, and cabin on board, Donghia's patterned carpeting supplanted those pools of primary color that, constantly demanding attention, had predominated under the ancien régime. The *Norway*'s interiors are sumptuous, with a vivid, textured elegance that remains as timelessly fresh as it is distinctive. Indeed, Donghia's work on board NCL's flagship remains a benchmark for all contemporary cruise ship interiors.

The *Norway* feeds her passengers, as does all Newpassenger tonnage, at separate consecutive sittings. Old Guard vessels pride themselves on offering a single sitting only; more than one, it is implied, betrays crowding. Moreover, single-sitting passengers need not be herded into the dining room, but can drift in at leisure. Then, too, company and clients alike prefer not to divide the passenger body, inevitable on a two-sitting ship: those first into the dining room enjoy their evening's entertainment while the second sitting dines, and it is very late before the two sittings are reunited. Sometimes they never are: older passengers, who rise early and prefer first sittings in consequence, tend to have retired by the time second sitting streams out of the main lounge after their evening's cabaret. For cruise directors, consecutive passenger meals make for cumbersome scheduling: double sittings require the duplication of other events—two shows, two screenings—with correspondingly fewer free hours in which to offer single events to everyone on board.

The lengths to which companies will go to avoid what they perceive as the stigma of double sittings is perhaps best illustrated on board the vessels of Sea Goddess Cruises. In the mid-eighties, their pair of small but lavish "cruise yachts" were entered into service, their passengers ensconced within only fifty-eight splendid cabins *en suite*. But the company's Achilles' heel was the dining room, which, reflecting the size of the vessel and its passenger load, was small. In consequence, planners were confronted with the Scylla of cramped tables or the Charybdis of consecutive sittings. The company's solution, which seems to have worked, was to adhere to a single long sitting yet encourage passengers to drift down to dinner à deux rather than en masse. Presumably, on a vessel that offers free drinks among its other perks, encouraging delay of this kind is easy; a free cocktail hour of indeterminate length is a persuasive way of diminishing dining room crush. A second and unique innovation in the Sea Goddess dining room is that passengers choose a different table—and different dinner companions —each evening. Since tipping is discouraged, this presumably liberates passengers from steward dependence.

But Old Guard opprobrium notwithstanding, back-to-back sittings spring from a perfectly respectable transatlantic lineage. Most fascinating about two sittings is the way companies designate them; depending on the sociological origins of a particular passenger load, a subtle war of words is waged as a means of diverting clients toward a neglected session. Encouraging enrollment for late dinner service, the generic First Sitting is renamed Early Sitting, an etymological slight suggesting inferior meals on a detrimental par with nursery tea; driving the psychological nail home, Second Sitting is hailed as Main Sitting. Conversely, in the rare instances when the first dining room shift needs bolstering, First Sitting becomes Main Sitting and the second turns into the somehow sinister Last or Final Sitting, subliminal inference that upturned chairs will be stacked atop tables moments after the coffee has arrived.

In fact, first sittings on cruise ships today are invariably overbooked, reflecting perhaps the advanced age of most passengers. On the *Norway*, I had already booked by mail for second sitting, inestimably preferable in my view because one need not rise at dawn for breakfast and it affords, toward evening, time for a cabin-bound hiatus before descent to dinner in the Windward Dining Room.

The Windward Dining Room. Models descending, passengers dining. Every spoon reflects lights in the dome. The wall murals remain unchanged from *France* days. Welcome additions since these photographs were taken are individual table lights, which permit reduction of the French fluorescent fixtures overhead. *(Norwegian Caribbean Lines)*

One of the evocative things about a table in the Windward is that the room retains so much of the look of the *France*'s Chambord Restaurant. As the original First Class dining room, it obviously boasts handsomer proportions than the former Tourist Class dining room located farther aft. That room, however, renamed Leeward after the Bremerhaven conversion, has been dramatically upgraded. Acting on a company mandate to equalize decoration in both spaces, Angelo Donghia connected the room's two levels with a spiral staircase and hung a startling, "dense-pack" chrome chandelier overhead.

Carpets and furniture common to both rooms replaced the original French furniture. The new oversized chairs, structured of rounded chrome rather than naked steel, are as comfortable as they are space-consuming. Windward Dining Room stewards in particular pay the unfortunate price: the larger the chair, the more crowded the aisles. As a result, working space is at a premium. It is this concentration of diners—as dense as the Leeward's chandelier—more than anything else that sets Windward apart from Chambord. But whatever the shortcomings, the overriding emotion that first night at dinner was delight that the *France* was *Norway* rather than fragments of Formosan scrap, that the ship was still in glorious service.

On the way out from dinner, I was pleased to find, after conducting a discreet experiment, that the blue-black circular ceiling over the Windward's central section still works as a "whispering dome." From a point anywhere beneath its rim, the most subdued conversation is broadcast clearly to a point diametrically opposite. This remains a curious architectural feature of the ship, as *France* stewards found to their chagrin when, occasionally, scraps of their candid backchat were overheard with ease by French-speaking passengers seated half a room away.

The earliest *Norway* schedule included Sunday-evening departures out of Miami, an incidental marketing inducement for newlyweds from all over the country who, married in their hometowns on Saturday, could reach Miami in time for a honeymoon cruise. Since then, the *Norway* has adopted Saturday sailings, in company—and competition—with most of Miami's ships. Initially, she called at only two ports, St. Thomas and a deserted Bahama out-island for a barbecue and swim on the beach. This latter remains an NCL innovation, an ingenious shore excursion that avoids the humidity, hassle, and expense of island taxis to a swim. The *Norway*'s pair of tenders, parked forward of the bridge and each capable of carrying four hundred, unload passengers clad in bathing suits directly onto their beach. Little San Salvador, the *Norway*'s originally designated

The *Norway* off St. Thomas. The two white specks along the portside plating forward are the blocks of the shore-tender davits. The tender is alongside, loading passengers. *Right,* the tender *Little Norway II,* named after a pilot-training facility in Canada during World War II, being lowered to the water. The white diagonal (upper right) is one of the special oversize davits installed at Bremerhaven to lower and retrieve the 400-passenger craft. *(Norwegian Caribbean Lines and author's collection)*

out-island, had been partially developed when it was discovered that storms could shoal the beach approaches, making them too shallow for the tenders; operations were than transferred to Great Stirrup Cay, another out-island already in use by the company, where four of the five ships of NCL's fleet call on different days of the week.

Since then, the *Norway*'s itinerary has twice been amended. Initially, the out-island call came first, but so much sun that early in the cruise necessitated a rearrangement. St. Thomas became the week's first port of call, and Little Stirrup Cay was relegated to day six—the night before reentry into Miami—by which time passengers could tolerate more tropical sun. In 1982, there was a second change, adding a third port to the ship's itinerary. Passengers were given the option of an evening—or a night—ashore in Nassau. The move made sense for crew morale as well. With a one-day turnaround in Miami each weekend as well as only daytime calls in between, *Norway* crew members seemed confined on board for months at a time, more, ironically, than had they sailed on the farthest-flung global itinerary. Nassau has its limitations as a liberty port, but for them, more important than a night on the town was a night away from the ship.

The *Norway*'s enviable capacity—in excess of two thousand passengers—produces income sufficient to guarantee the most lavish entertainment: cabaret, multimedia, Broadway musicals, big bands, name entertainers, the ship has them all, as well as a decisive edge over the competition. Just as outstanding hulls on the North Atlantic—the largest or the fastest—traditionally appealed, so the record-breaking *Norway*, surfeited with Las Vegas glitz, attracts Newpassengers to the Caribbean's *Wunderschiff*. Where she sails seems irrelevant. However the company juggles her itinerary, it is scarcely innovative: dozens of vessels call at Nassau and St. Thomas, and an out-island barbecue is standard for all NCL ships but one. The *Norway* compels not merely because the company hypes her as "the playground of the Caribbean" but, quite simply, because of the prestige of her size. During her first five years stationed out of Miami, I sailed on her half a dozen times; on each occasion, I was struck by the number of brand-new Newpassengers of every age on board. Travel agents apparently have no trouble selling a wide variety of clients seven days on the world's largest ship. And for every passenger confused by her size, dozens more revel in it. Over the slow Christmas cruise season of 1983, for instance, she enjoyed a better occupancy rate than any rival hull sailing from Florida.

For me on that August cruise of 1980, the *Norway*'s allure was part evocation of the *France* and part delight in sailing on any vessel anywhere.

More than half of her seven days are spent at sea, where ships of that lineage belong. A thousand nautical miles separate Miami from Charlotte Amalie, so that, at 16 knots, sixty hours of indolent sailing were in order. There can be no more pleasant antidote to the hugger-mugger of airports and embarkation than two days in Caribbean transit before landfall at St. Thomas. They are ideal passenger decompressants, an inaugural outbound voyage segment punctuated at its midpoint by the first of two captain's dinners.

Like every shipboard institution, whether crossing or cruising, origins of the captain's dinner are rooted in historical exigency. During early nineteenth-century crossings, immigrant passengers on board sailing packets were obliged to bring their own food. The company provided only cooking facilities and water. If crossings were delayed by adverse weather—not uncommon in the North Atlantic—these humblest passengers often ran short or completely out of food. Hence, owners gave masters of their ships dispensatory powers to distribute, gratis, company rations, held in reserve for that purpose, throughout the steerage compartments. Naturally, this gesture of gastronomic largesse became known as "the captain's dinner" and, more often than not, it occurred during final days at sea. From that compassionate expedient, the ritual has survived to the present, not so much as a charitable feed at voyage's end as a welcoming binge at its beginning. It is very much the master's evening, during which he shakes every passenger's hand, dispenses free drink, and sits at his table as host in the main dining room.

On the Monday afternoon, the first day at sea, an envelope was slipped beneath our cabin door; inside was an invitation to join Captain Torbjorn Hauge for dinner. (There is a probably apocryphal story about a nouveau riche passenger who, receiving that coveted summons, was supposedly heard to remark, "I didn't shell out all this dough to eat with the crew.") For the captain, poor man, the dinner that bears his name is a biweekly ordeal, endured for months on end. He seldom chooses his guests but must accept the catchall dozen or so recommended either by headquarters ashore or the purser or hotel manager on board. On the North Atlantic, unless imprisoned on the bridge by fog, captains ate regularly in the dining room, at a central table occupied by assorted glitterati—film stars, tycoons, politicians, the rich, or, when in doubt, repeaters, clients whose continuing patronage deserved reward. In common, those at the table sailed frequently and most could hold up their conversational end at what was, in effect, an extended dinner party lasting for nearly a week.

On cruise ships, in the absence of distinguished passengers, the selection of captain's tablemates seems a matter of accident more often than not, although one or two unattached pretty females will tend to be included. On some vessels, entire tables are summoned to dine with the master, with the result that, for the awkward or tongue-tied, conversational links already forged make for an easier evening. Sadly, on more and more ships, husbands' and wives' placecards are arranged side by side, denying the captain's table that irreplaceable random symbiosis of a conventional dinner party. Such was the case on board *Norway*: Mary and I sat side-by-side on the captain's left and five additional couples made up the rest of the table. No other officers were present; sometimes, guests will include a staff captain, hotel manager, or chief engineer to relieve the master of some of the social load.

Seated opposite us were amusing table companions: Bill Snead, a *Washington Post* photographer, and Louise Mangieri. Captain Hauge himself, with whom we had sailed on the previous May's maiden voyage, was an old friend, a man I had first met years earlier when he commanded *Sea Venture*. It was a pleasure to see him presiding in the Windward Dining Room, enjoying the less demanding requirements of command after a year spent wrestling with the conversion. Although I cannot remember much of our conversation, I do recall an especially agreeable burgundy that the stewards poured only too willingly. It was late when the long meal was over and, after the ship's photographer had snapped his obligatory group, I was surfeited with good talk, food, and wine and ready for bed.

Near midnight that Monday evening of August 19, our cabin lights blinked and began a long, irreversible fade, passing momentarily through an orange twilight before blacking out altogether. With the lights went television, music, air-conditioning, and the occasional chatter of bathroom plumbing: all the background sostenuto associated with a seaborne cabin vanished. In the eerie silence that followed, alarmed voices could clearly be heard through the cabin walls, followed shortly by that of our recent host, Captain Hauge, over the cabin speakers, regretting the inconvenience.

Normally, I bring a flashlight on cruises, but on this occasion, unaccountably—perhaps because it would have proved so invaluable—I had left it at home. Though the cabin was impenetrably dark, bleak emergency circuits, glowing pallidly every dozen yards, illuminated the corridors. Like moths drawn to a flame, passengers dressed and half-dressed forsook their cabins to begin a plaintive pilgrimage in search of more information than the captain's announcement had conveyed. A woman in a neighboring cabin, whose retarded child had gone on deck, was frantic that he would be unable to find his way back in the dark. My wife departed for a brief nocturnal tour of the public rooms, returning to report that a few couples were dancing in the dark, free drinks were being served, and, ominous news, the *Norway* was dead in the water. My response, as abrupt as it was unhelpful, was "So am I" before falling into a dreamless, burgundian sleep.

The next morning, the cabin was lit by the sun. Far below our sealed porthole, we could hear the unmistakable lapping of water against a stationary hull, clear indication that we were still adrift. Already, it was uncomfortably hot; opening the cabin door brought no relief, only the reek of the drains. I heard later that another passenger, using some judicious muscle and a clandestinely borrowed fire-ax, had unscrewed the lugs securing his porthole and succeeded in opening it. He had fresh air in his cabin over Black Tuesday, but most of us did not; if he had gone into the business of wrestling those sealed portholes open, he could have made a killing.

Conventional breakfast in the Windward and Leeward dining rooms had been aborted. Passengers, feeling their way down darkened stairways, had fared no better than stewards fumbling from galley to table with flashlights. The dining rooms were abandoned and, for the duration, picnic meals were served on Pool Deck or above, in public rooms that admitted daylight.

Pool Deck, in fact, was by then a cruel misnomer. Both pools, drained each evening at sea, remained empty. As the sun climbed, their comfort was sorely missed. Water of any kind was at a premium: there were no flushing toilets, no showers, and no way to cool off. Mercifully, there was ice, produced in quantities by emergency generators, and all the complimentary wine, beer, and soft drinks one could absorb. There was nothing to do about the heat except to find a shady spot on deck, preferably one cooled by a breeze. The encircling promenade on International Deck was stifling. Over the southern horizon lay Cuba. One of our tablemates, a Cuban from Miami, told me that several Cuban emigrées on board were convinced, some hysterically, that Castro had disabled the *Norway* with a Soviet laser so that she and all on board would drift helplessly into captivity.

Short of listening to rumors of this kind, there was surprisingly little to do. One really wanted, somehow, to help. Without electricity, the shops could not ring up their cash registers and the casinos were short-circuited.

I had a book, but reading out on a humid deck palled. Mary and I finally spent a dripping afternoon in the library, playing solitaire at a card table and listening to encouraging bulletins that, periodically, an exhausted Captain Hauge would broadcast to the passengers. "We hope to have things fixed by four o'clock," came the announcement at noon. The hour approached and passed without comment. Occasionally, we heard massive start-up efforts as the generators were turned over: a low whine would crescendo, then falter and die within seconds. From the adjacent Checkers Lounge, we could hear a talented amateur pianist thumping out show tunes for hours. Since every door was wedged open to promote circulation, he commanded a wide audience. Korean stewards, toiling far below in the gloomy humidity, carried buckets of seawater, hoisted in through an open port on E-deck, throughout passenger decks to flush out hundreds of fouled cabin toilets.

So the afternoon passed. As the inevitability of another powerless night approached, passengers all over the ship appropriated turf: confined to their cabins for the first night, they were determined to sleep outdoors for the second. Traffic in deck chairs became intense, at times heated. Scavenging families assembled chairs like wagon train encampments along stretches of deck, laying stubborn claim and departing only in relays for sustenance or relief. Armloads of bedding were brought up from below and, as the sun sank, a refugee squalor accumulated everywhere, as depressing as the sense of inertia that pervaded even the most disciplined constitution. In retrospect, I sense that Black Tuesday's ennui had as much to do with lack of the ship's movement as anything else. Drift was inescapable that endless, muggy day, and passengers were adrift as hopelessly as the vessel on which they were trapped.

That evening, after an improvised flashlight buffet served in Checkers, most passengers stayed out on deck. We ended up on the starboard side of Sun Deck, hard by the number 2 funnel, joined by Bill and Louise, friends made the previous night at Captain Hauge's table, an occasion that, already, seemed weeks earlier on another ship. It was an incomparable tropical night. Unsullied by deck lights, a skyful of stars and a full moon burned brilliantly overhead. Cool breezes ruffled the moon-burnished sea and set the *Norway*'s idle hull into gentle motion. Passing strollers shared new rumors: Cuban gunboats were gathering over the horizon, the *Mardi Gras* was steaming to evacuate all passengers. We stayed on deck until well past midnight; then, circumventing dozens of oblivious, recumbent forms, picked our way down to Viking Deck and bed.

Norway at sea, conventionally *(above)* and on "Black Tuesday" *(right)*. The wake's telltale turbulence is missing as NCL's giant flagship drifts in the Caribbean. *Opposite,* international signal of distress. Though the Norwegian postal flag flutters in the breeze, two black balls, one above the other, serve notice that the vessel is without power. *(Norwegian Caribbean Lines and author's collection)*

Power was restored sometime early the next morning. Every light in the cabin came on, fluorescent tubes flickering joyously to life. We staggered from switch to switch, rejoicing in the stirrings of machine-cooled air that issued once again from the deckhead vent and, even more welcome, the explosive return of rust-colored water from bathroom faucets. Up on deck, passengers awakened by the glare from light stanchions they could not turn off, draped and knotted swimming pool towels over the offending globes so that they could sleep on undisturbed until the sun came up.

The dining rooms were back in business for breakfast. Public rooms and open decks were restored to order. It was extraordinary how quickly the hardworking crew—for whom the power failure had been far more trying than for passengers—put things to rights. All over the vessel, evidence of Black Tuesday's dissolution had vanished with the finality of waking from a nightmare. The only reminder was the reassuring silhouette of a Coast Guard cutter sailing discreetly nearby. Emotions on board were back to normal as well: indulgent camaraderie, galvanized and sustained by a common emergency, was supplanted by discomfiture, a strange inversion of accommodation to angst. The first signs of disaffection were triggered midmorning when Captain Hauge announced over the speakers that the *Norway* would not be calling at St. Thomas but had turned back toward Florida, a call at Nassau the vessel's only scheduled stop.

There was an immediate outcry in the public rooms, the storm after the calm. Sea lawyers among the passengers composed indignant petitions demanding that the vessel proceed to St. Thomas; they were circulated aggressively for signature. Astonishingly, it seemed that the primary grievance was deprivation of the duty-free drink allowance synonymous with St. Thomas. The brouhaha served as an intriguing example of misplaced financial priorities: couples who had put down more than $3,000 for a seven-day cruise were infuriated at the prospect of losing out on a gallon of cut-rate whiskey.

Despite the petitions, Hauge remained adamant, a classic case where the captain's word was law. Though unpopular, his decision, reached after long radio-telephone conversations with company headquarters in Miami, was inevitable: engineers had been struggling for more than twenty-four hours in intolerable heat and would be too exhausted to cope in the event of a subsequent mechanical breakdown. And since Nassau was unpopular —"a dull port" scorned one petition—then the ship would return instead straight to Florida. That *Norway* cruise would be to nowhere, a trip to sea and back again.

Top, the morning after, port side, Sun Deck. Passengers camped outdoors awake to the good news that power has been restored. *Bottom,* resourceful Alan Farina, of Keene, New Hampshire, swung his hammock from the vessel's giant illuminated sign. *(Author's collection)*

En route, we met a California family on board recovering from a second *Norway* disappointment. Earlier that year, Larry and Diana Midland had taken their three children out of school and flown them to London for a whirlwind tour of the United Kingdom. The treat was to have concluded with the *Norway*'s maiden voyage westbound from Southampton to New York. But at Waterloo Station on the appointed day, within sight of the boat train, harried booking personnel from NCL's London office broke the news that their cabins were incomplete, escorted them to a hotel for the night, and presented them with plane tickets back to Los Angeles. They were promised a full refund of their maiden voyage tickets as well as half-price on a cruise of their choice out of Miami. The cruise the Midlands had chosen was the one we were incompleting, so to speak, at that moment.

Once again, Norwegian Caribbean Lines made handsome restitution to them and to every passenger on board: full refunds—air and sea alike—as well as half-price reductions on a subsequent cruise, on either *Norway* or another ship of the NCL fleet. Overwhelmed, even the most vociferous petitioner stood down. Early Friday morning, as we steamed up toward Miami's turning ground, crewmen on vessels lining Dodge Island, astonished at seeing the *Norway* midweek, waved and shouted incomprehensible greetings. Press helicopters circled overhead and a seething entourage of reporters and cameras awaited us pierside.

Before passengers disembarked, company ticketing agents set up shop in Checkers, where, three nights previously, canned meats, salad, and melting ice cream had been dispensed in the fetid dark. Now, NCL handed checks to every passenger and, for those ready to try again, accepted reservations on cruises to come. (The half-price gesture was shrewd, designed to divert some of the enormous cash flow back to NCL.)

More than one refunded passenger, uneasily fingering his check, requested a private audience with the purser: they could not, it seemed, accept repayment by check, for they were not officially on board, nor, for that matter, were their traveling companions. Paid in cash instead, these illicit voyagers lingered on board long after passengers had been released onto the pier; they were not anxious to appear inadvertently in television news footage among their fellow castaways.

Léon Tardy-Panit, the *France*'s *chef de patisserie* who had been so distressed when his ship had been laid up, finally came around to my point of view, that the *Norway* in service was infinitely preferable to the *France* laid up. He knew that Mary and I were making the maiden crossing and wrote from retirement:

. . . Would you be kind enough to stroke the *France*'s hull for me, saying that I am one of those that loved her, one of those who will never forget her? Thank you. . . .

It was a heartfelt commission and one that I was pleased to execute on his behalf as we disembarked at Pier 88, just before she set sail for Miami and her present-day renaissance.

Two years and many sailings later, we endured a grueling flight from New York to Manila, joining the *Rotterdam* for the Far Eastern portion of her 1982 world cruise. We would be on board for two and a half weeks, making that traditional southwesterly sea-loop around Asia, touching at Hong Kong, Singapore, Bangkok, and Colombo before disembarking at Bombay.

Only recently have companies divided these global itineraries, allowing passengers to choose portions of the voyage that suit both their schedule and purse. World cruises used to be, exclusively, cruises "round the world": passengers were obliged to book for the entire circuit or not at all. The only newcomers occasionally seen on board the *Caronia*, for instance, might be friends or relatives of permanent passengers who had been lent cabin accommodations by their temporarily disembarked benefactors. But in 1982, the *Rotterdam*'s passenger load was divided in half: 50 percent were full-time, the other 50 percent part-time. The latter would appear and disappear while the regulars stayed on as the great Dutch flagship churned her majestic way around the globe. Some of the diehard regulars are openly scornful of the fortnighters, accusing them of upsetting the balance of the ship. I always find this attitude curious, for, to me, passengers are passengers, whatever the duration of their stay on board.

For my part, I have never had time enough to embark on a complete world cruise and wonder whether I would enjoy it if I did. Though I stand second to none in my love of ocean liners, the prospect of a quarter of a year confined aboard one ship seems daunting. Staff who sail on world cruises find consistent pitfalls. Jean-Paul Giquel, an assistant purser on board *France* for both her global marathons, told me once that couples embarked for ninety-one days were *"toujours les uns sur les autres"*—in other words, never out of each other's sight. Whereas ashore they might separate for golf, tennis, bridge, shopping, or any one of a dozen day-to-day errands, on board they were nearly always *en face* for months on end. Giquel's solution, suggested by his superior, Commissaire Ermel, was

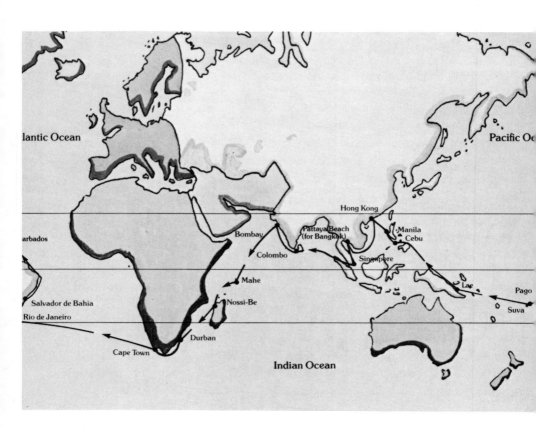

An exotic necklace of ports, from Manila
to Bombay. The *Rotterdam*'s Far
Eastern itinerary, world cruise, 1982.
(Holland America Line)

to improvise an instructional class for men only, a time each day when they could "go to the office," gathering together away from their wives. As it happened, among the young purser's talents was making sailing-ship models that could be fitted inside a bottle. With a supply of empties from Raimond, barman of the Salon Riviera, wood scraps from the ship's carpenter, and knives, thread, and glue bought at the next port, Giquel set up shop in the Salon Débussy. It was a tremendous success, consistently oversubscribed, and it greatly helped alleviate the problem of an overkill of world-cruise togetherness.

Additional disaffection can erupt beyond marital parameters. According to Peter Farranto, who has handled shore excursions on dozens of world cruises, on board *Kungsholm, France*, and *Rotterdam*, shipboard tensions arise less out of boredom than overfamiliarity between newly made friends: paired couples get so close that friendships deteriorate in consequence. Most trying, he recalls, are long sea passages between ports, either the waters between Japan and Hawaii or Atlantic crossings. But, inevitably, cruise's end always healed the stubbornest wounds, and days before final disembarkation, passengers who had been at each other's throats only weeks earlier wept at the prospect of separation.

The existence of these erratic, sociocircumnavigational moods has been authenticated by a recent archaeological find on board the *Norway*. All cabin bureaus on the original *France* were of steel, bolted to the deck; incorporated into the top drawer of each was a sliding cover that served as a writing desk. If the drawer was inadvertently closed with letters still on the desk's surface, they sometimes slid out of sight and fell beneath the bottom of the bureau. During some cabin renovations on board the *Norway*, a lost *France* page was discovered, part of a letter received by a passenger from her daughter in London. In it, the daughter quotes a former world-cruise hostess:

She said it was very amusing watching all the passengers on such a long cruise. She said the first month, everyone was very polite and friendly and obviously trying to make a few friends, generally weighing everybody up; by the second month, everyone had been sized up by their fellow passengers and they had all made friends; toward the end of the second month, they were beginning to get on each other's nerves and by the third month, everyone was screaming at everyone else but then, as the end of the cruise drew near, everyone is crying because they don't want to leave each other and they've had such a marvelous time!

Bill Archibald, the shore-excursion manager for Thomas Cook on *Caronia* world cruises, remembers an annual inescapable low point as the vessel approached her antipodal extreme:

> It was hot. People were getting on one another's nerves and the crew was getting uptight. It was called Hate Week. We knew it was coming and we knew it would go away. Bombay was the place where we broke Hate Week.

In the days of those stately *Caronia* progressions, the vessel would tie up at Bombay for a week, to be deserted by most passengers—"all but the infirm," recalls Archibald crisply with the relish of a successful promoter of excursions. The crew, in consequence, had the ship to themselves and "a chance to unwind." Their unchanging ritual of sea and port days broken, they would clean and paint the empty ship by day, spending riotous evenings ashore each night. When passengers reembarked after an exhausting week in the hinterlands, all rancor had vanished; clients and crew sailed for Suez, their equanimity restored.

Then, too, a paradoxical aloneness exacts its own toll on world cruises. A high proportion of the passengers are widows. Even though surrounded by others also traveling alone, many suffer from chronic loneliness, isolation that rankles. Violence may erupt over what may seem an insignificant slight. Knox Godfrey, a veteran of countless cruise staffs, recalled the following incident from a long Pacific crossing. A German woman on the *Rotterdam* came into the lounge one evening after dinner. She passed a table occupied by a single female acquaintance and asked if she might join her. The woman demurred, saying that friends would be arriving momentarily. Rebuffed, the German retired to a nearby table to watch. When, by the end of the cabaret, no friends had materialized, she paused at the table on her way out and, with one roundhouse swing of her evening purse, opened a gash on the woman's cheek that had to be sewn up by the ship's surgeon. Loneliness is pervasive for too many of these peripatetic widows. A night stewardess on board the *Royal Viking Sea* once told me that she regularly received late-night summonses from cabins occupied by elderly women traveling alone, asking for a sandwich or pot of tea. She found out later, from the respective cabin stewardesses involved, that the trays usually remained untouched; what the nocturnal callers wanted more than anything else was emotional nourishment.

If cruise ships were ball parks, and if teams from an American or National Maritime League played there, their world series would be world cruises. It is archetypal, big-league stuff. To please the fans, owners and operators field their best lineups. In addition, pinch-hitting tenors and comedians are sent to the plate: those scoring a base hit will stay in the batting order, those striking out will be relegated back to the Caribbean minors. Entertainment is—literally—jazzed up as extra musicians are booked to keep spirits up in the doldrums. World-cruise menus are enriched no less than passenger lists: "celebrities"—that twentieth-century showbiz catchall—are invited to sail on long cruise segments. Their value is as great, if not greater, offstage than on, bewitching blasé Old Guard passengers suddenly confronted with a world-famous face sharing the queue for a noontime buffet.

As on any cruise, maintaining on-board esprit is most demanding on the cruise staff. Cruise directors are run ragged; they must juggle their own performances (most seem to be singers) with the other entertainment, cope with conflicting star egos and complaining passengers, and oversee excursions—all the while soothing anxious superiors at headquarters with buoyant telexes. Some years ago, Holland America tried dividing up the load, replacing cruise directors halfway around the world. The move, however, was abandoned, not because the cruise directors objected, but because it was greeted with such suspicion and scorn by the passengers. Therein lies a recurring global headache: the need to placate and accommodate world-cruise regulars.

The members of this Oldest Guard, booking repeatedly on the same annual junket, are touching as they board each January. For the older ones, the cruise is less an excursion than a testament to survival. They greet each other with especial pleasure and close protective ranks about newly made widows or widowers. For all of them, a world cruise is the pleasantest indulgence, three months on board a ship where they will be spoiled to death. But, inevitably, some assume the proprietary covetousness of what the navy calls plank-owners. They like the ship run the way it always has been, yet improved each year as well, echoing in spirit the director exhorting his opening night cast: "Louder and better!" They are not anonymous tourists flocking on board for a week in the sun, forgotten the moment they disembark; world-cruise regulars are family, complete with all the stresses the word implies, experienced *amis de maison* who, each year, invest tens of thousands of dollars for a winter's travel and diversion. They know the ports, the ship, the captain, and all the officers; they know each other and what they want; and they know how to speak up if they feel they are shortchanged.

The view over the stern: *Rotterdam*
completing a turn to starboard. The two
cylindrical structures aft of the pool
are shower stalls, no longer painted with
the same multicolored pattern. The pool
itself is surrounded by a flagstone terrace.
(Holland America Line)

Keeping them happy is a compelling company preoccupation. The financial stakes are awesome. A flawed seven- or fourteen-day cruise can be shrugged off, an acceptable syncline in the company's economic bedrock, offset by the week that follows. But a world cruise, consuming more than a quarter of the vessel's operational year, is an extravaganza, requiring months of planning and one-shot logistical contingencies, that demands success. Not only that year's bottom line is at stake, but those for years to come as well. Passenger recidivism is paramount. The disaffected may transfer their allegiance to rival lines as a result of any dereliction, real or imagined. With what they perceive as a dwindling actuarial and financial pool of world-cruise passengers from which to draw, companies perceive defections—singly no less than en masse—as catastrophic. Worse, the Oldest Guard knows this and are not above a little cold-blooded, geriatric blackmail.

The evening we reached the Philippines, I caught sight of the *Rotterdam* approaching her berth in front of the Manila Hotel, where I was hoping to sleep off the effects of that murderous flight from New York. A window on the sixth floor offered an incomparable vision of the ship as she glided imperceptibly landward. It was the first time I had ever seen the vessel's three-quarter view from that height. Suddenly, that pair of tall, mastlike stacks across the stern, bathed by floodlights, were united with the single mast forward, making glorious design sense, an elongated tripod connected by festoons of pearl necklace. And just as my elevated vantage point revealed a new *Rotterdam* perspective, so an overview of that pressured world-cruise ethos would illumine the dynamics of the specific voyage to follow.

A raffish charm attends embarkation at Asian ports, and Manila proved no exception. We were abandoned by our taxi at the margins of a wasteland of rubbled concrete separating us from the pier. Luggage was surrendered to a gang of rascally porters who—one for each suitcase— formed up in single file and led us through the makeshift bazaar that throngs the pier wherever a cruise ship docks in the Far East. Among the crowds of shoppers we recognized friends from the ship—officers, stewards, and passengers. At the gangplank we were greeted by the starched white bulk of Cor Meijer, the *Rotterdam*'s security officer, beaming over his great sweep of moustaches. Our porter train was paid off—exorbitantly—and stewards assumed their load. We trailed them on board, first to Main Deck's foyer, then forward along the port side of Lower Promenade Deck to cabin 108.

Among the *Rotterdam*'s architectural delights are her spacious decks, hallmarks of a venerable design. They are kept so spotless that when Indonesian paint crews are working along their length, one cannot tell in which direction they are painting. *(Author's collection)*

Nothing equals that moment of shipboard bliss when the airport/ hotel hegira ends in the cabin. Suitcases packed three days earlier on the far side of the globe disgorge their cumbersome loads, if only for a matter of weeks. This particular bliss is doubled on the *Rotterdam*, where cabin storage spaces are extensive and as faultlessly maintained as the public rooms above. Accommodations on contemporary newbuilding seem extruded exclusively of steel and formica, with only an occasional wood veneer for relief. But those on Holland America's flagship rejoice in cabinetry, endless bookshelves, cupboards, and bureaus. Even the dividers between the wall panels are prettily routed strips of elm, their finish as clean and smooth as the day they were installed. So, too, cabin bathroom fixtures bear the uncompromising stamp of shoreside authenticity, stolid porcelain monuments spaced imperiously around a generous expanse of grouted tile floor. Though fifties ships may be the despair of cost-conscious company accountants, their cabin perks are worth cherishing.

Once recovered from jet lag, we realized that boarding the vessel at Manila had made good sense. Though chronologically the *Rotterdam*'s world cruise was a third over, in terms of reward it was only beginning. The route thus far had been less adventurous than routine. The passage from New York and Florida to Cartagena, Panama, Acapulco, and Los Angeles was as familiar as it was inevitable. Large numbers of the Californian world-cruise clients—more passengers of every kind originate from the Golden State than any other— picked up the *Rotterdam* at Los Angeles, avoiding the long, anticipatory Panamanian approach altogether. Company people admit that passage west from the continental United States inaugurates the world cruise proper, but crewmen on board suggest that it does not really begin until the Pacific has been traversed and the prospect of Asia's great ports lies just over the horizon.

Passenger vessels sailing west from Hawaii have three choices: dead ahead for the Philippines, starboard to Japan, port to the South Pacific and Australasia: in common, all involve a week or more of undiluted sea days. The *Rotterdam* had turned half-south, steaming to Pago Pago and Suva before veering northward again, touching at New Guinea's northern coast before reaching the Philippines. Now, she was poised on the threshold of Asia, from Hong Kong—*primus inter pares*—along a great circumferential sweep to Bombay. The Asian land mass is a compelling lure for world-cruise passengers, a succession of teeming, picturesque port cities, remote from Western experience, full of the smells and sounds of the East and chockablock with exotic shopping. Already, a neglected stretch of the *Rotterdam*'s starboard Lower Promenade Deck had been transformed into

The Far Eastern harvest begins. A corner of *Rotterdam*'s starboard Promenade Deck serves as storage warehouse for an increasing accumulation of passenger purchases. *(Author's collection)*

a mobile storage warehouse for passenger purchases in Manila that would otherwise have discommoded even the grandest suites. There were piles of paper-wrapped loot, carpets, tables and chairs, lacquered gimcracks, brassware, and other assorted Eastern exotica, lashed in place against the fearful day of disembarkation and off-loading in New York.

Yet however exquisite our timing, the mood on board was less so. Beneath the conventional languorous glamour lay unmistakable angst. Passage north to Hong Kong was marred. The staff may have been unsettled at the prospect of that landfall, for it is the port to which the brass invariably jet in midcruise to descend on the ship; visits from headquarters make for perennial butterflies in the stomach. But this neurosis was not confined to crew or staff ganglia: the entire soma was afflicted. If not quite one of Bill Archibald's Hate Weeks—it was too soon for that—a vague but persistent discontent lay everywhere.

During the one sea day before Hong Kong, without any effort on our part, we were put in the picture. A confidence trumpeted from an adjacent deck chair pronounced the cruise "not as good as last year," that insidious world-cruise comparative that company officials have learned to dread. Our first evening in the Ambassador Club, a bejeweled crony advised us, "The ports, so far, have been terrible." Not to be outdone, her companion disposed of the *Rotterdam*'s catering staff and dining room, to which we were about to descend. "The food's bad this year," she revealed—not putrefied, she meant, just dull. (Our dinner that night and for many to follow was at odds with her verdict.) But overwhelming passenger asperity was directed at that most tempting and vulnerable target: the entertainment. "There's got to be something good this evening," a couple assured us outside the Main Lounge. "It's been awful so far." On board were half a dozen performers—singers, instrumentalists, and comedians—a better-than-average shipboard mélange. Some we knew to be first-rate. It seemed extraordinary that so much talent, so expensively assembled in mid-Pacific, could have so disenchanted an entire shipload. Since blanket condemnation is always easier than constructive analysis, it was never made clear why the ship's entertainment had been so disparagingly received—until Singapore, that is.

Of any of the many things that can be wrong with a cruise, cabaret is the most often criticized. For my taste, it should not make or break a voyage; ideal shipboard is a far more complex sum of parts, including books, conversation, friendship, indolence, and exhilarating changes of scenery. But for too many—and not just world-cruise passengers—a consuming need to be entertained dominates, far beyond the perfectly adequate capacity of yesterday's films, bingo, and horse racing. Teatime on board ships today serves as a perfect case in point. No longer merely a restorative pause between lunch and dinner, it has become, invariably, tea with bingo, tea with a quiz, tea with a fashion show. Why not just tea? Similarly, lounges have been transformed into music halls, festooned with speakers, cables, consoles, spotlights, and those chrome-encrusted electronic boxes that litter the stage and assault the ears. Some Newpassenger lounges are no longer furnished with social chair groupings around tables; instead, they are fixed-row auditoria with terraced seating for better sightlines. The sole concession to sociability is a narrow shelf attached to each chair-back on which to rest drinks; only the most agile and wiry stewards can work their assigned areas of responsibility. These rooms are not ship's lounges in the old sense, they are performance halls; once nightly back-to-back shows are over, they are unusable, with all the charm of deserted cinemas.

Worse, contemporary passengers have been conditioned to expect a nightly entertainment fix. Marketing surveys indicate that the quality of a vessel's entertainment is a decisive factor in achieving that elusive company ideal, passenger satisfaction. So we can only expect more of the same in future. Television may be to blame, a medium that is less sinister than the consuming receptiveness it engenders. It has spawned a generation of passive passengers, boredom's pensioners who believe, somehow, that evenings on board should be surfeited with the same televised deluge laving them at home. For the hard-pressed companies, the entertainment conflagration has raged out of control, costing millions each year. Keeping a furtive eye on the competition is inevitable: passenger service directors board rival ships less to savor the food or ambience than to count the chorus.

Two ports subsequent to Manila—on a Singapore pier, in fact—I conducted an impromptu survey. It was midmorning and tour buses had already lumbered toward town. Mary and I waited in the heat for a shuttle bus that would carry us within reach of Rasa Singapura, an outdoor restaurant at which we were looking forward to lunching. Standing with us in the welcome shade of a warehouse were two women who, we discovered, had been on board since New York. Here, with nothing to distract us, I leaped at the chance to decode the 1982 world-cruise cypher, if not of all of its conundrums, at least cracking the puzzle surrounding the ship's entertainment. I introduced myself—not as a writer, merely a recently boarded passenger—and asked the women what they thought of the cruise in general and the entertainment in particular.

"It's been bad, very bad," responded the first, an angular midwestern widow.

Her companion—shorter, plumper, Floridian—agreed. Thus far, I had encountered consistency, not only with each other but with their fellow passengers as well. I probed further.

"If it was bad, how would you have improved it?"

"More singers," said the taller of the two.

"But there were singers nearly every night," I suggested. I had done my homework the day before, reviewing a backlog of daily programs.

"I don't like singers," interrupted the Floridian. "I liked that magician we had before Hawaii."

"So did I," was the midwesterner's rejoinder. "He was cute."

"What about the other one, the juggler?" recollected the first. "He was good."

"Sure, they were both great."

We were cut short by the arrival of the shuttle, though I had heard more than enough. Clearly, my instant poll—Trendex, Arbitron, and Nielsen all rolled into one—had rewarded me with naught save sympathy and admiration for those charged with hiring performers for cruise passengers. Shipboard audiences like or do not like what they see at a given time but, on reflection—if they reflect at all—derive pleasure nonetheless. Moreover, the collective passenger psyche, what nuclear scientists might term the critical mass, is as complex as it is quirky: no one can predict what it will enjoy, no one can be blamed for what it does not.

Sometimes, however, the choice of entertainment seems, at the least, inappropriate. Once, in a Royal Viking lounge on the Caribbean, I saw or, rather, heard an energetic female singer, pacing the stage like a caged lioness, backed by her pianist-arranger and half a dozen hardworking sidemen. For nearly an hour, she belted lyrics into a microphone held only millimeters from her persuasive lips. Sitting to the side, I saw less of her than her audience. It was a short cruise, and a standard Old Guard/ Newpassenger mix had booked. The penumbra of the followspot periodically grazed them as it swept the stage in pursuit of its prey. Many times, those mainly white heads seemed to recoil under the decibellian assault. Audience defection was marked, and the concluding applause perfunctory. I could not help wondering why that evening's interminable gig had been selected for an audience that might well have preferred something less relentless. I wondered, too, why they submitted. Perhaps because older people, especially, like to be plugged into whatever is current. Those oldster-hipsters certainly absorbed more wattage than they had anticipated.

Amplification of amplification. *Top*, the stage of the *Pacific Princess*. Is all that noise necessary? *Bottom*, on board the *Royal Viking Sky* there is a small bar at the stern, where a lone musician plays and sings. This is the amount of equipment he apparently needs to be heard. *(Author's collection)*

There is a final footnote to this entertainment riddle as well as a resolution of sorts to the *Rotterdam*'s Manila angst. Later on, between Hong Kong and Singapore, came the moment during 1982's world cruise when company marketing people on board announced specific details of 1983's cruise. The Silver Cruise—Holland America's twenty-fifth consecutive world cruise—promised, as always, to be memorable. A Rolls-Royce Silver Sprite would be raffled off to a full-fare passenger in order to alleviate mid-Pacific doldrums. Bookings of high-caliber entertainment were announced as well: joining the *Rotterdam* in 1983 at Rio would be Victor Borge, that comical pianist who plays so beautifully when he chooses but makes his hilarious reputation by procrastinating on the piano stool instead. He appeared during the Silver Cruise as promised but was received, I am told, with less than enthusiasm by one couple in the balcony. After twenty minutes of his performance, they swept out of the theater. "My God, he can't even play!" scoffed the wife to her husband. I rest my case and, sharing the confused inadequacy of my two Singapore informants, state nolle prosequi.

As it turned out, residual passenger distress was dispelled once the *Rotterdam* steamed into Victoria Harbor, that protected 50-square-mile crescent of water separating Hong Kong from the Asian mainland. It was overcast, with a persistent drizzle that discouraged the customary passenger gallery from assembling on dock. But the apparent disinterest was misleading: an urgent undercurrent of anticipation could be sensed throughout the vessel. Hong Kong—in its early years, "the Graveyard of the East" and, at the height of the British raj, "the brightest gem in the colonial diadem"—lay over our bows or, indeed, all around us. No city so crowds the water's edge. Victoria Island's steep elevation tilts Hong Kong's cityscape into a dramatic perspective, like a glorious shop window display, the better to entice shipboard visitors who would shortly swarm ashore. A century and a half earlier, Lord Palmerston had dismissed it as "a barren rock with nary a house upon it." Now, the formerly stark granite slopes have been wrought into a bustling warren of achievement where banks, offices, apartments, and warehouses jostle for every expensive square foot of space. The vigor and excitement of the fabled free port reached us across the water; here was Hong Kong—air-conditioned, neon-fired, accommodating China—at our feet.

In the old days, when Hong Kong was first established as the East's most rewarding port, cruise ships dropped their hooks at the western margin of Victoria Harbor. The central anchorage was reserved for warships only, underscoring the Crown Colony's significance as an armed outpost of the empire. Every Hong Kong hotel of the time—and they were all on the island, none on the mainland—dispatched launches to incoming passenger ships. Those who planned to sleep on board but shop by day hired one of a multitude of sampans that crowded the companionway, clamoring for patronage. (In 1916, 12,777 licensed rowing boats crisscrossed the waters of Victoria Harbor.) But as Hong Kong grew, overflowing from island to mainland, changing suburban Kowloon into a metropolitan extension, a ferry ashore was unnecessary, as cruise ships tied up at the Kowloon Wharves. Today, those wharves have been consolidated into the Hong Kong Ocean Terminal, a single, enclosed finger pier that can accommodate a pair of cruise ships at a time and contains within its glittering multiple levels the largest shopping complex in Asia. Passengers need only stagger ashore to find themselves, within feet of the gangway, inside an incredible marketplace. Betaking themselves only slightly farther, they can find the ubiquitous Star Ferry, that enchanting, waterborne link crossing the Hung Hom Fairway between Kowloon and Victoria Island.

Hong Kong's bountiful shops, combining Japan's technical wizardry with the riches of Chinese craftsmanship, make it irresistible. The *Rotterdam*'s urbane port lecturer and historian, Waldemar Hansen, estimated that a million dollars would be left in the city by passengers and crew combined during the ship's three-day stay in port. Pearls, jewelry, lacquer, silks, clothing, cloisonné, antiques, furniture, carpets, as well as an electronic cornucopia from radios to calculators to cameras, can be found in extraordinary variety at manipulable prices. The entire ship is preoccupied with things material, Hong Kong days and nights spent in a frenzy of buying. Passenger/shoppers return to their ship only to dump armloads of parcels before picking up more traveler's checks and returning to the fray. Orson Welles said it all: "You go broke saving money in Hong Kong." The vessel's profile seems as bizarrely infected as its passengers: the sides of the Ocean Terminal, covered with outsized neon hoardings, tint the white superstructure alongside with a lurid, pink, acquisitive glow.

During the final hours before we sailed, near midnight on our third day in port, deliveries from a hundred Hong Kong tailoring ateliers swamped the Main Foyer. Suits, dresses, jackets, shirts, and pajamas were awaited and retrieved. During ensuing sea days on board *Rotterdam*, there were echoes of the *Victoria Luise*'s misfit parade as new finery pervaded every public room. But more significant than the sartorial enrichment was equanimity's return. The pointer of the ship's socioemotional barometer swung firmly to Fair. Years ago, Moss Hart, writing in *Act One* about

The *Rotterdam* in Hong Kong. At night, pink spill from the shoreside neon washes over the vessel. *Below,* glimpsed between Ocean Terminal and still-moored *Rotterdam,* the outbound *Sagafjord.* *(Author's collection)*

out-of-town tryouts for Broadway, reached the celebrated—and accurate—conclusion that if the show were in trouble, then the hotel's food, room service, elevator service, mattresses, and hot water were similarly affected. The same mysterious disability had descended on the ship as she crossed to the Orient: Holland America's show was in trouble and passenger disaffection had soured everything. A ship's officer talked about it as we stood at the rail one day; he suggested that the world cruise's trap lay in its very globalness. To achieve the Far East, one had to travail across what Robinson Jeffers called "the deep, dark-shining Pacific." Once passed, in touch with Asia, the cure seemed to have been instantaneous, what a Stoppard might characterize as a "Cathay-sis."

Sea days to follow saw resumption of those nocturnal events that are fixtures of world cruises: elaborate private parties. Several hundred hosts and hostesses were confined on board, each anxious to leave their imprimatur on the cruise calendar. The sense of carousel was the same as in any resort's accelerated season: in a blur passed the same faces, the same smiles, the same small talk—though seldom the same dresses. The only variable was the decoration of the public rooms, miraculous transformations achieved by ingenious Indonesian stewards with nothing more than yards of fabric and scissors. On board ships today, the private dinner party is, sadly, a rarity; the conventional invitation is for cocktails, either a full-blown extravaganza in the Ritz Carlton or a smaller assemblage elsewhere, perhaps a roped-off corner of the Ambassador. Wherever, an immutable ritual is preserved: captain, officers, and staff head every list, summoned to join a constantly changing but painstakingly selected kaleidoscope of passengers. Social pitfalls abound: couples invited to conflicting parties must attend both, others invited a previous year can be inexplicably cut, failure to appear is remarked and never forgotten. During the *Rotterdam*'s first week at sea en route to Rio in 1984, an enterprising woman absolved herself of all social obligations for three months by inviting the entire passenger load, so vast a gathering that it was divided by sittings. She had achieved an inspired, if expensive, solution; unlike a conventional shipboard guest list, no one could claim to have been either inadvertently or purposely excluded.

(At the opposite end of the private party spectrum comes a parable from the *France* during her last world cruise in 1974. A very rich couple, new to shipboard, occupied one of the largest suites. After a week at sea, the husband asked a ship's entertainer how he could give a private party. "Buy some liquor," he was advised, "and invite your friends." Cases of drink were bought and delivered but no party materialized. Weeks went

...ll ashore. Including passengers and crew, over 5,000 ...vid buyers had swarmed ashore to the fabled crown ...olony when this picture was taken a week after the *...otterdam*'s departure in the winter of 1982. To the ...ft is P&O's *Canberra*; to the right, Cunard's *Queen ...lizabeth 2*. *(Hong Kong Tourist Association)*

by and the entertainer inquired about the delay. "I haven't found anyone I want to invite," was the explanation.)

So our enchanted pantechnicon continued its westerly quest, the longitudinal spread lengthening days already surfeited with pleasure. We would disembark in Bombay after more than a fortnight on board, two weeks that flew by. In retrospect, what made that and every world cruise memorable was a by-product of its length, an abiding rapport that springs up between passengers and crew, uniting normally adjacent but parallel shipboard components. We were all old friends, sharing a long sunlit voyage over remote seas. It is perhaps for this reason that I recall especially an afternoon at anchor off Pattaya, Bangkok's port, when local merchants crowded on board to set up shop in the Card Room. For the rest of the day, a crosscurrent of disparate cultures huddled together over those exotic displays, American passengers, Dutch and Indonesian crew, and affable Thais. Spared the aggravation of the shoreside bazaar, the ship's people passed leisurely hours poring over silks, jewelry, ivory, jade, and sandalwood. For me, the most pleasurable aspect of that day lay less in gentle haggling with the shopkeepers, less in the silk cushions that changed hands after our amiable discussion, than the afternoon itself, the sun streaming over the riches spread out for us as we swung idly at anchor off that incomparably lush coast. If a shipboard moment can best conjure up world cruising, perhaps it was that more than any other.

There can be no more marked contrast to that single ship, gliding along her solitary, languid itinerary, than the competitive summer rush-hour traffic that streams up North America's west coast to Alaska. From June to September, Alaskan waters are as thronged with cruise ships as the Caribbean. In the six years between 1978 and 1984, the tonnage of passenger vessels in Alaskan waters more than tripled. Serving that summer market are all three Holland America hulls, another trio from Princess Cruises, two ships from Cunard (one from either end of their market spread), and one each from Sitmar, Royal Viking, Costa, and Paquet: a dozen vessels on almost identical itineraries attest to the established success of the seabound Alaskan dream.

The continental United States is blessed by the geographical diversity of its diagonal extremes, each embracing a complementary cruise market. While at the country's southeast corner Florida's peninsula dangles contiguous to the sun-drenched Caribbean, the country's northwest quadrant anticipates a striking seasonal reverse. Alaska's cruise ambiente is balmy to cool. Suntan and swimming are suddenly and, for many, pleasurably redundant. Obligatory dress includes stout shoes, sweaters, or slickers; the probability of moisture—either drizzle or downpour—is acute. The character of the stern Alaskan itinerary is reflected in the northern passenger profile; older, staider, and solider country types book in overwhelming numbers, sharing a pride of destination and insatiable curiosity that hark back to the origins of American cruising.

A broad temperature range distinguishes the Alaskan voyage. Passengers packing during a midsummer heat wave in the lower forty-eight may find it difficult to believe that they will welcome a down jacket, scarf, and gloves at the cruise's climactic call in the waters of Glacier Bay. This compelling natural wonder, lying at latitude 58°30′ north, is the apogee of the archetypal Alaskan itinerary. Whereas Caribbean brochures flaunt vessels anchored off palm-fringed beaches, Alaska's scenic come-ons invariably portray ships humbled by glittering, glacial façades. Glacier Bay is every cruise's pièce de résistance, outweighing all the spurious frontier nonsense of intermediate calls en route. The conventional circuit is Inland Passage, Ketchikan, Juneau, Glacier Bay, Sitka, and back. Seven-day ships load up at Vancouver; fourteen-day vessels originate in San Francisco or, occasionally, Los Angeles, offering the double advantage of more sea days as well as Canadian calls at Vancouver northbound and Victoria on the return.

Passenger/readers still on board will have little trouble guessing that my obvious predilection for achieving Alaska by sea entailed the fortnight voyage. If for no other reason, it meant embarkation at San Francisco—after New York, America's most hypnotic city. There is a dreamlike quality to the San Franciscan sun that sets the famous bay as well as the hills surrounding it into dazzling perspective. There is magic, too, in a glimpse of one's inbound ship at dawn of embarkation day, the toylike hull slipping in toward land spied from a hotel window atop those preposterous slopes that are one of the city's most remarkable features. It is only sad that so few vessels sailing from San Francisco nowadays continue west to span the ocean, evoking those haunting Pacific shades of *Mariposa* and *Monterey* and the Japanese fleets from the other side. Once the pilot has cleared the port these days, it is, to paraphrase Matson Line master John Kilpack, "under the Golden Gate and turn right" for Alaska. San Francisco has almost been relegated from continental terminus to coastal port; nevertheless, the summertime flurry of docking at Pier 35 is heartening rejuvenation for a once-proud Pacific waterfront.

Launched at John Brown's yard in the fifties as the *Carinthia, Fairsea* boasts the thoroughbred lines of a midsize, North Atlantic sea boat. She is one of four vessels of the Sitmar Line, short for Società Italiana Maritima. Her bow is plain, the counter austere and uncompromisingly blunt. The Promenade Deck slopes up sharply at her after end and the same relentless banana curvature pervades every interior space. Deck and bulkhead junctions on board vessels of that vintage are complex. The sheer—that upward slope just remarked—combined with each deck's camber—an athwartship downslope to either side—must have made cutting and fitting interior partitions an agonizing business. Only the verticals were parallel, everything else a confusion of curves. *Fairsea* belongs to a more intricate shipbuilding era: solid, conservative, and well considered, similar, again, to the passengers crowding her passageways as we embarked. As no-nonsense as her clients, she is a doughty ex-Cunarder from thirty years back, admirably suited to any northern rigors she might face.

I have seldom met a steward I did not like, and almost all those on board *Fairsea* were delightfully attentive. Sitmar ships are crewed by Italians and Portuguese; the service—in cabin as well as public and dining rooms—was impeccable. Considering that Sitmar caters largely to Newpassengers, the level of expertise and concern is remarkable. The Italian waiter is a venerable fixture in fact and fiction, and Tony, the senior of our two dining room stewards, had been cast in that classic mold. He was Neapolitan, and his malleable features, only occasionally frozen in solemnity, more frequently radiated a mischievous southern warmth.

Tony's obverse, unfortunately, was stationed on the opposite side of the same dining room, as we would find out while tied up at Ketchikan. On port days, open-sitting lunch prevails. Passengers are seated indiscriminately as they enter, denied their customary tables and stewards. We were consigned by ill luck to a table whose steward was a company liability. I did not take the trouble to learn his name and shall call him Scaramuccio, after that celebrated braggart and bully from the commedia del l'arte. He was younger than Tony, with none of his accomplished charm. He bullied our tableful of naive, spinster Newpassengers, alternating between familiarity and scorn. Clearly, he was bored, venting his frustration on those he was obliged to serve. Mercifully, Scaramuccios are in the minority on board cruise ships though, conversely, too many of them survive in service professions ashore. The wonder is that they choose to serve as stewards, a calling that demands special patience and dedication. I kept my peace and was grateful that evening to return to Tony's endearing ministrations at table 18.

e *Fairsea*'s single funnel, its only
:oration the letter *V*, initial of Sitmar's
ner, Boris Vlasov. Just below the
me board is a tender dock that rides
 with the lifeboats when not in use.
uthor's collection)

Sitmar boasts very few tables for two, so Mary and I found ourselves dining for the duration of the Alaskan cruise with three fellow passengers. (I say dining with reason: we tend to breakfast in the cabin and take lunch on deck.) Our preference for eating by ourselves derives less from snobbism than from dietary caution. Larger tables take longer to serve, and though the pace may be retarded, consumption inevitably appreciates. Dining room captains hover around large tables with tempting specials; on board Italian ships, with reserves of that incredible pasta at their disposal, they can be devilishly persuasive. Our tablemates that cruise were three women. Two stunning blondes from Houston masqueraded for about half an hour of our first encounter as traveling companions; somewhere into the fettuccine Alfredo, Carole confessed to being Julie's mother. Her husband, who apparently dislikes shipboard, often sent his wife and stepdaughter on summer cruises. Both were, by that time, veteran passengers. The third woman was not: Ethel, a heavyset hospital nurse from California, was on her first cruise. She was a trencherwoman, compensating for any shyness by eating enormously, as though determined that nothing on the menu should escape her. We made an amicable group and, as the days passed, developed into a close-knit table. Relationships with satellite tables sprang up as well; that irresistible passenger web was spun.

Every bit as fascinating as our destination was sailing through Canada's Inland Passage. It was already September, making this the last of the *Fairsea*'s summer runs. But the early-fall weather was perfect, just the right temperature for sitting on deck with a rug. Whether from a canal barge or ocean liner, there is nothing quite as gratifying as the montage of scenery that unspools to either side of a moving deck. Surrounded by richly forested slopes, we were at a latitude equivalent to Copenhagen. The Inland Passage is not as spectacular as Norway's fjords, but the views, as we threaded our way through that lovely archipelago, were every bit as rewarding. Paradoxically, though we passed our day ostensibly at sea, it was the continuous proximity of land over both rails that so enriched shipboard.

That auditorium, if you will, of deck is extensive. In addition to a spread atop the ship, there were two flanking vantage points. The *Fairsea*'s Promenade Deck is unencumbered by glass, though protective clear plastic panels are lashed in place along a portion of it in Glacier Bay. In warmer waters, however, the open shelter was ideal for lunch. Sitmar has sensibly furnished its length with tables and chairs rather than deck chairs, thus offering a shaded seat within sight of whatever lay over the rail. Up one flight on Ocean Deck, the company had provided an additional sheltered

This is the view along the starboard side of the *Fairsea*'s Promenade Deck, a traditional and useful shipboard vista. Lunch is dispensed around the pool aft and passengers can carry their plates forward for a meal in the shade with a view. The sheer increases in the distance as one approaches the stern. *(Author's collection)*

vantage point by roofing over the narrow walkway beneath the lifeboats with a lean-to of green corrugated plastic panels. Jarring and plebeian by day, the green plastic enriches the *Fairsea*'s profile at night from afar, adding a band of emerald enchantment to the customary incandescent or fluorescent layers of light.

Alaskan cruises are heavy tour cruises. It is the stiff competition that does it: companies are anxious to break out of the similarity of their itinerary by enriching the seagoing portions with overland options, whether a flight over a glacier, a salmon-bake picnic near an abandoned gold mine, or a waterfront tour of Ketchikan. On board *Fairsea*, the cruise staff handles all shore excursions (to their profit) and, during our first day at sea, sold our one thousand fellow passengers $83,000 worth of tours. Though Mary and I seldom go ashore on tours, we enjoyed a surrogate berth on all of them courtesy of our tablemate Ethel, who had apparently booked excursions as relentlessly as she ordered meals. We were assured of a full report each night.

But before those total recall reprises began, during our first meals together, we learned something about Ethel's background. It was one of chronic deprivation. She had been the only child of a mother who had died giving birth; in consequence, her embittered father had relinquished his daughter's upbringing to both sets of grandparents, with whom the child had spent alternate six months of each year. Once she had completed her training as a nurse, Ethel resolved to leave the scene of her unhappy childhood and start afresh somewhere else, perhaps in Alaska. But she never broke away, thwarted by a latter-day inverted dependency: grandparents who had raised her had need of her in their old age and Ethel had to stay on. She had never married and hinted at an unsatisfactory relationship with an unnamed man who did not seem to need her. Now, finally, she was at least touching the Alaskan dream that had escaped her until she was middle-aged.

But from the beginning of the cruise, it seemed that everything Ethel attempted became flawed. She had trouble sleeping from her first night on board; even the gentlest sea motion was upsetting, and her inside cabin depressed her. The ship's hairdressers were unable to set her hair the way she preferred it. And all those tours ashore only unleashed further unhappiness. There was a group of benign, retarded children booked on the cruise, and Ethel inadvertently boarded their bus for the three-hour return from an abortive view of Mount St. Helens. On another bus waiting in the parking lot at Victoria's Burchart Gardens, a couple of passengers spent too long in the souvenir shop; Ethel was infuriated, upbraiding everyone on board, including the driver, for delaying the remainder of her tour. Reboarding after a full day ashore in Juneau, Ethel confessed to hysterical terror during a small plane flight over a glacier; even more distressing than her fear had been mortification at having made a fool of herself.

But Ethel was learning the ropes. "On my next cruise," she announced one evening, "I'll know just what to do." I suspect that she enjoyed her meals at table 18, for it was the only time she was not alone. Most of her days she spent by herself. Ethel did not, apparently, make friends easily. But travel evidently agreed with her, for she was planning a visit to Hawaii in October, only weeks after her return home.

The *Fairsea*'s day in Glacier Bay was as exhilarating as it was exhausting. We were glued to the rail for as long as a negotiation of the Panama Canal. Almost the entire passenger load, muffled against the cold, remained on deck, all save those who, either incapacitated or inadequately dressed, were confined indoors, the outdoor glories brought to them via black-and-white television monitors. On deck, the persistent, muted sound track was the click, buzz, and whir of shutters and advance mechanisms as miles of film unspooled past lens apertures. We were fortunate with the weather: a flawlessly clear sky that clouded only near day's end. Some ships spend their day in Glacier Bay drenched with rain, a condition endemic to southeast Alaska—Ketchikan's annual rainfall is 13 feet. But for us, mountain ranges to the east, capped with glistening snow mantles, shone in the sun. There was almost no wind. The waters of Glacier Bay were dotted with growlers, miniature icebergs that floated, seemingly immovable, in the clouded, gray-green water that glaciologists call glacial milk.

By lunchtime, after countless restorative mugs of bouillon, we were adrift off the face of the Margerie Glacier. This is the most famous of the bay's trio—the other two are the John Hopkins and Pacific—the one used as a ship's backdrop in every Alaskan cruise brochure. Its crenellated, Gaudiesque façade is a torment of white and an extraordinary blue that seems intemperately selected, as though from a paint store's sample card, too ridiculously intense to be real. Half a dozen crewmen went down the starboard side in a motorized lifeboat, off on Glacier Bay's obligatory iceberg retrieval. They carried a cargo net that, after an hour's complex maneuvering, was secured beneath a 5-ton growler, towed to the ship's side, and hoisted on board.

While they wrestled with their quarry, the port rails were packed the length of the vessel as passengers waited, cameras poised, for stunning falls of ice that topple randomly, without warning, from the glacier's face.

In Glacier Bay. With sunlight illuminating the mountaintops, *Fairsea* off the John Hopkins and Pacific glaciers. The temperature was bitter; stewards circulating with bouillon did a brisk trade. *Below,* dwarfed by the Margerie Glacier, the *Fairsea* and her passenger-load wait for the calving of a new iceberg. *Opposite,* another view shows the vessel from water level, surrounded by growlers. *Opposite bottom,* crewmen in a ship's boat snare and retrieve a glacial fragment to bring on board. *(Sitmar Cruises and author's collection)*

There was a time when captains of cruise ships in Glacier Bay would, in an effort to gratify their passengers, sound consecutive blasts on their whistles in hopes that reverberating sound waves might fracture an embryonic berg's last remaining link with its parent cliff; but in this era of ecological concern, the practice has ceased. A Glacier Bay National Park ranger, on board for the day to provide a running commentary over the ship's speakers, suggested instead that a fall might be precipitated by a mighty yell from all the passengers.

He counted a preparatory "One-two-three" before the command "Now!" and a great shout went up along the *Fairsea*'s decks. At the glacier face, nothing moved. There was a murmur of disappointment before the ranger urged the passengers to try again. This time, the chorus was appreciably louder and longer, almost desperate. Still nothing happened ashore but, for a fleeting, hallucinatory moment, I felt there had been a chilling re-creation of a moment in maritime history. Perhaps it was the intense cold, perhaps the lifeboat off our starboard bow, perhaps the unusual aspect of our vessel adrift, engines stopped, surrounded by ice fragments. But, in any event, that second shout, despairing in its intensity, seemed an eerie echo of that spontaneous awful cry from the *Titanic*'s people left struggling in the water when their ship vanished from sight.

Though the noise triggered no falls, we were not to be disappointed. Several times, long after any possible effect from the shouting, bergs calved from the face of the Margerie Glacier, thundering majestically into the bay. Though we were half a mile distant, the sound reached us clearly as massive chunks of ice, seeming to fall in a kind of awesome slow motion, plunged with a roar beneath the surface before rearing up again, jostling and tumbling into immobility. The *Fairsea* bobbed gently in response to the watery shock waves. Once the propellers turned again and we cleared the glacier's face, passengers clambered down to the forward end of Monte Carlo Deck to pose in front of the captive growler, a fragment that doubtless, months earlier, had fallen and floated from its glacial parent, effecting the same drama we had just observed. That evening, chunks of Glacier Bay ice, sculpted by carvers in the galley and draped with salmon carcasses, served as decorative Arctic still lifes in each dining room.

Only near voyage's end did a curious finality manifest itself. For Sitmar, our cruise was significant historically, not only the last Alaskan voyage of the season, but the *Fairsea*'s last forever in those waters. The new *Fairsky* would take over the following season, leaving *Fairsea* to complete her cruising life voyaging to Panama and back. Our final port of call before San Francisco was Astoria, at the mouth of the Columbia River;

as we sailed, after a sodden day ashore, townspeople gathered on the pier unfurled a homemade banner that read GOODBYE FAIRSEA WE LOVE YOU.

The sense of that cruise's finality was even more poignant at table 18. We discovered that, earlier that summer, Carole's only son had been killed in a helicopter accident in Houston and that she and her surviving child, Julie, had booked on the cruise in an effort to forget. Then again, Tony, our simpatico steward, was signing off the ship, giving up his life at sea to return to Naples and his family. That final night's dinner would be the last he would ever serve as a steward.

But it was Ethel who provided the ultimate bathos. After she had left the table, a shaken Julie passed on her news. She had been joshing Ethel earlier that day, suggesting that we would doubtless all meet again on another cruise.

"I shan't be back," had been Ethel's response.

"Sure you will," countered Julie. "Why not?"

"You don't want me to spoil your day, do you?" Ethel replied. Then it came out: she was suffering from a terminal, inoperable cancer and was not expected to live beyond Christmas. Hence the Alaskan cruise, hence the tours, hence the mammoth food consumption, hence the Hawaiian trip so soon to follow. Poor Ethel, she had left it all too late.

The next morning, as we were tying up in San Francisco, table 18's occupants gathered for the last time. Ethel had almost finished her meal by the time we appeared. She spoke not a word, as though California's proximity had struck her dumb. She left us as she had met us a fortnight earlier, suffused with misery. She rose abruptly from the table, handed each of us a scrolled tourist souvenir of an Irish prayer, and left the table, too moved to do more than mutter a choked, incomprehensible farewell. Tears at last breakfasts are not uncommon on board cruise ships, but these tears, we knew, sprang from the deepest wellspring one can know.

Two summers earlier, almost to the day, Mary and I had embarked on the *Sagafjord* in San Francisco and, turning left instead of right outside the Golden Gate, set sail for Panama and, ultimately, New York. We had made the same transit a year earlier on Holland America's *Veendam*, but this was our first time on board one of the two remaining vessels of the Norwegian America Line, or, as most ancient "lines" have been renamed, Norwegian American Cruises. *Sagafjord* and *Vistafjord* are the final product of seventy years of Norwegian American service on the North Atlantic, proud descendants of vessels like *Oslofjord*, *Bergensfjord*, and *Stavangerfjord*. Norwegian American's naming policy for its fleet is as geographically

Vistafjord on trials in the North Sea. She is most distinguished from *Sagafjord* by the supplementary row of large windows just above the strength deck; these provide daylight to the dining room. *(Norwegian American Cruises)*

evocative as it is convenient: each ship distinctive yet allied by the *-fjord* suffix for instant company identification.

From a distance the two vessels pass as sisters, though their interior configurations are markedly different: reflected are contrasting shipboard expectations prevalent in the consecutive decades into which each was launched. *Sagafjord* is the older of the two, built at Seyne-sur-Mer by the Société des Forges et Chantiers de la Mediterranée. She entered service in 1965, at a time when cruising was beginning in earnest and crossing was near its end. The *Amerikabatene*—Norwegian for the America boats—no longer carried passengers from Oslo to New York. Though she came equipped with nearly eight hundred berths on board, it was anticipated that no more than half that plus would be carried on one-class, Old Guard cruises. By the time the *Vistafjord* joined the fleet in 1973, cruising was even more in the ascendancy and the interior arrangements of the British-built ship—she had been launched into the River Tyne from Swan Hunter's yard—reflected those times. The *Vistafjord*'s dining room was moved one deck higher than the *Sagafjord*'s and furnished with windows to either side. A dining room with a view is a consistent feature of the new cruise ideal: *Queen Elizabeth 2* offered the same chic when she appeared in 1969. In the seventies, windowless dining rooms were thought of as old-fashioned and claustrophobic.

But elevating the dining room on Norwegian American's final ship involved a dimensional tradeoff, typifying the delicate spatial dilemmas posed for naval architects when designing Old Guard public rooms. By thrusting the dining room higher in the ship, directly under the Veranda Deck, ceiling height was sacrificed. *Vistafjord* passengers scanned the horizon as they lunched, but did so beneath a conventional deck-height ceiling. On the other hand, if one examines the *Sagafjord*'s deckplan, a revealing blank rectangle amidships on Upper Deck labeled simply DOME heralds the difference: an extra-high ceiling gives the older ship the decisive decorative edge. In fact, since most passengers—save on northern cruises—usually dine indoors after dark, the dining room window crusade seems pointless. But in 1983, when Cunard bought Norwegian American Cruises, the entire dining room differential on the two ships was made academic: one of Cunard's first orders of business was to open up the *Sagafjord*'s shell plating in way of the dining room on Main Deck so that she now boasts a view as well as height.

On both vessels, the galley is directly below the dining room, so that stewards must do the same as stewards on the *Rotterdam*: ride with their trays between pantry and serving station on high-speed escalators. Yet

Contrasting dining rooms on ships of the same company. *Top,* that of the *Sagafjord,* the older of the two, as it appears now with its original high ceiling and Cunard's fenestration complete. The *mise-en-scène* is curious: only four apparently celebrated passengers are lunching, conferring with the chief steward, while ten stewards, as though about to burst into song, hover in the background. *Bottom,* the low-ceilinged *Vistafjord* dining room lacks comparable architectural clout. *(Norwegian American Cruises)*

there the similarity between the two ships ends. The *Sagafjord* galley is off-center, pushed against the port-side shell plating with only a starboard row of outside cabins amidships. The *Vistafjord* galley lies directly over the keel with no outside view to either port or starboard; hence, cabins bracket both sides of the galley space on the newer ship. Indeed, the *Vistafjord* has nearly eighty more cabins than the older vessel, and it was this imbalance that prompted Cunard, in 1983, to add a set of suites on the *Sagafjord*'s upper deck as well as to reshuffle crew/passenger accommodations below, all with an eye to bringing the ship's capacity closer to parity with the more efficient *Vistafjord*. The magic number for vessels of the *Sagafjord*'s size is six hundred passengers—that many clients need to be accommodated in today's market to make an Old Guard vessel economically healthy. *Sagafjord*'s old cruising capacity of 450 was hopelessly low for post-OPEC cruising; nowadays, with Cunard's red-and-black funnel amidships, capacity has been increased to 588, within reach of that desirable six-hundred-passenger load factor.

But the deck that has remained intact on both ships regardless of changed ownership is the splendid sweep of Veranda Deck, which, indoors and out, save when dining, constitutes the social focus for all passengers at sea. The centerpiece, appropriately amidships, is the ballroom. On *Vistafjord* it is called the Grand Ballroom, but grand or no, significantly, the space is never described as a lounge. Why? Simply to advertise the fact that it is an extra-height room. One must go back to the years immediately following World War I, after the Hamburg-Amerika Linie's *Imperator* was given over to Cunard as the *Berengaria*. The British removed all tables and chairs from the extra-tariff Ritz Carlton Restaurant and, instead, designated the handsome space The Ballroom. Ever since, that transatlantic cognomen has served to convey an impression of height as well as grandeur. The Norwegian American ships' ballrooms are not as tall as the *Berengaria*'s—a height and half rather than double height—but the rooms still offer a sense of occasion and elegance. This architectural uplift occurs on board some Newpassenger tonnage as well; the *Song of America*'s Can-Can Lounge, so inadvisedly named, incorporates the same noble height. Conversely, the *Rotterdam*'s Queen's Lounge, originally a Tourist Class space, is made disappointing by a low overhead.

With several hundred critical feet of deck at their disposal, it is interesting to compare how rival Old Guard companies have grouped their public rooms. Royal Viking, as we shall see, made the decision to include both dining room and lounge contiguously on the same deck. Moreover, the kitchen is sited on the same level forward. The result is that the for-

Ballroom versus lounge. The *Sagafjord*'s ballroom remains essentially a tall, hence grand, room. *Below,* its equivalent on the *Royal Viking Star,* the Bergen Lounge, is hurt by a low ceiling. *(Norwegian American Cruises and Royal Viking Line)*

ward end of Scandinavia Deck—Royal Viking's equivalent to NAC's Veranda Deck—is an unusable blank. (Coincidentally, once Royal Viking ships had been lengthened, stewards with tables in the new after end of the dining room faced a gruelling marathon to the pantry and back, an ordeal their colleagues on *Sagafjord* and *Vistafjord* are spared since they ascend and descend by escalator.) Norwegian American, having buried dining room and galley below, rejoices in a *boulevard principal* of impressive dimension, along which can be clustered a wide variety of public rooms. Forward of the aforementioned ballroom, corridors around either side of the funnel casing embrace casino, shop, library, cinema, card room, and bar; farther forward—where Royal Viking houses its galley—a splendid circular Garden Lounge nestles within the hemispherical bulge of the bridge screen. Royal Viking, on the other hand, because it has grouped galley, dining room, and lounge all on one deck, has had to disperse the rest of its public rooms—theater far below, casino, bars, and nightclubs up above. Norwegian American has preserved an essential sense of continuity and adjacency.

Descending to dine is a time-honored ritual, whether ashore in a hotel or at sea in a ship. There seems no disadvantage in having the dining room removed, noncontiguous with the other public rooms where passengers dance, play, drink, gamble, or read. Day and night en route to Panama, we experienced a strong sense of community on board the *Sagafjord*. The ship's plan works admirably, as well as any I have ever known, with an effortless and convivial flow between public rooms. The majority of Old Guard passengers prefer small-ship ambience and, in this respect, the *Sagafjord* undoubtedly delivers. But it is no accident, no trick of management; it arises out of sound architectural planning. Keeping the dining room apart on another deck makes the critical difference.

Off the Baja peninsula one morning, the cautious, polite tones of the *Sagafjord*'s officer of the watch came over the loudspeakers: "Ladies and gentlemen, there is a whale on the port side." Deck chairs and pool emptied as passengers craned over the port railing for a glimpse. Whales became commonplace thereafter, no occasion for announcements; they were pilot whales for the most part, with an occasional finback, glistening black apparitions that surfaced abruptly and submerged as suddenly, evading all but the most dogged photographers, somehow all the more wondrous for their elusiveness. Dolphins and porpoises were more cooperative, schools of them paralleling our course, arcing repeatedly into the sunshine like shooting gallery targets, or surging through our bow-wave with no other motive, scientists assure us, than a display of high spirits. And as the sea calmed at day's end, there were incomparable Pacific sunsets, not merely smudging the horizon but daubing the entire western quadrant of the sky with such lavish pyrotechnics that dinner in that windowless *Saga-fjord* dining room waited, more than once, the descent of passengers transfixed at the starboard railing.

In cruise literature, a voyage through Panama's canal is described as a crossing, a miraculous vault across a continent. Eastbound, at least, fast passage down Central America's west coast seems an old-fashioned line crossing as well. With Mexico's ports behind us, three or four purposeful sea days presage the isthmus as itinerary shifts gear up to deep-water overdrive. Vessel, passengers, and crew are reformed with that recondite subtlety to which all ships are subject. Regardless of what calls bracket it, Panama is the voyage's logistical and emotional climax. Masters must arrive on station well before the appointed hour of transit, for passenger vessels are accorded priority and may jump the queue of tankers and cargo carriers anchored offshore awaiting their summons. So, midway between marimba and calypso, *Sagafjord* buckled down to some plain Pacific sailing.

Near noon one peerless sea morning, I leaned over the ship's after Promenade Deck railing. A tropical aviary was spread at my feet. Around its periphery, within thickets of chaises longues, nested the sun cultists—glistening, spread-eagled, somnolent—lost in dreams or deep in books. Water creatures splashed in a central clearing, feet immersed for respite from the equatorial heat. There were also compulsive athletes who, re-luctant to brave deck circuits in the heat, slipped afloat and stroked a dogged mile or more, breasting the pool's languid surge. Along the out-door bar to port perched the morning drinkers, like starlings on a power line, chattering with each other or the patient barman, enjoining passing flocks to join their vigil. In between outer baking arc and inner tiled oasis brooded the elders, idle/busy with bridge or Scrabble, knitting or needle-point, wives in muted confabulation, husbands nodding in umbrella'd shade. The men stirred imperceptibly, turning sun-glassed, rheumy eyes as a pretty woman, pool laps completed, rinsed salt from her hair, then smoothed oiled droplets from her thighs and forearms. The eyes followed as she wended her languorous way aft, leaving a trail of damp footprints that faded successively behind her until the teak's heat, stinging the soles of her feet, prompted a spontaneous little *pas de chat* before she alit at her chaise nest. Scarcely raising his eyes from his book, a mate acknowl-edged her return with a proprietary caress of her spandexed flank, and the old eyes turned back once again.

Only the bar birds actually faced the sea, staring outboard through salt-encrusted glass. The rest of the flock might have been anywhere, idling away a morning on an alpine terrace or at a sandy resort. They seemed oblivious of the vast blue Pacific surrounding them, unconscious of their vessel's southern progression. The ocean reeled past unseen, the unchanging horizon spread to every side. The passengers at my feet endured shipboard with a kind of patient neglect, each passing those morning hours with book, knitting, nap, or chatter. What a contrast with those emigrants on board ancient steamers who sat out the pointless sea days awaiting landfall that would signal change or challenge, a beginning rather than an end; instead, their passenger/successors embrace that same seaborne wait, cherishing rather than chaffing at the long sea days, allotting their pleasures and relishing days on board that would end with no more challenge than a resumption of life ashore.

Over the ship's loudspeakers, the noon announcement gave us our position and the news that we were traveling south at 19 knots. That was the tenor of the deckscape below me, sun-spawned indolence juxtaposed with relentless, maritime purpose; beneath our trembling fantail, the *Sagafjord*'s tireless propellers throbbed as we rumbled south to Panama.

That midocean insouciance recalled Kingsley Amis on cruising:

The trouble with a holiday in that sense is you get no free time. There are no changes of gear from what must be done to what need not be done, no moment when you can relax and put your feet up and have a drink. You have been able to do that all day. A man who marries his mistress is in something of the same position (admittedly for longer than most holidays). Once he could enjoy planning to go, then going over to her place, look forward to a nice bit of his life that was quite different from the rest, cut off from it; now, here she is, week in, week out.

So we, too, cruise passengers, marry our mistresses during those enchanted weeks—confined yet resigned and blissfully content.

At one untraceable moment during that sunny passage south, total blissfulness began to fade. It was like a cloud no larger than a man's hand obscuring our horizon: perceptibly and irrevocably, the ship's air-conditioning system sickened and died. It was a lingering demise. Though our cabin remained supportable, the dining room stewed. Waiters sweated, menus doubled as fans. The breakdown, on every passenger tongue, was never officially acknowledged until after the canal when, near Fort Lauderdale, a printed apology from the master was slipped beneath each cabin door. A sizable component had failed, according to a candid engineer with whom I talked at the rail one evening as he cooled off in his oil-stained, white boiler suit. Sure enough, when we pulled into our Florida destination, there was a large blue compression tank waiting on the pier.

The heat was worse on that cruise than in the old days because machine-cooling had failed and none of the time-tested appurtenances were there to fill the breach. There were no fans in the dining room, no awnings on deck, no wind chutes or scoops—in fact, no open ports on which to mount them and divert the ship's breeze of passage. But passengers suffered less than the crew, whose workpace continued unabated. On Norwegian Night, members of the crew entertained passengers with an evening of folk dancing in the Ballroom. For the occasion, they had donned woolen northern peasant finery and, in the Panamanian humidity, performed pink-faced and dripping. But it was a marvelous evening. No ship's professional entertainment, however prestigious, compares with that offered by well-rehearsed and enthusiastic crewmen. For that evening, they appropriated the Ballroom dance floor, bringing ship and country into compelling focus, stewards and stewardesses displaying another dimension of their already proud stance.

The ninth of September—our ninth day since boarding in San Francisco—began our canal transit. The entire ship rose to a dank, humid dawn; passengers with cameras and binoculars at the ready prowled every deck. Landfall had been presaged the night before by an insect assault from shore: thousands of 2-inch black day-moths of the genus *Urana* had been drawn to our floodlit superstructure and, that morning, littered the scuppers with their corpses. Still they came, in droves, fluttering from the jungle, lemminglike, across the water, a kind of reverse confetti greeting the ship. We passed beneath the Bridge of the Americas and approached the first step of our transatlantic ascent at the Miraflores Lock.

The engineering marvel that engulfed us is a geographical and historical delight, a waterway that is made even more fascinating by perusal of David McCullough's *The Path Between the Seas*, required reading for all Panama-bound passengers. Whereas Suez remains a sea-level ditch connecting the Red and Mediterranean seas, it is Panama's incredible locks that make the canal so enduringly appealing. Each time I pass through it, I am struck by their incredible size no less than their comprehensibility: one can see everything work from the deck of one's ship.

Today, few passenger ships let their people ashore at either Colón or Panama City, the canal's terminal ports. Only the ship's photographer dis-

The point of entry at Miraflores. Graphics are large and easy to read. As *Sagafjord* approached the lock, the red arrow, illuminated with neon for night locking, guided us to the left hand of the two parallel ascending steps. Then it returned to the vertical. *(Author's collection)*

embarks, stalking the vessel through each flight of locks, snapping telephoto candids of passengers at the rail. In the late sixties, one of the last ships to call at Colón was the *United States*. The city was crawling with pimps who approached passengers in singsong proposition: "Chinese girls? Spanish girls?" (then the capper) "*American* girls?" Rebuffed, they would shift gears effortlessly: "Chinese boys? Spanish boys?" etc., etc., ad nauseam. It was unsafe to wander anywhere. One woman asked a policeman how to avoid the red light district; she was told to remain on Front Street, for it was everywhere else. A man who ignored warnings not to explore the port's seamy back streets returned on board with his back pockets sliced open with a razor and his money gone. The *United States*, incidentally, never entered Gatun Locks, thus avoiding hefty lockage fees; passengers who wished were sent across the isthmus by train with the option of returning via a specially chartered excursion boat.

I have helped negotiate many a canal barge in and out of locks and so, in a sense, Panama's vast concrete canyons were familiar. Only their scale astonishes, again and again. A single gate leaf, for instance, which on a Burgundian canal can be swung closed by one man, weighs at the isthmus 660 tons and stands sixteen stories high, so huge that they had to be built while suspended on their hinges. To lighten their deadweight, they have watertight integrity and float through the ninety-degree closing arc. In common with all lock gates of any dimension, they are not parallel when closed but point slightly toward the water they exclude. Hence, the hydrostatic head—or height of water against them—helps jam them shut and tighten the seal. That particular lock refinement is an ancient one, devised originally by Leonardo da Vinci.

Periodically, as with any steel hull, lock gate leaves must be detached from their hinges and towed to dry dock for painting or repair. This is accomplished during Panama's dry season and reserves of spare metal leaves, the size of steel barges, can be seen floating in the backwaters of Gatun and Miraflores lakes. Lock chambers are drained at the same time. Replacing the gates are huge, lozenge-shaped plugs, the shape of turn-of-the-century dreadnoughts, complete with skylights and ventilators; they are floated into place beyond the hinge points, sealing the lock between opposing concrete walls. It is essential to clear debris from the gate sills at either end: waterlogged timbers or tires that fall from barges are menaces in this respect. Once a whale got into the system from the Pacific end and its carcass had to be grappled out of Miraflores Lock. The only other wildlife that plagues the Panama Canal Commission are frogs, and, at one point, a boa constrictor that had got lost in the network of underground

Far left, most of one's Panama Canal day is spent at the rail. *Left,* through the Gaillard Cut, the jungle almost brushes the *Sagafjord*'s bridge. *Below,* an archetypal midday in Gatun Lake on board the eastbound *Franconia* during her world cruise of 1935. Lunching on deck are, from right to left, Moss Hart, Cole Porter, Monty Woolley, Linda Porter, Howard Sturges, and travel writer William Powell. Three weeks earlier, Porter had composed "Begin the Beguine" on board. *(Author's collection; below, photograph used by permission of Robert H. Montgomery, Jr., Trustee of the Cole Porter Musical and Literary Property Trusts)*

culverts beneath the locks, terrifying workers before it was caught and dispatched.

Not one pump is employed anywhere in Panama's locking complexes: locks are filled and drained by gravity alone. Panama's notorious rainfall— several inches a day are common in the autumnal wet season—maintains a superabundant supply of water. During our transit, 55 million gallons of fresh water would be expended raising and lowering the *Sagafjord* up to and subsequently down from Gatun Lake, the man-made body of water that spans two-thirds of the isthmus. The first step upward is the most exhilarating, particularly for passengers new to the canal. Once the lock gates close behind us, water floods in below the surface through seventy openings spread evenly across the chamber floor below the surface, an engineering expedient to reduce turbulence within the lock. The ship moves in a novel, third dimension, ascending within minutes above the formerly confining concrete bluffs, so close that we could exchange greetings with workmen on each bank or crewmen of an adjacent ship passing in the opposite direction down to the Pacific. This is a striking Panamanian phe- nomenon, with passengers in surreal proximity to land and neighboring vessels. We would repeat the process six times—three up and three down —before the day was over, but the novelty never palled. An accompanying tug that locked up with us in tandem celebrated its arrival in freshwater Miraflores Lake by turning on all its hoses, less a salute than an opportunity for its chief engineer to flush saltwater out of his vessel's piping.

Maneuvering *Sagafjord* through all six locks was a mechanical ritual controlled almost exclusively from shore. Two dozen Panamanian line- handlers had boarded with the pilot at Balboa and were divided between fantail and fo'c's'le head. As we approached each lock, the first lines over the bow were retrieved from the water by men from shore in skiffs rowing beneath our bows trailing lines from shore. (After years of experimenta- tion, it had been discovered by canal authorities that a man at the oars was the most efficient and reliable motive power for this vital initial con- tact; that such a primitive and simple system has survived increasing mechanization elsewhere is somehow pleasing.) The messenger lines, joined with an almost magically swift knot, are attached to steel cables that, in turn, are hauled on board, their terminal loops snugged over the *Sagafjord*'s towing bits, fore and aft. Grinding along noisily at the other end of those cables was a sextet of landbound tugs called mules. These are the canal's workhorses, stout electrical locomotives with twin tension winches mounted at either end. Those specialized vehicles—unique to Panama—shepherd all vessels through every lock. Three to a side, they travel a priority route along the margins of each lock, rolling on four rails: two conventional, a buried third that picks up electrical power, and a fourth, cogged, that is needed to negotiate the steep slopes between locks. They can pull in either direction, but their drivers, sheltered by louvered steel awnings, face inward, their attention directed toward the vessel between them.

The mules' control is amazingly precise. The *Sagafjord* was held rigidly in midlock by a dozen, bar-taut cables that, as the vessel rose or, later, fell, had to be played like tackle hooked to a salmon. To all intents and purposes, the ship lay dead in the water during locking, her rudder amidships. Only occasionally were the engines used, and then only a SLOW AHEAD nudge to help overcome the inertia of a full stop. At the same time, the umbilical cables to the mules tautened and, charging the concrete slopes before them, the locomotives moved ahead into the next lock. From the bridge, the combined effects of ship's engine and shore-based mules hurried us toward the far end of the new lock chamber at intemperate speed. We were traveling, in fact, at no more than 3 knots, but in those confined waters, it seemed reckless. Yet once in position, at a command over the pilot's radio, all six mules fell back, cables checking rather than towing, their weight and winch power braking us to a surprisingly abrupt stop in moments.

So that fascinating day passed; we were completely through in a little over eight hours. It was a long day and like no other, neither at sea nor in port but somewhere in between. The routine was broken conveniently at midday when, after having negotiated the terraced slopes of Gaillard Cut, we steamed through the broad, palm-fringed waters of Gatun Lake, 85 feet above Pacific and Atlantic. Lunch at the rail in those smooth, quiet waters is a far cry from the concrete landscape of the locks at either end. The lake's innumerable islands are peaks of former hills atop the continental divide, flooded from uplands into islands that border a tropical lagoon. At the far end, Gatun's flight—for such is the admirable noun of multitude in this instance—of locks is a triple one, three successive steps down followed by a long, straight channel out into the Caribbean.

Though there were other ports remaining before we reached Florida, the high point, literally as well as figuratively, had passed with Panama. And yet, whatever scenic or engineering marvels beyond our railings, I cannot leave that *Sagafjord* cruise without reporting on two of the most anomalous passengers I have ever encountered. A woman had booked with her daughter, a girl of no more than six years with a pretty smile and a poisonous disposition. She was the only child on board, fellow passenger to a host of potentially doting grandparent figures, all of whom were,

GATUN LOCKS
PANAMA CANAL
1913

Descending the triple flight of Gatun Locks. *Opposite,* off-duty crew members forsake their sunbathing to peer over the port side. The lock is draining because the hull is moored to bollards. *Above,* mule number 44 grinds down the slope, checking the port bow. *Below,* the view aft from the bridge, showing the triple set of mule tracks as well as the adjacent lock gate closed; the weight of water they contain helps jam them tighter shut. *(Author's collection)*

within a day, discouraged from making friends; one who tried in the gymnasium was repelled with a bite. The two sat at a small table in the dining room, arriving late each evening, long past what might be considered a child's bedtime. Routinely, the mother ordered the entire menu for her daughter each night, conspicuous and formidable consumption for even the hungriest adult. The little girl refused it all, toying only with a hamburger and french fried potatoes. Throughout the dinner hour, ignored by her mother, she would wander unchecked among the tables, bane of laden stewards. After several futile warnings came a drastic measure indeed: mother and child were banished from the dining room, obliged to take their meals alone in their cabin (incidentally, one of the best on board). Regardless, the woman persisted: the same gargantuan—and ignored—meals were ordered every night. Even worse for the harassed cabin stewardess, each morning the cabin bedsheets were covered with crayon scribbling, as it turned out, not the work of the child but that of her bizarre mother. Despite graffiti'd sheets and a full load of untouched trays each evening, the hardworking stewardess was tipped, at voyage's end, a grand total of $10. Who was the woman? Where did she come from? American to be sure, but nobody knew more.

The last of these Cruises Present was also the longest, combining as it did a coastal detour before a "slow boat" crossing of the Western Ocean. We were booked on the *Royal Viking Sea*, sailing from Copenhagen to the North Cape, then westward to Iceland and touching at a scattering of Canadian and New England ports before disembarkation in New York. In company parlance, the crossing was a positioning cruise, one of those vernal/autumnal maritime rites for shipowners whose vessels must be redeployed for seasonal markets. The *Prinsendam* was on a positioning cruise when she came to grief in the Bay of Alaska, departing North America's coast for her Indonesian haunts. So, too, each fall and spring, the Sun Line's *Stella Solaris* makes a long Atlantic/Mediterranean crossing between Aegean and Caribbean. The *Royal Viking Sea* had just completed a summer of fourteen-day Baltic cruises out of Copenhagen, and many American passengers had booked on the last Baltic cruise in order to remain on board and sail home. We would be twenty-four days at sea with some ports thrown in along the way and, incomparably appealing, passage up and down Norway's coast before heading west.

I am always attracted by positioning cruises; there are sea days galore, the ports are off-beat and interesting, and one meets on board dozens similarly inclined, flocks of *Peregrinator transatlanticus inveteratus,* who are especially pleased with a re-creation of the old crossing days. But this pleasure is not a universal sentiment. The following summer, during another positioning cruise on the *Royal Viking Sky,* I overheard the following conversation at the bar:

FIRST CHOLERIC OLD GENTLEMAN: What do you think of this cruise?

[We were on a crossing, pure and simple, Southampton to New York, never billed as anything else.]

SECOND CHOLERIC OLD GENTLEMAN (Bleakly): Hate it. Goes on too long. Cooped up in the ship with no ports. Why do they do it?

FIRST CHOLERIC OLD GENTLEMAN: God knows! It's claustrophobic. And, do you know what? There are lots of people—a couple at my table—*who have done this before and they still come back for more!* (Italics mine)

The ship, incidentally, had been recently enlarged, what is popularly called stretched. By the early eighties, all three Royal Viking ships had been extended, their hulls elongated by 93 feet, the capacity of each increased by two hundred passengers. It was an ambitious effort, requiring the dry docking of a Royal Viking vessel for each of three consecutive summers at Bremerhaven. Each ship was put in dry dock and cut in half; then the two halves were separated. The new midsection had already been prebuilt at the yard, awaiting the moment of union with its ship, looking like a huge, rusted Rubik's cube; workers on their lunchbreak picnicked in the open honeycomb at each end, eating stolidly in the shade, like squatters in a ravaged tenement. Once it had been floated into dry dock, all three sections were rewelded together. The first modern cruise ship to be extended in this fashion was the *Song of Norway* of the Royal Caribbean Cruise Line.

But the practice of shuffling or replacing ship sections is almost as old as steel ships. One of the most celebrated examples of maritime surgery resulted after the grounding of the White Star liner *Suevic* outside Plymouth Harbor in 1907. Her bow was a write-off, the rest of her hull sound. Once cargo and passengers had been removed, the free-floating after end was blasted clear of the fore part with dynamite; propelled by her own engines, she proceeded stern first up-Channel to Southampton. A new bow was built at Harland & Wolff's, the original Belfast builders. It was launched stem first and towed to Southampton, where it was riveted onto the waiting hull. The *Suevic* sailed on, as good as new, until 1942.

Stretching a ship. *Royal Viking Star* was lengthened in the fall of 1981. *Top,* ready for surgery, the newly arrived *Star* at the A. G. Weser yard *Center,* the vessel is separated into two halves. *Bottom,* the bow, stabilized by a pontoon under the prow, floats clear. *Opposite: Top,* the new midsection is positioned in place. *Center,* now a third rather than half a ship, the bow is realigned. *Bottom,* the finished vessel, 93 feet longer, with room for 200 additional passengers. *(Royal Viking Line)*

But though replacing a damaged bow or stern was commonplace, lengthening a passenger hull was difficult: with main engines located amidships, the structural complications were prohibitive. But today, cruise ships position their engine rooms aft, profiting from shorter propeller shafts as well as quieter passenger spaces amidships. Hence, when the cruise market expanded, Royal Viking decided to enlarge each of their existing vessels rather than build a fourth. While the cost of that fourth ship would have been comparable to the $100 million cost of lengthening the other three, the years required to plan and build a new hull could not match the mere eighty-four days required to effect each stretching. In addition, the carrying costs of crewing a fourth vessel from scratch were eliminated.

But however straightforward and logical in theory, in practice, the rejoining of hull and deck plating in way of the two incisions was not simple. It was found at Wärtsilä, at the time the *Song of Norway* was operated on, that when the sections were reassembled, enough sag had occurred to leave a gap: the bottom shell plating met but the plates atop the superstructure were still an inch or so apart. Pull-jacks had to be installed on each deck, bridging the gap, and these were used to draw the new sections together with the old. But a narrow gap remained, wider on the upper decks than the half inch that Veritas—Norway's answer to Lloyds—would have permitted to be filled with welding material. So a pie-shaped sliver of steel was needed to finish the job.

But other complications resulted from the stretching. Insertion of a new midsection had cumulative logistical ramifications as well. Two hundred additional passengers would require more food, more linen, more water, more sewage capacity, and more service electricity. They would take up more room in the lifeboats, pools, lounges, and dining room. After stretching, the dining room was expanded because the Scandinavia Deck level of the insert incorporated a dining room extension; but the main lounge, aft of the new section, remained the same size and had to be adapted accordingly. On the *Royal Viking Star*, the first of the trio to undergo surgery, the Bergen Lounge lost its corner bar and was refurnished with smaller chairs so that it could comfortably absorb 670 rather than 520 passengers. (Strictly speaking, the stretched ship's capacity is seven hundred, but the chances of every passenger on board assembling in it at one time is remote: the theater, casino, or cabins take care of potential overflow crowds, avoiding the hazard of what traffic planners might term loungelock.)

Overall, dividends were substantial. The Royal Viking fleet's capacity had been increased by 40 percent while, at the same time, fuel consumption for each vessel had been increased by only 20 percent. The ships looked better, too. The original superstructure had seemed foreshortened and confined, on the top deck especially, funnel base too close to the forward bridge and mast assembly. The longer hull was also more seaworthy. Deadloading across from the shipyard to Fort Lauderdale, the *Royal Viking Star* ran into a gale off the Azores; everyone on board agreed that their longer hull rode out the bad weather better than before. Finding the new hull's joints, incidentally, is not easy; the after seam lies just forward of the main staircase but, whether outside or in, neither deck nor carpeting betrays its existence, a credit to the standards of Royal Viking housekeeping on a ten-year-old ship. There must have been an enormous backlog of postcards showing the ships in their original configuration for, months after the stretching, short-ship postcards are still found in each cabin's letter paper portfolio.

I have boarded ships half a dozen times in Copenhagen and, each time, the scene at the d'Angleterre—unquestionably the city's prettiest hotel—is the same: a deluge of inbound and outbound passengers sprawling on every lobby chair and the concierge's diminutive *consigne* bursting with suitcases. Whether embarking or disembarking, we are all captives in that awful limbo between ship and home. I always try to arrive at a port the day prior to embarkation; it makes that limbo more supportable, as well as avoiding that sword of Damocles hanging over every airline passenger's head: lost or delayed luggage. We have only once lost suitcases en route to a cruise and then, fortunately, in San Diego, where airport is only minutes from downtown. Even so, the experience left its scar, and ever since, our vigil at the carousel is one of suspense and dread until all suitcases have appeared. One only wishes that airlines spent as much time perfecting their baggage handling and routing as they do on pretentious commercials.

On nearly every ship in the Caribbean, there are continuous horror stories of passengers with lost luggage who must embark deprived of all or some of the clothing they had packed for their cruise. Either they wear the same thing for days on end or fit themselves out with temporary finery bought on board. Lost luggage destined for Caribbean cruise clients is customarily forwarded on to St. Thomas's airport—mecca of most Newpassenger cruises—for almost tearful reunion with their distraught owners halfway through their cruise. Perhaps the most bizarre lost suitcase story concerns a passenger who, having boarded his ship early, was watching baggage being loaded on board by crane. One pallet-load was so clumsily secured that a suitcase fell into the water; unseen by either crew or longshoremen, it floated momentarily before vanishing below the surface. The observant passenger noted where it lay, then notified the officer of the watch: a grapple was produced and the lost suitcase was hoisted, streaming, from the depths. The company made good on its sodden contents and the owner was forever grateful to her fellow passenger, who had, fortuitously, tracked down a piece of baggage that might otherwise have disappeared, mysteriously, forever.

By sailing time that summer's day in Copenhagen, all our luggage had reached the cabin without incident. On deck, the weather was Scandinavian perfection, a bright afternoon sun in a cloudless blue sky; just as we were to quit the pier, the *Prinsesse Margrethe*, the outbound overnight ferry to Oslo, slipped past our stern. The only thing marring the moment—as it mars every Royal Viking departure—was the broadcasting of "The *Royal Viking Star* Waltz." Music to accompany sailings is traditional, whether from a band playing on board or on the pier or, as Sitmar does so well, over the loudspeakers with recorded military marches. But the theme that assaults one during Royal Viking undockings is always the same, a piece commissioned by Wärtsilä to commemorate delivery of the first Royal Viking hull and presented as a gift to the company. The most distressing thing about the tune is its inevitability: whatever the mood, however beautiful the sunset, however evocative or bittersweet the moment of sailing, it squawks over the speakers, trivializing everything.

Our first night and day were spent at sea, passing through the Skagerrak out of the Baltic into the North Sea and across to Scotland. A Sunday-morning call at the sleepy Shetland port of Lerwick followed before we turned back east for Bergen, our first Norwegian port of call. It was a banner day for, coincidentally, another ship of the same company, *Royal Viking Sky*, was in port as well. We tied up at opposite sides of the same pier and the crew members of both ships with no family in Bergen spent their day visiting each other's vessel. We sailed that afternoon to a heartfelt accompaniment of whistled salutes exchanged by the two sisters. Then, with a brace of coastal pilots on board, we started our northern journey. It is a voyage I have made on a variety of vessels, from the little Bergen Line coastal steamers that call at three or four ports each day to the *Queen Elizabeth 2*. Large tonnage works to a scenic disadvantage in Norwegian coastal waters; although *QE2* can call at the larger ports, during intervening days at sea she tends to stay offshore. But Royal Viking hulls can adhere to the inland passage route that is wedded so intimately to that unforgettable coastline.

Bergen rarity: two Royal Viking Line
ips, the *Sea* and the *Sky,* tie up across
om each other on August 8, 1983.
uthor's collection)

The day after Bergen, the *Royal Viking Sea* anchored off the town of Hellesylt. Hundreds of our fellow passengers disembarked into a shore tender for a day's tour, a bus ride across the mountains that, after lunch, would rejoin the vessel in Geiranger Fjord. It is an overland journey I have never made; for me, the sea passage into the fjord is so breathtaking that I cannot bear to miss it. Geiranger is a long arm of the sea ending far inland at a picturesque cul-de-sac ringed by mountains. For decades, the little village of Merok—current population, three hundred—perched along the southeastern coast of the fjord, has played host to the world's cruise ships. Every Norwegian itinerary includes Geiranger simply because it is the archetypal Norwegian fjord, remote, peaceful, and majestic, seemingly small but accessible to the largest hulls afloat. Passage into the fjord is irresistible, through a narrow S-shaped defile between vertical cliffs. Each side is adorned with waterfalls, to port the haloed multiple ribbons of the Seven Sisters plunging directly into the waters of the fjord; to starboard, a stunning gossamer curtain of white called the Bridal Veil. A recurring anxiety-provoking dream of mine is that of being a passenger on a large ship racing through a bewildering shoal of reefs and skerries; miraculously, that dream vessel never comes to grief. I suspect that the image originates from passages through Geiranger, where it seems impossible that the vessel will not touch either side.

One of our fellow passengers, Colonel George S. Carrington, USMC-retired, told us that his mother, as a girl of nineteen, had been invited by her future parents-in-law to join them for a Norwegian cruise on the *Arcadian*. One summer evening, toward the end of July, they sailed into Geiranger; the only other vessel sharing their idyllic anchorage was an imposing white craft that turned out to be the *Hohenzollern*, Kaiser Wilhelm's yacht, flying the royal standard. Very early the next morning, a pair of German naval frigates entered the fjord. Moments after their arrival, the decks of the *Hohenzollern* were a scene of feverish activity: steam was raised, the anchor came up, and the yacht turned and steamed down the fjord in convoy with its naval escort. It was the summer of 1914, and the significance of the German emperor's precipitous, early-morning departure became clear to the *Arcadian*'s passengers only after they had disembarked two days later in Bergen: war was imminent, and obviously His Majesty's cruise off Norway's coast had been cut short by impending hostilities. Quite understandably, the German navy retrieved their emperor in person, not only to provide escort but to bring him firsthand dispatches as well; even present-day radio communication in Geiranger is difficult. Alan Holmes, wireless officer on board *QE2*, told me once that every time

Two visitors in Geiranger Fjord a summer apart. *Above, Royal Viking Sea* at anchor off Merok in August 1983; we were on our leisurely way back to New York. *Below,* the following year, the world's longest vessel, *Norway,* made two visits to the celebrated fjord. Despite her bulk, she seems to dwindle among the surrounding mountains. *(Royal Viking Line and Chip Hoehler Collection)*

the ship enters the fjord, communication is lost for a considerable period of time, just as consistently as spacecraft on the far side of the moon are cut off from Houston.

Indeed, Merok's most endearing charm is its remoteness, hidden from approaching ships until the last turn of the channel, a wondrous prize at the heart of a seaborne, granite maze. Like all fjords, Geiranger's surface is dead calm for much of the time, so placid that it seems more a mountain lake than what the Scots would call a sea loch. Four ships joined us there before we sailed—a not uncommon summer's day visitation—materializing silently and splendidly around the turn of the cliff. Their anchors momentarily ruffled the limpid expanse, and tenders ferried boatloads of eager passengers ashore. Lord knows, there is little enough to do in Merok; there is, however, a souvenir shop, or one can tramp half a mile up the main road past the waterfall for lunch at the comfortable Union Hotel. Another walk leads around the rim of the fjord, past a campground where an acre of brightly colored nylon indicates that Geiranger is as magnetic for campers as cruise ships. And for the taking from any vantage point ashore, there is that passengers' invariable prerogative, a photograph of their vessel against a mountainous backdrop. Despite the almost continuous intrusion of oceangoing hulls, the great event of Merok's day is the arrival, near noon, of the Hellesylt ferry, delivering automobile traffic that bounces across the ramp connecting bow with pier to vanish up the steep roads into the mountains. The flotilla of cruise ships at anchor is, after all, commonplace for Merokians and, in another sense, transient, so that none of them really compare with the solid prosaism of the ferry that remains such an integral and essential part of the villagers' lives year round.

It is curious that most brochures about fjords rely heavily on aerial views. Tourist board photographers are forever clambering into the mountains to cliff ledges overlooking the fjords, posing models in peasant dress thousands of feet above the glistening waters. Presumably, they have been instructed to encompass everything, to do scenic justice to a panorama of mountain, sea, and sky to suit driver and hiker as well as sailor. For me, the magic of the fjords is their exquisite navigability and, hence, appearance at altitude zero. The water is a rich green in shadow, malachite depths disturbed only by an occasional wake. All vessels—cruise ships, two-stroke diesel fishing boats, humble skiffs—leave their own languid signature on that mirrored surface, a perfect, spreading herringbone. The air above is still as well, an inversion of the deep below, where all rests in breezeless calm so that our funnel smoke creates an air wake, a ghostly blue wraith that hangs, suspended midway between mountaintop and water,

424   LINERS TO THE SUN

for minutes on end. The fjord passage, protected and ethereal, is unique in all the world, an unending delight for passengers and ships within its magical boundaries.

The next day, we crossed the Arctic Circle, that abstract geographical concept that, on Norway's coast, is appropriately marked by a monument, a skeletal globe erected atop a skerry along the inland channel. On coastal steamers, the couriers charged with entertaining full-fare passengers commemorate the occasion with the same kind of high-jinks attending equatorial crossings; but on *Royal Viking Sea*, no special ceremony was observed. The character of the shoreline changed with our northward progression: green forested slopes were replaced by wilder country, a rocky fastness that evoked Scotland without its softening mantle of heather. We passed yet another Seven Sisters, a septet of granite peaks, forbidding and vast, unrelieved of any green or living thing, the Alps from a deck chair. It was somehow moving, against so majestic a backdrop, to see a lone fisherman's craft or cottage miles from anywhere, isolated human presence incongruously juxtaposed with almost lunar barrenness. In fact, the waters off the coast seem more populous than the shore. Each day, we would pass a little coastal steamer, making heavy weather against the rolling swells that washed us north. We swept by in a flurry of salutes, two contrasting Norwegian vessels—a workhorse maintaining its vital daily schedule, dwarfed by the vast white cruise liner. Passengers and crew of each lined the port rails, waving and cheering across the windswept waters separating us.

During one night at sea between Geiranger and the North Cape, we had to evacuate our cabin. Mary—fortunately, in this case—is a light sleeper. In the middle of the night, she heard rain and wondered drowsily why it was so loud in a cabin with a sealed port. In fact, it was water dripping with increasing urgency. She woke me on the instant. We turned on the lights and saw water streaming down through the ceiling near the shell plating. We tried containing the worst of it in wastebaskets, but the cascade spread inboard like Geiranger's Seven Sisters, inundating the tops of our bureaus against the forward wall. Though their raised edges—designed to keep articles in place during rough weather—puddled the water efficiently, we managed to sweep watches and cameras out of harm's way. At first, we dumped everything on the beds.

Ceilings on board cruise ships are nearly all made by a Danish company called Daempa; they are composed of modular panels, allowing piecemeal removal for maintenance of air-conditioning ducts, electrical wiring, or plumbing overhead. The only disadvantage to the system is that

A circuit of every promenade deck invol▾
a continually changing vista of sun,
sea, and structure. On *Royal Viking Sea*,
passage narrows around the curve of the
bridge screen. *(Author's collection)*

water leaking from above is distributed over a wide area by the Daempa ceiling's impromptu guttering. Miniature cataracts soon engulfed the entire room. Clearly, we needed help.

With admirable calm, Mary tasted the water—a housekeeper's trick we had learned from the *Rotterdam*—before telephoning the front desk to report "freshwater leak in cabin 111." A charming night steward arrived on the double, buckets in one hand and huge garbage bags in the other. In a frenzy, the three of us began stuffing our belongings into the bags and hurling them into the corridor. (It is appalling how many possessions one has when they must be gathered in haste. Don Westlake and his wife, Abby Adams, once wrote a piece in praise of an indulgency of luggage entitled "Traveling Heavy"; it can be said that most shipboard—as opposed to airline—passengers subscribe to their rationale.)

The duty receptionist assigned us to a smaller cabin down the passage amidships, and the three of us shuttled between the two laden with suits, dresses, dinner jackets, typewriter, shoes, suitcases, binoculars, the lot. Shipboard corridors are carpeted these days so our safaris back and forth were achieved in surreal silence. It was just after three in the morning, and neighbors along that deck, oblivious of the flood in their midst, slept on, all save those poor souls just aft of our new accommodation, who must have been awakened and confused by the commotion of banging closets and drawers as we tried stowing the possessions heaped on our bunks.

Additional crewmen gathered in cabin 111. A bridge officer was there as well as two wonderfully reassuring engineers, complete with boiler suits, flashlights, and wrenches. Though they claimed to have located the appropriate cutoff, the torrents persisted, and I emptied a forgotten closet just moments before it was inundated. Cabin furniture was piled high in the bathroom and the comfortable, pleasant space we had called home for nearly a week was suddenly a wasteland, a carpet swamp squelching underfoot, occasional patches of naked steel deckhead above, sofa, mattress, bedding, furniture, and lopsided electrical fixtures a Picassoesque dereliction. The night steward, a tower of strength and solicitude, did his best to bring us a nightcap or at least a cup of tea; what we craved more than anything was to go back to bed.

The next morning we were installed in an empty suite on the boat deck. We took stock; remarkably, the only permanent damage sustained was a slight stain on a suede sunglasses case. Everything else, despite its pandemoniac salvage, was unharmed. Cabin 111 was forward on the starboard side of Atlantic Deck, directly under the galley; apparently, the culprit was a newly installed kitchen fixture improperly plumbed. Though the effect of a flood in the middle of the night had been jarring, how much better then—when we were both in the cabin—than at some time during the day when the deluge might have continued undetected for hours. Floods of this kind are occasional but inevitable shipboard emergencies that go with the cruise passenger's territory; the response of all the Royal Viking staff was exemplary and the damage, as it turned out, minimal.

The following day we moored at Honnigsvaag, the port where passengers these days disembark for a hair-raising bus ride to the North Cape. The cape is on Magerøy Island (Meager Island). Before the present road, earliest visitors to the cape had to be rowed ashore on the island's south coast, hiking for hours over a succession of ridges before achieving the coveted outlook from the landward side. But on July 17, 1873, the North Cape received its first royal visit: King Oscar II, monarch of the then-combined kingdoms of Sweden and Norway, landed from his yacht on the cape's eastern shore in Hornvik Bay. He inaugurated a special ascent to the top, a thousand feet up by laborious steps—half path, half staircase—lined with stanchions sunk deep into the rock and connected by a rope handrail. At the summit, His Majesty dedicated a commemorative obelisk; from that moment on the Nordkapp was big business. Steamers crammed with visitors anchored in the same bay and passengers hardy enough duplicated the royal ascent. Visits were and still are stage-managed to coincide whenever possible with the midnight sun, imparting a sense of wonder and mysticism to the occasion. An English guidebook from the turn of the century records that not everyone need necessarily disembark; it was recommended that those "not attracted to the summit nor drinking the health of *gamle Norge* in champagne ashore" (at a refreshment stand operated during the season) remain on board and fish instead! Apparently there is a fine fishing ground directly under the cape and, by midnight, early steamers' decks were awash with flapping cod and tangled lines. On our ship, too high above the water for this novel North Cape entertainment, we made do with an outdoor buffet as we steamed back and forth beneath those brooding cliffs.

Whether the midnight sun shines or cape and view are shrouded in mist, the visit is worthwhile—at least once. King Oscar's monument still stands along the edge. At the center of the plateau, surrounded by a parking lot, sprawls a huge stone combination refreshment center and post office where one can find shelter, if necessary, from the cold north wind. The view in that direction is impressive; from that elevation, an empty ocean is a stunning sight, especially after such an island-rich passage north. Far over the horizon, nothing save the twin archipelagos of Spitzbergen

...counter at Honnigsvaag. The *Mikhail*
...montov approaches to let her passen-
...s go ashore for a visit to the North
...e. *(Author's collection)*

and Franz Josef Land separate one from more than 500 miles of ocean and ice to the pole. Far to the east lies the Nordkyn, Europe's northern-most mainland point, and below, on one's left hand, is a low-lying island peninsula that, wonder of wonders, obviously extends farther north! It is called Knivskjelodden, or "knife edge," a scimitar-shaped spit reaching several hundred feet closer to the pole. So, the North Cape, that august tourist destination, is, one regrets to say, a sham; Knivskjelodden has a decided edge. But by the same token, the North Cape is undoubtedly the more splendid of the two, a massive, towering eminence, a press agent's dream of an attraction compared to the indifferent neighboring point to the west. Whoever made the decision to site King Oscar's monument on the former was obviously choosing the more dramatic of the two. But the ruse remains, common knowledge long before the royal blessing; a memoir of the mid-1850s remarks without much excitement that the smaller cape has "the right to Northern supremacy."

The lookout bars high atop the forward end of all three Royal Viking ships are among their most successful design features. Half a century ago, the concept of capping a ship's navigation bridge with a public room would have seemed outrageous to naval architects and owners alike. The bridge was a vessel's headquarters and profiles of the period show it isolated, separated from all passenger spaces. Not only was the bridge officer coun-try, its environs were as well; the only space above it—forbidden to pas-sengers—was an open-air, railed enclosure called, for reasons unknown, the monkey island. Forward-facing public rooms awaited vessels whose bulk was considered large enough to have their bridge screens glazed with impunity. Even so, the lookout bars or winter gardens that appeared on ships the size of the *Queen Mary* and *Normandie* remained below the bridge, leaving that essential maritime fixture in undisputed command.

But the modern cruise ship's wedge profile has changed all that. With one huge class and less concern about green water over the bow, passenger spaces have been extended forward as well as aft. The bridge has been outflanked and overwhelmed; formerly sacrosanct navigational preserves have been absorbed within the passengers' domain. Now, a vessel's topmost deck is given over to either splendid penthouse suites or splendid public rooms; invariably, one of these latter is perched atop the bridge. In truth, while it must obviously have an unobstructed view forward as well as over the side and open-air wings for officers' and pilots' use in port, there is no navigational reason for the bridge to be the highest point. (Several vessels built recently—*Scandinavia* and *Tropicale* among them—have their bridges

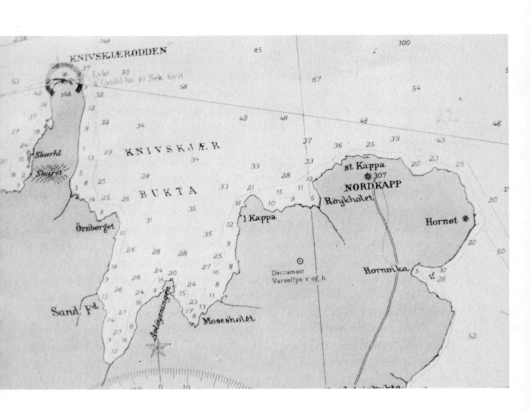

On the *Royal Viking Sea*'s chart, the
bulkier North Cape on the right is clearly
exposed as farther south than the little
point to the left. *(Author's collection)*

entirely enclosed; pilots docking the *Scandinavia* must peer through a plate-glass panel in the bridge deck to see what's happening beneath them.)

On *Royal Viking Sea*, the forward end of Sky Deck is occupied by the Windjammer Lounge, a U-shaped bar located directly over the bridge. It is surrounded by glass and achieves essentially the same visual effect as the Crown Lounge wrapping the funnel on *Song of America.* But whereas the Royal Caribbean facility's forward side is minimally furnished for maximum seating, the front of the Windjammer has been fitted with deep swivel chairs of such commodious depths that they are difficult to move and, for elderly passengers, nearly as difficult to rise from. They line an expanse of plate glass with a superb view forward, a seating and prospect that seem to have been contrived specifically for cruising Norway's coast. The sense of overview is Olympian, on an automotive par with the front seat atop a London bus or, aerially, within the observation gondola of a dirigible. In those calm coastal waters one feels suspended in midair, detached from the ship, floating above the seascape.

Between the North Cape and our departure west for Iceland were sixteen hours of inland steaming. (Strictly speaking, "steaming" is not applicable to describe a motor vessel's progress; but it has assumed a generic status fully as acceptable as "sailing.") Our route lay due west as far as Hjelmsoy (Helmet Island, so called because of its conical shape), a famous bird sanctuary where, some years earlier, one of Royal Viking's ships had struck the bottom and been forced to return south for dry docking. Giving it a wide berth, we turned south into the Ullsfjorden toward Tromsø, where we would tie up for a day's visit.

Tromsø is the largest city of Troms, Norway's second-northernmost county, situated on an island that lies like a loose stopper in twin channels between larger islands. It is connected to its eastern neighbor by a bridge; although small Russian cruise ships that call at the port can fit beneath it, we could not and so had to retrace our path northward around the island in order to continue south. The growth of automobile routes along Norway's coast has impinged on cruise ship traffic to the extent that larger vessels cannot pass beneath some of the car bridges; Narvik was, at one time, a stop for the *Queen Elizabeth 2* but a new bridge lower than the Cunarder's height above the water has necessitated a prohibitively time-consuming detour to the port's approaches.

We sailed from Tromsø at six o'clock that evening. It was raining slightly—an August snow in Tromsø is considered good luck—which did not bode well for the evening's sail; although by mid-August the midnight sun has departed for the year, a long twilight continues right up to mid-

432   LINERS TO THE SUN

The company's prototypical vessel departing San Francisco. The thirteen square windows of the bridge are surmounted by the curving facade of what is called on the *Star* the Stella Polaris Room. *Below,* the unencumbered view from the *Royal Viking Sky*'s equivalent is remarkable. *(Royal Viking Line and author's collection)*

night. But we were in luck: the rain stopped and the mist cleared. Whatever diversion was planned on board the evening after Tromsø, our preference was a seat forward in the Windjammer Lounge. Our ship would meander for the last time through fjord and island on its way south to Lodingen, where we would disembark our coastal pilots and leave Norwegian waters. Sensibly, the designers of those forward lounges have eschewed all but minimal interior lighting, so there is no reflection whatsoever, and the panorama ahead predominates. The room was nearly empty—cabaret somewhere aft had attracted most of our fellow passengers—and we were left in almost sole possession of that delightful aerie with no sound for distraction save—for once—some exquisitely appropriate Bach over the ceiling speakers.

Ruffled by only the faintest breeze, silver-gray water in our path stretched far ahead, bordered to port and starboard with brooding, somnolent peaks. For nearly an hour, we seemed bound only for a distant shore like a lake ferry; but steady, silent progress, unreeling almost imperceptibly to either side, revealed a narrow sea defile between headlands connected by a bridge. Once that exit came clear, then it was the bridge we awaited, attending the moment when the span approached, languidly yet inevitably, then rose above our bows to vanish overhead. One cannot, and hence does not, look back—the impetus is irrevocably forward.

Once past that bridge, we started another phase of that dream journey. The land relented, a new water route opened before us and our course changed noticeably as, on the bridge below us, the pilot transmitted his charted wish to the helm. Up in the tranquil peace of the Windjammer, we searched for new landmarks, as if aiming our bows toward the next exit through the surrounding hills. We sighted other ships, distant beacons at first that, as we approached, obviated collision by skirting to either side of our bow, fishermen or cargo vessels that slid twinkling beneath our flank. At Finnsnes there was another bridge, requiring an appreciably cautious approach. The channel narrows radically there—"cranky" is how the navigation officer characterized it in retrospect—to only half a cable's width. A cable is one-tenth of a nautical mile so the pilot had to maneuver us through a slot only 100 yards wide.

I suppose what we enjoyed vicariously that long evening in the Windjammer Lounge was the sense that we were at the tiller of a small boat, our cruise ship transformed into a manageable, adventurous yacht. The hypnotically slow approach toward distant landmarks, the close observance of passing shore features, and the continuous inland proximity combined the pleasures of an amateur voyage. It continued until after midnight, when an impenetrable northern dusk finally blotted out all but the navigation lights. That nocturnal progression had been exquisite; I know of no more enchanting coastal waters, nor any more magical evening light, nor any more captivating shipboard space from which to observe them. We had completed our farewell segment of the Norwegian coast, an irreplaceable journey, the memory of which stayed with us all the way across the Atlantic.

Our first North American stop was at St. John's, Canada's closest port on Newfoundland's eastern tip, not to be confused with Saint John on the Bay of Fundy. It has a splendid harbor, fjordlike, entered between cliffs, a remote, northern backwater that is a refreshing change from conventional ports of call, encountered only on positioning cruises. At Saint-Pierre, our next port, some new arrivals embarked, the first since Copenhagen. These were invited rather than paying passengers: a dozen models had been flown in from all over the United States, from as far west as California. Together with a team of public relations people and photographers, they had endured ghastly air connections in order to join us on board for a location shoot as *Royal Viking Sea* approached the United States. The company needed new pictures for their *1984/1985 Cruise Atlas*, and the models who assembled on board in Canadian waters had clearly been selected with an eye to reinforcing Royal Viking's special passenger image.

The matter of image in general—and passenger image in particular—is of supreme importance. As I mentioned earlier, Carnival Cruise Lines publishes brochures using photographs of actual passengers. Very few companies follow their example because Old Guard passengers, in general, are neither young nor photogenic enough—at least not in the rapturous style espoused by the image-makers. I asked one of the public relations people on board how the trade defined the look she had achieved in assembling her passenger/models: "Upscale country club" was her immediate response. Then, too, however successful an Old Guard company, it is always interested in attracting a younger clientele, in order to buttress future prospects.

So Old Guard brochure passengers are selected to be chronologically ambiguous, distinguished yet lean and tanned. They are represented as indefinably middle-aged, éminences grises tempered with an overriding youthfulness. Jawlines are well defined, bellies concave, heads luxuriantly coiffed. At sunset and dawn alike, they linger, entwined, at the rail; they order extravagant cabin breakfasts—delivered on silver trays—or nibble at splendiferous buffets on deck; they gather jovially for drinks in the most expensive accommodations; in black tie and evening dress, they dine in

A question of image. *Above,* models
assemble on the *Royal Viking Sea*'s
deck to pose as passengers. *Left,* cha[
complete. Anchored off Bar Harbor,
vessel surrenders to the beautiful peo[
There are some real passengers in th[
background, but the focus is on the
graceful swimmer and two couples c[
ting in the sun. *Opposite top,* Holland
America models on board *Nieuw An[
sterdam.* In all my years at sea, I hav[
never seen anyone in black tie playing
shuffleboard. *Opposite bottom,* passer[
gers unvarnished, infinitely preferabl[
(Author's collection, Royal Viking Li[
Holland America Line, and author's
collection)

broad daylight; and after dark, they throng the gaming tables up in the casino, smiling whether winning or losing. In fact, whatever Old Guard brochure passengers do anywhere on board, they always smile, as benevolent as the weather and the surface of the sea. By the same token, brochure cruise passengers manage to avoid all fog or storm and seldom read a book; if they do, they never doze off in a deck chair with their mouths open.

Creating convincing brochure shipboard vignettes is an art form. Some shipping lines shoot public rooms full of real passengers blurred in the background while "upscale country club" postures to the fore. But during the photographic session on our cruise, the company had decided to populate their vessel almost entirely with models. Booked exclusively by beautiful people, the *Royal Viking Sea* set sail on a Kodachrome cruise, Main Chance *Outward Bound*.

Though the weather southwest from Canada to Bar Harbor was sunny, the casual groupings required were not easily achieved. Once our *vrai* outdoor buffet had ended, dirty plates, napkins, and glasses were gathered up by hardworking stewards; fresh teams from the galley appeared with a duplicate buffet, pristine *faux* fare for the *faux* passengers who had assembled with combs and hairspray for a *faux* lunch on deck. Later, dressed for the evening, the *faux* passengers would assemble for *faux* cocktails in an empty penthouse suite. An off-duty stewardess had to change into evening uniform, and trays of canapés had to be summoned far ahead of conventional ship's schedule.

Alas, however excruciating the effort, the end product remains unconvincing. Between chores, the models lived in our midst, a Pirandellian paradox, twice six characters in search of a cruise. For central casting had erred: aping passengers, garbed as passengers, playing at passengers, that divine dozen remained actors, hopelessly isolated by their very perfection from the lesser mortals they strove to emulate. It occurred to more than one of us that these spurious intruders in the ship's life, dispatched specifically to immortalize it, only perpetuated an antiseptic charade.

Saddest of all, these counterfeit clients do a disservice to those who book legitimate passage. The Old Guard en masse may lack panache; not all are fashion plates and, admittedly, some would not decorate a glossy brochure to advantage. But they have the advantages of character, zest, and honesty so lacking in the two-dimensional cutouts displayed in their place. To capture a valid image, companies should dispatch only photographers: passengers are already on board. It seems clear that passenger/models do not make model passengers.

But that vexing charade notwithstanding, the cruise continued pleasantly. Conventional crossings are sea affairs exclusively, a near-week or more at sea without sight of land. But during *Royal Viking Sea*'s leisurely westward journey, we hugged the shore, so to speak: the North American coastline trends in a southwesterly direction, and we followed its crescent shape, touching at Canadian and New England ports before reaching final landfall at New York.

We crossed the Canadian border for a stop in Bar Harbor on the type of crisp, late-August Maine day for which there is no substitute. The town itself is a tourist trap as well as a lobster trap, and the conifered hills seemed of a piece with Bergen, as though we had, on that cruise, closed a kind of grand scenic circle. Then we sailed south to Boston and Newport before a last, laggardly overnight approach to New York.

I have noticed a curious thing as ships near their final destination: the engines seem to balk. On a normal sea day, one wakes each morning attuned to a certain fixed tremor, a pulse that governs life for several weeks. That machine regime falters at journey's end; the vessel's heart fibrillates into a reluctant episode, either in actuality or in susceptible passengers' minds, a kind of engineering *ritardando*. I had once thought that the phenomenon owed its existence to passage through shallow waters, as though the propellers' regular beat were distorted by a premature sonic response from the closer channel bottom; but the engineers tell me this is not so. Yet whatever tune the *Royal Viking Sea*'s engines played that final morning, it was markedly different, more complex than mere speed limitation occasioned by our movement under the pilot's care up through the Narrows.

Perhaps it reflected passenger unease. The cruise tempo, as always, had vanished with the luggage. The cabin was strangely ordered now, its former cozy domesticity evaporated. We had donned sober shoreside dress, the voyage behind us a forgotten idyll, fading like an ancient daguerreotype. All that remained were addresses, promises, and extravagant farewells over breakfast. (Never say good-bye to shipmates in the dining room; you encounter them again half a dozen times on board or on the pier.) Though twenty-four days at sea was no world cruise, we had enjoyed an extended occupancy, not easily abandoned.

Last sight of the *Royal Viking Sea*, towering inviolate over the Hudson's Passenger Ship Terminal, was evocative, a symbol as full of promise as regret, signaling, in some sublime mystical semaphore: not the end of a cruise, the vision of many more to come.

Of all five cruises present, the most evocative moment occurred late one night in the Caribbean on board Sitmar's *Fairsea*. At dinner, it had been confirmed that, near midnight, we would pass *Fairwind*. *Royal Viking Sea* and *Sky* had shared a Bergen pier earlier that summer but this encounter between sister ships would take place, as the French say, *en pleine mer*, two original Cunarders, *Carinthia* and *Sylvania*, renamed now *Fairsea* and *Fairwind*, still in service after three decades, cruising rather than crossing.

Like elderly but sprightly sisters of advanced but useful years who share an especial familial longevity, so these two ships converged port to port on an empty moonlit sea. On our vessel, every rail was packed with passengers who, as the bow lines overlapped, broke into spontaneous cheers. *Fairsea* and *Fairwind* were united by a dappled light river spanning the intervening sea. The other ship's decks must have been packed too, for her profile, already ablaze with light, flared explosively with the flashes from a thousand cameras as the two ships, like steel against flint, struck a shower of strobe sparks. For a few exhilarating seconds, at a passing speed of thirty knots, the two sisters and their passengers were linked in sweet resolution before passing and vanishing, withdrawn once again within our respective hulls. We had each seen, momentarily, our reflected selves slide by.

*Sea Goddess I sails the Mediterranean
like no other ship. She takes you to out-
of-the-way places untouched by other cruise
ships as well as popular playgrounds favored
by royalty.*

—SEA GODDESS CRUISES BROCHURE

*Set your course by distant stars . . . not
by the light of passing ships.*

—PHOENIX PRELIMINARY STUDY

10.
Cruises to Come

In the fall of 1984, I talked with the president of a new cruise line. "Over the next five years," he warned, "there will be continuing depression in the cruise industry. So many ships are entering the market. There's just too much newbuilding." The speaker was Ron Kurtz, originally with the French Line, then Norwegian Caribbean Lines, and now head of Sea Goddess Cruises.

"But some of those are replacements for old tonnage," I pointed out. "Carnival, for one, is merely bringing its ships up to date. They'll phase out the older ones."

"Carnival may get rid of them," was Kurtz's response, "but someone will continue to operate them. There's going to be a glut of passenger berths in the Caribbean for some time to come." Then he brightened. "But I like to think that we will be insulated from that kind of problem."

"We" was Sea Goddess Cruises. Our conversation took place in the oriental-carpeted lobby of the first of his two vessels, *Sea Goddess I*. I had just enjoyed its maiden transatlantic crossing, a positioning cruise marking the vessel's transfer from inaugural Mediterranean season to inaugural Caribbean season out of St. Croix. Sea Goddess Cruises had been designed to attract a very special market segment with an expensive, yacht-like ambience.

Kurtz and Sea Goddess Cruises are in a challenging position. If there is one broad sociological lesson to be learned from today's cruise phenomenon, it is that the market's upper end involves the highest risk. In the mid-eighties, while *Sea Goddess I* was on the ways at Wärtsilä, two top-of-the-line companies, Norwegian American and Royal Viking, had faltered and been absorbed by larger rivals. Trafalgar, the holding company that owns Cunard, announced in early May 1983 that they had bought Norwegian American Cruises for $73 million. It was a move, Cunard's press release hinted, that would enable Cunard to "achieve greater penetration of the luxury market."

Fifteen months later, the other shoe dropped. Knut Kloster, chairman of Klosters Rederi A/S, the Oslo holding company that controls Norwegian Caribbean Lines, bought Royal Viking Line from her Norwegian owners. There had been talk the winter before that the line was to be sold to Whitney Enterprises; Kloster's surprise move kept the trio of vessels not only flying the Norwegian flag but also under control of a shipping visionary as well. Kloster now owns five Caribbean cruise ships—the *Norway* as well as what is called "the white fleet"—and the trio of Royal Viking vessels, a fleet with a passenger capacity of 7,200 and hence the largest cruise line in the world. Bob Perez, who works for rival RCCL in Miami, said wryly that Kloster has now become the General Motors of the cruise industry, "with a selection of models for every taste!"

Similarly, by absorbing Norwegian American, Cunard's fleet was increased to five ships. For a time, the company seemed hungry for further acquisition. Shortly after the NAC takeover, there were indications of a Trafalgar stock purchase of P&O's fleet. Had the deal gone through, Cunard would have absorbed *Canberra* and *Oriana*, as well as P&O's highly profitable subsidiary, Princess Cruises, including the *Royal Princess*, which entered service at the end of 1984. As it happened, Trafalgar backed down a year later; however, if the takeover had occurred, Cunard would have rejoiced in the position it enjoyed some years ago with the largest fleet in the world.

The trend, or rather trends, toward this kind of consolidation are significant. It seems obvious that, under present market conditions, the luxury end of the market cannot survive on its own: Old Guard tonnage flagships steaming majestically around the world need an underpinning of Newpassenger dollars from the Caribbean. Does this spell the end for the Old Guard? Is that top-dollar luxury cruise market doomed? One hopes not. Both Royal Viking and Norwegian American, their new owners assured the public, would continue unchanged. This crucial reassurance came in response to shocked disbelief in the northeast when news of Kloster's purchase was announced. Old Guard passengers—who saw Royal Viking as a last bastion for *Peregrinator transatlanticus*—were terrified that their palatial white goddesses would be downgraded to Caribbean tourist vessels. Similarly, Cunard's Norwegian American takeover seemed to some of the company's oldest passengers a threat that the exclusive *Sagafjord/Vistafjord* service they had always enjoyed was in jeopardy. Both companies have been at pains to assure their Old Guard clients—bought, so to speak, with their newly acquired tonnage—that the quality of life on board would remain the same.

The profitability and, hence, the survival of Old Guard ships depend on Old Guard clients. An invaluable sales tool for Old Guard ships is fostering a sense of familial loyalty among the regulars. Holland America treats their repeaters with particular care. Those who sail with the company more than once are assured of a special reception on board; for long-term repeaters, special certificates and ribbons, as well as photographs with the captain, are handed out. Sitmar has their Circolo del Commandante, Royal Viking their Skald members (derived from the old Norse word for storyteller), and Norwegian American their Fjord Club.

But very few Newpassenger vessels bother with this kind of stroking. Royal Caribbean grants no special perks to clients who come back, nor do Carnival or NCL. Former passenger names are fed into the computer for mailings but no attempt is made to fête their owners on board. The Newpassenger companies work Main Street, U.S.A., relying for their marketing clout on a huge, almost infinite potential passenger pool: that 95 percent of the American public which has never booked a ship's cabin. So, fresh waves of Newpassengers clamber up cruise ships' gangplanks each week. Newcomers and old-timers alike are welcomed with universal enthusiasm and, curiously, no special ceremony or keepsake rewards those who come back.

"*We would like a no-disco, no-social-director, no-casino cruise.*"

(Drawing by B. Tobey; © 1984 The New Yorker Magazine, Inc.)
There may be millions of potential clients out there who share the sentiments of the couple above, not only those new to cruise ships but those tired of conventional offerings as well.

Ron Kurtz's concern is that that pool of new consumers may not be as deep as some of his opposite numbers believe; or at least not deep enough to replenish the fleets of newbuilding steaming over the horizon. His company, Sea Goddess Cruises, represents one of the most significant and interesting attempts to pull ahead of the pack. At a time when the Old Guard luxury market seemed terminally soft, when only Newpassenger tonnage seemed profitable, *Sea Goddess I* set sail on a radically new course. The company's two ships are small—purposely so—originally the brainchild of an ex-head of Norwegian Caribbean Lines in Miami, Helge Naarstad. He and Ron Kurtz were after affluent but elusive customers, those who would hesitate to board a conventional cruise ship but might be tempted by something different and special. Sea Goddess Cruises was marketed to attract Newpassengers of a different sort—first-time cruisers who had never booked passage for reasons of disdain rather than frugality. They were to be welcomed aboard small, select vessels of yachtlike proportions to be shared, it was inferred, with a yachtlike clientele. Sea Goddess advertising copy makes no bones about it: "a renaissance of the golden age of travel when only a privileged few could afford to venture abroad." Prices were steep. In the early spring of 1984, when *Sea Goddess I* first sailed out of Monaco, each passenger occupying one of the fifty-eight almost identical cabins was paying in excess of $500 a day: a week's cruise for a couple ran to more than $7,000 excluding airfare, but including almost everything else. Drinks were on the house, so was postage; gratuities were "discouraged." Moreover, hinting at the riches on board, Sea Goddess Cruises claimed that they spent more per passenger for caviar than other companies spent for all meals.

Originally, there were to have been sixty cabins, all but two of them identical suites. But the pressure of crew accommodation—a perennial problem on board through the planning and design phase at Wärtsilä—meant that passenger capacity had to be decreased by four in order to create enough room for ship's personnel. Crew accommodation on board remains tight; there are as many as three in some stewards' cabins, and there is just not room enough for a crew dayroom larger than a mess that accommodates only a portion of the crew at one time.

Not surprisingly, clients are more comfortably ensconced. Each Sea Goddess cabin is divided in half, with a sleeping area near the shell plating and a living room area inboard. The entire cabin/bathroom block is 200 square feet, well above the industry average. Still, the sense of suite has been achieved only by cutting crucial corners elsewhere. The Sea Goddess bathroom is diminutive; though handsomely finished, well-appointed, and

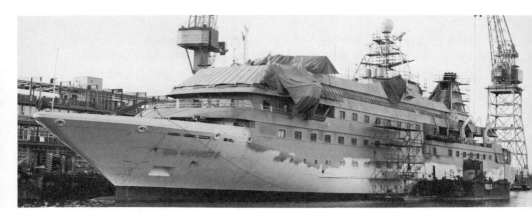

Sea Goddess I. Top, fittin
out at Wärtsilä, Newbuild
466 nears completion. *Ce*
after a courtesy call in
London, Helge Naarstad
first cruise yacht sails for
Mediterranean to enter
service in the spring of
1984. *Left,* a landing doc
at the stern encourages w
sports. The expert—henc
fully dressed?—officer on
board the windsurfer is th
vessel's first master, Capt
Johann L'orange. *(Wärtsi
Helsinki Shipyard and Se*
Goddess Cruises)

stocked with free unguents, it is scarcely commodious, not at all of a piece with the luxurious aura the company has established elsewhere. Similarly, cabin closets are small, too crowded for the amount of clothing with which the Old Guard prefers to travel—again, obviously restricted in order to increase cabin size and pretension. The trick, I realized as I unpacked, is to "think yacht"; then it all makes sense.

But however disappointing the bathroom and closet, the detailing within the cabin itself is impressive. Furniture, paneling, and cabinetry are finished in handsome white oak. Berths may be single or double at will, either as separate twin beds or joined into a queen-size bed. An icebox and bar are concealed in uniform cupboards as is a safe with a passenger-originated computerized combination for valuables. In front of the sofa is a coffee table with a pedestal that can be elevated to become a dining room table. One of Sea Goddess's ingenious passenger options is to dine—à quatre if so desired—in one's own cabin with the identical exquisite service enjoyed in the ship's dining salon. This is not merely a room-service dinner delivered on a tray; it is a complete meal, served course by course under the discreet supervision of a steward. Overall, the Sea Goddess cabin, splendidly thought out and beautifully executed, works well.

The dining salon is down on Two deck, approached through a tiny lobby where a pianist, one of no more than three musicians on board, plays during dinner. Every deck above his head, all the way up to Six deck, has an identical railed opening, one above the other, creating an intriguing, vertical well that carries his music throughout the ship; it is pleasantly reminiscent of the *lichtschacht* on board the *Victoria Luise*. Passengers— whom the company insists, alas, on calling guests—come down to dine at tables of their own choosing. As a result, every night there is a continuous turnover of passengers, tables, and stewards, which, more than any other departure, serves to discourage tipping. The traditional rapport is never established with any one steward. The system has its disadvantages: ship-board passengers throughout history have enjoyed relying on a specific steward who, in turn, knows every nuance of his passengers' likes and dislikes. But the compensatory pleasure of making new friends over drinks, and then, on impulse, dining with them as well, is a novel—and unique— Sea Goddess perquisite today; it brings to mind the casual luxe of the *Queens*' Veranda Grills. Moreover, on a seven-day crossing, with a passenger load of only thirty-four, it meant that by voyage's end, we had managed to dine consecutively with almost everyone on board.

Sea Goddess food was, without exception, superb, whether in the dining salon at night or at an outdoor buffet up on Five deck. The menu

The *Sea Goddess I* ordinary is beautifully designed and executed. *Above,* the view outboard, showing double bed, mirrored dressing table, and greenery. *Below,* inboard, the cabinet to the left of the chair conceals the television set; its videotape player will rest on the bookshelf above. Cabinets to the right contain icebox, safe, and a stocked bar. On the far right is the patent coffee table that can be raised and enlarged to serve as a dinner table for four. *(Wärtsilä's Helsinki Shipyard)*

clearly reflects a predilection for nouvelle cuisine, no longer very nouvelle but, on board ship, where food seems the major passenger preoccupation, an advisedly wise company decision. The choices are adequate but not overwhelming, the arrangement and presentation of every dish stunning. Indeed, Sea Goddess food may be too good; I was told that passengers on Mediterranean cruises used to forego lunch ashore, even in the South of France, in favor of a return to the buffet on board. During the crossing, with seven uninterrupted sea days, we had no such choice thrust upon us and, in fact, were very glad not to have had one.

Regularly scheduled entertainment does not exist, an omission designed to please passengers surfeited with cabaret and amusement on board every other cruise ship: there is no bingo, horse racing, or masquerade; no dance lessons, cooking demonstrations, or lectures. As a result, the atmosphere on board is, as Commander Whitehead used to say about Schweppes, curiously refreshing, a re-creation of Atlantic Conference days, when passengers were encouraged to amuse or entertain themselves. Sunbathing and swimming occupied most mornings; some passengers parboiled themselves in the on-deck Jacuzzi, a few walked around Five deck, ten circuits to the mile. Almost no one bothered with the gymnasium in the base of the funnel. Extraordinarily, out of thirty-four passengers on board, not one foursome could be mustered for bridge. Passengers talked, read, gambled, or watched films on the videotape players that are standard equipment in every Sea Goddess cabin. No one complained about being deprived of a nightly fix of cabaret. Indeed, each evening's main event was an excellent dinner; anything to follow would have been anticlimactic. The chief steward told me that we drank a great deal, that more champagne had been consumed on that crossing—by one-third the ship's customary capacity—than ever before.

Perhaps the most endearing effect of the size of the Sea Goddess ships is the close camaraderie that springs up instantly between passengers and crew. On such a small vessel, the captain and his senior staff are very much in evidence, not only at mealtimes but all day as well. Save for the dining room stewards on duty in the evening, dress is unconventional: officers wear shorts as part of their uniform, and cabin stewardesses a kind of neutral yachting rig of gondolier shirts with white slacks. There is a lot of doubling among certain crew members: the assistant purser on duty behind the desk in the ship's square deals blackjack in the evening. Passengers are encouraged to visit the bridge whenever they wish, a shipboard courtesy that benefits those interested and has never yet abused the master's hospitality. Traveling westbound from Las Palmas, we sailed directly into incomparable sunsets; so, every evening, just before six, an informal Sunset Club would congregate on the bridge. In fact, the front of the bridge windows are surrounded by a crescent of passenger deck, so that occasionally, when the ship is full, the officer of the watch has to clear the railings directly ahead in order to navigate the vessel. But most in-port navigation is achieved from either bridge wing, standard shipboard features that Petter Yran, the naval architect, had originally thought to exclude from his design.

Though every mile of our transatlantic crossing was smooth, I was told that the little ship copes with rough weather well. She seemed to travel very fast, partly because we were assisted for most of the way by a 2½-knot current and partly because one is so close to the water. Approaching or in port, the vessel can be maneuvered with a single bow-thruster. The only thing lacking in her navigational arsenal is, I was advised, a second rudder. The single one amidships does not impart adequate torque to the hull whereas a pair—one in each propeller's wash —would have made tight work in confined harbors far easier. For her length, *Sea Goddess I* stands tall in the water, with high superstructure and funnel that, like the *Caronia*'s, are subject to considerable wind pressure, acting like a giant, steel-and-aluminum sail. Those surprisingly large, flanking surfaces, together with the vessel's single rudder, make dockings and undockings tricky, especially when the Mediterranean's notorious afternoon wind picks up.

An analysis of our small shipload revealed that Sea Goddess Cruises's appeal had failed on the one hand, though succeeded handsomely on the other: all but one honeymoon couple had sailed on cruise ships previously. For our crossing, the elusive, affluent Newpassengers had not materialized. If that cross section was typical, Sea Goddess Cruises has attracted less the untried rich than jaded Old Guard anxious to travel on a new and promising ship. The steep price seems not to have discouraged anyone; in fact, during the vessel's first Mediterranean season, several clients had intimated that the cost of a ticket was too low for the quality of service provided. So, presumably, there is no limit to what an enterprising company can charge, provided they have gauged—and can deliver—an elitist cruising clientele's predilection for *grande luxe*. My last morning on board, a Swiss passenger on the bridge told me that after having sailed on *Vista-fjord*, the *Pearl of Scandinavia, Queen Elizabeth 2*, and two Royal Viking ships, he felt that *Sea Goddess I* had displaced all former company loyalties at a stroke.

450

Goddess I on trials in the Gulf of
*...*nd: A benefit of small passenger
... is that not one of the four lifeboats
*...*ks a cabin view. The pool lies
*...*tly aft of the funnel. *(Wärtsilä's*
...inki Shipyard)

I heard subsequently that for Sea Goddess's first Christmas cruise in the Caribbean, their coveted target market had begun to materialize. My informant was Myrtle Loewenstern, who, with her husband, Walter, had flown from Houston to embark on the new ship. The Loewensterns are inveterate Old Guard passengers, having sailed on eight consecutive *Rotterdam* world cruises. They found the Sea Goddess crowd different, "like the jet set," reported Myrtle, "all young, in their forties." Apparently, some older men on board were accompanied by much younger traveling companions. One young woman had appeared on deck in a bathing suit of such startling abbreviation that older female passengers had complained to the chief steward. But the lady in question—asserting that "It's my vacation, after all"—outdid herself that same evening with an even more revealing evening dress as though re-asserting her right to deshabille. Myrtle also told me that one of her fellow Houstonians on board had proposed that she and her husband fly home with him in his private sixteen-seat jet, which was waiting at St. Croix's airport the day they disembarked. It seems that Sea Goddess's painstaking market research is paying off; perhaps Old Guard and Newpassenger should be joined by a third client category, Nouveaupax.

Another pair of small ships is on the drawing boards for debut in 1986. Jean-Claude Potier, ex–North American manager for TRANSAT and subsequently with Sun Line and Paquet Cruises, will head his own company, Windstar Cruises. Each of his ships will carry 150 passengers within a hull approximately 300 feet long; the first was laid down on France's Channel coast at the Société des Ateliers et Chantiers du Havre in early 1985. The same length as Sea Goddess ships, they will boast a novel refinement, a quartet of masts carrying a spread of computer-operated canvas. The ships' design is based on research studies made at Wärtsilä for cruising sailing vessels; they will have a small funnel amidships to vent diesel exhaust from auxiliary engines. Potier hopes to attract a younger, "more swinging" passenger than Sea Goddess and, because of fuel economies, expects to do so for only $250 a day per passenger, less than half his rival's fare. He is convinced that there is a sizable and growing number of clients who are fed up with conventional cruises on large vessels, remote from the feel and life of the sea and regimented in cliché activities. "If you tell a travel agent that you are going to do away with the midnight buffet," he points out in articulate English, "they think you have abandoned Christmas." Time will tell if he is correct; once again, innovation is the key.

dstar's sail cruiser as seen by an artist before the
was laid in January 1985. Although Wärtsilä's
nal "Windcruiser" had only three masts, *Windstar*'s
have four. Incorporated into the number 2 mast
funnel with the same branching *cheminée aux*
ons design of the *France* to keep diesel soot off
white sails aft. *(Windstar Cruises)*

And if the Old Guard has new toys, the ultimate Newpassenger novelty may lie over the horizon as well. By the late eighties, an extraordinary innovation will titillate the public, not with reduced size or increased luxury but with gargantuan immensity. Knut Kloster, the man who rescued the *France* from oblivion and turned her into the popular and profitable *Norway*, is obsessed with yet another record-breaking hull. His dream is called *Phoenix*, and she will be, quite simply, the largest passenger vessel ever built, garlanded with festoons of multiple-zero integers: 1,200 feet, 250,000 tons, $400,000,000 to build. She will have a divided, catamaran stern inside which the *Sea Goddess I* could be comfortably accommodated. When Norwegian Caribbean Lines inaugurated Miami's cruise boom in the early seventies, no one could have guessed that, within less than two decades, the company would commission a vessel surpassing in size anything that has ever sailed before.

She will be designed by Tage Wandborg, the same Danish naval architect charged with converting *France* into *Norway*. The vessel was initially conceived to carry four thousand passengers but, by reworking his basic cabin design, Wandborg has increased that figure by a quarter, to five thousand. (Even so, the standard outside cabin is generous, 230 square feet [nearly forty bathmats] in addition to a private terrace outside.) *Phoenix* is awesome in concept, what Wandborg describes as a "floating universe." In a structural and logistical class with supertankers, she is scheduled to be laid down at a West German yard at Kiel in 1986. A basic feature of her design will be an inversion of conventional cruise ship priorities: public rooms will be placed down inside the hull while all cabins will be stacked above the strength deck, contained within a quartet of superstructure towers thrusting high into the air. The cabins farthest forward will incorporate the bridge, those aftermost the vessel's single funnel; the two midship towers will be positioned, for design variety as well as a better ocean view for their occupants, with their axes diagonal to the keel. Hence, save for those who elect to book inside cabins, every *Phoenix* passenger will enjoy a prospect of the sea from a private balcony, elevated accommodations of a kind that, on conventional cruise ships, are restricted to only a score of the ship's elite.

For sailor and landlubber alike, first sight of the *Phoenix*'s improbable profile is startling. Although longer than her closest competitor, what astonishes is less the horizontal than the vertical. Her deckhouse roof will be on the same plane as the tops of the *Norway*'s pair of funnels. Traditionalists, only recently resigned to contemporary wedge ships, tend to be struck dumb when confronted with four ziggurats perched atop a tanker.

...wn here at Trondheim, the *Phoenix* and her two
...t ardent champions. On the left is Tage Wandborg,
...Danish naval architect; seated with him in the
...hy is Knut Kloster, head of Klosters Rederi, the
...shipping concern that is NCL and Royal Viking's
...nt company. *(Klosters Rederi A/S)*

For some, it seems a land/sea anomaly, downtown Miami afloat, or a plundered Mesopotamian ruin en route to the British Museum by barge. Others balk at the scale, as though man were—as in the case, incidentally, of *Great Eastern, Olympic,* or *Queen Mary*—tempting fate. There are passengers who avow they would hate sailing on anything that size as well as ships' officers who are concerned about the *Phoenix*'s maneuverability.

But in time, assorted disbeliefs relent, and the image grows clearer, losing its initial bizarreness. One must think of the *Phoenix* ziggurats as merely separated components of a conventional cruise ship superstructure. Tage Wandborg is rhapsodic about his giant creation, especially because it behaved so well in model form. After testing in Trondheim's Ocean Laboratory over the winter of 1983, he was astonished and delighted to discover that, despite her top-heavy appearance, the *Phoenix* had almost too much stability; Wandborg debated about dispensing with stabilizers altogether. In the long run, the *Phoenix* bewitches all who come in contact with her, even the most skeptical corporate types from Norwegian Caribbean Lines's Miami office. One marketing executive has a fixed fantasy image of the operational *Phoenix*, steaming along a sun-drenched Caribbean course, never coming ashore save to fuel and victual every two months, embarking and disembarking passengers by helicopter or even airship in the interim.

Inside that monster hull will be a theater seating two thousand with broadcasting facilities that would allow the *Phoenix* to host, for instance, a televised Miss Universe contest early in the nineties. There will be half a dozen contrasting restaurants—perhaps one extra-tariff—and a reproduction of a New England village shorefront, with waterfall, where passengers will wait to board one of four identical five-hundred-passenger tenders for a ride to shore. The tender fleet will be housed in a special dry dock inside the stern. Once the *Phoenix* is at anchor offshore, her passenger load ready to disembark, the stern will open, flooding the dry dock. The two aftermost tenders will sally forth from their sternbound grotto to load along either *Phoenix* flank, while the forward pair embark passengers below deck. While all four tenders are on shuttle station, the open stern will remain flooded, creating an Olympic-size-plus interior swimming hole for those who opt to remain on board. (It will be the first pool to have been constructed inside a vessel since the late sixties.) For those who prefer swimming in the open, the *Phoenix*'s upper deck (eleven above that interior lagoon) will offer a sand-encircled lake spanned by a bridge. For quieter swimming, two additional outdoor pools will be sited at diagonal corners of the vast strength deck. Elsewhere in the hull will be an

456

Hypothetical views. If we can trust the renderings, amidships on board *Phoenix* will look like this. Whether the square island will be surrounded by a palm-lined La Croisette is questionable, but real sand is promised around the bridged pool. *Below,* a passenger-laden tender enters the catamaran stern of its mother ship. *(Klosters Rederi A/S)*

enormous shopping complex. The evening's entertainment possibilities available with a five-thousand-passenger handle are almost limitless.

Indeed, the "floating universe" and all the galaxies it contains may preclude the necessity for ports at all. By the early nineties, there should be a growing number of veteran passengers who would rather stay contentedly on board for a week and forego tender rides ashore to dubious island enchantments; the island, in fact, is already out on deck. Or will there always be enough Newpassengers on board every *Phoenix* cruise to make at least one traditional port call advisable? Whatever the mix, it seems obvious that with the advent of the *Phoenix*, the industry will be closer to that cruising paradigm, the port-less—hence tender-less—ship.

Another intriguing spin-off of a vessel that size might be the return of two-class service, less a function of *Phoenix*'s size than her form. With passengers housed in separate, autonomous towers, Norwegian Caribbean Lines could easily designate one or even a portion of one as a First Class enclave. Insulated geographically from that special section, regular passengers would not come in contact with—and thus not feel excluded from —an area of the vessel to which their ticket does not authorize them access. The aftermost ziggurat, for instance, could become a separate First Class complex with its own pool, terrace, and restaurant. First Class passengers would enjoy the traditional privilege of descending at will to any part of the ship for shopping, shows, specialty restaurants, a swim in the central pool, or a jog around the decks, only two and a half circuits of which will log a mile. They could always retire to their more luxurious cabins and service when they wished.

The potential for a *Phoenix*-class vessel seems limitless, an evocation of Le Corbusier's image in *La Ville Radieuse*; his "radiant city" remains, in fact, an appropriate synonym for all passenger vessels—past, present, and future—whether micro-*Sea Goddess*, macro-*Phoenix*, or any of the assorted fleets of meso-ships in between. The landbound will continue to flock to the radiant city, its attraction as changeless as its cosmos. Surely one reason for sea travel's enduring appeal is that ever since the first ships crossed any ocean, the seascape has remained the same. In a world where surroundings are at peril, where environment is often no more than a catchword, where fragile urban and rural landscapes can be brutalized overnight, the open ocean survives untouched. Beyond our railings, the ever-present horizon—that great arc of adventure and contentment—remains circumferentially intact. It is as it ever was and so, regardless of how *Peregrinator transatlanticus inveteratus* may nostalgically lament, are the

ee-quarters view of the *Phoenix* as
h photographed from the air. The
from a pier can be seen by inverting
cture. *(Klosters Rederi A/S)*

ships and that magical passenger life on board. There is no more blessed reprieve from care than that whistled blast dispatching us to sea, the engines' tremble underfoot, the cabin and its comforting steward, and the lure of ports ahead.

Appendix: A Postscript to Crossings

Since the publication of *The Only Way to Cross*, many readers have been kind enough to write. I have excerpted below the most interesting and pertinent selections on the assumption that readers of the present volume who are familiar with its predecessor may find matters of interest and amusement therein. My most grateful thanks are extended to the correspondents who graciously consented to be quoted.

On page 72 of *The Only Way to Cross*, in connection with the *Titanic* disaster, I had remarked on the peculiarly maritime collective noun "souls," used to describe a shipload of combined passengers and crew, commenting that "souls" never seem to board trains, planes, or buses. From California, Phyllis Jordan suggested:

A possible answer to your musings about the use of "souls" with regard to those who travel by sea might be found in the first Epistle of Peter, chapter iii, verse 20: "Which sometimes were disobedient, when once the long suffering of God waited in the days of Noah while the ark was a preparing, wherein few, that is, eight souls were saved by water."

Subsequently, an air force officer who attended one of my lectures proved me wrong. "Souls On Board" is apparently a common air force cognomen, reduced, as are so many service references, to the unfortunate acronym "S.O.B.'s"!

Anent *Titanic*, I had included an account of the late Violet Jessop, the White Star Line stewardess who survived the *Olympic/Hawke* collision as well as the sinking of both the *Titanic* and *Britannic*. Vernon Finch, a steward living in retirement in Vancouver, wrote that he had sailed with Jessop years earlier. I lent him the tape cassettes of my long interview with her in her retirement cottage near Bury Saint Edmunds in 1970. He returned them with the following recollections:

> It gave me great pleasure to hear the voice of Violet Jessop again after nearly 45 years. At the same time it was sad to think of her lonely existence to the very end. She had given so much comfort and care to so many during her lifetime. After hearing the tapes, I realized for the first time why she was so like a mother to us youngest members of the ship's company. No doubt the memories of the bell boys who perished on the S.S. *Titanic* and the frightened ones on the *Britannic* made her so forgiving when at times we disappeared to have a smoke in the gloryhole when we should have been on duty.
>
> When I told her I wanted to start a little sideline business in supplying Belgian cigarettes and tobacco to some of the members of the crew when they ran out half-way across the Atlantic, she thought this was a good idea and gave me a one dollar bill for luck. When the enterprise failed at the end of the trip, due to verbal promises of payment either in New York or on our return to Antwerp, not being kept by my customers, I told Violet. She smiled and said, "Well, at least you tried."
>
> She would not tolerate any word or conduct from anyone which went against her strict code of living, and everyone respected her for this. During the daily inspections at sea, the Captain or the officers would always have a few words with Violet. Although I knew from the other crew members that she had survived the *Titanic* and the *Britannic* sinking, she never mentioned either experience to anyone. Although my curiosity as a youngster was very strong at times, I

refrained from asking any questions, fearing that the memories could be sad or painful for her. She was a remarkable woman who loved the sea and ships as very few women ever can, and I only regret I did not know where to contact her when she was still alive.

I am indebted to Russell Makepeace of Wareham, Massachusetts, for advising me about another *Titanic* connection:

> Have just finished *The Only Way to Cross*. It has had my almost undivided attention during reading hours since we received it Christmastime. The enclosed will bring you up-to-date on your reference to "Edith Russell gave her trunk keys to Wareham, her steward. . . ." Cyril A. Wareham . . . is the son of Robert Arthur Wareham, who was "Chief Bedroom Steward." Mr. Wareham's mother died about three years ago age 94 and his older sister Doris about a year ago. He is the last surviving child and presently functions as head dining room manager of Cunard, presently serving on *QE2* for training purpose.

In fact, I knew Cyril Wareham well, one of the many "*Titanic* orphans," as they were called, who had followed in his late father's footsteps and gone to sea. He was known in the Veranda Grill of both *Queens* as "Flamer" Wareham because he "suzetted" crepes with such flair that he endangered flammable furnishings. It was said that he once so singed one of Doris Zinkeisen's mural panels that it had to be touched up.

In the chapter entitled "On Board," I mentioned John Finley, one of the North Atlantic's most celebrated and indefatigable walkers. Frank Waters of the *New York Times* was kind enough to elaborate:

> What especially interested me was the evocation of daily life aboard the ships, a life I enjoyed so much and that is almost gone now. On page 193, you mention a Dr. Finley who clocked 100 miles in walking on one crossing. Not just another walker, but Dr. John Finley, once editor of the *New York Times*, president of City College in New York, State Education Commissioner and all-around strider in the city. He celebrated his birthday every year by making the complete circuit of Manhattan Island on foot—and then going to work. He died in 1940.

The *Normandie*, of course, dazzled all who knew her. One of her staunchest aficionados was Ludwig Bemelmans, several of whose recollections I reprinted from *I Love You, I Love You, I Love You*. One I apparently neglected, and David Binger of Mount Kisco, New York, was kind enough to paraphrase it. In fact, it happened on the *America*:

I have just finished your delightful book. I was enthralled. You left out the episode of Ludwig Bemelmans's toy poodle, which he kept in his cabin. The purser started shadowing him when he aired the little dog, trying to catch Bemelmans in the act of taking his pet to his quarters instead of to the ship's kennel. One day Bemelmans bought a toy stuffed poodle at the ship's souvenir store and then made a big fuss about carrying it around on deck until the purser was hot on his heels, at which point he stepped to the rail and threw it overboard!

But one Bemelmans story that I did reproduce in extenso on page 313 was about a celebrated lady passenger on board the *Normandie* and her daughter, "a sad little girl," according to Bemelmans. That little girl is now Mrs. Thomas D. Hill of Winnetka, Illinois. She wrote:

Before she died this year, my mother had one of the grandest laughs of her life, over page 313 of *The Only Way to Cross*. On her behalf and mine, I thank you. Discussion of Mr. Bemelmans's memoir filled in the memory gaps of the "sad little girl." Going through Mother's belongings I found a few things which represented the best of her sentimentality. In a small white box is about six or eight ounces of black chiffon with no back, very little bosom, and a narrow skirt relieved with an intriguing slit. Mother had, indeed, wonderful legs and, in the days of the *Normandie*, wonderful everything else! The bracelets are gone, but I saw them just as Bemelmans did. Alas, they were paste, but one set with square green stones and rhinestones made a fine headband for my spontaneous ballet recitals years ago. Another fiction is the "junior mink." It was gray lamb, cut from a coat belonging to my grandmother, and the strings on the matching hat were wool and itched my chin furiously.

Also, Mother's popularity put me in constant tow of a French nursemaid who, for all her warmth for Americans, might have been a German agent. "Sad"? I was bored to tears. The whole atmosphere made me long for the *Britannic*, on which a dining room steward did magic tricks for solitary characters like me. There was also the fellow who set up the muffin stands for tea and told me to be very early to avoid the adults and get the best selection. To this day I am not certain the French really like children.

I can give you a full-length description of what it was like to have dinner with all the well-tended children in the children's dining room, how I stood with that ghastly French nursemaid for over an hour outside our stateroom door while my mother wondered where the deuce I was (ah, you see, there was ze gentleman inside!).

A dear friend, staring at my mother, once said that her resemblance to the popular Garbo was startling, but wasn't it a shame that Garbo had such large feet and coarse hands. You get the picture. Suffice to say, the ladies in the nursing home where she spent almost a year frequently commented that she was not only pretty but sweet. On my last visit there the head nurse repeated the phrase and I answered, "You should have seen her when." Just like the great old ships.

A *Normandie* architectural anomaly—to which I was unable to respond with any accuracy—was uncovered by David C. Townson, a sharp-eyed reader from Rexdale, Ontario:

> Facing page 282 are two pictures of the *Normandie*. But the ship's name is much higher—and somewhat farther aft—in the upper plate than is apparent in the lower one and any other picture in the book that shows the name—although those that do are all of her starboard bow. Do you know whether the *Normandie*'s name was moved at some time between her trials and her maiden voyage or whether she simply suffered the unlikely inconsistency of wearing it higher on the port bow than on the starboard one?

Indeed, sharp-eyed readers abounded. Stephen M. Payne, a young naval architect from London, was kind enough to point out that I had misidentified a vessel in the process of being scrapped:

> The vessel being scrapped (top photo, page 348/349) in *The Only Way to Cross* cannot be the *Caledonia*-ex-*Majestic*. The remaining funnel and two masts of the vessel in the photograph have clearly not been shortened. A photograph of the *Majestic* leaving Southampton's King George V dry dock for Rosyth and renaming to H.M.S. *Caledonia* appears in *The Great Luxury Liners 1927–1954* by William H. Miller (introduction by you!) on page 67. The funnels have been cut down to the buff color level and the masts reduced to stumps. Clearly the vessels cannot be the same. I believe the vessel in your book to be the *Berengaria*.

Payne's evidence is incontrovertible, and the caption has been corrected. So, too, has another one that, I am ashamed to admit, still contained no less than three separate errors twelve years after publication! J. D. Hill of Warrington, Cheshire, another sharp-eyed Englishman, wrote:

> May I say what a superb book yours is. I initially read it from cover to cover and now I plunge in at random for "bedside reading" most evenings. It does not matter which chapter chance gives me, my enjoyment is always secured. . . . I am particularly fascinated by the White Star story. My favorite photograph in the book is the one on

page 55 showing Lord Pirrie and Captain Smith conferring on the boat deck of the *Olympic*. Apart from the interest in seeing these two men together who were so bound up in the White Star fortunes, the impression of immense deck space is well shown.

May I indulge in some detective work? The caption states that the funnel in the photograph is No. 1! I think it is No. 4. Looking at the boat deck plan, I think that they are standing on the starboard side, just aft of the gymnasium. It looks like the edge of No. 3 funnel is just visible. Needless to say, for June 6th I read June 14th for the maiden voyage Sailing Day.

By great good fortune, several people recognized either parents or themselves in some of the passenger photographs, including Curt Segeler from Brooklyn:

If you will reach for a copy and turn to page 336, you will see a laughing lady in the picture at the bottom left. That lady was my mother. The man struggling with the trunk was William Strong, our handyman who always came to help us on our return. Back of the lady is a second one and that was my grandmother. Undoubtedly, I was around somewhere since I would have been about eight years old at the time. You can see the letter "S" on the trunk required, as you know, to help in sorting baggage of the returning traveler. Your book brings back many memories.

Another passenger/reader recognized her parents and a friend in the photograph of Southampton's boat-train platform on page 224. She is Anna Glen Vietor, since then a friend and fellow trustee on the board of New York's Ocean Liner Museum:

As I looked at the picture, I recognized my parents, Mr. and Mrs. Arthur W. Butler and a friend, Miss Zelina Blagden, all of New York City. My mother has a coat over her arm—my father is not the man in the immediate foreground but the one behind my mother with a wide black band on his hat. Miss Blagden, who often traveled in our family party, is seen only from the back but both her clothing—a light coat with a large fur collar, a wide-brimmed picture hat—and her stance are unmistakable. Unfortunately, I am not in the picture— I must have been somewhere else on the dock as I was along on that trip. I think it was May 1937, and [the ship] was the *Queen Mary*. I traveled to Europe so often, something like forty ocean crossings, that I become a bit vague. As I recall, we went over twice in 1937. Anyway, it is certainly reminiscent of all arrival scenes. Again, let me say how surprised I was to see them while I was just idly glancing at the pictures in *The Only Way to Cross*. I think the news people were lined up as this sailing was bringing a good number of Americans over for the Coronation [George VI and Elizabeth].

But the "news people" to whom Mrs. Vietor referred were not, as I had put in the original caption, newsreel cameramen at all. Two readers set me straight, the first, Gary Franklin of Canoga Park, California:

> Page 224 . . . customs clearance . . . Southampton Docks, 1937 . . . and the inevitable newsreel camera. Uh-uh. I'll bet that's neither a newsreel camera nor a newsreel crew. That's a technicolor camera— with a production crew—shooting process shots for a feature or a promotional film or a short subject. But newsreel? Unlikely.

Garry Coxall, from Toronto, echoed Franklin's suggestion and even had an idea of the film in question:

> As a matter of passing comment, I would like to offer a possible explanation for the presence of a film crew at Southampton Docks. The camera is an unblimped Technicolor three-strip and, therefore, the unit is probably doing some pick-up shots for a feature; probably for *Wings of the Morning* which was made at about that time with Anabella.

Mrs. Franklin W. Bahler recognized herself as a young lady among the owners at the *Aquitania*'s impromptu dog show:

> I just finished reading your book *The Only Way to Cross*. It was just great and brought back so many memories of sailings as a child when I'd see my parents off and of the one crossing both ways on the *Aquitania* I made in 1929. I almost cried when I came to page 331 when I saw myself (second from the left, age 12) with my cairn that Mother had bought me in Paris before we left for home. I remember the day well but have searched for the photo I know I have. It was the end of November or beginning of December 1929, not 1932 as stated. No one could have enjoyed that crossing more, walking not only my dog but the others who had no masters on board.

The same photograph impressed Miss M. Sybil Churchill of Horsely in Gloucestershire, chairman of the Cairn Terrier Association. She thought it quite remarkable that four out of the five dogs pictured were cairn terriers. The picture was republished in the Cairn Terrier Association's journal with the footnote: "Perhaps some of the Association's senior members can identify the owners of these cairns." (Thus far, none have come forward.)

A correspondent from San Francisco, William Clark, thought he recognized a participant in a fancy-dress competition:

> I derived such pleasure from reading *The Only Way to Cross* that I gave five copies as gifts to my brothers and sisters and friends. A picture in your book on page 410 depicts a Funny Hat Competition on the *Queen Elizabeth* and it has touched off quite a debate in our family circle. My wife and I are convinced that the lady on the right is my late stepmother, Mrs. Harold T. Clark, who came from Cleveland, Ohio, but my brothers and sisters do not agree. I am writing you with the hope that in your files there might be some identification of the ladies in the picture. Failing this, is there any chance of pinpointing the year the picture was taken as I might be able to determine if my father and stepmother (both of whom are now deceased) made a crossing on the *Queen Elizabeth* that year.

Alas, the original, reproduced from Cunard's publicity files, carried no caption or date so I was unable to help resolve the Clark family's dilemma.

Ralph Whitney, a steamship historian now living in retirement in Florida, remembered some details of the first great auction of shipboard furniture and fittings held in Southampton in 1935:

> Which reminds me that I just missed having an interesting *Mauretania* souvenir. I was Art Editor of *Cosmopolitan* (long before the nude male centerfold era) at the time [the *Mauretania*] was being broken up and wrote to ask a friend in the London office of Hearst International if he could pick up a souvenir for me at the great sale, at a not too high price. (No dining saloon paneling, that is.) I eventually received a small—about 6-inch—Basset-Lowke model, in the white paint of her cruising days, *sous cloche*, cost, as I recall, about two pounds. My friend reported that the only other moderately reasonable items were WC seats; many visitors to the sale were walking out with them, horse-collar fashion, around their necks.

Amplification about an incident from the early days of World War I on the North Atlantic discussed on page 121 was supplied by Florence Pyne of Short Hills, New Jersey:

> It has been many years since I read a book which I enjoyed more than *The Only Way to Cross*. I was amused when I read about the return of the *Kronprinzessin Cecilie* to Bar Harbor during the first war. The man (American) on the bridge was my father, C. Ledyard Blair. He had an ocean-going yacht, the *Diana*, and as my grandparents lived there in summer he knew every rock and depth in that area.

From England, Lord Geddes wrote to point out another misnamed vessel in the text—since corrected—as well as some intriguing detail about the death of a famous Cunard master:

> It was in the summer of 1928 that Cunard first gave engine-room round voyages to New York to Cambridge engineering undergraduates. Lord Pentland was the first of these in *Mauretania* and I followed a week later in *Aquitania*. Sir James Charles had already retired but was brought back for this final voyage. On the return passage, we reached Cherbourg early on July 14th. The date is easy to remember because the French fleet was there and dressed overall for their national holiday. About 6 a.m. I was in the wheelhouse and an officer came up to say that Sir James Charles was very ill. Guy Dolphin was the staff captain and he took command and brought the ship back to Southampton. There was always some doubt about the time of Sir James's death. It was said at the time that if he was still alive the Staff Captain could deputize for him in closing articles, but if he was deceased then a new Master would have to be appointed for this purpose. A quick turn round was intended and Sir James was carried off the ship on a stretcher and it was reported that he died in the ambulance en route to Southampton hospital, thus leaving Dolphin able to close articles. The point of all of the above is to substantiate my certainty that it was *Aquitania* and not *Berengaria*.

Also from the United Kingdom, an Ulster reader sent an interesting addendum to my discussion of cardsharps and confidence men working the North Atlantic liners (pages 207–211, "On Board"):

> Your stories about confidence men interested me as you say they always liked privacy. My father told me this tale about a friend of his traveling on his own out of season to New York. He was reading on deck on the second day out when he was approached by an elderly retired English colonel and asked if he would like to make up a four at bridge. Father's friend said he would if the stakes were small. So for the next few days they played bridge for small stakes in one of the men's cabins. The day before landing the colonel came up to him and suggested a farewell drink in the smokeroom. In the smokeroom they were joined by the other two and the colonel said to one of them "Show our friend the game I saw you playing yesterday."
>
> "Oh no," he said, "it was only a child's game, our friend wouldn't be interested." However, he was persuaded to demonstrate. (I think it was a version of Slippery Sam.) Father's friend fell for it, cut a king, was talked into making a bet, and of course his "friend" cut an ace! He found out he was stung for a large sum of money, and

the bet had been made in public and he felt he couldn't get out of it and save face. He hadn't anything like the amount of money with him, nor had he his cheque book, so he signed an IOU. Afterwards, the colonel came up to him and said he had lost money to these other men too and he was not sure they were honest! Luckily father's friend knew a New York police superintendent and went to him rather ashamed of himself and told what had happened. The policeman laughed and said not to worry but to send any threatening letters to him. The trio were well-known characters on the boats. It certainly bears out your remarks—they do go for the loner.

George Webber of Morristown, New Jersey, had a valid question about one of the *Imperator* photographs:

Why does the *Imperator* (picture facing page 105) have one of the very old type anchors with a stock on her starboard bow instead of the modern stockless type?

The response I addressed to him was that probably the photograph was taken at the end of the ship's fitting out. Presumably, engineers from the Vulcan Werke used a temporary yard anchor as a precaution while towing the *Imperator* from fitting-out berth to dry dock, where, presumably, the ship's proper, modern anchors—by then salvaged from the harbor bottom where they fell the day of her launch—would be restored to the hawsepipes.

From Georgetown, in our nation's capital, the Reverend Gerard Yates wrote of his boyhood shipping memories as well as pointing out the real color of United States passport covers of the period, an error long since corrected:

As a boy, I lived on Staten Island; my father was in shipping; until I left home in the 20's, all the great ships mentioned in your book were familiar sights and part of my surroundings. I remember visiting the *Olympic* with my father and mother when she came into New York on her maiden voyage. . . . Anyway, thank you for several hours of keen pleasure and for much information that was quite new to me. I trust it will not be thought ungracious if I point out one small error: on page 352 you refer to the "distinctive green passports" of American travelers trying to return from Europe in 1939. Actually, the U.S. passports in those days were maroon. Mine was taken up when I returned in the *Washington* from Le Verdon, below Bordeaux in France, in October of 1939. I was able to get it back in 1950.

Ernest May, a frequent ocean traveler between the wars, imparted some invaluable data about steamship rivalry:

On page 220 there is a sentence beginning, "One of the ironies of intense Anglo-French competition . . ." to which I can contribute a little explanation.

Twice in the 30's, when I was crossing eastbound on two different British ships, I was told independently by two different separate ship's officers that one advantage TRANSAT had was that French ships would save time by consistently cutting across the Grand Banks —spring, summer made no difference. This was, of course, breaking the international safety agreements after the *Titanic*, and the Britishers did *not* like it.

I understood the Britishers to mean that instead of following the prescribed ship lanes, the French luxury liners (and I have crossed on them, too) would go east from New York along 41°–42° North to about 62° West, whereupon they would cut directly up to approximately 50° North and 38° West, where they would get back on track again. The chart inside the covers of *The Only Way to Cross* can illustrate this beautifully.

Finally, among the most interesting and amusing correspondence is a series of letters from retired Cunard captain J. D. Armstrong, D.S.C., R.D. He wrote on a wide variety of liner-related subjects, among them some memories of the *Aquitania*'s first wartime crossing from New York in September 1939:

> We sailed immediately after the *Bremen*. She backed into the North River after being held up by the Coast Guard for a passenger certificate but as she sailed without any passengers they could not hold her any longer. Her ship's company were mustered on the foredeck, the band played "Deutschland Uber Alles" and they gave the Nazi salute. We followed her down river, and saw her switch off all her lights. She disappeared into the night and re-appeared off Murmansk a couple of weeks later.
>
> We sailed as a full ship, our own passengers and all the *Normandie* passengers who could be accommodated. We missed the Cherbourg call, all the passage home passengers were slapping paint (grey) on anything they could reach. We came in on a mid-Channel course and as we approached the Nab Tower, an elderly British "V & W" class destroyer obviously dug out from Reserve and making dense clouds of black smoke called us up on the Aldis Lamp: FOUR FUNNEL SHIP PLEASE INDICATE. [Captain] George Gibbons's remark when told the signal was classic: "We are the only f——ing four-funnel ship in the world and that so-and-so wants our name. Tell him to read *The News of the World*." The next signal was DO YOU REQUIRE AN ESCORT, [our] reply CAN YOU KEEP UP. The final signal as

we drew away, still at full speed: YOUR FINE SPEED REQUIRES LITTLE PROTECTION.

Captain Armstrong also supplied additional details about the Prince of Wales's crossing westbound on the *Berengaria*, described on pages 227–232 of *The Only Way to Cross*:

> John Croaisdale, who was duty officer on the *Berengaria* when the Royal Party boarded, told me the following:
>
> He was called to the gangway door on the off side of the ship around four A.M. The Royal Party had arrived unexpectedly from the Isle of Wight. They were not due until later in the morning when all kinds of civic functions had been laid on. According to Croaisdale, none of the party were feeling any pain and the Prince of Wales wanted to be taken to the Suite and for more refreshment to be served. Staff were called. Customs seals were broken. The Southampton manager arrived, and high jinks were continued so much so that none of the party were fit to function at the appointed time. The P.O.W. was propped up in the wing of the bridge by a couple of Bridge Boys from where he waved good-bye. . . . Prior to arrival in New York an aide arrived in Haughty Bill's [Captain William Irvine] cabin with a handsome gold watch. "With the compliments of His Royal Highness." To which Bill replied "A present suitable for a Chief Steward. If His Royal Highness feels like making a gift, I'd like a signed photograph." This duly arrived by hand of a very apologetic P.O.W.

Years later, the same passenger, traveling this time with his wife as the Duke and Duchess of Windsor, crossed the Atlantic regularly. Captain Armstrong had some additional insight into Their Royal Highnesses' transfer of allegiance from Cunard to the United States Lines:

> Page 406. The reason the Windsors left the *Queen*s (I had them several times on the *Queen Mary* when I was staff captain) was that they demanded minimum bed rate for a suite and Cunard would not play but the U.S. Lines did, 47 pieces of baggage and all.

Finally, Armstrong told me a story that I am not sure I believe but which, for an Anglo-American, is too irresistible not to use as a conclusion:

> During the McCarthy era . . . the U.S. Immigration Authorities processed all the crews of the big ships, with the full Immigration procedures, and the threat of no shore leave if the crews refused to submit to the questions. The French and Italian crew members mostly refused. They said they were not in port long enough to miss one

night of shore leave. The *Queen Mary* got the first full treatment and I was horrified at some of the questions asked. "Had they ever been guilty of unnatural practices? Had they been inmates of a disorderly house?" (this to the stewardesses) and various other searching questions. One was, "Is there any insanity in your family?" To which a young kitchen porter replied with a perfectly straight face, "Yes, sir, my sister married a GI." The subsequent uproar ended the proceedings.

So, too, will end these proceedings.

Bibliography

ADAMS, WILLIAM M., ed., *Tsunamis in the Pacific Ocean,* East-West Center Press, Honolulu, 1970.

ALBERTS, A., *Per Mailboat Naar de Oost,* De Boer Maritiem, Amsterdam, 1979.

ANCHOR LINE, *The Book of the Anchor Line,* ed. J. Burrow & Co. Ltd., London, 1932.

ARNOTT, CAPTAIN ROBERT H., and ROLAND L. SMITH, *Captain of the Queen,* New English Library, Sevenoaks, Kent, 1982.

ASHE, GEOFFREY, *The Tale of the Tub,* Newman Neame Ltd., London, 1950.

BRAYNARD, FRANK, and WILLIAM MILLER, *Fifty Famous Liners,* Patrick Stephens, Cambridge, 1982.

BUSHELL, T. A., *Royal Mail: A Centenary History of the Royal Mail Line,* Trade and Travel Publications, Ltd., London, 1939.

CARMICHAEL, W. A., *Practical Ship Production*, McGraw-Hill Book Company, Inc., New York and London, 1941.

CHADWICK, F. E., *Ocean Steamships*, Charles Scribner's Sons, New York, 1891.

COEN, MARTIN J., *Ship Welding Handbook*, Cornell Maritime Press, New York, 1943.

COLEMAN, TERRY, *Passage to America*, Penguin Books, Harmondsworth, 1974.

COURSE, A. G., *Ships of the P & O*, Adlard Coles Ltd., London, 1954.

DODMAN, FRANK, *Ships of the Cunard Line*, Adlard Coles Ltd., London, 1955.

EDMONDS, FREDERICK, *The Atlantic Liners*, Drake Publishers Inc., New York, 1972.

GIBBS, C. R. VERNON, *The Western Ocean Passenger Lines and Liners 1934–1969*, Brown, Son & Ferguson, Ltd., Glasgow, 1970.

GREENHILL, BASIL, and ANN GIFFARD, *Travelling by Sea in the Nineteenth Century*, Adam and Charles Black, London, 1972.

HAMBURG-AMERIKA LINIE, *Nordland-Fahrten*, Hamburg-Amerika Linie, Magdeburg, n.d.

HAMILTON, WILLIAM, *A Diary of My World Cruise*, privately published, n.d.

HARD, A. C., *Motorships*, Chapman and Hall, Ltd., London, 1925.

HASKIN, FREDERICK J., *The Panama Canal*, Doubleday Page & Company, Garden City, N.Y., 1913.

HENSHALL, S. H., *Medium and High Speed Diesel Engines for Marine Use*, The Institute for Marine Engineers, London, 1972.

HOBBS, WHIT, *At Home Aboard*, Holland America Lines, New York, 1893.

HUNGERFORD, EDWARD, *Planning a Trip Abroad*, Robert M. McBride & Company, New York, 1923.

HYDE, FRANCIS E., *Cunard and the North Atlantic 1840–1973*, The Macmillan Press, Ltd., London and Basingstoke, 1973.

ISHERWOOD, J. H., *Ships of the Orient Line*, Adlard Coles Ltd., London, 1953.

JACKSON, G. GIBBARD, *British Railways: The Romance of Their Achievement*, Sampson Low, Marston & Co., Ltd., London, n.d.

KENNEDY, LUDOVIC, ed., *A Book of Sea Journeys*, Fontana Paperbacks, Huntington, N.Y., 1982.

KIRKHAM, STANTON D., *Cruising Around the World and the Seven Seas*, G. P. Putnam's Sons, The Knickerbocker Press, New York, 1927.

LEIGH-BENNETT, E. P., *History of a House Flag*, Willem Ruys & Zonen, Rotterdam, 1939.

LLOYD-ZEITUNG, *The Progress of German Shipbuilding*, Hobbing & Co., G.M.B.H., Berlin, 1909.

LORDS COMMISSIONERS OF THE ADMIRALTY, *The Application of Electric Arc Welding to Ship Construction*, H.M. Stationery Office, London, 1946.

LUEHRING, FREDERICK W., *Swimming Pool Standards*, A. S. Barnes & Company, New York, 1939.

MABER, JOHN M., *North Star to Southern Cross*, T. Stephenson & Sons Ltd., Prescot, Lancs, 1967.

MACDONALD, JOHN D., and CAPTAIN JOHN H. KILPACK, *Nothing Can Go Wrong*, Fawcett Crest, New York, 1981.

MacLean, Donald, *The Captain's Bridge*, Doubleday & Company, Inc., Garden City, N.Y., 1965.

McCullough, David, *The Path Between the Seas*, Simon and Schuster, New York, 1977.

Miller, William, *The First Great Ocean Liners in Photographs*, Dover Publications, Inc., New York, 1984.

Morris, Charles F., *Origins, Orient and Oriana*, Teredo Books Ltd., Brighton, 1980.

Morton, Margaret, *Around the World*, privately published, 1931.

Parker, Earl R., *Brittle Behavior of Engineering Structures*, John Wiley & Sons, Inc., New York, 1947.

Potter, Neil, and Jack Frost, *Queen Elizabeth 2: The Authorized Story*, George C. Harrap & Co., Ltd., London, 1969.

Prinzhoffer, Renato, *Le Città Galleggianti*, Ifotolibri/Longanesi & Co., Milan, 1978.

Royal Mail Steamship Company, *A Link of Empire*, Royal Mail Steamship Company, 1909.

Saunders, Jeraldine, *Cruise Diary*, J. P. Tarcher Inc., Los Angeles, 1982.

Schaap, Richard, *A Bridge to the Seven Seas*, Meijer Pers bv, Amsterdam, 1973.

Stoddard, S. R., *The Cruise of the Friesland*, privately published, Glens Falls, N.Y., 1896.

Swinglehurst, Edmund, *Cook's Tours: The Story of Popular Travel*, Blandford Press, Poole, Dorset, 1982.

Taggart, Robert, *Marine Propulsion: Principles and Evolution*, Gulf Publishing Company, Houston, 1969.

Taylor, David W., *The Speed and Power of Ships*, volumes I & II, Ransdell Incorporated, Washington, D.C., 1933.

Van Herk, Captain Cornelius, *De Schepen van de Holland Amerika Lijn*, Uitgeverij de Boer Maritiem, Bussum, Netherlands, 1981.

Waugh, Evelyn, *Charles Ryder's Schooldays and Other Stories*, Little, Brown & Company, Boston, 1982.

——, *When the Going Was Good*, Penguin Books, Harmondsworth, 1951.

White Star Line, *The White Star Line of Mail Steamers Official Guide*, Ismay, Imrie & Co., London, 1877.

Wright, Lawrence, *Clean and Decent*, Routledge & Kegan Paul, London, 1960.

X and Y, *A Long Vacation Ramble in Norway*, Macmillan & Co., Cambridge, 1857.

Index

Figures in boldface indicate illustrations